CALIFORNIA REAL ESTATE PRINCIPLES

SIXTH EDITION

Prentice Hall Series in California Real Estate

Dennis J. McKenzie, Editor

CALIFORNIA REAL ESTATE PRINCIPLES, 6th EDITION
Dennis J. McKenzie, Lowell Anderson, Frank Battino, Cecilia Hopkins

CALIFORNIA REAL ESTATE PRACTICE
William L. Mansfield

LEGAL ASPECTS OF CALIFORNIA REAL ESTATE,
3rd EDITION
Louis Hansotte

CALIFORNIA REAL ESTATE FINANCE, 6th EDITION
Robert Bond, Alfred Gavello, Carden Young

BASIC REAL ESTATE APPRAISAL, 4th EDITION
Richard M. Betts, Silas Ely

ESSENTIALS OF REAL ESTATE ECONOMICS,
4th EDITION
Dennis J. McKenzie, Richard M. Betts

THE CALIFORNIA REAL ESTATE CONSULTANT
Lorraine Norton

CALIFORNIA REAL ESTATE LICENSE PREPARATION,
10th EDITION
William H. Pivar, Dennis J. McKenzie

CALIFORNIA MORTGAGE LOAN BROKERING & LENDING
D. L. Grogan, M. C. Buzz Chambers

CALIFORNIA REAL ESTATE PRINCIPLES

SIXTH EDITION

Dennis J. McKenzie, Realtor®
McKenzie Real Estate Seminars,
College of the Redwoods

Lowell Anderson, Professor
Cerritos College

Frank Battino, Realtor®
Merritt College

Cecilia A. Hopkins, Ph.D.
College of San Mateo

PRENTICE HALL
Upper Saddle River, New Jersey 07458

Library of Congress Cataloging-in-Publication Data

California real estate principles / Dennis J. McKenzie . . . [et al.]. —
6th ed.
    p.   cm. — (Prentice Hall series in California real estate)
Includes index.
ISBN 0-13-082661-8
    1. Real estate business—California. I. McKenzie, Dennis J.,
  — . II. Series.
HD266.C2C25 1999   98-47266
333.33'09794—dc21   CIP

Acquisitions editor: *Elizabeth Sugg*
Production: *Holcomb Hathaway, Inc.*
Production liason: *Barbara Marttine Cappuccio*
Director of manufacturing and production: *Bruce Johnson*
Managing editor: *Mary Carnis*
Manufacturing buyer: *Marc Bove*
Creative director: *Marianne Frasco*
Cover design: *Miguel Ortiz*
Editorial assistant: *Maria Kirk*

Updated 4/99
© 1999, 1997, 1994, 1988, 1983, 1981 by Prentice-Hall, Inc.
Simon & Schuster/A Viacom Company
Upper Saddle River, New Jersey 07458

Printed in the United States of America

10 9 8 7 6 5 4 3

ISBN 0-13-082661-8

Prentice-Hall International (UK) Limited, *London*
Prentice-Hall of Australia Pty. Limited, *Sydney*
Prentice-Hall Canada Inc., *Toronto*
Prentice-Hall Hispanoamericana, S.A., *Mexico*
Prentice-Hall of India Private Limited, *New Delhi*
Prentice-Hall of Japan, Inc., *Tokyo*
Pearson Education Asia Pte. Ltd., *Singapore*
Editora Prentice-Hall do Brasil, Ltda., *Rio de Janeiro*

Contents

Preface

This book is an outgrowth of years of teaching real estate principles at California community colleges and working with private vocational schools. The material is current and designed to maintain student interest. This new edition incorporates all the latest changes that apply to a course in California Real Estate Principles. Plus practical application exercises have been added to the multiple choice review questions at the end of each chapter. These exercises will help students focus on the real world of real estate. **For readers who are planning to take the California Real Estate Sales Examination, in addition to the extensive preparation material in this current edition, readers are encouraged to purchase the book *California Real Estate License Preparation Text* by William H. Pivar and Dennis J. McKenzie, published by Prentice Hall.** Although this current edition of *California Real Estate Principles* explains the content of the California real estate examination and contains hundreds of practice test questions, the preparation text noted above follows the format of this principles textbook and contains over a thousand additional practice questions that will be extra helpful in preparing for the California real estate sales examination.

It is impossible to acknowledge all the assistance we have received from students, colleagues, and friends. We hope we have successfully communicated the insights that they have given us. Particular thanks go to the many other real estate instructors who have participated at instructor and coordinator workshops sponsored by the California Department of Real Estate, the California Community College Real Estate Education Center, and the California Real Estate Education Association.

Special recognition is given to Carden Young, instructor at American River College, Sacramento City College, and Shasta College; James Black, real estate coordinator/instructor, San Jose City College; and Mary Ann Zamel, real estate instructor at Mt. San Antonio College in Walnut, California. They were extremely helpful with this current edition. They have been true friends and we are grateful. Many of the original illustrations were provided by Allison McKenzie Michel. We also thank National Real Estate Editor, Elizabeth Sugg, and the rest of the staff at Prentice Hall for helping us through the publishing maze.

Dennis J. McKenzie
Lowell Anderson
Frank Battino
Cecilia A. Hopkins

Chapter 1

Introduction to Real Estate

Welcome There are a variety of reasons why people study real estate. Some wish to become real estate agents, and they are reading this book because a course in Real Estate Principles is required before a person is allowed to sit for the state real estate license examination. Some people study real estate to be better-informed consumers as they work with agents to buy or sell a personal residence. Still others study real estate as a way to acquire long-term investments that could generate rental income for their retirement years.

Whatever the reason, this book provides a strong basic understanding of the principles of California real estate. The format of the book has been designed to logically take a reader step by step through the study of real estate. The book ends with a complete discussion of the requirements to become a licensed real estate salesperson or broker and a 150-question practice examination similar in format to the state test.

Why are the licensing requirements at the end rather than the beginning of the book? Two reasons: (1) Those who think they may be interested in a career as a real estate professional should first study the information in the book to see if they are comfortable with the topic. (2) Some readers wish to become informed consumers and real estate investors and are not interested in a career as a real estate agent.

However, if you wish to know the California real estate license requirements before you begin your study of real estate, you are encouraged to begin your reading with Chapter 15, then return to Chapter 1. The choice is up to you.

Chapter Preview

In this first chapter, the historical, legal, civic, and economic importance of real estate is stressed. This chapter also highlights the characteristics and differences between real and personal property and their effect on today's real estate market. At the conclusion of the chapter, you will be able to:

1. Trace the history of real estate property ownership in California

2. List the four-part definition of real property

3. Explain the term "bundle of rights" and list each of those rights

4. List the five legal tests of a fixture and explain their meaning

1.1 PRESENT AND HISTORICAL IMPORTANCE OF REAL ESTATE

Real estate touches the lives of more people than any other single commodity. Real property represents a significant portion of wealth and contributes to a substantial amount of commerce in the United States.

Impressive Statistics

Of the almost 2.5 billion acres of land in the United States, over 100 million acres are in California. According to the U.S. Census Bureau, the population in California is presently over 33 million, with a projected increase of millions more in the next century. These statistics are important only if they help people to become aware of the significance of real estate in their lives.

Historical Importance of Real Estate

California has perhaps the most interesting and romantic history of any state in the Union. The historical story of California can be told in terms of the use and occupancy of its land.

The earliest inhabitants of California were the Native Americans. Although they led a nomadic existence, they were still governed by tribal rights to the land they occupied, including hunting, fishing, and gathering. The Native Americans respected and cherished the land, because they recognized that their survival was based on products derived from the land.

Spanish Rule

In 1513, a Spanish explorer by the name of Balboa first sighted the Pacific Ocean and claimed it for the king of Spain. Many other Spanish explorers followed in the ensuing years. The years 1542 to 1822 were known as the period of exploration, discovery, and colonization.

The Spanish colonizers established forts called *"presidios"* in selected areas along the California coast to protect against invaders. Communities and agricultural villages known as *"pueblos"* appeared throughout the land to supply food for colonizers. During this period, the land was under Spanish domination. All land was held in the name of the king of Spain, and private activities were governed by Spanish law. Spain did not recognize the ownership rights of Native Americans.

During the Spanish occupation of California, missionaries strived to spread Christianity among the natives by establishing a string of 21 missions ranging from San Diego to Sonoma, north of San Francisco.

Mexican Rule in California

In 1822, Mexico, then a territory of Spain, established its independence and, in the process, took over the territory of California. During the Mexican reign, colonization of the territory of California continued to expand. Large Mexican land grants, called *"ranchos,"* were created and given to private citizens. Much of this rancho land was converted to agricultural use.

Under Mexican rule, colonization was encouraged, and land grants made extensive private ownership a reality for the first time in California history.

American Rule in California

American settlers coming from the east were confronted by Mexican authorities, and these tensions led to the Mexican-American War in 1846. In 1848, the Treaty of Guadalupe Hidalgo ended the war with Mexico, and California became a territory of the United States.

California achieved full statehood on September 9, 1850, and from that time on, the population rapidly increased,

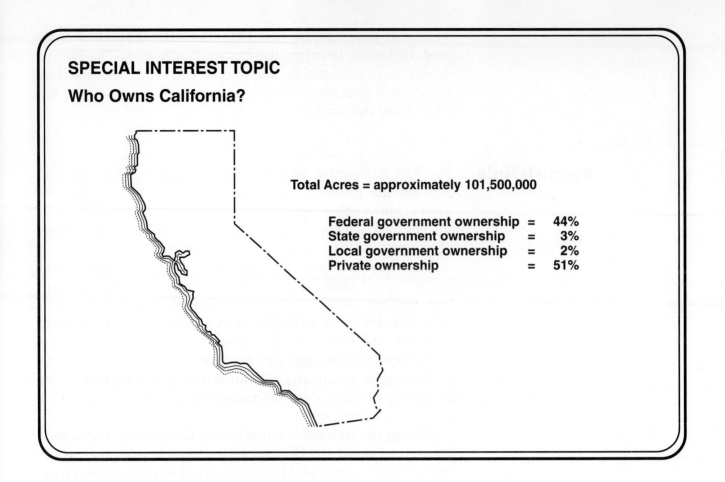
aided by the gold rush in the Sacramento Valley. The new California legislature adopted a land ownership recording system, which recognized and protected some, but not all, of the early Mexican land grants.

1.2 PROPERTY RIGHTS

As you launch into your study of real estate, it is important to differentiate between real estate in a physical sense, such as land and buildings, and real property in the legal sense, such as property rights. The law defines property as "that which is the subject of ownership." It explains ownership as essentially "the right of one or more persons to possess and to use the thing which is owned, to the exclusion of others." Technically, then, in a legal sense, the word "property" does not refer exclusively to the physical thing owned. The law is also concerned with the rights and the interests that the owner has in the thing he or she owns.

What kind of rights does an individual have as an owner of real property? The law designates the rights that accompany ownership as the "bundle of rights."

BUNDLE OF RIGHTS

The right to own property

The right to possess property

The right to use property

The right to enjoy property

The right to encumber property or borrow money on property

The right to dispose of property

The right to exclude those who do not share ownership of the property

Although owners of real estate have a bundle of rights, they have certain responsibilities to other persons regarding the use they can make of their property. Their rights are not absolute, or unlimited. Ownership rights are subject to government control to promote public health, safety, and welfare. Zoning, building codes, and antidiscrimination laws are all examples of government control of property rights.

1.3 REAL PROPERTY VERSUS PERSONAL PROPERTY

To better understand regulations relating to the acquisition and transfer of real property, you need to distinguish between real and personal property.

The law states that anything that is not real property is personal property. Likewise, any property that is not personal property is real property. To fully understand this concept, you need to understand what is meant by "real property."

Real property consists of:

1. land
2. that which is affixed to the land
3. that which is appurtenant or incidental to the land
4. that which is immovable by law

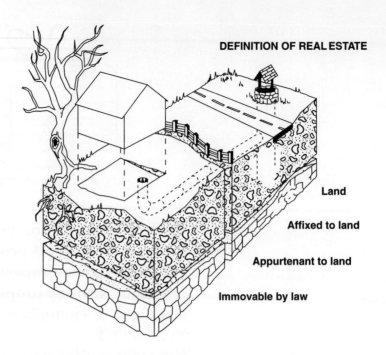

DEFINITION OF REAL ESTATE

Land

Affixed to land

Appurtenant to land

Immovable by law

LAND Land is the solid material of the earth such as soil, rock, or other substances. It can be composed of mountains, valleys, swamps, or any other kind of terrain. The technical definition of land includes:

1. Surface of the land
2. Airspace above the land
3. Materials and substances beneath the surface to the center of the earth

Surface of the Land The surface of the land is defined as the space on the surface of the earth, upon which we live. This includes lateral support—support from adjoining land, and subjacent support—support from underlying strata.

Airspace Airspace (air rights) is more difficult to define. Modern theories, based on air travel, generally agree that an owner of real property owns a reasonable amount of airspace above the land, with the remainder being public highway. Moreover, landowners have the right to prevent a use of airspace that would interfere with their use and quiet enjoyment of the land. However, the issue of what constitutes a "reasonable amount" is currently determined by the courts on a case-by-case basis whenever a lawsuit arises between disputing parties.

Minerals in the Ground

Solid minerals contained in the land—such as coal, iron ore, gold, or silver—are real property until they are taken from the ground, at which time they become personal property. A landowner who deeds the land to another conveys the minerals contained in the land, unless the mineral rights are reserved or have already been sold to some other party. When mineral rights have been reserved by the former owner or conveyed to another person, the owner of the mineral rights has an implied easement to enter upon the surface of the property to extract the minerals. Oil and gas are special classes of minerals and, because of their shifting nature, are not considered capable of ownership until reduced to possession. However, the right to drill for oil and gas rests with the surface landowner or the owner of the mineral rights, if they belong to someone other than the surface landowner. Once oil and minerals are brought to the surface, they are considered personal property.

WATER RIGHTS

A working knowledge of the water rights of a property owner should include an understanding of the following issues:

1. Underground water rights
2. Riparian water rights
3. Right of Appropriation

Underground Water

Underground, or percolating, water is water that is not confined to a well, a defined channel, or a water bed. In California, the landowner has no ownership of specific underground water, nor absolute ownership of waters running across or bordering property, such as a lake or a stream. Under the Concept of Reasonable Use, the landowner may take, in common with other owners, only his or her share of underground (percolating) waters for beneficial use.

Riparian Rights

Owners of land that borders on a river or other water course enjoy certain benefits regarding use of the water, under a concept known as "riparian rights." Although they have no absolute ownership of the waters, each owner has a personal right, along with other landowners, to the use of such waters in a "reasonable manner." Basically, each owner has a right to an amount of water in proportion to the amount of land owned that borders the water course, and in light of the needs of all interested parties.

Right of Appropriation   The right of appropriation is that right given to the state to give permission to a nonriparian owner to take water from a river or lake.

Affixed to the Land   The second component of the definition of real property is "that which is affixed to the land," or anything regarded as a permanent part of the land. This includes:

1. Things permanently resting on the land, such as buildings
2. Things permanently attached to a building, such as fixtures
3. Things attached to the land by roots, such as trees and shrubs

Natural trees, shrubs, and vines that are rooted in the ground are generally considered to be part of the land. In other words, natural vegetation is real property until severed or gathered, at which time it becomes personal property. On the other hand, farm produce and growing crops that are the result of annual labor are considered to be goods and are governed by laws of personal property. Growing vegetable crops are sometimes referred to as "emblements."

Appurtenant to the Land   The third component of the definition of real property is that which is appurtenant or incidental to the land. That which is appurtenant to the land is anything that, by right, is used by the land for its benefit and "goes with the land." Examples might be:

1. Easements, such as the rights of way over adjoining lands, or even passages for light, air, or heat from or across the land of another. (Easements are discussed in detail in a subsequent chapter.)

2. Stock in a mutual water company. A mutual water company is a nonprofit company organized by or for water users in a specific district to develop and furnish water to its stockholders at reasonable rates. Usually each share is considered to be appurtenant to a specific piece of real property and cannot be sold separately. In other words, the stock is considered real property and transfers with the property.

Immovable by Law   Real property is also defined as any property that is immovable by law. When the law declares that an item of personal property is required to stay with the land, that item becomes real property.

Personal Property

As was indicated previously, anything that is not real property is personal property. Personal property is movable, whereas real property is considered to be immovable. Other names for personal property are "chattels" or "choses." Examples of personal property include bonds, money, contracts, furniture, automobiles, mortgages, and so on.

Other distinctions that might be made between real and personal property are:

1. Contracts involving the sale of real property must be in writing and signed by the person whose title is being transferred. In the sale of some personal property, the transaction need not be in writing if the price is low enough. However, prudence suggests that all personal property sales contracts should be in writing to avoid misunderstandings. The contracts themselves are personal property even though the contracts might refer to the sale of real property.

2. Personal property, when sold, is usually transferred by use of a bill of sale. Real property is transferred by delivery of a written instrument called a "deed."

The Status of Property Can Change

Real property can become personal property, and personal property can become real property. For example, trees growing in a forest are considered real property. The trees are cut and transported to the sawmill, where they are made into boards, thus becoming personal property. The boards are used in the construction of a building, changing them back to real property. The building eventually outlives its usefulness and is torn down. The salvaged lumber becomes personal property once again.

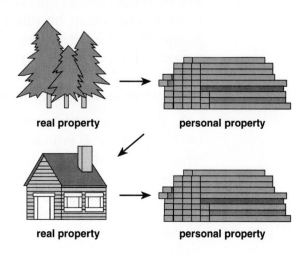

real property   personal property

real property   personal property

1.4 FIXTURES

Fixtures are items that were originally personal property but are now attached to the land in such a manner as to be considered part of the land itself, thus becoming real property. Depending upon the specific circumstances, certain items of personal property may become so integrated with the land that they are considered to be part of the real property and, consequently, belong to the current owner of the real estate.

The concept of fixtures can become a touchy question when land is bought or sold, or when a tenant makes improvements on the property. If a legal dispute arises, the court must make a decision as to whether the property in question is a fixture and must remain with the real property, or whether the item is still personal property and can be removed and taken by the seller or the tenant. If allowed to be taken, the seller and/or tenant must repair all damage caused by the removal.

Tests of a Fixture

To help determine whether an item is a fixture and consequently real property or is not a fixture and consequently personal property, the courts have established **"five tests of a fixture,"** which include **method of attachment, adaptability, relationship of parties, intention of parties, and agreement between parties.**

1. The courts are concerned with the method by which the property is incorporated into or attached to the land and its consequent degree of permanence. In other words, is it nailed, cemented, welded, or bolted down? Or is it simply leaning against the building or hanging on the wall?

2. The courts are concerned with the adaptability to ordinary use of the attached personal property. In other words, is the item in question customized, or can it easily be used in some other building? Wall-to-wall carpeting would be considered a fixture because it had been cut for a room of a particular size and shape, and the carpet is attached to a tack strip that is nailed to the floor. Customized draperies or fireplace screens may also become fixtures.

3. The courts are concerned with the relationship between the person who adds the article and the party with whom he or she may be transacting business. In other words, is the dispute between a landlord and a tenant, a buyer and a seller, or a borrower and a lender? In a dispute between a landlord and a tenant, the courts today tend to favor the tenant; between a buyer and a seller, the courts tend to favor the buyer; between a borrower and a lender, the courts will lean toward the lender.

4. The intention of the person attaching the personal property to the land is a very important issue. Intention is indicated by action or agreement of the parties, whether it be expressed or merely implied. If intention can be proved, the courts will consider this the most important test.

5. The courts will also look to the existence of any agreements between the parties regarding the item in question. In other words, has a right to the property in question been established by the signing of an agreement? Is the item mentioned in the real estate listing or purchase contract?

Take Proper Precautions

Many times problems arise between buyers and sellers regarding fixtures. Therefore, it behooves people to clearly spell out, in the purchase contract, the intentions of the seller and the buyer regarding the items of personal property or fixtures to be included in the sales price. The purchase contract should state whether the carpets, stove, or any other questionable item is included as a part of the sales price or if the seller reserves the right to remove these items after the sale.

Exception to the Fixture Rule

For every good rule, there is often an exception. In the case of fixtures, there are certain items that remain personal property after they have been affixed to real property. Articles of personal property that a business tenant has attached to real property because of their need to be used in a trade or business are called "trade fixtures." Examples are shelving, counters, or cash registers used by a business but not sold as merchandise to customers.

These trade fixtures are viewed as the personal property of the business tenant, and the tenant has the right to remove these items. However, a residential tenant in a house or apartment might install room dividers or different light fixtures. These fixtures may or may not be viewed as the personal property of the tenant. As noted earlier, the courts do tend to favor the tenant. In many cases, these fixtures may be removed by the tenant, provided the premises are not damaged in the process of removal. However, the right to remove is not absolute; it depends upon the circumstances in each and every case.

CHAPTER SUMMARY

California's colorful history is closely tied to the concept of land ownership. A study of the early inhabitants of the state gives a better understanding of the foundation upon which real estate laws and regulations have been built.

Ownership of real property includes certain property rights called the "bundle of rights." The bundle includes the right to own, possess, use, enjoy, encumber, dispose of, and exclude.

Real property is defined as (1) land; (2) that which is appurtenant to the land, such as easements or stock in a mutual water company; (3) that which is affixed to the land, known as fixtures; and (4) that which is immovable by law.

The status of property can change. Real property can become personal property and personal property can be changed to real property. In determining the status of real versus personal property, the courts have developed five tests to determine whether or not an item is a fixture. These tests are Method of attachment, Adaptability, Relationship of the parties, Intention of the parties to the transaction, and the existence of an Agreement between the parties involved (the MARIA memory tool).

IMPORTANT TERMS AND CONCEPTS

Appurtenant

Bundle of rights

Emblements

Fixture

Personal property

Real property

Riparian rights

Tests of a fixture

Treaty of Guadalupe Hidalgo

PRACTICAL APPLICATION

1. After purchasing a home, the new owner applies for a building permit to add another bedroom and bath. The city building department requires a $500 application fee and refuses to issue the permit until acceptable plans are submitted showing that the project meets all construction codes. How does this building department requirement conflict with the basic bundle of rights?

2. After the close of the sale, the seller of a home removes a 8' x 10' metal prefab storage shed from the property. The buyer states that the shed is real property and should stay on the property as part of the sale. Who is right? How could this problem have been avoided?

3. How do trade fixtures differ from regular fixtures?

1. Which group of explorers and colonizers set up presidios and pueblos in the early days of California?
   a. Mexicans
   b. British
   c. Spanish
   d. Native Americans

2. Which of the following is *not* considered to be one of the bundle of rights? The right to:.
   a. own property
   b. pay taxes
   c. enjoy
   d. encumber

3. Which of the following is considered "land" and therefore is real estate?
   a. oil deposits beneath the surface
   b. harvested crops
   c. trade fixtures
   d. airspace above the land

4. The right of the owner of land bordering on a river to use the river water in a reasonable manner is called:
   a. appropriation rights
   b. take out rights
   c. riparian rights
   d. subjacent privileges

5. Wall-to-wall carpeting in a single-family dwelling is usually considered to be:
   a. a fixture
   b. a chattel
   c. removable
   d. separate property

6. Which of the following is considered appurtenant to the land and upon sale, or other transfer, stays with the land and is not taken by the former owner?
   a. stock in a mutual water company
   b. trade fixtures
   c. an easement
   d. both a and c

7. In a dispute between a buyer and seller over a fixture, the courts would tend to favor the:
   a. seller
   b. buyer
   c. one with the most money
   d. neither party

8. In what year was California granted statehood?
   a. 1821
   b. 1846
   c. 1848
   d. 1850

9. The main feature of personal property is:
   a. title is transferred by a deed
   b. its immobility
   c. its value is always less than real property
   d. its mobility

10. Which two terms do not belong together?
    a. bundle of rights—use and enjoyment
    b. real estate—land
    c. reasonable use—water rights
    d. personal property—easement

11. An orange tree in a suburban backyard is real property. An orange on the ground in that yard is:
    a. real property
    b. fixture
    c. personal property
    d. real estate

12. Unless otherwise noted, mineral rights:
    a. transfer with the land
    b. are the personal property of the owner
    c. are always reserved by the former owner
    d. never carry an implied right to enter the land for extraction

13. Mortgages and deeds of trust are:
    a. real property
    b. personal property
    c. fixtures
    d. emblements

14. The right of the state to give permission to a nonriparian owner to take water from a river or lake is called:
    a. riparian right
    b. possessor right
    c. percolating rights
    d. right of appropriation

15. Which mineral is not considered capable of ownership until reduced to possession?
    a. gold
    b. oil
    c. iron
    d. silver

16. The words "chattel" and "chose" stand for:
    a. fixtures
    b. real estate
    c. personal property
    d. real property

17. Which of the following is *not* considered a test of a fixture?
    a. relationship of the parties
    b. method of financing
    c. intention of the parties
    d. method of attachment

18. Personal property that is attached to the land in such a manner that it becomes part of the real property is called:
    a. a fixture
    b. a chattel
    c. a chose
    d. an emblement

19. Arnold and Sally Williams are tenants in an apartment. They add temporary shelves in the kitchen. When they move, the shelves will probably be considered:
    a. trade fixtures
    b. real property
    c. appurtenances
    d. personal property

20. Jane Garcia leases a retail store and operates a jewelry business. When she moves, her business machines and shelves will probably be considered:
    a. trade fixtures
    b. real property
    c. appurtances
    d. personal property

Chapter 2

Part I: Legal Description, Method of Acquiring Title, and Deeds

Chapter Preview, Part I

In Part I of this chapter, you will study land descriptions, stressing the lot, block, and tract; metes and bounds; and U.S. Government survey methods for describing and locating land.

You will also explore five ways of acquiring title to real estate, including an explanation of deeds used in California. At the conclusion of Part I, you will be able to:

1. List the three major methods used to legally describe and locate land

2. Find a parcel of land using each of the three location methods; be able to calculate acreage

3. Outline five ways of acquiring title to real estate

4. Discuss the difference between a grant deed, quitclaim deed, and warranty deed

5. Briefly describe the purpose of the California recording system

2.1 LAND DESCRIPTIONS

Three reasons the description of real property is essential are:

1. To specifically identify and locate areas of real property ownership

2. To satisfy buyers who are interested in the precise dimensions and area of their property
3. To minimize land description disputes between neighbors by establishing set boundary lines

In addition to these three reasons, the law requires that every parcel of land sold, mortgaged, or leased must be properly described or identified. Legal descriptions are usually based upon the field notes of a civil engineer or a surveyor. When dealing with property, recorded descriptions usually can be obtained from title insurance policies, deeds, deeds of trust, or mortgages.

Engineers and surveyors establish exact directions and distances by means of transits and measuring devices. Aerial photography is also used in modern mapping.

Early Methods Used

Today's survey methods are a far cry from the methods used in early California. One early method of land measurement employed two people on horseback. Each would drag an end of a cord or rawhide strip called a *thong,* which was about 100 *varas* in length. (A vara is about 33 inches.) One rider would remain stationary while the other rode past. When the length of the thong was reached, this would be repeated by the other rider until one of them arrived at the end of the property. The number of thong lengths passed would then be counted and the dimensions of the property would be determined.

In another early method, the circumference of a wagon wheel was measured. A leather strip was tied to a spoke and then, by rolling the wheel on the ground, the revolutions of the wheel could be counted and the distance recorded.

Present-Day Land Descriptions

There are three major methods used today to legally describe and locate land. They are:

1. Lot, block, and tract system
2. Metes and bounds system
3. U.S. Government survey, commonly called the U.S. section and township system

Lot, Block, and Tract System

When a large parcel of land is divided into smaller parcels, it is called *subdividing.* The California Subdivision Map Act requires that all new subdivisions be either mapped or platted. A map of each subdivision is recorded in the recorder's office of the county in which the land is located.

At the time a subdivision map is filed in the county recorder's office, it is assigned a tract name and/or number. Once subdivision maps are recorded, legal descriptions are created by making reference to a particular lot in the block in that tract in which the property is located.

EXAMPLE. "All of lot 4 in Block A of Tract number 2025 in the city of Bellflower, Los Angeles County, California. As per map recorded in Book 76 page 83 of maps in the office of the recorder of said county." This type of identification is commonly found in urban areas of California, where extensive subdividing has taken place. (See Figure 2.1.)

Metes and Bounds System

The metes and bounds system of land location is used most often when the property in question is not covered by a recorded subdivision map or when the property is so irregular in shape that it is impractical to describe under the section and township system.

Metes refers to the measurement of length, using items such as inches, feet, yards, rods, meters, and miles. *Bounds* refers to the use of boundaries, both natural and artificial, such as rivers, roads, fences, boulders, creeks, iron pipes,

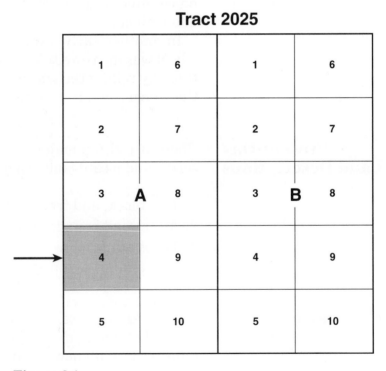

Tract 2025

Figure 2.1

and so forth, so metes and bounds means to *measure the boundaries.* This system is one of the oldest methods used to describe land, and it is used in both rural and urban areas. A common term used in the metes and bounds system is *bench mark.* A bench mark is a mark on a fixed or enduring object, such as a metal stake or rock, and it is often used as an elevation point by a surveyor.

Another term is *angular lines.* Many surveys using metes and bounds descriptions are based on angles and directions from a given north-south line, which is obtained with a compass. Angles are a deflection from this north-south line. Deflections will be to the east or west of the north-south line.

There are 360° in a circle and 180° in a half-circle. Each degree is divided into 60 minutes and each minute is divided into 60 seconds. The bearing of a course is described by measuring easterly or westerly from the north and south lines. (See Figure 2.2.)

Although the metes and bounds land description is one of the oldest forms, it is also one of the most complicated. The system ranges from just simple distances between given landmarks to surveyor readings based on angles found in the arc of a circle.

In using the metes and bounds method, three important points must be stressed:

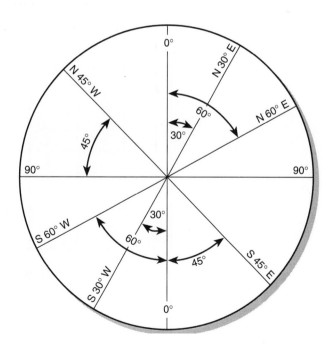

Figure 2.2

1. You must start at a given point of beginning.
2. You must follow, in detail, the boundaries of the land in courses, distances, and directions from one point to another.
3. You must always return to the point of beginning, thus enclosing the boundary lines.

EXAMPLE. Here is a legal description using the metes and bounds method. "Beginning at a point on the southerly line of Harbor Ave., 200 ft. westerly of the southwest corner of the intersection of Harbor Ave. and 8th St.; running thence due south 300 ft. to the northerly line of Cribbage St.; thence westerly along the northerly line of Cribbage St., 200 ft.; thence northerly and parallel to the first course, 300 ft. to the southerly line of Harbor Ave., thence easterly along the southerly line of Harbor Ave., 200 ft. to the point of beginning." (See Figure 2.3.)

One major weakness in using a metes and bounds system is that markers or points of beginning often disapp   or have been moved or replaced. In later years this ma   it difficult to find the exact corners of a parcel.

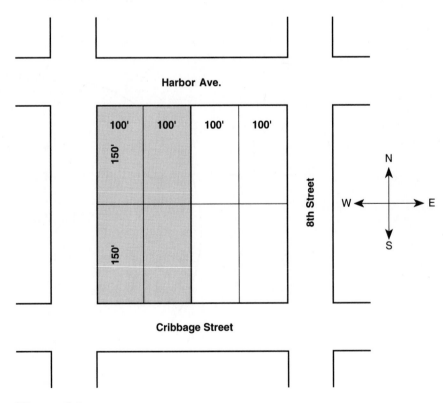

Figure 2.3

U.S. Government Section and Township System

The U.S. Government section and township method of survey is used primarily to describe agricultural or rural land. The system originated in the 1800s with a survey of public lands made by the U.S. Surveyor General. The U.S. Government survey system establishes monuments as points of beginning. The monuments are intersected by two imaginary lines, one running east and west called a *base line,* and another running north and south called the *meridian line.*

Because of its peculiar shape, the state of California requires three of these principal base lines and meridians, as shown in Figure 2.4. They are:

1. *Humboldt Base Line and Meridian,* which is the point of beginning for describing land in the northwestern part of California. The actual point of beginning is on Mt. Pierce, just south of Eureka, California.
2. *Mt. Diablo Base Line and Meridian,* which is the point of beginning for describing land in the central part of California. The actual point of beginning is on Mt. Diablo near Walnut Creek, California.
3. *San Bernardino Base Line and Meridian,* which is used to describe land in southern California. The actual point of beginning is the intersection of Base Line Street and Meridian Avenue in the City of San Bernardino, California.

CALIFORNIA BASE LINES & MERIDIANS

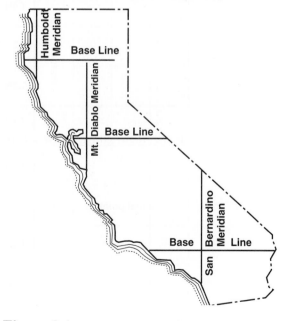

Figure 2.4

Range lines run parallel to the principal meridians at six-mile intervals. *Township lines* run parallel to the principal base lines at six-mile intervals. The result is a grid of squares, or *townships,* each township containing approximately 36 square miles.

In order to identify each of these townships, a numbering system utilizing an assignment of two location numbers has been devised. The identity of each township is determined by its position north or south of the base line, and east or west of the meridian line. A legal description might be, for example:

"Township 2 North, Range 3 East, San Bernardino Base Line and Meridian. (T2N, R3E, SBBL & M)." The X indicates the township. (See Figure 2.5.)

Sections in a Township

Townships are in turn divided into *sections*. Each township contains 36 squares, or sections. Each section is one mile square. These sections are uniformly numbered from 1 to 36, with Section 1 located in the northeast corner of the township.

Not only is each section one mile square, but each contains 640 acres. Each section can be divided into smaller parcels of land, such as:

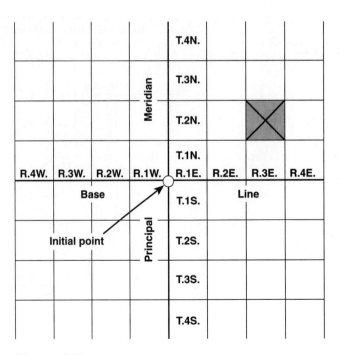

Figure 2.5

TOWNSHIP

6	5	4	3	2	1
7	8	9	10	11	12
18	17	16	15	14	13
19	20	21	22	23	24
30	29	28	27	26	25
31	32	33	34	35	36

Figure 2.6

A quarter of a section = 160 acres

A quarter of a ¼ section = 40 acres

A quarter of a ¼ of a ¼ section = 10 acres

The division can be smaller and smaller until the size of the parcel is identified. The division need not be in quarters; it may also be in halves. (See Figures 2.6 and 2.7.)

Pitfall Because of the earth's curvature, some sections in townships are distorted and may not contain a full 640 acres; thus, computing acreage under the U.S. Government system will

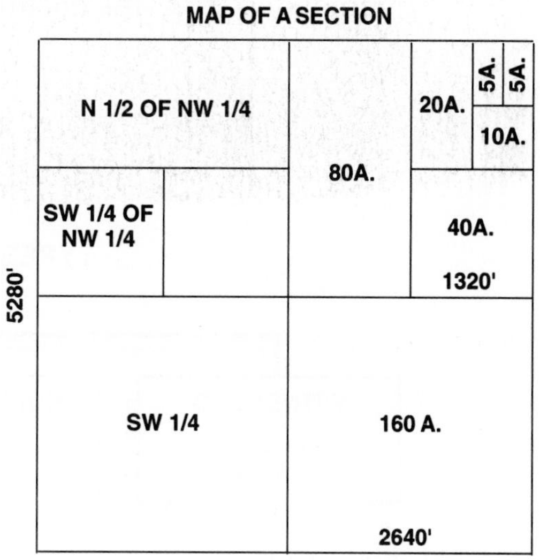

MAP OF A SECTION

Figure 2.7

give approximate figures. An accurate measure of actual acreage is best left to licensed engineers or surveyors.

The following additional measurements will help in computing land measurements:

One mile = 5,280 feet or 320 rods

One rod = 16½ feet

One acre = 43,560 square feet

One square acre = 208.71 feet × 208.71 feet

Commercial acre = standard acre less land needed for streets, sidewalks, curbs

2.2 METHODS OF ACQUIRING TITLE

Chapter 1 discussed the difference between real and personal property. Section 2.1 of this chapter illustrated the three main ways of legally describing real property. The next logical step is to describe how a person goes about acquiring legal title to real property. According to the California Civil Code, the five ways of acquiring property are by *will, succession, accession, occupancy,* and *transfer.*

Acquiring Property by Will

A will is a legal instrument by which a person over the age of 18 and of sound mind disposes of property, upon his or her death. California law recognizes three types of wills: (1) a witnessed will, (2) a holographic will, and (3) a statutory will. (See Figure 2.8.)

A *witnessed will* is a formal typewritten document signed by the individual who is making it, wherein he or she declares in the presence of at least two witnesses that it is his or her will. The two witnesses in turn sign the will. It is recommended that this document be prepared by an attorney.

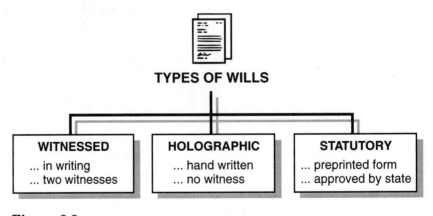

TYPES OF WILLS

WITNESSED	**HOLOGRAPHIC**	**STATUTORY**
... in writing ... two witnesses	... hand written ... no witness	... preprinted form ... approved by state

Figure 2.8

A *holographic will* is a document written, dated, and signed in its entirety in the handwriting of the maker. It requires no witnesses.

A *statutory will* is a preprinted form, approved by the state, in which a person merely fills in the blanks, usually without formal legal assistance. This statutory will requires at least two witnesses.

At one time, another will—an oral will in contemplation of death, called a *nuncupative will*—was occasionally recognized. But today oral dying declarations are for the most part ignored by the probate courts.

Special Terms
A will is also called a *testament.* Special terms relating to wills are:

Testator: Male person who makes a will

Testatrix: Female person who makes a will

Executor: Male person named in the will by the maker to handle the estate of the deceased

Executrix: Female person named in the will by the maker to handle the estate of the deceased

Administrator: Male person appointed by the court to handle the estate, when no will is left

Administratrix: Female person appointed by the court to handle the estate when no will is left

Devise: A gift of real property by will

Devisee: Person receiving real property by will

Bequest, legacy: A gift of personal property by will

Legatee: Person receiving personal property by will

Codicil: A change in a will

Intestate: A situation where a person dies without leaving a will. He or she is said to have died intestate.

Testate: A situation where a person dies leaving a will

Probate

Legal title to property being acquired by will is subject to the control of the probate court. The purpose of a probate hearing is to identify the creditors of the deceased and pay off these creditors. Then if any property remains, the probate court determines the identity of the rightful heirs and distributes the remaining property.

The law requires that upon the death of the owner, all property is subject to the temporary possession of an *executor(trix)* or an *administrator(trix).*

Probate action takes place in superior court, and the estate property may be sold during the probate period for the benefit of the heirs or to cover court costs. If a probate sale takes place, certain guidelines are set by the court. The general guidelines are:

1. The initial offer in a probate real estate sale must be for at least 90% of the appraised value of the property.
2. Once the initial offer is made, the court is petitioned to confirm the sale, and at the hearing the court may accept additional bids.
3. The first additional bid must be an increase of at least 10% of the first $10,000 of the original bid and 5% of any excess. Subsequent bids may be for less.
4. The court confirms the final sale and sets the broker's commissions, if a broker is involved.

Probate fees paid to executors, administrators, and attorneys are set by the courts and vary depending upon the size and complexity of the estate. It should be noted that certain types of property holdings need not be probated. This is discussed in Part II of this chapter.

Acquiring Property by Succession

When a deceased person leaves no will, the law provides for the disposition of his or her property. The state of California dictates who will get the property under the law of *intestate succession,* with succession meaning the handing down of property to another person. (See Figure 2.9.)

When a person dies intestate, the property of the deceased is divided into two categories: separate property and community property. The laws of intestate succession are different for each of these categories. When a person dies

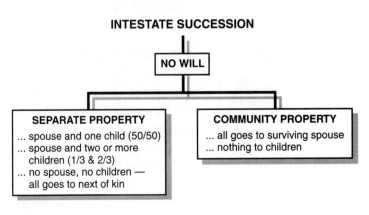

Figure 2.9

without a will and leaves separate property, this means that the surviving spouse did not have an interest in said property. If a person leaves community property, this means a surviving spouse has a one-half interest in the property.

When *separate property* is involved, the following disposition of property is made:

1. When a deceased person leaves a spouse and one child, the separate property is divided one-half to the spouse and one-half to the child.
2. When a deceased person leaves a spouse and two or more children, the spouse receives one-third and the children equally divide the other two-thirds.
3. There are other divisions made by the courts in the event that a person dies leaving no spouse or children. The usual rule is the property goes to the next of kin, such as parents, brothers, sisters, and so on.

If a person dies intestate and leaves *community property,* the deceased person's community interest always passes to the surviving spouse. The children, if any, get nothing.

Key Point | On matters regarding wills and estates, *always* consult an experienced attorney! Do-it-yourself estate planning is not recommended!

Acquiring Property by Accession You may acquire title to property that is added to your existing real estate. This process is called *accession.*

Examples include (1) accretion, (2) avulsion, (3) addition of fixtures, and (4) improvements made in error. (See Figure 2.10.)

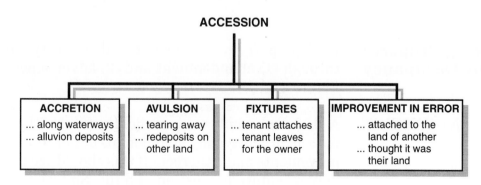

Figure 2.10

ACCRETION	The gradual accumulation of soil on property bordering a stream, river, or an ocean shore line is called *accretion.* The soil thus deposited is referred to as *alluvion,* or *alluvion deposits.* The gradual wearing away of land by the action of water and wind is known as *erosion. Reliction* occurs when the waterway, sea, or river recedes permanently below the usual water line. When this takes place, the owner of the property that borders on the waterway, sea, or river may acquire title to the newly exposed land.
AVULSION	*Avulsion* occurs when a river or stream, during a storm or earthquake, carries away a part of the bank and bears it to the opposite bank or to another part of the same bank. The owner of the part carried away may reclaim it within one year after the avulsion. However, the owner must reclaim the title by applying some act of ownership, such as cultivation of the soil, within one year; if not, then the land belongs to the property owner to whom the land is now attached.
	For urban readers, this discussion regarding rivers and water rights may seem out of place. But in rural California, especially northern California, those topics are an important aspect of real estate principles.
ADDITION OF FIXTURES	Addition of fixtures occurs when a person affixes something to the land of another without an agreement permitting removal. The thing so affixed may then become the property of the landowner.
IMPROVEMENTS MADE IN ERROR	An *improvement made in error* occurs when a person, in good faith, erroneously affixes improvements to the land of another. In some cases these erroneous improvements may pass to the landowner. But in most cases the person who made the improvements in error is permitted to remove the improvements and pay the cost to restore the property to its original condition.
Acquiring Property by Occupancy	Real property or the use of real property can be gained through (1) abandonment and (2) adverse possession. (See Figure 2.11.)
ABANDONMENT	A party who holds a leasehold interest (the tenant) in a piece of property may abandon his or her interest or any improvements made thereon. If this should occur, the landlord may reacquire possession and full control of the premises. In other words, when a tenant leaves before the lease ex-

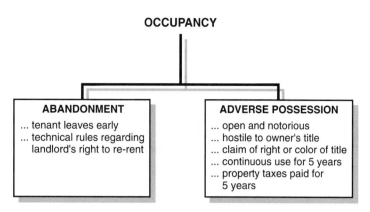

Figure 2.11

pires, the landlord may reacquire the use of the property at that time, and in some cases not be obligated to refund rental payments or return any improvements made on the property. There are technical rules regarding the landlord's right to re-rent the property. If a tenant abandons the premises and leaves personal property, the landlord may, after due notification, dispose of such personal property.

ADVERSE POSSESSION   Adverse possession is a method of acquiring physical possession of property by a person who is not the actual owner. This physical possession may develop into legal title if five conditions are met.

Five elements of adverse possession

1. There must be actual occupation, *open and notorious.* This means that the claim of possession must not be kept a secret. In other words, if the present owner inspects the property, the possession or use by another person should be apparent. You do not actually have to reside on the property, but you must show your intentions of holding and possessing the land through some type of improvement to the land. For example: If the property were farmland, the cultivation of crops, the grazing of cattle, or the fencing of the property might constitute possession.

2. There must be occupancy *hostile* to the true owner's title (wishes). Hostile does not mean physical confrontation. Hostile means a person is using the property without permission and not making rental payment of any kind to the owner. Permission to use the property defeats the hostile use and prevents acquiring title by adverse possession.

3. There must be a *claim of right or color of title.* Under claim of right, the claimant enters as an intruder and remains; under color of title, claimants base their right on some court decree or upon a defective written instrument.

4. There must be *continuous and uninterrupted* possession for a period of five years.

5. There must be the *payment of all real property taxes* levied and assessed for a period of five consecutive years. The fact that the true owner is also paying the taxes does not necessarily defeat the rights of the adverse possessor, as long as the possessor also pays the taxes.

Adverse possession is not common in California because of the five requirements listed previously. It is not possible to obtain title by adverse possession to public lands, nor against an incompetent private landowner. Title insurance and marketable title cannot be obtained until a court, under a quiet title action, rules that the adverse possession vested valid title. In short, if you acquire title by adverse possession, it will be difficult to finance or sell the property without first going to court.

Acquiring Property by Transfer

Without question, the most common method of acquiring property is by transfer. When property is conveyed from one person to another by act of the parties or by act of law, it can be said that title is acquired by transfer. There are five basic types of property transfers: (1) private grant, (2) public grant, (3) gift, (4) public dedication, and (5) court action (or involuntary transfer). (See Figure 2.12.)

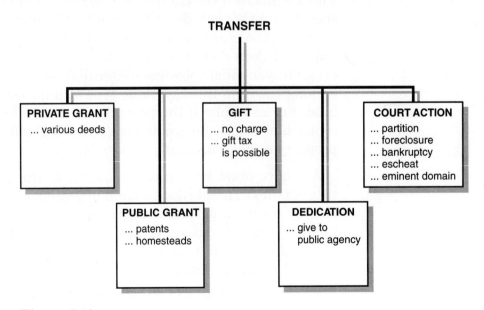

Figure 2.12

PRIVATE GRANT	Private grant occurs when an owner voluntarily conveys his or her ownership rights to another. The basic instrument used in this transaction is a deed. (Deeds are discussed in detail in Section 2.3.)
PUBLIC GRANT	When a governmental agency deeds property to an individual or institution, it is called a public grant. In the early years of our country's history, public grants were made through laws enacted by Congress.

PUBLIC GRANT (continued)

The Preemption Act of 1862 allowed persons living on federal land, who were known as squatters, to acquire 160 acres of land at a small fee.

The Homestead Act of 1862 allowed vast stretches of public land to be homesteaded. The heads of families or persons over 21 years of age could obtain 160 acres. They had to file a declaration of homestead with the county recorder or at a land office and had to agree to occupy and improve the land. After residing on it for five years and paying a small fee, they received a document from the government called a *patent,* which conveyed ownership to the homesteader.

Other public grants were made by the government for railroads, educational institutions, national parks, cities, and towns.

GIFT

A property owner may voluntarily transfer property to a private person or organization without giving or receiving any consideration or compensation. In case of real property, the transfer normally would be evidenced by a gift deed. Depending upon the value of the gift, there may or may not be a gift tax liability. The person who gives the gift is called the *donor,* the person who receives the gift is called the *donee.*

PUBLIC DEDICATION

A property owner may also give land to a public body for a particular use such as a street, a park, bridges, schools, playgrounds, and so on. This act is called public dedication. The dedication is valid only if the public body accepts the property.

COURT ACTION (INVOLUNTARY TRANSFER)

There are a variety of situations in which a court of law may be called upon to transfer legal title. The most common of these involuntary transfers are partition action, foreclosure action, bankruptcy, escheat, and eminent domain. (See Figure 2.13.)

Partition action is a court action wherein the co-owners of property may sue other co-owners for severance of their respective interests. If the property cannot be physically

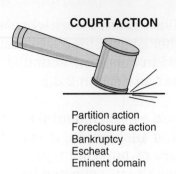

COURT ACTION

Partition action
Foreclosure action
Bankruptcy
Escheat
Eminent domain

Figure 2.13

divided, the court can order a sale, and divide the proceeds among the former owners.

Foreclosure action takes place when a person, holding a delinquent lien on a property, institutes proceedings requesting the forced sale of property. In California, delinquent real estate loans are foreclosed using a process called a "trustee's sale," which is discussed in Chapter 7.

Bankruptcy can be either voluntary or involuntary. When an individual cannot meet credit obligations, he or she may voluntarily file bankruptcy or may be adjudged bankrupt by the courts. Title to real property is then vested in a court-appointed trustee, who sells the property to pay the claims of creditors. Under certain circumstances a family home can be protected against forced sale by the bankruptcy court.

Escheat is the legal process whereby ownership of real property reverts to the state, for lack of heirs or want of legal ownership. The probate courts will do all in their power to locate possible heirs. After escheat proceedings are instituted, the title is held in trust by the state for a set time. If at the end of that time no heirs have been located, title to the property will transfer to the state. Every year millions of dollars worth of property escheats to the state of California because of the lack of heirs.

Eminent domain is the power of the state to take land from private ownership by due process of law. Use of eminent domain is often referred to as "condemnation proceedings." These proceedings may be instituted by all levels of government and by public utilities or railroads.

Two conditions are legally required to use the power of eminent domain:

1. The property must be taken for a public use.
2. The owner must be paid just compensation. Most courts have ruled that the "fair market value" based upon an appraisal is the proper method for determining just compensation.

2.3 INSTRUMENTS USED IN THE TRANSFER OF REAL PROPERTY

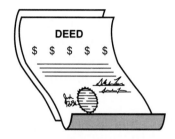

Under English common law, a written document was not needed to transfer title to real property. Rather, a twig, a stone, or a handful of dirt passing from one owner to the next owner in the presence of witnesses was symbolic of the transfer of property. Other methods of transfer were simply a statement made before witnesses in sight of the land, followed by entry upon the land by the new owner. Today under California law, the transfer of ownership of real property may be done by a single written instrument known as a deed.

A *deed* is a written document by which (when properly executed, delivered, and accepted) title to real property is transferred from one person, called a *grantor,* to another person, called a *grantee.* The grantor is the person who gives title and the grantee is the person who receives title. In a real estate sale, the grantor is the seller, and the grantee is the buyer. Throughout this book you will find words to designate the parties in an agreement that end in the letters *or* and *ee,* such as:

Trustor and trustee
Lessor and lessee
Vendor and vendee
Optionor and optionee

To understand these terms, remember this rule:

The *or* ending denotes the *giver,* and the *ee* ending indicates the *receiver.*

EXAMPLE. A lessor (owner or landlord) gives a lease to the lessee (tenant).

Essentials of a Valid Deed

To be valid, a deed must contain certain essential elements:

1. *Deed must be in writing.* Legal instruments required to be in writing come under the *Statute of Frauds.* According to this statute, when the title to real property is to be voluntarily conveyed, it must be accomplished by an instrument in writing, usually a deed.

2. *Parties must be correctly described and identified.* In order for a deed to be valid, the parties must be properly described. This means that the grantor (seller) and the grantee (buyer) must be certain and absolute.

EXAMPLE. A deed from A to B or C is not absolute. The word "or" creates the problem. A deed from A to B and C is absolute. The word "and" makes it certain.

Since there are so many individuals with like or similar names, it is also important that the parties to a deed be identified as clearly as possible in order to avoid any later confusion as to true identity.

If possible, the full legal name should be used and the legal status of the individual should be shown. Remember, the full name includes middle name or initial, if any, and the legal status should refer to the relationship between parties, such as husband and wife.

3. *Grantor must be competent to convey and capable of receiving title.* Everyone is competent to convey except:

a. *minors* . . . persons under the age of 18 years, unless the minor is classified as emancipated, in which case a minor can legally contract for real estate. An emancipated minor is normally a person under 18 years who is married or in the armed services.

b. *incompetents* . . . persons of unsound mind, judicially declared incompetent

c. *convicts* . . . persons imprisoned for life or under a death penalty

Question: Can an infant take title to real property?

Answer: Yes, an infant can receive title by gift or inheritance but cannot convey title without a guardian or other court approval.

Question: Can a person take title under an assumed name?

Answer: Yes, but upon resale it may be difficult to prove identity for a notary public.

4. *Description of the property must be clear.* The property in the deed must be correctly described. This means that any description which clearly identifies the property so that it can be located with certainty meets the test of the law. In most cases, the legal description is either a lot, block, and tract; a metes and bounds; or a U.S. Government survey description.

5. *There must be a granting clause.* A granting clause means that the deed must contain words indicating the intention of the owner to convey the property. The exact words are not specified; however, the words, "I hereby grant," "I hereby convey," or "I hereby transfer" will satisfy the requirements of a granting clause.

6. *Deed must contain the signature of the grantor.* To be valid, a deed must be signed by all grantors named in the deed. If there is more than one owner, all owners must sign. For instance, both husband and wife must sign a deed to convey community property.

Under certain guidelines, state law allows a grantor's name to be signed by an "attorney in fact," acting under a valid power of attorney.

California permits a person who is unable to sign his or her name to sign by mark, as long as two witnesses are present. One of the witnesses then signs the deed according to the manner prescribed by law.

Delivery of the Deed Is Required

A deed is not effective unless it is delivered to and accepted by the grantee. This does not mean a mere turning over of the physical possession of the document. The grantor must have a clear and honest intention to pass title immediately, before there is a legal delivery.

1. *Evidence of delivery.* The best evidence is actually handing the deed to the grantee. However, manual delivery is not necessary, as a deed may be delivered to a third party for the benefit of the grantee—for example, depositing the deed in escrow. Again, manual delivery does not in itself constitute delivery; the proof lies in the intent of the grantor to pass title. If and when the deed is recorded, recording of the deed presumes valid delivery.

2. *Time of delivery.* To be effective, a deed must be delivered to the grantee during the grantor's lifetime. It cannot be used to take the place of a will.

A deed that is delivered to a grantee with the condition that it is not to take effect until the death of the grantor is not valid since the intent to pass title would not occur during the lifetime of the grantor.

3. *Date of delivery.* A deed is presumed to be delivered as of its date of writing or execution. If no date exists on the deed, the legal date is presumed to be the date of delivery. The lack of a date on the deed does not invalidate the deed.

4. *Conditional delivery.* Delivery of a deed must be absolute. It cannot be delivered to a grantee subject to conditions. For example, in an attempt to avoid the cost of probate, A gives a deed to B telling B that she is not to record the deed until A dies. This is a conditional delivery and is not a valid deed or transfer.

Acceptance

The deed must be accepted by the grantee, and this acceptance must be voluntary and unconditional. It is usually accomplished by words, acts, or conduct on the grantee's part which lead to the presumption of voluntary acceptance. An example of acceptance would be the recording of the deed by the grantee.

Acknowledgement
A deed is a real estate document that need not be recorded to be valid. However, if the grantee wishes to record the deed, it must first be acknowledged.

An *acknowledgement* is a formal declaration before a duly authorized officer (usually a notary public) by the person who signed a document, stating that the signature is voluntarily given and that he or she is the person whose signature appears on the document.

Nonessentials in a Deed
Many of the items listed earlier are essential for a deed to be valid. Here are some items that are not legally required, but are commonly found in a deed.

Legally, a deed *does not* have to contain, but commonly has (1) an acknowledgement, (2) a date, and (3) a recording number issued by the county.

However, it must be remembered that a deed is *void* or *invalid* if the:

1. Grantor is incompetent
2. Deed is signed in blank
3. Deed is never delivered
4. Deed is a forgery
5. Grantee does not exist (fictitious or deceased)
6. Deed is altered in escrow

TYPES OF DEEDS

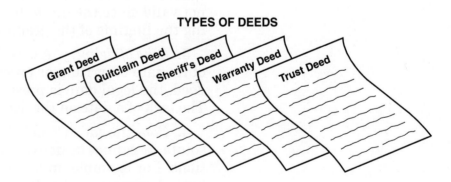

Grant Deed
In California, the grant deed is the most commonly used instrument for transferring title to real estate. A grant deed carries two "implied warranties"—meaning that although they are not written in the deed, the law says they apply. An example of a grant deed is presented in Figure 2.14.

AND WHEN RECORDED MAIL THIS DEED AND, UNLESS
OTHERWISE SHOWN BELOW, MAIL TAX STATEMENTS TO:

Name

Address

City &
State

TT-100 (Rev. 6/94) Ω

————— SPACE ABOVE THIS LINE FOR RECORDER'S USE —————

GRANT DEED

APN No.   **Title No.**   **Escrow No.**

THE UNDERSIGNED GRANTOR(s) DECLARE(s)
     DOCUMENTARY TRANSFER TAX is $ CITY TAX $
        ☐ computed on full value of property conveyed, or
        ☐ computed on full value less value of liens or encumbrances remaining at time of sale,
        ☐ Unincorporated area: ☐ City of   , and

FOR A VALUABLE CONSIDERATION, receipt of which is hereby acknowledged,

hereby GRANT(s) to

the following described real property in the

County of   , State of California:

Dated:

_____   _____

State of California

County of _____ } **ss.**

On_____ before me, _____ (here insert name) Notary Public,

personally appeared_____ ,
personally known to me (or proved to me on the basis of satisfactory evidence) to be the person(s) whose name(s) is/are subscribed to
the within instrument and acknowledged to me all that he/she/they executed the same in his/her/their authorized capacity(ies), and
that by his/her/their signature(s) on the instrument the person(s), or the entity upon behalf of which the person(s) acted, executed the
instrument.
WITNESS my hand and official seal.

Signature _____

————— affix seal within border —————

MAIL TAX STATEMENTS AS DIRECTED ABOVE.

Figure 2.14

The implied warranties in a grant deed are:

1. That the grantor has not already conveyed title to any other person
2. That the estate being conveyed is free from encumbrances made by the grantor or any other person claiming under the grantor, other than those disclosed to the grantee

Notice that these implied warranties do not state that the grantor is the owner or that the property is not encumbered. Rather, they state that the grantor has not deeded to others and that the property is free of encumbrances made by the grantor. This is why a potential buyer should always insist that a policy of title insurance be issued as a condition of the purchase.

In addition to transferring legal ownership, a grant deed can be used to create easements and land use restrictions. A grant deed also conveys any *after acquired title*. After acquired title means that after the grantor deeds the property to the grantee, if the grantor should later acquire an additional interest in the property that interest automatically passes to the grantee.

Quitclaim Deed

A quitclaim deed provides the grantee with the least protection of any deed. A quitclaim deed carries no implied warranties and no after acquired title provisions. Under a quitclaim deed, the grantor merely relinquishes any right or claim he or she has in the property. If the grantor has absolute ownership, then that is what is conveyed. If the grantor has no claim or ownership right, this type of deed transfers what the grantor has—nothing! In other words, a quitclaim deed merely says, "Whatever interest I have in the property is yours; it may be something or it may be nothing."

The quitclaim deed is usually used to remove certain items from the public record, such as the removal of an easement or recorded restriction. It is not normally used in a buy and sell transaction.

Sheriff's Deed

The court may order an owner's property sold after a lawsuit and the rendering of a money judgment against the owner. The successful bidder at this type of sale receives a sheriff's deed, which contains no warranties. In some courts, this sale is conducted by a commissioner instead of the sheriff, and the deed issued is called a commissioner's deed.

Gift Deed

A person who wishes to give real estate to another may convey title by using a gift deed. The legal consideration given in a gift deed is usually "love and affection." A gift deed is valid unless it is being used to defraud creditors, in which case the creditors may institute legal action to void the deed.

Tax Deed

A tax deed is issued by the tax collector after the sale of land which previously reverted to the state because of nonpayment of property taxes. The tax sale procedure is presented in Chapter 13.

Warranty Deed

A warranty deed is seldom used in California. Under a warranty deed, the grantor is legally responsible to the grantee for the condition of the title. Sellers in California are reluctant to assume this liability and rarely will sign warranty deeds. Instead, sellers sign grant deeds and leave the legal responsibility for the condition of the title to title insurance companies.

Trust Deed (or Deed of Trust)

A trust deed conveys "bare legal title" (but no right of use or possession) to a third party called a trustee. This deed differs from others in that title is held by the trustee merely as security for a loan (lien) until such time as the loan is paid off or until the borrower defaults on his or her payments. Trust deeds are financing instruments, and they are explained in Chapter 7.

Deed of Reconveyance

This deed is executed by the trustee to the borrower (trustor). When a beneficiary (the lender) notifies the trustee that the trustor has repaid a loan, the trustee reconveys the title back to the trustor using a deed of reconveyance. This instrument is also involved with the financing of real estate and is discussed in Chapter 7.

Trustee's Deed

This deed conveys title to a successful bidder at a trustee's sale (foreclosure). A trustee's deed contains no warranties.

A trustee's deed and the foreclosure process are discussed in Chapter 7.

2.4 THE RECORDING SYSTEM

The recording of a deed and many other title instruments, although not required by law, protects the new owner's rights. Under the Spanish and Mexican governments there were no recording laws in California. Shortly after California became a state, the legislature adopted a recording system by which evidence of title or interest in real property could be collected and held for public view at a convenient and safe place. This safe public place is the county recorder's office.

To be accepted for recording by a county recorder the deed must have:

1. An acknowledgement (be notarized)
2. Name and address to which future tax statements can be mailed
3. Basis for computing the transfer tax
4. Names of all parties involved in the transaction
5. An adequate legal description
6. Payment of a recording fee

Once a document is recorded, it is said that the world has *constructive notice* of the contents of the document.

The recording system also shows sequential transfers of property from the original owner to the present owner. This successive list of owners is called a *chain of title.*

Recorded documents are filed in books called grantor-grantee indexes. Most counties have reduced their title records to microfilm or microfiche for easy handling and storage. These title records are frequently transferred by title companies to computers, making it easier for the title company to research a property.

There is a general rule that says *"The First to Record Is the First in Right."*

EXAMPLE. A deeds to B, who does not record. If A then deeds to C, who does record, under the general rule, C would probably get the property because C recorded first.

However, there are two exceptions to this rule:

1. If the party who recorded first has knowledge of a prior unrecorded interest, the recording of a deed will not defeat the unrecorded deed.

2. If the first party failed to record, but took possession of the property, the possession by an unrecorded owner can defeat a later recorded deed.

EXAMPLE. A deeds to B who does not record, but B takes physical possession of the property. A then deeds to C, who does not make a physical inspection of the property. C then records the deed. Who will probably win? Answer: B, because physical possession gives actual notice to all parties, including C, that B has a prior interest in the property.

Moral: Always physically inspect a property before you purchase. Do not rely upon the public records only!

CHAPTER SUMMARY, PART I

There are three major types of land descriptions: lot, block, and tract; metes and bounds; and the U.S. Government survey system.

Five ways of acquiring title to property are by will, succession, accession, occupancy, and transfer.

To be valid, a deed must contain certain essential elements and the deed must have proper delivery and acceptance.

Major types of deeds are grant deed, quitclaim deed, warranty deed, sheriff's deed, and gift deed. The most common is the grant deed, and it contains two implied warranties.

California has adopted a recording system designed to protect the rights of property owners and lien holders.

IMPORTANT TERMS AND CONCEPTS

Accession
Accretion
Administrator(-trix)
Adverse possession
Alluvion
Avulsion
Codicil
Eminent domain
Escheat
Executor(trix)
Grant deed
Grantee
Grantor

Holographic will
Intestate
Lot, block, and tract
Metes and bounds
Probate
Quitclaim deed
Statutory will
Succession
Testator(trix)
U.S. Government survey system
Warranty deed
Witnessed will

1. S ½ of SW ¼ of the SW ¼ of the NW ¼, and the SW ¼ of Section 5. How many acres? Using the grid below, shade in the parcel.

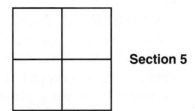

Section 5

2. At a probate sale, the initial accepted offer to purchase is $200,000. If you wish to place the next additional bid, what is the minimum you must bid?

3. Garcia deeds real property to Williams using a grant deed. Shortly thereafter the county abandons an alley easement at the rear of the property. Garcia maintains that the alley area is his, while Williams says it belongs to her. Based on your knowledge of grant deeds, who is probably right?

REVIEWING YOUR UNDERSTANDING

1. Ms. Jones was killed in an automobile accident. When the courts were called upon to distribute her property, they found she had died intestate. This means that she died:
   a. leaving no property
   b. leaving no heirs
   c. in debt
   d. without a will

2. If a married man with two children died without leaving a will, separate property purchased by him before he married and maintained as separate property during the marriage would be distributed as follows:
   a. one-half to the children
   b. one-half to the widow
   c. all to the widow
   d. one-third to the widow and two-thirds to the children

3. How many acres are there in a parcel of property which includes the following: the NW ¼ of the SW ¼; and the E ½ of the NW ¼; and the NE ¼ of the SW ¼ of Section 5?
   a. 320 acres
   b. 160 acres
   c. 40 acres
   d. 80 acres

4. The state urgently needs a piece of property to complete a project for public use. The owner did not wish to sell. Which method could be used to acquire the property?
   a. dedication
   b. escheat
   c. police power
   d. eminent domain

5. The term escheat is a legal term meaning that:
   a. a fraud has been committed
   b. an agent's license has been revoked
   c. property with a mortgage can be conveyed
   d. title has reverted to the state

6. The water flowing down a river gradually builds up the land along the bank by leaving deposits of soil; this action is called:
   a. accretion
   b. reliction
   c. avulsion
   d. erosion

7. All of the following statements concerning wills are correct, *except:*
   a. a statutory will uses a form approved by the state
   b. a holographic will can be signed by an X if it is witnessed
   c. an administratrix is appointed by a probate court
   d. a person who receives real property by will is known as a devisee

8. Deeds are used to transfer property. Which deed contains no implied or expressed warranties?
   a. warranty deed
   b. grant deed
   c. quitclaim deed
   d. interspousal grant deed

9. The executrix of an estate is:
   a. selected by the heirs
   b. appointed by the superior court
   c. named in the testator's will
   d. named by the decedent's attorney

10. To be valid, a deed must:
    a. contain a proper description of the property
    b. be signed by a competent grantee
    c. be recorded
    d. be dated

11. "Beginning on a point on the North line of Bard Avenue distant 218.00 feet East from the Northeast corner of Bard Avenue and Elm Street . . ." This legal description is:
    a. metes and bounds
    b. lot, block, and tract
    c. government survey
    d. townships and sections

12. Which of the following is *not* a base and meridian found in California?
    a. Humboldt
    b. Mt. Diablo
    c. Mt. Shasta
    d. San Bernardino

13. Which measurement is incorrect?
    a. acre = 43,800 square feet
    b. mile = 5,280 feet
    c. one square acre = 208.71 ft × 208.71 ft
    d. township = 6 miles square

14. Hostile, open, and notorious use of another person's land for five years is required for title by:
    a. will
    b. succession
    c. accession
    d. adverse possession

15. An instrument by which government grants title to a person:
    a. homestead
    b. partition action
    c. patent
    d. escheat

16. Recording of a deed gives:
    a. actual notice
    b. constructive notice
    c. physical notice
    d. vested notice

17. A deeds to B, who does not record the deed or take physical possession of the property. A then deeds to C, who had no notice of the prior deed to B. Then C records the deed. In a dispute over title between B and C, which rule would be important?
    a. All deeds must be recorded to be valid.
    b. He or she who records first is the first in right.
    c. All deeds must be acknowledged to be valid.
    d. The date of the deed determines who is first.

18. Which statement regarding deeds is false?
    a. A minor who is not emancipated can receive title but cannot convey title without court action.
    b. Incompetent persons cannot convey title without court action.
    c. A person cannot take legal title under an assumed name.
    d. A valid deed need not be recorded.

19. An "after acquired title" provision occurs in a:
   a. grant deed
   b. quitclaim deed
   c. sheriff's deed
   d. tax deed

20. Who signs the deed?
   a. lessor
   b. mortgagor
   c. grantee
   d. grantor

Part II: Estates and Methods of Holding Title

Chapter Preview, Part II

Part II discusses freehold and less-than-freehold estates. In addition, various methods of holding title including joint tenancy, tenancy in common, community property, and tenancy in partnership will be presented, stressing the characteristics, advantages, and disadvantages of each. At the conclusion of Part II, you will be able to:

1. Explain the difference between freehold and less-than-freehold estates

2. Describe the key differences in taking title to property as joint tenants as opposed to tenants in common

3. Explain the difference between community property and separate property

2.5 ESTATES

An estate is defined as the degree, quantity, nature, and extent of interest a person has in property. If the estate is in real property, you have a real estate interest. Real property estates fall into two major classifications: freehold estates and less-than-freehold estates.

46

Freehold Estates

A freehold estate refers to one's interest as an owner of real property. Freehold estates can be subdivided into fee estates and life estates. (See Figure 2.15.)

1. Fee estates or fee simple estates can be divided into:

   a. *fee simple absolute,* which the owner holds without any qualifications or limitations via private deed restrictions. All government ordinances and limitations still apply. This is the highest form of interest an individual can have in land.

   b. *fee simple qualified (defeasible),* which the owner holds subject to special conditions, limitations, or private deed restrictions that limit the use of the property.

   EXAMPLE. A parcel of land may carry a restriction that prohibits the sale of alcoholic beverages on the premises. If the owner fails to adhere to the restriction, the owner may be liable in a lawsuit for damages or, in extreme cases, the title may revert back to the grantor or creator of the restriction.

2. *Life estates* are created by deed or will for the life of one or more designated human beings. The life tenant has all the rights of possession, or income, during the life of the designated person(s). However, the holder of a life estate cannot deed or lease a property beyond the life of the designated person. If the person granting the life estate designates that the title is to go to some other person upon the death of the life estate holder, the person so designated is said to have an *estate in remainder.*

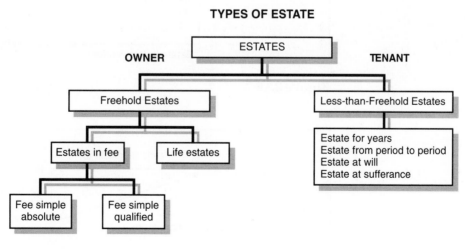

Figure 2.15

EXAMPLE. In Figure 2.16, A deeds a life estate to B for the life of B. When B dies, the property passes to C. B holds the life estate, C holds the estate in remainder.

If the property is to be returned to the person who gave the life estate or to the heirs, that person is said to have an *estate in reversion.*

EXAMPLE. In Figure 2.17, A deeds a life estate to B for B's life, with the provision that when B dies, the title reverts back to A. B holds a life estate; A holds the estate in reversion.

Another possibility is a *grant reserving a life estate.* Among life estates this is probably the most common situation.

EXAMPLE. In Figure 2.18, A deeds title to B, but A reserves or keeps a life estate for the rest of A's life. Upon death of A, possession and use passes to B.

As previously mentioned, a holder of a life estate cannot deed or lease property beyond the length of the life of the designated person. For example: Assume that A holds title for life and upon A's death, title is to pass to B, the remainder person. If during A's life, A leases the property to C, upon A's death, the lease is canceled and B, the re-

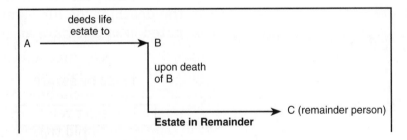

Figure 2.16

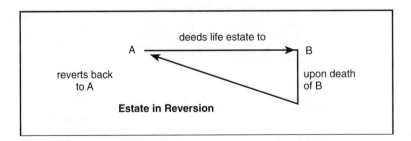

Figure 2.17

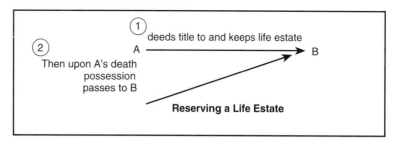

Figure 2.18

mainder person, will receive title free of the lease. If C wishes to continue to lease the property, C will need to negotiate a new lease with B.

Finally, it should be mentioned that freehold estates, both fee simple and life estates, are considered durable and capable of being transferred by inheritance upon death. Therefore, freehold estates are sometimes called "estates of inheritance."

Less-than-Freehold Estates

Less-than-freehold estates are interests held by *tenants* who rent or lease property. They are also called lessees, or leaseholders, and are discussed in detail in Chapter 11.

2.6 METHODS OF HOLDING TITLE

When people acquire ownership of real property, they must decide how to hold title. Title may be held separately in your name alone, or concurrently with other people.

Ownership in Severalty

When a person acquires real property and holds title solely in his or her own name, it is technically known as *ownership in severalty*. In other words, he or she alone enjoys the ownership benefits, including the complete bundle of rights, and "severs" his or her relationship with others.

A person can hold title in severalty in one of the following ways, depending upon the owner's legal status:

A single man	A married man
A single woman	A married woman
An unmarried man	A widower
An unmarried woman	A widow

A person who wishes to indicate separate property ownership can add the words "sole and separate property" to any of the choices listed. A corporation can hold title in severalty such as "Acme Company, a California Corporation."

Concurrent Ownership

Concurrent ownership is when two or more people hold title together. There are numerous types of concurrent ownership, but for our purposes the most important are joint tenancy, tenancy in common, community property, and tenancy in partnership.

JOINT TENANCY

Joint tenancy exists when two or more persons are joint and equal owners of the same undivided interest in real property. In order to create a valid joint tenancy, four unities must exist:

1. *Unity of time.* This means that the owners must have acquired their interest at the same time.
2. *Unity of title.* This means that all owners must come into title on the same document. Consider this example: A and B are joint tenants. B sells her interest to C. A and C are tenants in common because they each took title on a different document at a different time.
3. *Unity of interest.* This means that all owners must have equal shares or interest in the property. For example, if there are two owners, each must have a one-half interest; four owners, each must have a one-quarter interest; eight owners, each must have a one-eighth interest; and so on.
4. *Unity of possession.* This means that all owners must have equal rights of possession. No one owner can be prevented from using the property by the other owner(s).

If any of these unities are missing, the joint tenancy is invalid, and the rules of tenancy in common will apply.

IMPORTANT CHARACTERISTICS

The most important characteristic of joint tenancy is the *right of survivorship.* This means that if one tenant dies, the surviving joint tenant(s) acquires the deceased's interest without a court action.

EXAMPLE
1. A and B take title to property as joint tenants. B dies; A becomes the sole owner because of the right of survivorship.
2. A, B, and C take title to a property as joint tenants. C dies and her interest automatically passes to the survivors, A and B. A and B are still joint tenants between each other, each owning a one-half interest in the property.

OTHER
CHARACTERISTICS
OF JOINT TENANCY

In addition to the four unities (time, title, interest, possession) and the right of survivorship, joint tenancy has these important characteristics:

1. You cannot will your interest in joint tenancy property.
2. Interest in the property is undivided. In other words, each owner can use every square foot, and he or she cannot say, "this is my half, and this is yours."
3. No probate procedure is required to distribute the interest upon the death of one of the owners. The interest goes to the surviving co-owners. However, there is some paperwork required to shift the remaining interest to the surviving joint tenant. But this paperwork is minor in comparison to a complete probate.
4. A joint tenant may sell or convey his or her interest without approval of the other tenant(s). This action may break the joint tenancy and create a tenancy in common.

EXAMPLE. A and B are joint tenants. B sells her interest to C. A and C are now tenants in common. Why? Because B's selling to C violated the unities of time and title.

5. A corporation is not allowed to hold title as a joint tenant, because in theory a corporation never "dies."
6. A surviving tenant acquires the interest of the deceased joint tenant, free from the debts created individually by the deceased joint tenant.

TENANCY IN COMMON

When two or more persons are owners of an undivided interest in property, they can hold title as *tenants in common.* Tenancy in common has these characteristics:

1. There is no right of survivorship, meaning that upon the death of a tenant in common, his or her interest passes to the heirs, not the surviving co-tenants. This requires a probate proceeding.
2. Each owner may hold an unequal interest—that is, he or she may own unequal shares.

EXAMPLE. A, B, C, and D hold title as tenants in common. These owners might share their interest as follows:

A might own one-quarter interest.
B might own one-eighth interest.
C might own one-eighth interest.
D might own one-half interest.

Contrast this with joint tenancy, which requires all owners to have equal shares or interest.

3. Each owner has equal rights of possession and must pay his or her share of the expenses, such as property taxes.
4. Each owner may will his or her interest to his or her heirs, and upon death, the heirs take their place along with the other owners as tenants in common.
5. Each co-tenant may sell, convey, or encumber his or her interest without the consent of the co-tenants.

EXAMPLE.   A and B are tenants in common, A dies and his interest passes to his heir, X. X and B will be tenants in common.

OR

A, B, and C are tenants in common. If C sells her interest to D, then A, B, and D become tenants in common.

What If?   To test your understanding, answer the following questions:

1. A and B are joint tenants. If B dies, who gets what?
2. A and B are joint tenants. If B sells to C, what is the relationship between A and C?
3. A and B are tenants in common. If B dies, who gets what?
4. A and B and C are joint tenants. C sells his interest to D. What is the relationship between A and B and D?

Answers

1. B's interest passes to A, who now holds title in severalty.
2. A and C are tenants in common.
3. A and the heirs of B are tenants in common.
4. A and B are joint tenants to each other and tenants in common with D.

TENANCY IN PARTNERSHIP   Tenancy in partnership exists when two or more persons, as partners, pool their interests, assets, and efforts in a business venture, with each to share in the profits or the losses. This type of business organization includes general partnerships and limited partnerships, and there are many rules and regulations. The following discussion outlines only the real estate aspects of partnerships, not the legal or accounting aspects. Tenancy in partnership has the following real estate characteristics:

1. Each partner has an equal right with other partners to possession of specific partnership property for partnership purposes. This means a partner only has the right to use the property for business, not for personal purposes, unless the other partners agree to the personal use.
2. A partner's right in the partnership property is not assignable except in connection with the assignment of rights of all the partners in the same property.
3. A partner's right in the partnership property is not subject to attachment or execution, except on a claim against the partnership.
4. There is a form of survivorship when one partner dies.

EXAMPLE. A and B own property as partners. A dies; B receives title in trust until the disposition of the property. In other words, the title rests in the survivor only long enough to carry on the business for the sole purpose of winding up the partnership affairs.

Limited Partnership

Sometimes title to real estate is held by a limited partnership. Under a limited partnership there is one or more general partners who have unlimited liability, and usually a series of limited partners who have limited liability. Limited liability means that if all legal requirements have been met, the limited partners can lose only their investment and not be held liable for partnership debts. Most real estate syndicates hold title as a limited partnership.

COMMUNITY PROPERTY

Community property ownership is another form of ownership held by more than one person, but in this case it can be held only by a husband and wife. Community property is defined as all property acquired during a valid marriage. California is a community property state; therefore, all California property acquired by a husband and wife during marriage is presumed to be community property. However, there are a few exceptions:

1. All property owned by husband or wife before marriage can remain separate property after marriage as long as the property is not commingled with community property, causing it to lose its separate property identity.

2. All property acquired by gift or inheritance by either spouse during marriage remains separate property as long as it is not commingled with community property.

3. All income and profits from separate property as well as any property acquired from the proceeds of separate property remain separate property as long as said income and profits are not commingled with community property.

In effect, a husband and wife are general partners, each owning one-half of the community property. Each spouse has equal management and control of the community property. Neither spouse may convey or encumber real estate held as community property unless the other spouse also signs the contracts or documents involved.

Each spouse has the right to dispose of his or her half of the community property by will to whomever they wish. But if either spouse dies intestate, the surviving spouse receives all the property; the children, if any, get nothing.

Community property does not have to be probated if the deceased spouse leaves his or her interest to the surviving spouse. But if the deceased spouse's interest is left to someone other than the surviving spouse, the estate must be probated.

For Married Couples, Which Is Best: Joint Tenancy or Community Property?

The answer is complicated and should be discussed with a tax attorney. Some of the main issues to compare are income tax basis upon death, estate taxes, and probate procedures if any. Also, the trend toward deeding title into a "living trust" may need to be discussed with a tax attorney. Real estate licensees and escrow officers are not qualified nor allowed to give buyers and existing owners advice on how to hold title. (See Table 2.1.)

TABLE 2.1   The Basics of Co-Ownership

	Tenancy in Common	*Joint Tenancy*	*Community Property*
Who Can Hold Title?	Any 2 or more, including married couples	Any 2 or more, including married couples	Husband and wife only
Ownership Interest	Can be any percent, equal or not	All shares must be equal	Equal shares
Upon Death	Probate usually required	No probate, right of survivorship, no will allowed	Special probate, right to will, intestate goes to surviving spouse
Disposition of Title	Convey interest without others' permission	Convey interest without others' permission	Need both signatures to convey title

Cohabitation and Property Rights

In 1976, in the famous Marvin *vs.* Marvin case involving the late actor Lee Marvin, California courts held that unmarried persons who cohabitate may create property rights and obligations by oral agreement. In the years since this precedent-setting case there have been many others regarding who gets what when unmarried persons split up. The bottom line is that unmarried people who cohabitate might need to discuss this situation with an attorney. They may find it advisable to reduce to contract form an agreement on how to handle previously owned property and property accumulated during cohabitation, in the event they should separate at a later date.

Equity Sharing

Equity sharing is when an owner-occupant and a nonresident owner-investor pool their money to buy a home. The down payment is split according to an agreed percentage, and both parties are on the deed and mortgage. The owner-occupant pays rent to the nonresident owner-investor for a portion of the home owned by the investor. The nonresident owner-investor then uses the rent money to join with the owner-occupant to pay the monthly mortgage payments. The equity share contract spells out who is responsible for taxes, insurance, and upkeep. Some day in the future the home is either refinanced or sold, and the parties split the net proceeds according to a prearranged percentage.

The purpose of an equity share arrangement is to allow a person who otherwise could not buy a home on his or her own to at least acquire a partial interest, with a goal to eventually getting enough equity to acquire a home in his or her name alone. The nonresident owner-investor treats his or her interest as a rental property, with the investment and tax aspects of a landlord without the usual hassles of a regular tenant. The owner-occupant is more likely to treat the property better than a regular tenant because the owner-occupant has a partial ownership interest. Equity share arrangements are complicated and should not be undertaken without advice from legal and tax experts.

CHAPTER SUMMARY, PART II

Freehold estates consist of fee estates and life estates, representing the rights of an owner of real property. Fee estates may be either fee simple absolute with no private restrictions, or fee simple qualified with some limitations and restrictions. Life estates are granted for the life of one or more persons and may be a remainder, reversion, or reservation type.

Ownership in severalty is when title is held in sole ownership. Concurrent ownership is when title is held by two or more persons. Common examples of concurrent ownership are joint tenancy, tenancy in common, tenancy in partnership, and community property.

In California, property acquired by a husband and wife during marriage is considered to be community property. Property acquired by either spouse before marriage, or by inheritance or gift during marriage, is treated as separate property unless it is commingled with the community property. Methods of holding title have important estate and income tax consequences that should be discussed with a qualified attorney before a selection is made.

IMPORTANT TERMS AND CONCEPTS

Community property

Estate in remainder

Estate in reversion

Fee estate

Fee simple absolute

Fee simple qualified

Four unities of joint tenancy

Freehold estate

Joint tenancy

Less-than-freehold estate

Life estate

Ownership in severalty

Right of survivorship

Separate property

Tenancy in common

Tenancy in

PRACTICAL APPLICATION

1. Chan owns real property and deeds a life estate to Washington and upon Washington's death title is to pass to Adams. While holding a life estate, Washington leases the property for five years to Santos. Two years later Adams dies, then one year later Chan and Washington both die. Upon Washington's death who is entitled to possession of the property?

2. Nuygen and Harris purchased 20 acres as joint tenants. Harris then sold one half of her undivided interest to Battino. Shortly thereafter, Harris died. What is the legal relationship between Nuygen and Battino and what percentage interest is owned by each?

3. Bill and Sara Belinski, husband and wife, purchased a home in California as community property. Later Sara's parents died and left her a five-unit apartment in Los Angeles. The apartments are professionally managed and all rental proceeds are placed in a separate account under Sara's name alone. Sara then uses the rental proceeds to pay tuition for their children who are still in college. The Belinskis are now in the process of a divorce. What are the community property issues?

REVIEWING YOUR UNDERSTANDING

1. Which of the following statements is false?
   a. The right of survivorship is present in a tenancy in common.
   b. A life estate tenant is responsible for payment of the property tax.
   c. A leasehold estate is a less-than-freehold estate.
   d. Unity of possession is present in both joint tenancy and tenancy in common ownerships.

2. Which of the following terms do not belong together?
   a. joint tenancy–probate hearing
   b. tenancy in common–equal interest
   c. tenancy in common–severalty estate
   d. all of the above

3. Which of the following is considered to be a less-than-freehold estate?
   a. fee simple absolute
   b. life estate
   c. leasehold estate
   d. fee simple defeasible

4. The single most important characteristic of joint tenancy is:
   a. equal rights of use
   b. equal interest
   c. right of survivorship
   d. right to encumber

5. It is impossible for a corporation to legally hold title as a:
   a. trustee
   b. joint tenant
   c. tenant in common
   d. California corporation

6. Which of the following is not one of the four unities of joint tenancy?
   a. time
   b. interest
   c. security
   d. title

7. A deeds a life estate to B; upon B's death, title is to pass to C. This is an example of a:
   a. perpetual estate
   b. less-than-freehold estate
   c. remainder estate
   d. fee simple estate

8. The term fee simple defeasible is best described in which statement?
   a. Owner holds a title without limitations.
   b. Owner holds a less-than-freehold estate.
   c. Owner holds title subject to deed restrictions.
   d. Owner holds an estate in remainder.

9. Smith and Dang are joint tenants; Dang sells his half of the property to Brown. Brown will take title with Smith as:
   a. joint tenants
   b. tenants in common
   c. ownership in severalty
   d. separate property

10. Community property is defined as property acquired by a husband and wife:
    a. before marriage
    b. after marriage
    c. by either party, by gift or inheritance
    d. before or after marriage

11. Real estate syndicates usually hold title to property as:
    a. general partnership
    b. limited partnership
    c. tenants in common
    d. tenancy in partnership

12. Freehold estates are sometimes called estates of:
    a. inheritance
    b. will
    c. accession
    d. years

13. Ownership in severalty refers to holding title as:
    a. joint tenants
    b. an individual
    c. co-ownership
    d. partners

14. Garcia owned a life estate in a property. Garcia leased the property to Williams for five years. Two years later Garcia died. The lease is:
    a. valid and in force for the rest of the term
    b. valid for a two-year period after the death of Garcia
    c. invalid from the beginning; a life estate owner cannot sign a lease
    d. canceled and invalid upon Garcia's death

15. A, B, and C are joint tenants and they hold title to the NW ¼ of Section 24 in some township. C deeds her interest to D.
    a. D is a joint tenant with A and B.
    b. D acquired approximately 53.33 acres.
    c. D owns a one-third interest in 160 acres.
    d. A, B, and D are all tenants in common with each other.

16. In California, without any evidence to the contrary, a husband and wife are presumed to hold title as:
    a. tenants in common
    b. joint tenants
    c. community property
    d. tenancy in partnership

17. To be valid, all owners must have equal shares, except for:
    a. community property
    b. joint tenancy
    c. tenants in common
    d. all of the above must have equal shares

18. Which of the following is most likely to be separate property? Real estate recently acquired by:
    a. gift
    b. severalty
    c. purchase
    d. foreclosure

19. Which real estate owner is usually considered to be liable only for the amount of invested capital, not the owner's personal assets?
    a. tenant in common
    b. general partner
    c. joint tenant
    d. limited partner

20. Regarding the best method for buyers to hold title:
    a. real estate agents should tell buyers the best way
    b. buyers should seek advice from their attorney
    c. joint tenants is always the best method
    d. for married couples in California, community property is the only method allowed

Chapter 3

Encumbrances, Liens, and Homesteads

Chapter Preview In this chapter you will study money and nonmoney encumbrances. The discussion of nonmoney encumbrances centers on easements, encroachments, and private and public restrictions.

Money encumbrances are defined as liens. The liens discussed include mechanic's liens, tax liens, special assessment liens, attachments, and judgment liens.

In addition, the California homestead law is presented, illustrating how homeowners may protect their homes against a forced sale by certain types of creditors. At the conclusion of the chapter, you will be able to:

1. Define encumbrance, lien, easement, and encroachment

2. Explain the difference between private deed restrictions and public restrictions

3. Describe the key characteristics of mechanic's liens, tax liens, and judgment liens

4. Discuss the details of the California homestead law

3.1 ENCUMBRANCES

In real estate, an *encumbrance* is anything that burdens the owner's title. Any right or interest in the property, possessed by someone other than the owner, is called an encumbrance. In short, an encumbrance is anything that burdens the title with legal obligations.

Encumbrances fall into two basic categories: *nonmoney encumbrances* and *money encumbrances.*

Nonmoney Encumbrances

Nonmoney encumbrances affect the physical condition or use of the property. Examples include easements, public and private restrictions, and encroachments—as opposed to money encumbrances, such as real estate loans or property taxes, where the property is held as security for repayment.

Easements

An easement is a right to enter or use another person's property, or a portion thereof, within certain limitations without paying rent or being considered a trespasser. In California, the most common type of easement is a right of way, also called an easement for ingress (entering) and egress (exiting) from the property.

Two important terms used in connection with a right of way are (1) *dominant tenement* and (2) *servient tenement.* The property that benefits from the easement (Property B in Figure 3.1) is described as the "dominant tenement." The property subject to the easement or upon which the easement is imposed (Property A in Figure 3.1) is described as the "servient tenement."

A right-of-way easement is usually designated as *nonexclusive,* meaning that when it is created it doesn't prevent the owner from using the land, including that part covered by the easement. The owner's use (servient tenement), however, cannot interfere with the right of use by the dominant tenement.

In addition to a right of way, other examples of easements include the right to take water, wood, minerals, and other

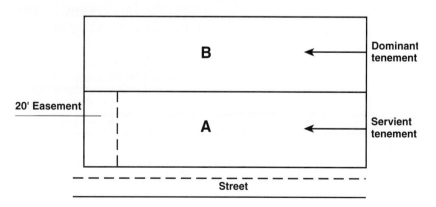

Figure 3.1

named items; the right to receive air and light; or the right to use a wall as a party wall.

When this type of easement is created, it is considered to be appurtenant or belonging to the land. This means the easement is considered real property and stays attached to the property in the event of a sale or other title transfer. When easements "run with the land" they are called *easement appurtenant.*

Some easements do not have a dominant tenement. This is known as an *easement in gross.* For example, when a utility company erects poles or strings wire over private lands, the utility company obtains an easement in gross. Easements in gross allow someone to pass over the land for a personal use, not to reach an adjoining parcel of land. This means there is no dominant landowner being served, hence no dominant tenement.

Creation of Easements

Easements can be created in a number of ways. The most common ways are by (1) deed, (2) necessity, (3) dedication, (4) condemnation, and (5) prescription. (See Figure 3.2)

BY DEED

Easements are not created orally; instead they are set forth in the form of a written grant (such as a deed or contract). An easement must comply with all the legal requirements of a deed and be signed by the owner of the property (servient tenement) over which the easement lies.

Examples: (1) **A** deeds an easement to **B** to cross **A's** property, or (2) **A** deeds title to **B,** but reserves an easement over **B's** property for **A's** use. Easements created by a written deed or contract are also called "expressed easements."

BY NECESSITY OR BY IMPLICATION

When a buyer discovers that he or she has no access to the street without passing over the property of another, the buyer's property is considered "landlocked." In this situation, the landlocked buyer can appeal to the courts and ask for an easement by necessity over the portion of land, if any,

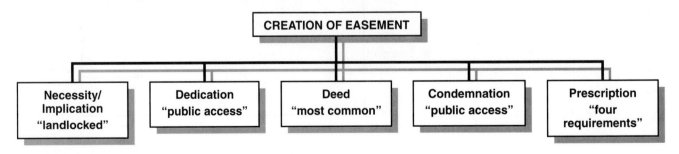

Figure 3.2

which the seller of the landlocked parcel may still own. If the seller of the landlocked parcel does not own an adjoining parcel to cross over, the buyer of the landlocked parcel may be permanently landlocked.

An easement can also be implied. For example, **A** deeds a portion of his or her land to **B** but fails to mention an easement. However, there is an existing road over the remaining portion of land owned by **A. B** usually has an implied right to use the road over **A's** property to get to **B's** land.

BY DEDICATION   An owner may voluntarily dedicate an easement for public access. An example might be when an owner gives the public the right to cross over his or her land to reach the beach.

BY CONDEMNATION   Often an easement is created through condemnation. This means that government, as well as utility companies and railroads, may acquire an easement against the wishes of an owner through a legal process known as eminent domain. The law states that the condemned easement must be acquired for public use and the owner reimbursed for the value lost to the property.

BY PRESCRIPTION   An easement by prescription is created when a person acquires an easement in another person's property by reason of use. In order to obtain an easement by prescription in another person's property, a person must comply with four basic requirements:

1. A person must openly and notoriously use the land of another.
2. The easement use must be continuous and uninterrupted for five years.
3. The easement use must be hostile to the true owner's wishes, meaning without the owner's permission.
4. There must be a claim of right or color of title. This means the easement user must feel that he or she has some right to cross the land of another, or have a document that falsely purports to give the easement user an easement right.

Termination of an Easement   Easements can be terminated in several ways. (See Figure 3.3.)

1. The most common way to terminate an easement is by express release. The dominant tenement usually issues a quitclaim deed to the servient tenement owner, and that extinguishes the easement.

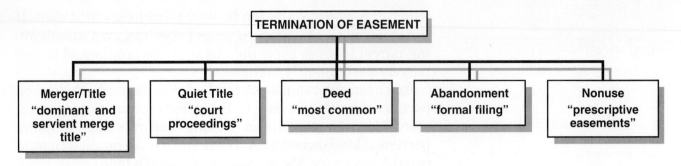

Figure 3.3

2. Another way easements can be terminated is by a court proceeding called a quiet title action.

3. When the owner of the dominant tenement property becomes the owner of the servient tenement property, the easement is terminated by merger of title. In other words, you cannot have an easement over your own property!

4. The filing of a formal abandonment can terminate an easement.

5. A prescription easement may be terminated automatically by nonuse for a period of five years. However, termination by nonuse applies only to prescriptive easements, not deeded easements.

Other Types of Nonmoney Encumbrances

In addition to easements, other examples of nonmoney encumbrances include private deed restrictions, public restrictions, and encroachments.

PRIVATE DEED RESTRICTIONS

A seller of property can place in a deed certain legal restrictions or limits on the use of the property being sold. The restrictions can apply not only to the new owner, but to all subsequent owners. These restrictions are often referred to as CC&Rs, which stands for covenants, conditions, and restrictions.

A *covenant* is a promise or agreement on the part of the individual accepting it to do or not to do certain things. If a grantee (buyer) violates a covenant, he or she has broken a promise or agreement, and the grantor (seller) may institute court proceedings. The grantor may sue for dollar damages or get an injunction against the grantee prohibiting continuation of the violation of restriction.

A *condition* is a restriction that places a limitation on the grantee's (buyer's) ownership. The main difference between a covenant and a condition is the degree of punishment if a violation occurs. If a condition is violated, it may give the grantor the right to demand the forfeiture of the grantee's title to the property, whereas a violation of a covenant normally only allows money damages or a court order to cease and desist.

Some restrictions are legal and some are not. A classic example of restrictions that are unethical, illegal, and unenforceable are those relating to discrimination.

Any discrimination based on race, color, creed, religion, national origin, sex, marital and family status, or physical handicap is prohibited by state and/or federal law. A detailed discussion of fair housing laws is presented in Chapter 12.

PUBLIC RESTRICTIONS When the government imposes restrictions on property, they are called public restrictions. Using a provision called *police power,* government has the right to impose restrictions on the use of private property in order to protect the health, safety, morals, and welfare of its citizens.

Police power includes such public restrictions as:

1. Zoning regulations that dictate what type of land use may exist in a given geographical area
2. Building codes that mandate rules and regulations governing quality and size of construction
3. Health codes to protect and regulate the quality of domestic water and the effectiveness of sanitation systems

ENCROACHMENTS Another type of physical nonmoney encumbrance is an encroachment. An *encroachment* is the wrongful construction of a building or improvement on or over the land of another. Examples of possible encroachments are shown in Figure 3.4.

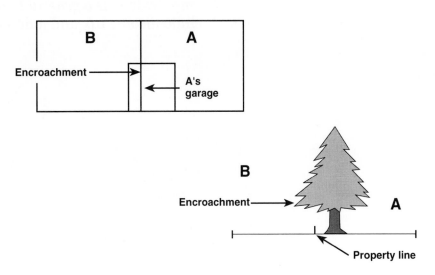

Figure 3.4

According to the Statute of Limitations, the party whose land is encroached upon has only three years in which to bring action for the removal of any such encroachment. If the owner allows the time limitation to run out, the owner runs the risk that the encroachment on the property may become permanent. However, some encroachments are above the ground, such as a neighbor's tree limb extending into your airspace. Above-the-ground encroachments have no statute of limitation, and an action for removal can be brought at any time.

3.2 LIENS

A *lien* is a money encumbrance. In this type of encumbrance, a specific property is held as security for the payment of a money debt. Liens can be classified as voluntary, involuntary, general, or specific. (See Figure 3.5.)

Voluntary Lien

A *voluntary lien* is a lien that is freely accepted by the property owner. An example of a voluntary lien would be a mortgage or a deed of trust, which an owner signs when obtaining a real estate loan. (Deeds of trust and mortgages are discussed in detail in Chapter 7.)

Involuntary Lien

Involuntary liens are liens that are imposed by law and that the owner does not freely accept. Examples of involuntary liens include mechanics' liens, tax liens, attachments, and judgment liens.

General Lien

A lien that applies to all the property of an owner, unless exempt by law, is a *general lien*. Examples of general liens include income tax and judgment liens.

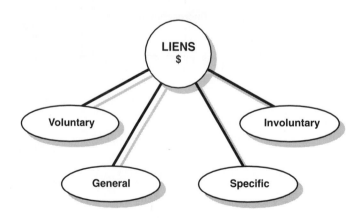

Figure 3.5

Specific Lien

A lien against a particular single piece of property is a *specific lien*. Examples of specific liens include mortgages, trust deeds, property taxes, and mechanics' liens.

Types of Liens

MECHANIC'S LIENS

Before discussing the details of this type of lien, we need to know what is meant by a "mechanic." A *mechanic* is anyone hired to do work that improves real property. In short, a mechanic is anyone who performs labor, bestows services, or furnishes material or equipment on a construction project.

This includes contractors, subcontractors, carpenters, plumbers, painters, plasterers, laborers, material and equipment suppliers, architects, and landscape gardeners, as well as those workers involved in the demolition and removal of old buildings and the grading and filling of land. The California state constitution allows any qualified mechanic who does not receive payment to file a lien against the specific property upon which work was done.

The mechanic's lien must be based on a valid contract, written or verbal, between the claimant and the owner, or the owner's general contractor. The mechanic's lien law is based on the theory that improvements contribute additional value to the land; therefore, the property's owner should be held responsible for wages and materials that led to the improvements.

The key provisions of the mechanic's lien law are illustrated in Figure 3.6.

Preliminary Notice

The law requires that all mechanics and material suppliers must give written notice to the owner, the general contractor, and the construction lender, if there is one, of their right to file a lien against the property if they are not paid. This notice should be served within *20 days* of the first furnishing of labor, services, equipment, or material to the job site.

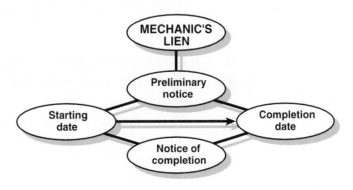

Figure 3.6

Failure to give the preliminary notice within 20 days does not preclude the right to give a preliminary notice at a later time, but the mechanic's claim rights may be subordinated to other claims.

Starting Date

In order to create a valid mechanic's lien, the law requires that the lien must be recorded within a specified period of time after completion of the project. The law has determined the following situations to be equivalent to completion:

1. Owner occupies the property, and work stops.
2. Owner accepts the work as being completed, and files a document called a *notice of completion.*
3. Work on the project ceases for a continuous 60-day period.
4. Work ceases for a continuous period of 30 days or more, and owner files a *notice of cessation.*

Notice of Completion

A *notice of completion,* if filed by the owner, must show the date of the completion, name and address of the owner, the nature of the interest or estate of the owner, a description of the property, and the name of the contractor, if any. To be valid, a notice of completion must be recorded within *10 days* after the completion of the project.

Statutory Time Period

There are two situations that establish time periods for filing liens.

1. If the owner files a notice of completion, the original contractor has *60 days* in which to file a lien; all others have *30 days.*
2. If no notice of completion is filed or if the notice is invalid, all parties, including the contractors and subcontractors, have *90 days* to file from the day work was finished.

Termination of a Mechanic's Lien

1. A mechanic's lien is terminated when the debt has been paid, either by voluntary action or by forced foreclosure sale.
2. A mechanic's lien is automatically terminated if the mechanic fails to institute a court foreclosure within 90 days after filing the mechanic's lien. In other words, once a mechanic's lien is recorded, a mechanic has only 90 days to bring foreclosure action. If mechanics wait more

than 90 days, they lose their rights to foreclosure upon the property. They still can personally sue the owner for the amount owed but cannot foreclose on the mechanic's lien and force the sale of the home.

Notice of Nonresponsibility

If a tenant orders work on a property without the landlord's approval, can the landlord be held responsible for any unpaid work? The answer is yes. However, a landlord can protect against mechanic's liens resulting from work ordered by a tenant if the landlord files a *notice of nonresponsibility*.

This notice of nonresponsibility must be filed within *10 days* of the date of discovery that the work is being done. It is filed by recording a copy of a notice of nonresponsibility in the county recorder's office and posting a notice on the property. This gives the workers notice that the owner will not be financially responsible for the work being done, and the workers must look to the tenant for payment.

Priority of Claim

When a mechanic's lien is placed against a given piece of property, its priority over a construction loan will be determined by the beginning date of the project. The law states that even though a mechanic's lien is recorded after a construction loan is recorded, the mechanic's lien is given priority if any work had been done or materials furnished prior to recording the construction loan. Ordinarily, a title insurance company will first inspect the property to make sure no work has been done or materials delivered prior to the recording of the construction loan.

If there are multiple mechanic's liens against a property, they all share on a parity with each other. This means that the first mechanic to record a lien does not have a superior right over the second mechanic's lien, and so on. If there are multiple mechanic's liens and the property is sold for lien payments, each mechanic receives a share of the proceeds based on his or her pro rata share of the work.

Summary of Mechanic's Liens Dates

1. Preliminary notice should be given within *20 days* of the beginning of work.
2. If the owner files a notice of completion within *10 days* of completion of the project:
   a. Original contractors have *60 days* to file
   b. All others have *30 days* to file

3. If the owner does not file a notice of completion or if the notice is invalid, all mechanics have *90 days* to file from the day work was finished.
4. Once a valid mechanic's lien is filed, the mechanic must bring a court foreclosure action within *90 days* to enforce the lien.
5. A notice of nonresponsibility must be filed by the landlord within *10 days* of the discovery of work ordered by a tenant.

Finally, a property owner who hires a contractor might consider having the contractor provide a performance bond in which, for a fee, an insurance company guarantees payment in the event the general contractor fails to complete the project and/or fails to pay the subcontractors.

TAX LIENS The purpose of taxation is to provide money to cover government expenses. A tax lien arises when a person does not pay taxes when due and his or her property is encumbered to ensure payment.

Tax liens may include:

1. Unpaid real property taxes
2. Unpaid income taxes
3. Unpaid estate taxes
4. Unpaid gift taxes

Taxes and their consequences are covered in detail in Chapter 13. The point stressed here is that government has the power to levy taxes. If the taxpayer refuses to pay the levy, government has the right to place a lien against the taxpayer's property and foreclose upon the property for back taxes.

SPECIAL ASSESSMENTS Special assessments are levied against property owners in a certain assessment district. The basic purpose is to defray the cost of specific local improvements, such as streets, sewers, schools, and so on. Even though assessments are usually paid with property taxes, they differ in that property taxes are a general tax levied to pay general government expenses, whereas assessments are for a single purpose. If a person refuses to pay the assessment, government and/or bondholders can foreclose upon the assessee's property. Special assessments are discussed in Chapter 13.

ATTACHMENTS AND JUDGMENTS

An *attachment* is a legal process whereby property, personal or real, is seized pending the outcome of a court action. A *judgment* is a decision of the court as a result of a lawsuit. A judgment is the final determination of the rights of the parties involved in a court proceeding.

The purpose of the attachment is to have the property of the defendant available to satisfy a judgment if it is rendered in favor of the plaintiff. In some cases it may take several months before the case is tried and a judgment issued. In that time an unscrupulous defendant might secretly sell or give away his or her property, making it impossible to satisfy the judgment.

Under an attachment, the seizure and holding of the property is merely symbolic. The defendant may still keep the property, but a notice is posted on the property and the attachment is recorded. The attachment remains a lien upon all real property attached, three days from date of levy. However, so much property is exempt from attachment, such as personal residence, most of the debtor's wages, and so on, that the use of an attachment has declined in recent years. Instead of seeking an attachment, many creditors go directly for a judgment.

A judgment (court decision) does not automatically create a lien on real property. In order for a judgment to become a lien, an abstract of the judgment (summary of the judgment) must be recorded with the county recorder. It then becomes a general lien on all real property located in the county in which the abstract is recorded.

The judgment lien normally runs for ten years. Any real property acquired during the ten-year period, in the county where the abstract is filed, automatically becomes encumbered by the judgment lien. The abstract of judgment may be recorded in any number of California counties. If a creditor wishes to tie up anything a debtor might own in California, the creditor can record the abstract of judgment in all 58 counties. Abstracts of judgments from California courts cannot normally be recorded in other states. It takes a separate court proceeding in each state.

WRIT OF EXECUTION

In order to collect on a judgment, the creditor will request a *writ of execution*. Under a writ of execution, the court orders the sheriff to seize and sell the property to satisfy the judgment. A public auction is then held, and the property is sold to the highest bidder.

In the event that the judgment is paid before the sale, the judgment creditor issues to the judgment debtor a satisfaction of judgment. When this notice is recorded, the judgment is released, and the lien is lifted from the property.

3.3 HOMESTEAD LAW

The California homestead law is designed to protect a homeowner's equity in a personal residence from forced sale by certain types of creditors. The term homestead means personal dwelling and should not be confused with the federal homestead laws of early American history, whereby the government gave away land to encourage settlement.

Declared versus Automatic Homestead

There are two types of homesteads in California: a formal declared homestead and an automatic homestead called *Dwelling House Exemption.*

The formal declared homestead requires an owner to correctly complete and file a homestead document at the county courthouse, whereas a dwelling house exemption is available to all valid homeowners who have not previously filed a document at the county courthouse. The dollar protections are the same, but there are some other differences that will be pointed out in the following discussion.

Requirements for a Formal Declared Homestead

There are certain essentials that must be observed in the filing of a formal homestead exemption. If these rules are not followed, the formal homestead is void and the automatic dwelling exemption will usually apply.

1. A formal homestead must be recorded to be valid. A homestead declaration must be recorded in the recorder's office showing that the claimant is a head of family, if such is the case, or when the declaration is made by the wife, that the husband has not made such declaration and that she, therefore, makes it for their joint benefit. In addition to a husband or wife, the state liberally interprets a "head of family" to be any person who lives in their home and provides for any relative living in the same home.

2. The formal homestead statement must declare that the claimant is residing on the premises and claims this as a homestead.

3. The formal homestead statement must include a description of the premises. The dwelling house may be a single- or multiple-family dwelling, a condominium, a stock cooperative, a community apartment project, a mobile home, or a yacht. Any owner-occupied residential

property can be used, but the owner may have only one homestead exemption at a time.

No previous formal filing is required for the automatic dwelling house exemption, but the home must be a principal residence and the debtor/homeowner must appear in court and claim the Dwelling House Exemption.

Dollar Protection for Formal and Automatic Homestead

A head of the household is entitled to exemption protection of $75,000 (as of January 1999). Heads of households 65 years and older, and certain low-income homeowners 55–64 years old, are allowed a $125,000 exemption. Single persons who are not considered low income and are under the age of 65 years are usually allowed a $50,000 exemption. These exemption figures do not reflect the actual value of the property. The homestead exemption is intended to protect the equity the owner has in the property.

When the courts rule that a home has too much equity and therefore is to be sold to satisfy the debts of the homeowner, the owner retains the exemption portion, and the creditor is awarded the difference.

EXAMPLE

        Homestead Property A $100,000 home
                            – 90,000 loan
                            $10,000 equity

This home cannot be sold by judgment creditors as the equity is within the homestead exemption.

        Homestead Property B $150,000 home
                            –0 loan
                            $150,000 equity

This home can be sold by judgment creditors as the equity exceeds the homestead exemption. However, the homeowner (debtor) is allowed to keep the amount of the exemption, and the creditor only gets the excess.

    $150,000 equity
    –75,000 exemption for
            head of family
    $75,000 excess to creditor

The proceeds from any forced sale will be allocated in the following order:

1. To the discharge of all prior liens and encumbrances exempt from homestead
2. To the homestead claimant (homeowner), the amount of the exemption
3. To the satisfaction of the execution
4. To the homestead claimant if there is a balance left over

The Six-Month Rule

In the event that the homeowner wishes to sell to move to another home or if the owner is forced to sell the home to satisfy an execution, and the homeowner's equity is converted to cash, a homeowner with a valid formal declaration of homestead applies what is known as the six-month rule.

The owner has six months in which to invest his or her equity money in a new home. The homeowner may then file a homestead on the new home and thereby continue to protect the equity against creditors up to the exemption amount. *The homeowner who relies on the automatic dwelling house exemption does not get to use this six-month rule to protect the equity exemption upon resale.*

Remember, the law states that a party cannot have more than one homestead at the same time, and that a homestead can only be placed on owner-occupied residential property.

Homestead's Protection

Homesteads, both formally declared and automatic, protect against forced sale of the family home because of bankruptcy and execution of judgments as long as the equity in the home does not exceed the homestead exemption.

Homesteads do not protect against forced sale of the family home resulting from mortgage or trust deed foreclosures and mechanic's liens. Even if the homestead is recorded before the trust deed and mechanic's lien, *a homestead never defeats a trust deed or mechanic's lien.*

Termination of Homestead

A homestead may be terminated in one of two ways:

1. The owner may sell the home, which automatically terminates a homestead. On the other hand, a formally declared homestead will not be terminated if the owner merely moves out and rents the home. The rule is that a property must be owner-occupied at the time of filing the

formal homestead. An owner can later move and rent the property and still have a valid homestead. *But if a homeowner relies on the automatic dwelling exemption and then moves out, this will cause a loss of the homestead protection.*

2. The homeowner who has filed a formal declaration of homestead can terminate a homestead by filing a notice of abandonment. If one spouse dies, the homestead stays in force for the surviving spouse. A dissolution of marriage will not terminate a homestead if one spouse remains in possession of the title. However, if death or divorce results in only one occupant, the exemption will be reduced from $75,000 to $50,000 unless the person is 65 years or older, or 55 years and of low income; then the exemption remains $125,000.

CHAPTER SUMMARY

Encumbrances are burdens on title that can be either physical or money encumbrances. Physical (nonmoney) encumbrances include easements, private and public restrictions, and encroachments. Money encumbrances are called liens, and they include mechanic's liens, tax liens, judgment liens, mortgages, and deeds of trust.

An easement is a right to use the land of another, with the most common easement being a right of way for ingress and egress. Easements are created by deed, implication, necessity, dedication, condemnation, and prescription. They may be removed by deed, court action, merger of title, filing of an abandonment, or nonuse for five years in the case of prescriptive easements.

Private restrictions placed in a deed are known as CC&Rs, which stands for covenants, conditions, and restrictions. Public restrictions such as zoning, building codes, health regulations, and so on are imposed by governments.

An encroachment is the wrongful extension of a building or improvement on or over the land of another. There are statutory time periods in which an owner must sue to force removal.

Liens (money encumbrances) may be voluntary or involuntary and may be general or specific. Mechanic's liens are involuntary liens that may be placed upon a property by anyone who performs labor, provides a service, or furnishes equipment or supplies on a construction project, in order to guarantee that they are paid for their services. Starting dates and completion dates are extremely important, and the law specifies the exact time limits involved in carrying out a mechanic's lien right.

Judgments are considered general liens and may attach all property owned by the debtor in the county in which the abstract of judgment is filed. An abstract of judgment creates a lien for 10 years on real estate located within the county where the judgment is recorded.

The homestead law provides a limited amount of protection in the event a judgment is obtained against a homeowner. If properly completed and recorded, the head of a household is entitled to a $75,000 exemption (persons 65 or over and low-income people 55–64 get $125,000), whereas a single person under 65 years receives $50,000. A homestead can be applied only on owner-occupied residential property, and only one homestead can be held at a time. Homesteads can be terminated by selling the property or filing a declaration of abandonment, or, in the case of the automatic dwelling house exemption, by moving out of the home.

IMPORTANT TERMS AND CONCEPTS

Attachment

Covenants, conditions, and restrictions

Dominant tenement

Easement appurtenant

Encroachment encumbrance

Homestead

Judgment

Lien

Mechanic's lien

Notice of completion

Notice of nonresponsibility

Servient tenement

Writ of execution

PRACTICAL APPLICATION

1. How does an easement by prescription differ from adverse possession?

2. You wish to have a contractor build a home on your lot. You insist that the contractor be licensed, bonded, and carry adequate work person compensation, and other liability insurance. You are also concerned about the mechanic's lien rules. Fill in the correct days for each situation.

   a. Preliminary Notice should be served within _____ days from the first furnishing of labor or materials on your home site.

   b. A Notice of Completion should be filed by you within _____ days after the completion of the home.

   c. After filing your Notice of Completion, the general contractor has _____ days to file a lien, while the subcontractors have _____ days.

d. If your Notice of Completion is filed incorrectly and hence is invalid, all workers have _____ days to file a lien.

e. If a mechanic's lien is filed, it will automatically terminate if court action is not instituted within _____ days.

3. A 45-year-old head-of-household has correctly filed a formal Declaration of Homestead. The home is worth $250,000 and has a first loan of $125,000, plus a $35,000 homeowner equity second loan. A judgment creditor petitions the court to force the sale of the home for the payment of a $25,000 debt. Assuming the court orders the sale of the home, how will the proceeds be distributed?

REVIEWING YOUR UNDERSTANDING

1. An easement on a parcel of land may be removed from the records by one of the following:
   a. reconveyance deed
   b. unlawful detainer action
   c. recording a quitclaim deed executed by the user of the easement to the servient tenement
   d. lis pendens action

2. Materials were delivered to a building site for the construction of a commercial building. In order to be sure of collection for the cost of the material, the supplier should file a:
   a. homestead declaration
   b. preliminary notice
   c. surety bond
   d. subordination lien

3. The terms ingress and egress refer to:
   a. utilities
   b. streams
   c. encroachments
   d. easements

4. An easement is defined as:
   a. a general lien on real property
   b. an encumbrance on real property
   c. an equitable restriction on real property
   d. a specific lien on real property

5. A formally declared homestead can be terminated in all of the following ways, *except by:*
   a. renting the property
   b. making untrue statements in the homestead declaration
   c. selling the property
   d. filing an abandonment of homestead

6. When a property owner discovers that a neighbor has built a fence on a portion of his or her property, how long does the property owner have to bring an action against the neighbor?
   a. six months
   b. two years
   c. three years
   d. indefinitely

7. A mechanic's lien can be filed and recorded for the benefit of:
   a. painters
   b. subcontractors
   c. material suppliers
   d. all of the above

8. Which document does *not* need to be recorded to be valid?
   a. mechanic's lien
   b. deed
   c. formal homestead declaration
   d. none of the above need be recorded to be valid

9. One way of acquiring an easement is by prescription. All of the following are required for the creation of this type of easement, *except:*
   a. pay the property taxes for five years
   b. use the property hostile to the true owner's wishes
   c. use the property open and notoriously
   d. have some right of claim or color of title

10. A plaintiff takes a case to court and obtains a judgment. In order to create a lien on the defendant's property, the plaintiff must record:
    a. a writ of attachment
    b. an abstract of judgment
    c. a writ of execution
    d. a lis pendens action

11. A telephone company's right to enter your property to maintain power lines is an example of:
    a. servient tenement
    b. mechanic's lien
    c. easement in gross
    d. easement appurtenant

12. A 35-year-old head of household files a legally declared homestead against a $180,000 home that has a $70,000 loan against the property. A judgment creditor attempts to force the sale of the home. If the home is sold, the judgment creditor will be allowed how much from the sale proceeds?
    a. $35,000
    b. $75,000
    c. $100,000
    d. nothing

13. If zoning laws allow a property to be used in such a manner that is prohibited by a lawful deed restriction, the:
    a. owner must file a quiet title action
    b. zoning laws always prevail over a deed restriction
    c. deed restriction should prevail
    d. owner must file a quitclaim deed

14. Which of the following is an involuntary lien?
    a. homestead
    b. encroachment
    c. mortgage
    d. judgment

15. Private deed restrictions are known as CC&Rs. The first C stands for:
    a. condition
    b. covenant
    c. convenient
    d. cooperative

16. Once properly recorded, an abstract of judgment is good for:
    a. 10 years
    b. 7 years
    c. 5 years
    d. 3 years

17. If an owner files a notice of completion, a general contractor has how many days to file a mechanic's lien?
    a. 90 days
    b. 60 days
    c. 30 days
    d. 10 days

18. If an owner files a notice of completion, a subcontractor has how many days to file a mechanic's lien?
    a. 90 days
    b. 60 days
    c. 30 days
    d. 10 days

19. If a landlord wishes to be protected from a mechanic's lien on work ordered by a tenant, upon discovery of the work the landlord must file a notice of nonresponsibility within how many days?
    a. 90 days
    b. 60 days
    c. 30 days
    d. 10 days

20. Which of the following is a general lien?
    a. property tax
    b. special assessment
    c. mortgage
    d. judgment

Chapter 4
Real Estate Agency

Chapter Preview

In recent years, the laws regarding a real estate agent's duties have changed drastically. This chapter defines the term agency, discusses the creation of agencies, and analyzes the duties and responsibilities of real estate agents. At the conclusion of the chapter, you will be able to:

1. Define agency and then list the three ways in which agencies are created

2. Discuss the fiduciary relationship that exists between a principal and a real estate agent

3. Explain the difference between a single agency and a dual agency

4. List and give examples of several real estate agency violations

5. Describe the agency differences between salespersons and brokers

6. List and give examples of six ways in which real estate agencies are terminated

4.1 AGENCY

The California Civil Code defines agency as "the representation of another person called a principal, by an agent, in dealings with third persons." An agent, therefore, is empowered to represent a principal in negotiating with a third party for the principal's benefit.

Agencies are not required by law. Because of the complexity of business and for convenience, however, principals frequently prefer to have experts represent them in transactions. Common examples of agents include travel agents, insurance agents, and real estate agents.

There are two broad categories of agency. The first category is called "general agency" and the second is called "special agency." A general agent is one who has broad powers to act on behalf of the principal. A special agent has limited or well-defined powers, perhaps confined to a single transaction. Most real estate agencies are special in nature, with powers normally limited to the sale of a specific property. (See Figure 4.1.)

Employer-Employee and Independent Contractor Distinctions

A real estate agency differs from an employer-employee pact. It also differs from an independent contractor relationship.

An employer-employee relationship exists when an individual is hired by another to perform certain services under the strict supervision of the employer. The degree of direct control over the individual hired is important in determining whether that individual is an employee or an independent contractor.

For example, assume that Santos hired Brown to perform office work. Santos requires that Brown work from 9:00 A.M. to 5:00 P.M. Monday through Friday. Santos carefully supervises the method in which Brown performs work duties. Further, Santos provides fringe benefits and deducts money from Brown's paycheck each week for income taxes and social security. Under these circumstances Brown is clearly an employee, and an employer-employee relationship exists.

An independent contractor relationship exists when an individual is hired to accomplish results with little or no supervision required. Assume that Santos hires West

Figure 4.1

Company to perform janitorial services for an office. Santos pays West Company a fixed amount of money per month and does not supervise West Company. West Company is free to clean the office at a self-determined pace and at the company's own time schedule, provided it is after business hours. Further, Santos does not provide fringe benefits and does not take deductions for social security or income taxes out of West Company's pay. West Company, under these circumstances, is probably an independent contractor and not an employee.

A real estate agency differs from both an employer-employee relationship and an independent contractor relationship. Whereas an employee works for an employer, and is under the control of the employer for all work activities, a real estate agent's activities are not under the complete control of a principal. For example, most sellers do not tell a real estate broker when to open the real estate office, when to take a lunch hour, or when to return home!

A real estate agency is also different from an independent contractor relationship in that the agent is not free to do anything to achieve a sale. An agent must respect the lawful instructions of the principal. For example, a seller engages a real estate agent to find a buyer under certain *terms and conditions* which the agents must do to receive a commission.

Creation of Real Estate Agencies

Agencies are created in three ways: by *agreement*, by *ratification*, or by *estoppel*. (See Figure 4.2.)

By far, the greatest number of real estate agencies are created by *agreement*. The principal (usually the seller) orally, in writing, or by their mutual actions, appoints a real estate agent. The authorization to sell (listing agreement) is the document most frequently used to appoint real estate agents. The authorization to sell specifies the powers delegated to the agent, the terms and conditions of the proposed sale of the property, and the circumstances under which a brokerage commission is earned, as well as the brokerage amount. As will be outlined in Chapter 5, there are

CREATION OF REAL ESTATE AGENCIES

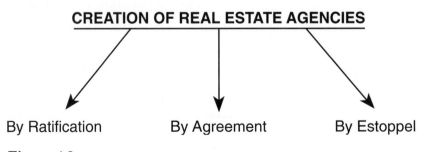

By Ratification   By Agreement   By Estoppel

Figure 4.2

different types of listing agreements, and each has different powers of agency.

The second method of creating an agency is by *ratification*. Under this concept no agency is currently in existence; however, a series of events then occurs which creates an agency relationship. In other words, an unauthorized agent performs a service on your behalf of which you were unaware. Upon learning of the service, which turns out to be beneficial, you accept the responsibility for the agent's act. As an example, assume that Chang, a real estate broker, approaches Johnson with an offer from a buyer to buy Johnson's store when Johnson had not previously considered selling the store. Johnson likes the price and terms and decides that it would be advantageous to sell the property. By accepting the offer and agreeing to pay a commission, Johnson has created an agency with broker Chang. In essence, Johnson ratified broker Chang's unauthorized actions by accepting the buyer's offer.

The third method of creating an agency is by *estoppel*. In an estoppel situation, an individual knowingly allows another person to purport to be his or her agent when in fact an agent has not been appointed. If an innocent third party is later damaged because of this action, the owner may not be able to deny that an agency exists. An example would be an owner who allows a real estate broker to pretend that the broker is the owner's agent. The broker solicits a buyer, who, relying upon the broker's statements, borrows money to purchase the owner's property. If the owner refuses to sell, stating that "the broker is not my agent," the owner may be prevented from denying that an agency existed.

Actual versus Ostensible Agent

Sometimes, on the state real estate examination and in agency discussions, this question comes up: What is the difference between an *actual agent* and an *ostensible agent*? Answer: An actual agent is directly appointed by a principal using a written contract where the agent is granted certain powers to act on behalf of the principal. An ostensible agent is appointed when a principal knowingly allows innocent third parties to believe that an unauthorized person is the principal's agent. If this occurs, the principal may be held liable for the unauthorized agent's actions.

Fiduciary Relationship

When a real estate agent is appointed by the principal (seller) to represent the seller in negotiations with a buyer, a *fiduciary relationship* is created. This fiduciary relationship is one of trust and loyalty and obligates the agent to act in the principal's best interest. It is probably the agent's most important duty. An agent cannot act in a manner that is detrimental to this fiduciary relationship. The agent (1) cannot profit from the agency without the consent of the principal, (2) must obey all lawful instructions of the principal, and (3) may not discriminate in the rental or sale of real property.

Seller's Agency

The majority of real estate agencies are created when a seller (principal) appoints a real estate broker to find a buyer for the seller's property. Therefore, the agency relationship is between the seller and the broker, not the broker and the buyer. Therefore, a real estate broker is legally bound to do the very best for the seller, which includes trying to get the best price and terms for the property.

Although the real estate broker may not be the buyer's agent, the broker owes a degree of allegiance to the buyer. The agent must be honest and truthful and disclose any known defects in the property. Above all else, an agent must not misrepresent the property to a prospective buyer.

Buyer's Agency

Although not as common, a buyer may appoint a real estate broker to be the buyer's agent to find property for the buyer. Under these circumstances the buyer's broker is bound to reveal this fact to the seller. When there is a buyer's broker agency, the fiduciary relationship is between the buyer and the real estate broker, not the seller and the buyer's broker.

Single versus Dual Agency

When a real estate broker acts as an agent to only the seller or only the buyer, this is called a *single agency*. A real estate agent may represent both the buyer and seller in the same transaction, but only with the knowledge and consent of both parties. This is called *dual agency*. Although common, dual agencies are considered by many attorneys as a conflict of interest ripe for lawsuits. Real estate agents often carry errors-and-omissions insurance to help protect against this problem.

Agency Disclosure Requirements

California law requires all real estate agents to disclose in writing to both the buyer and seller as to whether the real estate broker is the agent of the seller, the buyer, or both. Both the buyer and seller must sign a consent form approving the real estate agency status. The disclosure must be done before the seller signs the listing contract with the ~~broker~~ seller and before the buyer signs the purchase contract. The disclosure is done in three steps: disclosure, election, and confirmation. Step one, the real estate agent discloses or presents the choice of being the agent for only the seller, or only the buyer, or for both. Step two, the seller and buyer make their choices known. Step three, the agent, seller, and buyer sign the required form. (See Figure 4.3.)

Subagents

If the seller gives permission in the listing agreement, a real estate agent may assign some of his or her duties to other agents. This occurs when the real estate agent cooperates with other agents, called *subagents,* in attempting to seek purchasers for the property. The same fiduciary relationship exists between subagents and principal as exists between the real estate agent and the principal. Subagents are required to try to get the best price and terms for the seller even if they are from another brokerage office and they have secured a buyer independently. Likewise, subagents must be honest and truthful and not misrepresent the property to the buyers.

4.2 SOME AGENCY VIOLATIONS

There are several hundred thousand real estate licensees in California. The percentage of these licensees who violate agency laws is very small. Of those who are disciplined, most have committed violations unintentionally or through ignorance. Through education, examination, and on-the-job training, real estate licensees learn their duties and responsibilities and therefore reduce the possibility of agency violations. The following, from the Department of Real Estate *Reference Book,* are examples of types of agency violations. The appropriate sections of the Real Estate Law are cited as a reference.

Misrepresentation. Section 10176(a). Many complaints received by the real estate commissioner allege misrepresentation on the part of the broker or salesperson. This includes not only what was said but also the failure of a broker or salesperson to disclose a material fact about the property. Can a real estate agent legally withhold information about a defect in the property? No, failure to disclose is a type of misrepresentation!

False promise. Section 10176(b). A false promise and a misrepresentation are not the same thing. A misrepresen-

DISCLOSURE REGARDING
REAL ESTATE AGENCY RELATIONSHIPS
(As required by the Civil Code)
CALIFORNIA ASSOCIATION OF REALTORS® (C.A.R.) STANDARD FORM

When you enter into a discussion with a real estate agent regarding a real estate transaction, you should from the outset understand what type of agency relationship or representation you wish to have with the agent in the transaction.

SELLER'S AGENT

A Seller's agent under a listing agreement with the Seller acts as the agent for the Seller only. A Seller's agent or a subagent of that agent has the following affirmative obligations:

To the Seller:
A Fiduciary duty of utmost care, integrity, honesty, and loyalty in dealings with the Seller.

To the Buyer and the Seller:
(a) Diligent exercise of reasonable skill and care in performance of the agent's duties.
(b) A duty of honest and fair dealing and good faith.
(c) A duty to disclose all facts known to the agent materially affecting the value or desirability of the property that are not known to, or within the diligent attention and observation of, the parties.

An agent is not obligated to reveal to either party any confidential information obtained from the other party that does not involve the affirmative duties set forth above.

BUYER'S AGENT

A selling agent can, with a Buyer's consent, agree to act as agent for the Buyer only. In these situations, the agent is not the Seller's agent, even if by agreement the agent may receive compensation for services rendered, either in full or in part from the Seller. An agent acting only for a Buyer has the following affirmative obligations:

To the Buyer:
A fiduciary duty of utmost care, integrity, honesty, and loyalty in dealings with the Buyer.

To the Buyer and the Seller:
(a) Diligent exercise of reasonable skill and care in performance of the agent's duties.
(b) A duty of honest and fair dealing and good faith.
(c) A duty to disclose all facts known to the agent materially affecting the value or desirability of the property that are not known to, or within the diligent attention and observation of, the parties.

An agent is not obligated to reveal to either party any confidential information obtained from the other party that does not involve the affirmative duties set forth above.

AGENT REPRESENTING BOTH SELLER & BUYER

A real estate agent, either acting directly or through one or more associate licensees, can legally be the agent of both the Seller and the Buyer in a transaction, but only with the knowledge and consent of both the Seller and the Buyer.

In a dual agency situation, the agent has the following affirmative obligations to both the Seller and the Buyer:
(a) A fiduciary duty of utmost care, integrity, honesty and loyalty in the dealings with either Seller or the Buyer.
(b) Other duties to the Seller and the Buyer as stated above in their respective sections.

In representing both Seller and Buyer, the agent may not, without the express permission of the respective party, disclose to the other party that the Seller will accept a price less than the listing price or that the Buyer will pay a price greater than the price offered.

The above duties of the agent in a real estate transaction do not relieve a Seller or Buyer from the responsibility to protect his or her own interests. You should carefully read all agreements to assure that they adequately express your understanding of the transaction. A real estate agent is a person qualified to advise about real estate. If legal or tax advice is desired, consult a competent professional.

Throughout your real property transaction you may receive more than one disclosure form, depending upon the number of agents assisting in the transaction. The law requires each agent with whom you have more than a casual relationship to present you with this disclosure form. You should read its contents each time it is presented to you, considering the relationship between you and the real estate agent in your specific transaction.

This disclosure form includes the provisions of Sections 2079.13 to 2079.24, inclusive, of the Civil Code set forth on the reverse hereof. Read it carefully.

I/WE ACKNOWLEDGE RECEIPT OF A COPY OF THIS DISCLOSURE.

BUYER/SELLER _____ Date _____ Time _____ AM/PM

BUYER/SELLER _____ Date _____ Time _____ AM/PM

AGENT _____ By _____ Date_____
　　(Please Print)　　　　　　　　　　　　　　　(Associate Licensee or Broker-Signature)

This Disclosure form must be provided in a listing, sale, exchange, installment land contract, or lease over one year, if the transaction involves one-to-four dwelling residential property, including a mobile home, as follows:
(a) From a Listing Agent to a Seller: Prior to entering into the listing.
(b) From an Agent selling a property he/she has listed to a Buyer: Prior to the Buyer's execution of the offer.
(c) From a Selling Agent to a Buyer: Prior to the Buyer's execution of the offer.
(d) From a Selling Agent (in a cooperating real estate firm) to a Seller: Prior to presentation of the offer to the Seller.

It is not necessary or required to confirm an agency relationship using a separate Confirmation form if the agency confirmation portion of the Real Estate Purchase Contract is properly completed in full. However, it is still necessary to use this Disclosure form..

OFFICE USE ONLY
Reviewed by Broker or Designee _____
Date _____

FORM AD-14

M-SC-DEC-95

Figure 4.3 (Reprinted with permission, *California Association of Realtors*®. Endorsement not implied.)

tation is a false statement of fact. A false promise is a false statement about what the promiser is going to do in the future. To prove false promise, the injured party must show that the promise was impossible of performance and that the person making the promise knew it to be impossible. An example might be, "Buy this home and it will double in value in six weeks!"

Continued misrepresentation. Section 10176(c). This section gives the commissioner the right to discipline a licensee for "a continued and flagrant course of misrepresentation or making a false promise through real estate agents or salespersons."

Divided agency. Section 10176(d). This section requires a licensee to inform all principals if the licensee is acting as agent for more than one party in a transaction. An example is the licensee who receives a selling commission from the owner of a piece of property and, at the same time, receives an additional fee from the buyer without the knowledge of both.

Commingling. Section 10176(e). Commingling takes place when a broker has mixed the funds of his or her principal with the broker's own money. To prevent commingling, most real estate brokers establish a trust fund account at a bank and the funds of a principal are deposited into this account. Conversion is not the same thing as commingling. Conversion is misappropriating and using the client's money. This is a crime that carries a jail sentence.

Definite termination date. Section 10176(f). This section of the law requires a specified termination date for all exclusive contracts between a real estate agent and a principal relating to transactions for which a real estate license is required. What is a definite termination date has been the subject of a number of lawsuits. Generally, it can be said that if a definite date is specified in the contract or if a definite period of time is indicated, the requirement is satisfied. However, if it cannot be determined from the exclusive listing contract when the listing is to expire, then the real estate agent may be in violation of the law.

Secret profit. Section 10176(g). Secret profit cases usually arise when the broker, who already has a higher offer from another buyer, makes a low offer, usually through a "dummy" purchaser. The difference is the secret profit.

Many attorneys contend that an agent is guilty of secret profit if the real estate agent derives any profit other than the agreed commission without disclosing the nature of the profits to the principal.

Listing-option. Section 10176(h). This section requires a licensee who has used a form which is both an option and a listing to inform the principal of the amount of profit the licensee will make and to obtain the written consent of the principal approving the amount of such profit, before the licensee may exercise the option. This section does not apply where a licensee is using an option only.

The reason for this requirement in the law is that a licensee, acting as an agent, occupies a highly confidential position of a fiduciary nature. The law imposes upon an agent the responsibility to do nothing that will act to the detriment of the principal, and to keep the principal informed of any fact of which the principal should be aware. This section is provided to prevent unauthorized profits by requiring the broker to give the principal full information.

Other possible violations include dishonest dealing, obtaining license by fraud, false advertising, conviction of crime, negligence, misuse of trade name, inducement of panic selling, plus many others.

TRUST FUNDS   A broker is required to keep an official record of all deposits that pass through his or her real estate business. This account must be kept using acceptable accounting procedures and is subject to audit by the California real estate commissioner.

Although not required by law, most real estate brokers also open a trust fund account at a financial institution where all monies received on behalf of clients and customers can be deposited for safekeeping. Withdrawals can be made only by the broker or other authorized persons. The broker cannot put his or her personal funds in this trust fund account, with the exception of up to $200 to cover bank service fees.

If a broker receives a deposit from a prospective buyer *who does not ask that the deposit be held uncashed,* the broker must within three business days either:

1. Give the deposit to the seller.
2. Put the deposit in escrow.
3. Put the deposit in a trust fund account.

If the broker fails to do one of these three within three business days, the broker could be found guilty of commingling.

Recovery Fund

The state of California has a unique program whereby the public can recover money when there are uncollectable court judgments obtained against a real estate licensee on the basis of fraud, misrepresentation, deceit, or conversion of trust funds in a transaction. Called the Recovery Fund, this program is financed using a portion of real estate licensing fees. The maximum amount of money a person may receive from the fund is currently limited (1999) to $20,000 per individual claim, up to a $100,000 maximum for multiple claims against any one real estate licensee.

Responsibilities of Principals to Agents and Buyers

Agency is a two-way street. Real estate agents owe certain duties and responsibilities to principals, and principals in turn owe certain responsibilities to agents. A principal must tell the real estate agent of any defects in the property so that the agent may properly disclose the defects to a prospective buyer. If the seller knows of a property defect and fails to tell the real estate agent, the seller can be held legally accountable. In short, a seller should not withhold pertinent information or distort facts about the property. In California, sellers of 1–4 residential properties are required to complete and hand to the buyer, prior to the sale, a complete written disclosure regarding the property. (See Chapter 5.)

Sellers usually enter into a contract (listing agreement) to have an agent sell their property. Those contracts should be honored, and commissions should be paid when the property is sold. Sellers should not deal directly with prospective purchasers, procured by the agent, to evade the payment of a commission.

"AS IS" SALE

This brings up the concept of an "as is" sale. Although an "as is" sale is legal, laws and regulations require that the buyer be fully informed as to the condition of the property, including any known defects, before the buyer becomes bound by a purchase contract. If the buyer is fully informed and still wishes to proceed with the sale, then an "as is" transaction is permissible. "Caveat emptor," the old Latin phrase meaning "let the buyer beware," is no longer a defense in court in a real estate transaction. If a seller withholds material facts about the property, such as structural defects known to the seller, the seller can be sued by the buyer.

"I want a real estate license so I will be able to get a share of the commission when I buy and sell my own properties." There are people who do not wish to become real estate agents to serve the public, but want a license to deal for their own account. Is this a good idea? The answer is not clear cut—it depends!

When a licensee buys and sells real estate as a principal, regulations require the licensee to disclose to the opposite party that he or she has a real estate license. Sometimes sellers and/or buyers refuse to deal with licensees as principals for fear that the licensee will take advantage of them. In some cases the seller will allow the buyer-licensee a portion of the commission. However, there have been cases where the seller absolutely refused to allow the listing broker to share the commission with a buyer-licensee.

Working Out-of-State Properties

Problem: A California broker wants to sell a property in another state where the California agent is not licensed.

Solution: The California broker cooperates with a licensed broker in that particular state. Both brokers may then share the commission.

4.3 REGULATION OF BROKERS AND SALESPERSONS

Real Estate Broker versus Salesperson

Although both brokers and salespersons are licensed by the state of California Department of Real Estate, a salesperson's license is valid only when working for a real estate broker. It is through this affiliation with an agent (the real estate broker) that a salesperson also becomes an agent. Therefore, only a real estate broker can contract directly with a principal. A real estate salesperson must use the broker's name when signing a listing agreement with a seller. (Requirements to become a licensed real estate agent are discussed in detail in Chapter 15.)

Considered an employee of the broker by the Department of Real Estate for supervision purposes, a real estate salesperson is usually considered an independent contractor with the broker for other purposes such as income tax withholding, social security, and so on. The broker must supervise the real estate activities of all salespersons under the broker's jurisdiction. In other matters, however, the broker usually treats the salesperson as an independent contractor and does not require the salesperson to be at work at certain hours, or so on. The salesperson is responsible for final results, not the method used to attain the results.

By law, real estate salespersons are required to have a written employment contract with their broker. Commission details between the broker and salesperson should also be in writing. A real estate salesperson can receive compensation only from his or her broker. When escrow is closed, the escrow company usually sends the entire commission to the employing broker, who in turn writes a separate check to the salesperson for his or her share.

Violation of agency law by a real estate salesperson may subject the salesperson to disciplinary action and may also be a cause for disciplinary action against the employing broker who by law is responsible for certain of the salesperson's acts. (See Figure 4.4.)

Regulation of Real Estate Agents

Real estate agents are regulated by government agencies and professional trade associations. The California real estate commissioner, using the employees of the California Department of Real Estate, is empowered to enforce the real estate law and to issue regulations that are enforced in the same manner as law. (See Chapter 15 for details regarding the real estate commissioner's regulation of licensees.)

Commissioner's Former Code of Ethics

At one time the California real estate commissioner had established, by regulations, a code of ethics and professional conduct that applied to all real estate licensees. The code of ethics listed examples of unethical behavior by real estate licensees and required that licensees refrain from such behavior. In addition, the code of ethics outlined positive steps real estate licensees can undertake to improve the public's image of a real estate agent. In 1997, a new regulation repealed the code in an effort to reduce the number of regulations over the real estate business. However, many topics in

BROKER-ASSOCIATE LICENSEE CONTRACT
(Independent Contractor)
THIS IS INTENDED TO BE A LEGALLY BINDING CONTRACT — READ IT CAREFULLY.
CALIFORNIA ASSOCIATION OF REALTORS® (CAR) STANDARD FORM

THIS AGREEMENT, made this _____ day of _____, 19____, by and between

_____

_____ (hereinafter "Broker") and

_____ (hereinafter "Associate Licensee").

IN CONSIDERATION of the respective representations and covenants herein, Broker and Associate Licensee agree and contract as follows:

1. **BROKER:** Broker represents that he/she/it is duly licensed as a real estate broker by the State of California, ☐ doing business as _____
_____ (Firm name), ☐ a sole proprietorship, ☐ a partnership, ☐ a corporation.
Broker is a member of the _____ Board(s)/Association(s) of REALTORS®, and a Participant in the
_____ multiple listing service(s).

2. **ASSOCIATE LICENSEE:** Associate Licensee represents that, (a) he/she is duly licensed by the State of California as a ☐ real estate broker, ☐ real estate
salesperson, and (b) he/she has not used any other names within the past five years except _____
_____. Broker shall keep his/her/its license current during the term of
this agreement. Associate Licensee shall keep his/her license current during the term of this agreement, including satisfying all applicable continuing education
and provisional license requirements.

3. **LISTING AND SALES ACTIVITIES:** Broker shall make available to Associate Licensee, equally with other licensees associated with Broker, all current listings
in Broker's office, except any listing which Broker may choose to place in the exclusive servicing of Associate Licensee or one or more other specific licensees
associated with Broker. Associate Licensee shall not be required to accept or service any particular listing or prospective listing offered by Broker, or to see or
service particular parties. Broker shall not restrict Associate Licensee's activities to particular geographical areas. Broker shall not, except to the extent required
by law, direct or limit Associate Licensee's activities as to hours, leads, open houses, opportunity or floor time, production, prospects, sales meetings, schedule,
inventory, time off, vacation, or similar activities. In compliance with Commissioner's Regulation 2780, et seq. (Title 10, California Code of Regulations, §2780,
et seq.), Broker and Associate Licensee shall at all times be familiar with, and act in compliance with, all applicable federal, California and local anti-discrimination
laws.

4. **BROKER SUPERVISION:**
   (a) Associate Licensee shall submit for Broker's review:
       i. All documents which may have a material effect upon the rights and duties of principals in a transaction, within 24 hours after preparing, signing, or receiving
          same. Broker may exercise this review responsibility through another licensee provided the Broker and the designated licensee have complied with
          Commissioner's Regulation 2725 (Title 10, California Code of Regulations, §2725).
       ii. Any documents or other items connected with a transaction pursuant to this agreement, in the possession of or available to Associate Licensee, (i) immediately
          upon request by Broker or Broker's designated licensee, and/or (ii) as provided in Broker's Office Policy Manual, if any.
       iii. All documents associated with any real estate transaction in which Associate Licensee is a principal.
   (b) In addition, without affecting Associate Licensee's status, Broker shall have the right to direct Associate Licensee's actions to the extent required by law, and
   Associate Licensee shall comply with such directions. All trust funds shall be handled in compliance with Business and Professions Code §10145, and other
   applicable laws.

5. **OFFICE FACILITIES:** Broker shall make available for Associate Licensee's use, along with other licensees associated with Broker, the facilities of the real
estate office operated by Broker at _____
and the facilities of any other office locations made available by Broker pursuant to this agreement.

6. **ASSOCIATE LICENSEE'S EFFORTS:** Associate Licensee shall work diligently and with his/her best efforts, (a) to sell, exchange, lease, or rent properties
listed with Broker or other cooperating Brokers, (b) to solicit additional listings, clients, and customers, and (c) to otherwise promote the business of serving the
public in real estate transactions to the end that Broker and Associate Licensee may derive the greatest benefit possible, in accordance with law.

7. **UNLAWFUL ACTS:** Associate Licensee shall not commit any act for which the Real Estate Commissioner of the State of California is authorized to restrict,
suspend, or revoke Associate Licensee's license or impose other discipline, under California Business and Professions Code Sections 10176 or 10177 or other
provisions of law.

8. **LISTING COMMISSIONS:** Commissions shall be charged to parties who desire to enter into listing agreements and other contracts for services requiring
a real estate license, with Broker,
   ☐ as shown in "Exhibit A" attached which is incorporated as a part of this agreement by reference, or
   ☐ as follows: _____
   _____
   _____ .
   Any proposed deviation from that schedule must be reviewed and approved in advance by Broker. Any permanent change in commission schedule shall be
   disseminated by Broker to Associate Licensee.

9. **COMPENSATION TO ASSOCIATE LICENSEE:** Associate Licensee shall receive a share of commissions which are actually collected by Broker, on listings
and other contracts for services requiring a real estate license which are solicited and obtained by Associate Licensee, and on transactions of which Associate
Licensee's activities are the procuring cause,
   ☐ as shown in "Exhibit B" attached which is incorporated as a part of this agreement by reference, or
   ☐ as follows: _____
   _____
   _____
   _____
   _____ .
   The above commissions may be varied by written agreement between Broker and Associate Licensee before completion of any particular transaction. Expenses
   which must be paid from commissions, or are incurred in the attempt to collect commissions, shall be paid by Broker and Associate Licensee in the same proportion
   as set forth for the division of commissions.

10. **DIVIDING COMPENSATION WITH OTHER LICENSEES IN OFFICE:** If Associate Licensee and one or more other licensees associated with Broker
both participate on the same side (either listing or selling) of a transaction, the commission allocated to their combined activities shall be divided by Broker and
paid to them according to the written agreement between them which shall be furnished in advance to Broker.

11. **COMMISSIONS PAID TO BROKER:** All commissions will be received by Broker. Associate Licensee's share of commissions shall be paid to him/her, after
deduction of offsets, immediately upon collection by Broker or as soon thereafter as practicable, except as otherwise provided in (a) Paragraph 9, above, (b) Broker's
Office Policy Manual, or (c) a separate written agreement between Broker and Associate Licensee. Broker may impound in Broker's account Associate Licensee's
share of commissions on transactions in which there is a known or pending claim against Broker and/or Associate Licensee, until such claim is resolved.

12. **UNCOLLECTED COMMISSIONS:** Neither Broker nor Associate Licensee shall be liable to the other for any portion of commissions not collected. Associate
Licensee shall not be entitled to any advance payment from Broker upon future commissions.

FORM I-14

Figure 4.4a (Reprinted with permission, *California Association of Realtors®*.
Endorsement not implied.)

☐

13. **ASSOCIATE LICENSEE EXPENSES; OFFSETS:** Associate Licensee shall provide and pay for all professional licenses, supplies, services, and other items required in connection with Associate Licensee's activities under this agreement, or any listing or transaction, without reimbursement from Broker except as required by law. If Broker elects to advance funds to pay expenses or liabilities of Associate Licensee, Associate Licensee shall repay to Broker the full amount advanced on demand, or Broker may deduct the full amount advanced from commissions payable to Associate Licensee on any transaction without notice.

14. **INDEPENDENT CONTRACTOR RELATIONSHIP:** Broker and Associate Licensee intend that, to the maximum extent permissible by law, (a) this agreement does not constitute a hiring or employment agreement by either party, (b) Broker and Associate Licensee are independent contracting parties with respect to all services rendered under this agreement or in any resulting transactions, (c) Associate Licensee's only remuneration shall be his/her proportional share, if any, of commissions collected by Broker, (d) Associate Licensee retains sole and absolute discretion and judgment in the methods, techniques, and procedures to be used in soliciting and obtaining listings, sales, exchanges, leases, rentals, or other transactions, and in carrying out Associate Licensee's selling and soliciting activities, except as required by law or in Broker's Office Policy Manual, (e) Associate Licensee is under the control of Broker as to the results of Associate Licensee's work only, and not as to the means by which those results are accomplished except as required by law, or in Broker's Office Policy Manual, if any, (f) this agreement shall not be construed as a partnership, (g) Associate Licensee has no authority to bind Broker by any promise or representation unless specifically authorized by Broker in writing, (h) Broker shall not be liable for any obligation or liability incurred by Associate Licensee, (i) Associate Licensee shall not be treated as an employee with respect to services performed as a real estate agent, for state and federal tax purposes, and (j) the fact the Broker may carry worker compensation insurance for his/her/its own benefit and for the mutual benefit of Broker and licensees associated with Broker, including Associate Licensee, shall not create an inference of employment.

15. **LISTINGS AND OTHER AGREEMENTS PROPERTY OF BROKER:** All listings of property, and all agreements for performance of licensed acts, and all acts or actions requiring a real estate license which are taken or performed in connection with this agreement, shall be taken and performed in the name of Broker. All listings shall be submitted to Broker within 24 hours after receipt by Associate Licensee. Associate Licensee agrees to and does hereby contribute all right and title to such listings to Broker for the benefit and use of Broker, Associate Licensee, and other licensees associated with Broker.

16. **TERMINATION OF RELATIONSHIP:** Broker or Associate Licensee may terminate their relationship under this agreement at any time, on 24 hours written notice, with or without cause. Even after termination, this agreement shall govern all disputes and claims between Broker and Associate Licensee connected with their relationship under this agreement, including obligations and liabilities arising from existing and completed listings, transactions, and services.

17. **COMMISSIONS AFTER TERMINATION AND OFFSET:** If this agreement is terminated while Associate Licensee has listings or pending transactions that require further work normally rendered by Associate Licensee, Broker shall make arrangements with another licensee associated with Broker to perform the required work, or shall perform the work him/herself. The licensee performing the work shall be reasonably compensated for completing work on those listings or transactions, and such reasonable compensation shall be deducted from Associate Licensee's share of commissions. Except for such offset, Associate Licensee shall receive his/her regular share of commissions on such sales or other transactions, if actually collected by Broker, after deduction of any other amounts or offsets provided in this agreement.

18. **ARBITRATION OF DISPUTES:** All disputes or claims between Associate Licensee and other licensee(s) associated with Broker, or between Associate Licensee and Broker, arising from or connected in any way with this agreement, which cannot be adjusted between the parties involved, shall be submitted to the Board of REALTORS® of which all such disputing parties are members for arbitration pursuant to the provisions of its Bylaws, as may be amended from time to time, which are incorporated as a part of this agreement by reference. If the Bylaws of the Board do not cover arbitration of the dispute, or if the Board declines jurisdiction over the dispute, then arbitration shall be pursuant to the rules of the American Arbitration Association, as may be amended from time to time, which are incorporated as a part of this agreement by reference. The Federal Arbitration Act, Title 9, U.S. Code, Section 1 et seq., shall govern this agreement.

19. **PROPRIETARY INFORMATION AND FILES:** Associate Licensee shall not use to his/her own advantage, or the advantage of any other person, business, or entity, except as specifically provided in this agreement, either during Associate Licensee's association with Broker or thereafter, any information gained for or from the business or files of Broker. All files and documents pertaining to listings and transactions are the property of Broker and shall be delivered to Broker by Associate Licensee immediately upon request or upon termination of their relationship under this agreement.

20. **INDEMNITY AND HOLD HARMLESS:** All claims, demands, liabilities, judgments, and arbitration awards, including costs and attorney's fees, to which Broker is subjected by reason of any action taken or omitted by Associate Licensee in connection with services rendered or to be rendered pursuant to this agreement, shall be:

☐ Paid in full by Associate Licensee, who hereby agrees to indemnify and hold harmless Broker for all such sums, or

☐ Other: _____

_____

_____ .

Associate Licensee shall pay to Broker the full amount due by him/her on demand, or Broker may deduct the full amount due by Associate Licensee from commissions due on any transaction without notice.

21. **ADDITIONAL PROVISIONS:** _____

_____

_____ .

22. **DEFINITIONS:** As used in this agreement, the following terms have the meanings indicated:

(a) "Listing" means an agreement with a property owner or other party to locate a buyer, exchange party, lessee, or other party to a transaction involving real property, a mobile home, or other property or transaction which may be brokered by a real estate licensee, or an agreement with a party to locate or negotiate for any such property or transaction.

(b) "Commission" means compensation for acts requiring a real estate license, regardless of whether calculated as a percentage of transaction price, flat fee, hourly rate, or in any other manner.

(c) "Transaction" means a sale, exchange, lease, or rental of real property, a business opportunity, or a mobile home which may lawfully be brokered by a real estate licensee, or a loan secured by any property of those types.

(d) "Associate Licensee" means the real estate broker or real estate salesperson licensed by the State of California and rendering the services set forth herein for Associate Licensee.

23. **NOTICES:** All notices under this agreement shall be in writing. Notices may be delivered personally, or by certified U.S. mail, postage prepaid, or by facsimile, to the parties at the addresses noted below. Either party may designate a new address for purposes of this agreement by giving notice to the other party. Notices mailed shall be deemed received as of 5:00 P.M. on the second business day following the date of mailing.

24. **ATTORNEY FEES:**

In any action, proceeding, or arbitration between Broker and Associate Licensee arising from or related to this agreement, the prevailing party shall, in the discretion of the court or arbitrator, be entitled to reasonable attorney fees in addition to other appropriate relief.

25. **ENTIRE AGREEMENT; MODIFICATION:** All prior agreements between the parties concerning their relationship as Broker and Associate Licensee are incorporated in this agreement, which constitutes the entire contract. Its terms are intended by the parties as a final and complete expression of their agreement with respect to its subject matter, and may not be contradicted by evidence of any prior agreement or contemporaneous oral agreement. This agreement may not be amended, modified, altered, or changed in any respect whatsoever except by a further agreement in writing duly executed by Broker and Associate Licensee.

BROKER: ASSOCIATE LICENSEE:

_____   _____
(Signature)   (Signature)

_____   _____
(Name Printed)   (Name Printed)

_____   _____
(Address)   (Address)

_____   _____
(City, State, Zip)   (City, State, Zip)

_____   _____
(Telephone)   (Fax)   (Telephone)   (Fax)

NOTE: (1) Broker and Associate Licensee should each receive an executed copy of this agreement.

(2) Attach commission schedules Exhibits A and B if applicable.

This form is available for use by the entire real estate industry. The use of this form is not intended to identify the user as a REALTOR®. REALTOR® is a registered collective membership mark which may be used only by real estate licensees who are members of the NATIONAL ASSOCIATION OF REALTORS® and who subscribe to its Code of Ethics.

EQUAL HOUSING OPPORTUNITY
M-SC-JUN-93

Figure 4.4b

the former code of ethics are still illegal in other codes sections under California law.

Filing Complaints

If a person wishes to file a complaint about a real estate agent, the procedure is to send a written complaint to the real estate commissioner. The commissioner then assigns the complaint to a deputy for investigation. Statements about the incident are taken from witnesses and the licensee. In addition, the real estate agent's records and accounts may be audited. An informal conference may be called to allow the investigating deputy to determine the seriousness of the complaint. If a violation of the law has occurred, a formal hearing is called and the agent's license may be suspended or revoked. Every year, the commissioner receives several thousand complaints about real estate licensees, but after an investigation, a majority are dismissed as not being in violation of real estate law or regulations.

Trade Associations

There are several national, state, and local professional real estate trade associations, such as the National Association of REALTORS® and the National Association of Real Estate Brokers. The role of trade associations is presented in detail in Chapter 15. The point stressed here is that real estate trade associations have membership rules and codes of ethics to help monitor the activities of their members. This indirectly works as a form of self-regulation. Members who violate the real estate trade association rules of conduct can be suspended from membership and in the process lose many benefits.

4.4 TERMINATION OF A REAL ESTATE AGENCY

There are six basic ways to terminate a real estate agency.

1. Termination by *completion of the agency agreement.* The agent fulfills his or her responsibilities by securing a buyer who is ready, willing, and able to buy the property on the exact terms of the listing or on other terms agreeable to the seller. When this occurs, the agent is eligible for the commission and is normally paid at close of escrow.

2. Termination by *expiration of time.* If an agent fails to find a ready, willing, and able buyer by the termination date of the listing, the agency is terminated. Most list-

ings contain a clause, however, that provides for the agent to give the seller a list of prospects to whom the agent has shown the property during the term of the listing. If any of these prospects buys the property directly from the seller or through another broker during the designated protection period after the listing expires, then the agent is entitled to a commission. Additional details are presented in Chapter 5.

3. Termination *by death of the principal or death of the agent.* An agency is automatically terminated if either the principal or agent dies during the term of the listing. One exception is if the principal dies after a purchase agreement is signed, the agent is entitled to the commission. The sale is usually binding on the heirs of the decedent.

4. Termination *by destruction of the property.* If a major catastrophe such as an earthquake or fire occurs causing damage to the property, the agency is terminated.

5. Termination *by mutual consent.* The principals and the agent can mutually agree to terminate the agency.

6. Termination *by unilateral action of the agent or the principal.* Either party may terminate the agency unilaterally. However, the party that cancels the agency may be liable for damages. If a principal cancels the agency, the agent is usually entitled to the full commission or at a minimum, to reimbursement for expenses and time spent.

(See Figure 4.5.)

CHAPTER SUMMARY   An agency relationship is created when a principal appoints an agent to represent the principal in dealings with third parties. A real estate agency is usually created when a seller appoints a real estate broker to find a buyer for the

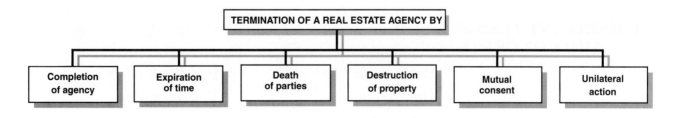

Figure 4.5

seller's property. There are two broad categories of agency: general agency and special agency. Real estate agents are usually special agents. When a real estate broker represents only the seller or only the buyer, it is called a single agency. If the broker represents both the buyer and seller, it is called a dual agency. A real estate agency differs from both an employer-employee relationship and an independent contractor relationship.

Agencies are created in three ways: by agreement, ratification, or estoppel. Most real estate agencies are created by written agreement. A fiduciary relationship is established when a real estate agent is appointed by the principal. This relationship is one of a binding trust and loyalty and obligates the real estate agent to act in the principal's best interest. The agent, nonetheless, owes the opposite party a full disclosure of all known defects. A real estate agent must be honest and truthful and must not misrepresent the sale.

Agency violations may include misrepresentation, false promise, divided agency, commingling, definite termination date, and secret profit. A principal should advise a real estate agent of any known defects to the property. A seller should not withhold information from the real estate agent or buyer. A seller can be held liable for distortion of facts about the property.

A real estate broker can contract directly with a principal, whereas a salesperson cannot. It is only through the real estate salesperson's association with a broker that the salesperson becomes an agent. Salespersons must have a written employment contract with a broker and can receive compensation only from the employing broker.

Real estate agents are regulated by the California Department of Real Estate and by professional trade associations, if they are members of those organizations.

Agencies are terminated by completion of the agency agreement, by expiration of time, by death of the principal or agent, by destruction of the property, by mutual consent, and by unilateral termination by the agent or the principal.

IMPORTANT TERMS AND CONCEPTS

Agent	Independent contractor
Commingling	Misrepresentation
Conversion	Principal
Dual agency	Recovery fund
False promise	Secret profit
Fiduciary	Single agency
General agency	Special agency

1. Real estate salesperson Ames from Vista Realty is the agent for the sale of the Alvarez home at 123 Main Street, Somewhere, CA. Salesperson Jones also works for Vista Realty and brings in an offer on the Alvarez home from Buyer Patel. Explain the agency relationship between Alvarez, Vista Realty, and Patel.

2. A real estate salesperson from Acme Properties shows a potential buyer a home listed with Lake Realty. While showing the home, the Acme agent mentions that based on the information supplied by Lake Realty, the home is 2,100 square feet and the lot is one-half acre. In fact, the home is 2,000 square feet and the lot is only one-quarter acre. Which real estate company is guilty of misrepresentation? How should the salesperson from Acme Properties have handled the situation?

3. Excellent Realty has a signed contract to act as the exclusive agent for the seller of a condo for a period of 90 days, at a price of $175,000. Within 60 days a buyer is found who makes an offer of $160,000. Prior to accepting the offer, the seller dies. The heirs then cancel the agreement with Excellent Realty. Excellent Realty contends that it is entitled to a commission based on the $160,000 offer. The heirs deny that they must pay the commission. Who is right and why?

REVIEWING YOUR UNDERSTANDING

1. A real estate agency exists between:
   a. seller and buyer
   b. broker and principal
   c. borrower and lender
   d. landlord and tenant

2. A fiduciary relationship is best described as:
   a. ethics and loyalty
   b. ethics and trust
   c. trust and confidence
   d. loyalty and trust

3. A real estate salesperson is:
   a. a direct agent
   b. an agent by virtue of his or her association with a broker
   c. an employee of the seller
   d. an employee of the buyer

4. A subagent owes a chief responsibility to the:
   a. buyer
   b. listing agent
   c. employing broker
   d. real estate lender

5. A real estate agency can be created by all of the following, except:
   a. by ratification
   b. by agreement
   c. by estoppel
   d. by doctrine of realty determination

6. All of the following are methods of terminating a real estate agency, except:
   a. estoppel
   b. mutual consent
   c. completion of agency
   d. expiration of time

7. A home seller must inform his or her real estate agent when the seller is aware of:
   a. termite infestation discovered earlier
   b. leaky roof
   c. an inoperative fireplace
   d. all of the above

8. All of the following are true, except:
   a. both real estate salespersons and brokers are required to be licensed
   b. a real estate broker, not the salesperson, is appointed by the principal to be the agent
   c. a salesperson collects the commission directly from the seller
   d. a dual agency means the real estate broker represents both the buyer and seller

9. A seller's real estate agent owes the buyer:
   a. the duty to see that the property is sold at the lowest possible price
   b. a disclosure of known defects
   c. a fiduciary relationship
   d. the right to know the seller's lowest acceptance price

10. The Real Estate Commissioner:
    a. administers the real estate law
    b. issues regulations that have the force of law
    c. heads the Department of Real Estate
    d. all of the above

11. If a real estate salesperson decides to work for a new broker, the existing listings obtained by the salesperson belong to the:
    a. salesperson
    b. former broker
    c. new broker
    d. seller, who can automatically cancel the listing

12. Unless instructed to hold the check uncashed, a buyer's deposit must be placed with the appropriated party or account within how many business days?
    a. three
    b. five
    c. seven
    d. nine

13. Ms. Lightdeer showed a property to Mr. and Mrs. Chu without having an agency agreement with the owner. Later the owner accepted the offer to purchase, which was submitted by Ms. Lightdeer on behalf of Mr. and Mrs. Chu. The owner consented to Ms. Lightdeer's unauthorized acts. Under these circumstances an agency could be created by:

a. fiduciary
b. estoppel
c. ratification
d. assumption

14. The maximum amount per individual claim against the Department of Real Estate Recovery fund is:

a. $10,000
b. $20,000
c. $50,000
d. $100,000

15. A real estate broker who has been appointed in writing to be a property owner's agent to find a buyer under a specified set of terms is best described as a:

a. general, ostensible agent
b. general, actual agent
c. special, actual agent
d. special, ostensible agent

16. A real estate agent mistakenly states that the portable dishwasher is included in the sales price of the home. This agent is guilty of:

a. false promise
b. misrepresentation
c. divided agency
d. secret profit

17. When a real estate agent mixes his or her personal funds with that of a principal, the agent is guilty of:

a. commingling
b. conversion
c. trust funding
d. embezzlement

18. When a seller specifically authorizes a real estate agent to use agents from other real estate companies to help find a buyer, the other agents are called:

a. principals
b. listing agents
c. subagents
d. finder agents

19. Homeowner Raymond appoints Broker Cecilia to find a buyer. Later a qualified buyer is found, and all papers are signed and loans approved. The home is scheduled to be transferred on June 1. On May 30, Homeowner Raymond dies. Which best describes the situation?

a. The real estate agency is canceled, and Broker Cecilia has not earned the commission.
b. The real estate agency is canceled, and Broker Cecilia has earned the commission.
c. The sale is probably not binding on the heirs of Raymond.
d. The sale and agency are terminated by expiration of time.

20. All of the following are true, *except:*
   a. all real estate brokers are required to establish reasonable procedures to supervise the activities of salespersons transacting business under the name of the broker
   b. "as is" home sales are allowed in California if proper disclosures are given
   c. by law, real estate salespeople are required to have a written contract with their employing broker
   d. a majority of real estate complaints against agents are valid enough to warrant disciplinary action by the real estate commissioner

21. A real estate broker is allowed to keep $————of his or her money in a trust fund to handle bank service charges.
   a. $200   c. $400
   b. $300   d. $500

22. When attempting to become an agent for a home seller, the seller asks the agent if he or she would be willing to reduce the amount of the commission. An acceptable reply would be:
   a. the commission is set by law, I cannot change it
   b. the commission is set by our local trade association, and I cannot change it
   c. the commission is set by our company policy, and I cannot change it
   d. the commission is set by the Real Estate Commissioner, and I cannot change it

23. Which of the following is an example of secret profit?
   a. Seller sells for 50% more than he or she paid for the property.
   b. Buyer believes the property is worth more than the asking price.
   c. Broker receives a referral fee from a title company without telling the principals in the sales transaction.
   d. Broker earns a commission after showing the property to only one buyer who then purchases within one week.

24. Under a buyer's agency, the fiduciary relationship is between the broker and the:
   a. seller
   b. buyer's broker
   c. buyer
   d. seller and buyer

25. When a California real estate broker sells a property in another state where the California agent is not licensed, the use of a licensed broker in the other state does not allow the California broker to share in the commission.
   a. true
   b. false

Chapter 5
Real Estate Contracts

Chapter Preview   This chapter presents the legal requirements for an enforceable real estate contract. The chapter includes a definition of a contract, outlines the essential elements of a valid contract, and then discusses how contracts are terminated. Two important real estate contracts, the authorization to sell (listing agreement) and the purchase agreement (deposit receipt), are discussed. These two contracts are presented in detail in the chapter appendix. At the conclusion of the chapter, you will be able to:

1. Define contracts and list the legal requirements for an enforceable contract

2. Describe how contracts are terminated or discharged

3. List seven provisions that should be part of a real estate contract

4. Explain the purpose of an authorization to sell (listing agreement) and then discuss the various types of listing agreements

5. Discuss the purpose of an option contract

6. Discuss the purpose of a purchase agreement (deposit receipt) and then explain the meaning of each clause that appears in a typical purchase agreement

7. Explain the use of a counteroffer form

5.1 LEGAL REQUIREMENTS FOR ENFORCEABLE CONTRACTS

A *contract* is generally defined as an agreement between two or more persons consisting of a promise or mutual promises to either perform or not to perform certain acts. If the contract is executed under proper conditions, the law will enforce the contract and require the parties to abide by the terms or incur damages.

A *unilateral contract* may be created by only one party extending a promise without a reciprocal promise by another party. An example is a reward. If you lost your wallet and offered $100 for its return, this would be a unilateral contract because you are the only person making an offer.

However, most real estate contracts are *bilateral* in nature, in which a promise is made for another promise. An example is a listing agreement in which an agent promises to use diligence to secure a purchaser if the owner promises among other things to sell the property under the terms outlined and pay a commission.

A contract may be created by expression or by implication. An *expressed* contract is one wherein the parties have agreed to perform an act or acts either verbally or under a written agreement. An *implied* contract is one wherein the parties have not formally agreed either verbally or through a written agreement to perform an act. Instead, they agree to perform by their actions rather than by words.

For example, say you reached agreement with a contractor to build a fence around your home and you mutually agree as to a style, size, costs, and starting date. Under these circumstances you have probably created an expressed contract. On the other hand, assume that you had talked to the contractor about the fence but that your discussions had been inconclusive with no promises made. The next day the contractor appears on your property with a load of materials and begins building the fence. If you do not stop the contractor and the fence is built, an implied contract may be established.

A contract can also be labeled as an *executed* contract or an *executory* contract. In an executed contract all parties have performed and fulfilled their obligations. An executory contract means that some act of the contract remains to be completed by one or more of the parties. A real estate listing agreement, discussed later in this chapter, is a good example of an executory contract. (See Figure 5.1.)

Legal Effects of Contracts

Once a contract is created, what are the prospects that the agreement will stand up in court in the event of a dispute? Four important legal terms are presented here.

TYPES OF CONTRACTS

UNILATERAL = PROMISE FOR AN ACT

BILATERAL   = PROMISE FOR A PROMISE

EXPRESSED   = VERBAL OR WRITTEN

IMPLIED   = CREATED BY ACTIONS

EXECUTORY = SOME ACTION NEEDED

EXECUTED   = COMPLETED CONTRACT

Most real estate agreements are expressed bilateral contracts.

Figure 5.1

1. *Valid.* A binding and enforceable contract. You can sue on it; it is considered the best type of contract that you can have.

2. *Void.* An agreement that the courts will not consider a contract—it has no legal effect. An example would be a contract by a minor (someone under 18 years of age) to purchase a home. A minor may acquire real property through will or by a gift. However, a minor may not buy or sell real property except through a court-appointed person acting on his or her behalf. An exception is a category of minor called emancipated minor. Examples of emancipated minors are those minors who are married or serving in the military service or whose parents have been relieved of legal responsibility for their minor's actions. Emancipated minors can legally contract for real property.

3. *Voidable.* A contract where one of the parties (the injured party) has the option of proceeding with the contract or calling it off. Example: contracts entered into because of duress (force), menace (threat of force), undue influence (pushed by a person with excess power), or fraud (misrepresentation).

4. *Unenforceable.* A contract which, although valid, cannot be sued upon. An example would be an oral agreement for the sale of real property by an agent for a commission. (See Figure 5.2.)

Essential Elements of a Real Estate Contract

The five essential elements for an enforceable real estate contract are (1) parties capable of contracting, (2) mutual consent, (3) lawful object, (4) a sufficient consideration, and

LEGAL EFFECTS OF CONTRACTS

✓ **VALID**
binding and enforceable

✓ **VOIDABLE**
one party can cancel due to fraud, duress, undue influence but the other side cannot cancel

✓ **UNENFORCEABLE**
appears valid, but cannot be enforced in court

✓ **VOID**
no legal effect, no contract

Figure 5.2

(5) according to the Statute of Frauds, must be in writing. (See Figure 5.3.)

PARTIES CAPABLE OF CONTRACTING

For a contract to be valid, there must be at least two or more parties with the capacity to contract. As a general rule anyone is capable of contracting. However, there are some exceptions. A minor is incapable of contracting for real property unless the minor is emancipated. Persons who are declared incompetent by the courts cannot contract. Like minors, however, incompetents may acquire title to real property by gift or by will. Certain classifications of convicts are considered incapable of contracting. On the other hand, foreigners may hold and sell real property, although there are certain federal restrictions. Partnerships and corporations are regarded as artificial beings, and may also hold and dispose of real property.

MUTUAL CONSENT

The parties to the contract must mutually agree to be bound by the terms of the contract. This is exemplified by an offer by one party and an acceptance by the other. The offer must be definite and certain in its terms. A typical example is where a buyer makes an offer to purchase real estate under

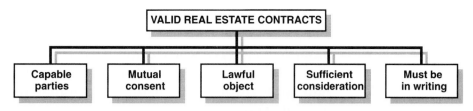

Figure 5.3

certain terms and conditions. The seller then accepts the offer, and the acceptance is communicated, in person or by mail or Fax, to the buyer. This offer and acceptance constitute mutual consent.

LAWFUL OBJECT

A contract must have a lawful object. An "object" refers to what is required to be done or not to be done. A contract is void if there is a single object and that one object is unlawful or impossible to perform. If there are many lawful objects in the contract and one or more unlawful objects, usually only the lawful objects will be valid, and the other objects will be void. A contract for a gambling debt in California, or a contract to commit a crime, would not be a lawful object. Therefore, the contracts would not be valid.

SUFFICIENT CONSIDERATION

Consideration is defined as "a benefit conferred or agreed to be conferred on the person making the promise or on any other person, or a detriment suffered or agreed to be suffered." Consideration can be as simple as the return of one promise for another promise. The consideration must have some value. In many cases the consideration is money, but it need not be. It must be something of value in exchange for something of value and is termed a "valuable" consideration. For example, love and affection might be considered "valuable" or "good" consideration on a gift deed. If there is a dispute as to what constitutes "sufficient" consideration, the parties to the contract may need to bring a court action to clarify the issue.

THE STATUTE OF FRAUDS

According to the Statute of Frauds in the California Civil Code, a real estate contract must be in writing to be enforceable in court. Similarly, any change from the original contract must also be in writing and dated and initialed by the parties involved. The purpose of the law is to prevent perjury, forgery, and dishonest conduct on the part of unscrupulous people in proving the existence and terms of certain important types of contracts. The so-called "parol evidence rule" applies. This rule states that oral evidence may not be used to modify a written contract that appears to be complete. Oral evidence may be allowed to prove fraud or other illegal aspects of a written contract. Practically speaking, a written contract is simply a good way to help eliminate ambiguities and misunderstandings that might arise at a later date.

The California Civil Code requires that the following contracts must be in writing to be enforceable:

1. An agreement that by its terms is not to be performed within a year from the making thereof.
2. A special promise to answer for the debt, default, or miscarriage of another, except in the cases provided for in Civil Code Section 2794.
3. An agreement made on consideration of marriage other than a mutual promise to marry.
4. An agreement to lease real estate for more than one year, or for the sale of real property, or of an interest therein. A lease for one year or less need not be in writing to be valid.
5. An agreement authorizing or employing an agent, broker, or any other person, to purchase or sell real estate, or to lease real estate for a period longer than one year, or to procure, introduce, or find a purchaser or seller of real estate or a lessee or lessor of real estate where such lease is for a period longer than one year, for compensation or a commission.
6. An agreement that by its terms is not to be performed during the lifetime of the promisor, or an agreement to devise or to bequeath any property, or to make any provision for any reason by will.
7. An agreement by a purchaser of real property to pay an indebtedness secured by a mortgage or deed of trust on the property purchased, unless assumption of said indebtedness by the purchaser is specifically provided for in the conveyance of such property.

Any contract that does not comply with the preceding is not void but is unenforceable.

Discharge of Contracts

Contracts can be discharged in a number of ways. *Full performance* is the normal situation, wherein the parties accomplish what they set out to do in the contract. At the other extreme is a *breach* of the contract, which means that one of the parties did not fulfill its part of the agreement. In the case of a breach, the injured party has a number of legal remedies available.

Two of the more common remedies are to (1) *sue for damages,* or (2) *sue for specific performance.* When you sue for damages, you are attempting to receive monetary compensation for the damage because the other party will not complete the contract. When you sue for specific performance, you are asking the court to compel the other party to perform according to the contract.

Statute of Limitations

In order to initiate a lawsuit, the *Statute of Limitations* states that you must begin the lawsuit within a legally prescribed time period. If you fail to initiate the lawsuit within the time period outlined in the Statute of Limitations, you may have no remedy in the courts and your rights to sue are said to have "outlawed." Four real estate examples of Statute of Limitation periods are:

1. Three years to bring action for removal of encroachments
2. Four years to bring action on a written contract
3. Five years to bring action for recovery of title to property
4. Ninety days after filing a mechanic's lien, the mechanic must bring a court foreclosure to enforce the lien

Sometimes, even though the issue is within the statute of limitations, certain rights may be set aside using the *Doctrine of Laches.* This doctrine states that if an unreasonable delay in bringing an action results in an unfair situation for a defendant, the extent of the lawsuit might be limited.

Other ways to discharge a contract include:

1. Part performance
2. Substantial performance
3. Impossibility of performance
4. Agreement between the parties
5. Release
6. Operation of law
7. Acceptance of a breach of contract

Provisions in Contracts

The following basic provisions should be part of a real estate contract:

1. The date of the agreement
2. The names and addresses of the parties to the contract

3. A description of the property
4. The consideration
5. Reference to the creation of new mortgages or deeds of trust, if any, and the terms thereof; also, the terms and conditions of existing mortgages, if any
6. Any other provisions that may be required or requested by either of the parties
7. The date and place for closing the contract

In the real world, most real estate contracts are preprinted forms that cover the current legal requirements per California law.

Real Estate Licensees Should Not Practice Law

It must be stressed that a real estate agent is not licensed to practice law. Therefore, a real estate agent should not create a contract from a blank sheet of paper. Current practice allows a real estate agent only to fill in blanks on a preprinted real estate form.

Another point—on some occasions a discrepancy occurs between a preprinted clause in a contract and a handwritten clause. The usual rule is that the handwritten clause supersedes the preprinted clause.

5.2 AUTHORIZATION TO SELL

Commonly referred to as the *listing agreement,* the authorization to sell is one of the most common contracts found in a real estate transaction. An authorization to sell is the formal contract wherein the owner of the property (the seller) agrees to sell the property under certain stipulated conditions. The listing agreement creates a contract between a real estate broker and the seller.

As noted in the previous chapter, the authorization to sell also establishes an agency relationship between the broker and the principal. This agency is referred to as a fiduciary relationship.

An authorization to sell is a bilateral contract in that there is an exchange of promises. The seller promises to sell at a stipulated price and to pay the broker a commission upon delivery of a ready, willing, and able buyer. The broker promises to use diligence in attempting to procure a purchaser. The seller may make additional promises regarding the terms. Thus there is a promise for a promise—the required ingredient for a bilateral contract. (See Figure 5-4.)

Different Types of Authorization to Sell

There are essentially four different types of authorization to sell: (1) open listing, (2) exclusive agency listing, (3) exclusive authorization and right-to-sell listing, and (4) net listing.

TYPES OF LISTINGS

Open
Exclusive Agency
Exclusive Right to Sell
Net

Figure 5.4

All of these should be in writing, and real estate regulations require that all parties must be given copies at the time of signature.

OPEN LISTING

The open listing is one that can be given simultaneously to more than one agent. Only one commission is payable and that is paid to the agent who first procures an offer acceptable to the seller. Even the owner may sell the property to his or her own prospective buyer, without paying a commission to any agent. For these reasons, most agents are generally reluctant to spend their time on this type of listing arrangement.

EXCLUSIVE AGENCY LISTING

In an exclusive agency listing one broker is named in the contract. The named broker may cooperate with other brokers and agree to share his or her commission with them if they bring in a buyer. The seller reserves the right to sell the property him or herself to prospects he or she finds without paying a commission. An exclusive agency listing must have a definite termination date.

EXCLUSIVE AUTHORIZATION AND RIGHT-TO-SELL LISTING

The exclusive authorization and right-to-sell listing is the most common form of listing used in the real estate business. The broker is entitled to a commission no matter who sells the property, including the owner, during a specific time period. Because the broker can expect compensation, assuming the property is reasonably salable, the broker is willing to spend considerable time attempting to find a buyer. The broker is also more likely to spend money to advertise and promote the property.

If authorized by the seller, the listing broker may cooperate with other brokers who then become subagents of the seller and agree to split the commission. An exclusive authorization and right-to-sell listing, like the exclusive agency listing, must contain a definite termination date. If a real estate agent accepts any exclusive listing without a definite termination date, he or she is in violation of the real estate law.

See Exhibit 5.1 in the appendix of this chapter for a completed Exclusive Authorization and Right-to-Sell listing form.

NET LISTING   Under a net listing, the seller stipulates a set sum of money that is to be received by the seller regardless of the sales price. An example would be the case wherein the seller of a small home stipulated that he or she needed to net $20,000 after paying off the first deed of trust of $125,000, pest control work, escrow, and other miscellaneous fees totaling $2,000. Assuming the broker sold the property for $155,000, the broker would be entitled to a brokerage fee of $8,000.

Costs
$125,000 first deed of trust
+   2,000 pest control, escrow, miscellaneous
+ 20,000 net to seller
$147,000 total costs

Brokerage Fee
 $155,000 sales price
 – 147,000 total costs
 $8,000 brokerage fee (Must be disclosed to seller prior to
                                       close of sale)

Under California real estate law, the broker must notify the seller of the amount of commission the broker is earning before the seller agrees to sign the purchase contract with the buyer. Failure to disclose this fact may result in revocation or suspension of the real estate agent's license. A net listing may be taken on an open, exclusive agency, or exclusive authorization and right-to-sell form.

The multiple listing service (MLS) is a listing service usually operated by a group of brokers who are affiliated with a real estate association. Listings are placed on the MLS and that information is then disseminated to all members of the MLS. The seller gets significantly greater market exposure through this type of service, given that most MLS systems have hundreds or even thousands of members. Through the use of computers, this kind of quick mass exposure gives the seller a better chance of receiving the best possible price and terms.

Virtually any type of listing can be placed on the MLS, but because of practical considerations, the exclusive authorization and right-to-sell listing is predominantly used. Under the terms of MLS, the listing broker controls the listing and agrees to split the commission in some manner with the cooperating agents.

5.3 PURCHASE AGREEMENT AND DISCLOSURE RULES

The *Real Estate Purchase Contract and Receipt for Deposit,* commonly called the *deposit receipt,* is a contract between the buyer and the seller that outlines the terms for the purchase of real property. It also acts as a receipt for the buyer's deposit toward the purchase of the property. In addition, the purchase agreement spells out the details regarding the payment of the broker's commission.

The Offer and Acceptance

The prospective buyer stipulates the price and terms of the offer, and the offer is then put on the purchase contract form. By regulation, all offers received by the broker must be presented to the seller. If the seller accepts the offer, communication of acceptance must be delivered back to the buyer in person or by mail or fax. At that time there is a binding contract, because offer, acceptance, and notification of the acceptance have occurred. At any time prior to receiving communication that the seller has accepted the offer, the buyer can withdraw the offer and not be liable on the contract.

California real estate regulations used to require the broker or the broker's designee to review and initial the purchase agreement within five business days. As of 1997, new regulations removed this 5-day requirement. The broker must now show that he has reasonably supervised the transaction. Signed copies of the offer and the acceptance must be left with all parties at the time they sign. Then a final completed copy with all signatures must be given to all the parties.

Rejection of the Offer

If the terms of the offer are unacceptable, the seller may reject the offer outright. The legal effect of this is that no contract exists, because there has been no acceptance. The buyer, however, may make another offer.

Counteroffers

If the seller feels that the offer is basically a good one, but that there should be a change in price or terms, the seller may make a counteroffer to the buyer. A counteroffer by the seller automatically does away with the buyer's original offer and, in effect, is merely an offer made by the seller to the buyer. As such, the legal requirements for withdrawal or acceptance and communication of acceptance exist in reverse order. If the buyer accepts the changes, that fact must be indicated in writing and communication of acceptance of the counteroffer must be delivered back to the seller. At any point prior to the communication of acceptance of the counteroffer, the seller may withdraw the counteroffer.

See Exhibit 5.2 in the appendix of this chapter for a completed Real Estate Purchase Contract and Receipt for Deposit form.

Real Estate Transfer Disclosure Statement

In California, sellers of residential 1 to 4 units must furnish buyers with a completed disclosure statement. This disclosure statement details various facts about the property—needed repairs, condition of appliances, improvements added with or without building permits, and so on.

The details noted are based upon an inspection conducted by the real estate agents involved in the sale and upon statements made by the seller. This statement must be provided even if the transaction is an "as is" sale. The responsibility for providing this disclosure rests with the real estate agents. If no agents are involved, the seller must provide the statement. The disclosure statement must be signed by the sellers and all real estate agents involved in the transaction. Ideally, the disclosure statement should be given to the buyers before they sign the purchase contract. If the disclosure statement is given after the purchase contract is signed, the buyer has a three-day right to cancel the sale.

See Exhibit 5.3 in the appendix of this chapter for an example of a Real Estate Transfer Disclosure Statement.

Other Required Disclosures

In addition to the disclosures required in the Real Estate Purchase Contract and Receipt for Deposit form and the Real Estate Transfer Disclosure Statement, potential home buyers must also be given a booklet regarding possible environmental hazards such as lead paint, asbestos, radon gas, and so on. In addition, disclosures regarding flood zones, earthquake areas, and other natural disasters must be given to the potential buyer. The requirement for these disclosures rests with the seller and/or the seller's real estate agent. As time goes on, it is expected that the list of disclosure items will continue to grow.

Options

An option is a contract between the owner of a property (the *optionor*) and a potential purchaser (an *optionee*). Under an option, the optionor gives to the optionee the right to purchase real estate under a set of terms and conditions, within a designated time period. To be binding, the optionee must pay consideration to the optionor.

Here is the key point—the optionee is not *required to exercise the option (purchase the property).* The optionee has the choice of buying or not buying. If the optionee decides to buy, the owner must sell under the terms of the option. If the optionee decides not to buy, the optionor (owner) keeps the option fee.

Sometimes a combination of lease and option is used, by which a person leases the property for a certain time and then has the option to purchase the property when the lease expires. The use of lease/option agreements usually increases during "tight" markets when sellers have a difficult time finding buyers. The seller attempts to entice someone to purchase by allowing the person(s) to rent for a while, then buy later—a sort of try-before-you-buy situation.

Broker Supervision and Record Keeping

A broker is required to exercise reasonable supervision over the activities of his or her salespeople. Reasonable supervision includes the establishment of policies, rules, procedures, and systems to review, oversee, inspect, and manage the activities that require a real estate license.

A real estate broker is required to keep copies of all listings, deposit receipts, canceled checks, trust funds, and any other documents in connection with any sale transaction for at least three years. Forms pertaining to acting as a mortgage broker must be kept for four years. As noted in Chapter 4, a broker must also maintain current trust fund records.

5.4 SAMPLE CONTRACTS

The appendix of this chapter includes samples of contracts typically used in a simple real estate sale. The forms are published by the CALIFORNIA ASSOCIATION OF REAL-

TORS®. All forms are reprinted with permission, but endorsement is not implied.

The forms are the:

1. Exclusive Authorization and Right-to-Sell listing
2. Real Estate Purchase Contract and Receipt for Deposit
3. Real Estate Transfer Disclosure Statement

The Exclusive Authorization and Right-to-Sell listing and the Real Estate Purchase Contract are presented as completed forms, based on a case study outlined in the chapter appendix. The Real Estate Transfer Disclosure Statement is self-explanatory and is presented in blank form.

CHAPTER SUMMARY

A contract is an agreement between two or more persons consisting of a promise or mutual promises to do or not to do certain acts. In a unilateral contract a promise is made by one party in exchange for an act by another party. In a bilateral contract one party exchanges promises with another party. Contracts may be created by expression or implication. Contracts can be valid, void, voidable, and unenforceable.

There are five essential elements of a real estate contract. They are: (1) parties capable of contracting, (2) mutual consent, (3) a lawful object, (4) sufficient consideration, and, according to the Statute of Frauds, (5) the contract must be in writing. An executed contract is one that has been completed or fulfilled. An executory contract is one that remains to be fulfilled.

Full performance discharges or terminates a contract. Contracts can also be terminated by expiration of time, mutual consent, plus other technical means. A breach of contract means that one of the parties did not fulfill its part of the agreement. The two most common remedies for a breach are to sue for damages or to sue for specific performance. The Statute of Limitations prescribes the time period within which a lawsuit must be filed. Beyond the prescribed period, a person's rights are said to have outlawed.

A real estate contract should contain the date of the agreement, names and addresses of the parties, a description of the property, the consideration, mortgage terms, the date and place of closing the contract, and any other provisions required or requested by the parties. A listing agreement is the contract between the principal, usually the seller, and the real estate broker. Types of listings include open, exclusive agency, exclusive authorization and right-to-sell, and net listing. Multiple listing service is an organization whereby member brokers agree to pool listings and share information and commissions.

The Purchase Contract and Receipt for Deposit is the contract between the buyer and seller. To be binding there are certain requirements that must be met. Common real estate forms are provided in this chapter, with an explanation of the various clauses contained in each form. For residential 1 to 4 unit properties, various disclosure statements must be presented to the buyer before the close of the sale.

IMPORTANT TERMS AND CONCEPTS

Bilateral contract	Mutual consent
Counteroffer	Net listing
Deposit receipt	Open listing
Disclosure statement	Options
Exclusive agency listing	Real estate transfer
Exclusive authorization and right-to-sell listing	Statute of Frauds
	Statute of Limitations
Executed contract	Unenforceable
Executory contract	Unilateral contract
Expressed contract	Valid
Implied contract	Void
Multiple listing service	Voidable

PRACTICAL APPLICATION

1. Sally Hennings, age 17, joins the Army and then signs a lease agreement and moves into an apartment near the base. Using correct contract language, describe in complete detail Sally's contract, beginning with words such as unilateral, bilateral, expressed, implied, executed, executory, valid, void, voidable, and unenforceable.

2. Homeowner Vargas signed a 180-day exclusive authorization and right-to-sell listing with Sunrise Realty. After 90 days, Vargas unilaterally cancelled the listing and gave it to Ambrosini Properties, who 10 days later brought in a full-price offer. The sale closed and a full commission was paid to Ambrosini Properties. Later Sunrise Realty filed a lawsuit for another full commission. What are the legal issues?

3. An old, run-down rental home is listed for sale with a real estate company in "as is condition." The seller knows that the roof leaks and that the electrical system frequently shorts out and blows fuses. The seller does not mention this to the listing real estate agent. A buyer agrees to purchase the home "as is." For the seller and the real estate agent, what are the Real Estate Transfer Disclosure Statement requirements?

REVIEW YOUR UNDERSTANDING

1. All of the following are covered by the Statute of Frauds, except:
   a. the payment of an agent's commission
   b. a two-year lease
   c. an agreement not to be performed within the lifetime of the promisor
   d. a six-month tenancy

2. Which of the following is not considered an essential element of a real estate contract?
   a. consent of the parties
   b. a lawful object
   c. consideration
   d. parol evidence

3. Contracts may be discharged by:
   a. impossibility of performance
   b. agreement of the parties
   c. choices (a.) and (b.) are both correct
   d. none of the above

4. The most common form of listing agreement found in California is:
   a. open listing
   b. exclusive authorization and right-to-sell listing
   c. net listing
   d. exclusive agency listing

5. By law, which of the following listings must have a definite termination date?
   a. net listing
   b. exclusive agency
   c. exclusive authorization and right-to-sell listing
   d. both b. and c.

6. Of the following listings, which stipulates that the agent may earn anything over the seller's stipulated amount after giving the seller proper disclosure?
   a. net listing
   b. exclusive agency
   c. exclusive authorization and right-to-sell listing
   d. open listing

7. A listing is a:
   a. unilateral contract
   b. bilateral contract
   c. both a. and b.
   d. none of the above

8. A deposit receipt:
   a. is a receipt for the deposit
   b. is a real estate contract when properly executed
   c. reaffirms the brokerage commission
   d. all of the above

9. Which of the following statements is true if, during the escrow process, but prior to closing the sale, a fire destroys the home being sold?
   a. Buyer must complete the purchase.
   b. Buyer need not complete the purchase, but seller retains the deposit.
   c. Buyer need not complete the purchase and is entitled to the deposit back.
   d. Buyer must complete the purchase for the land, not the remains of the building.

10. After signing a deposit receipt, the seller later decides not to sell. The buyer may do all the following, except:
    a. simply cancel the agreement and get a refund of any deposit
    b. sue for specific performance
    c. sue on criminal grounds
    d. sue for money damages

11. A contract that still needs some action by one or more of the parties is:
    a. executory
    b. executed
    c. valid
    d. voidable

12. Within the prescribed time period, an inexcusable delay might limit a lawsuit according to the:
    a. Statute of Frauds
    b. Statute of Limitations
    c. Doctrine of Laches
    d. Stoppel of Contracts

13. Which best describes a voidable contract?
    a. valid and enforceable
    b. valid on its face, but for some reason cannot be sued upon
    c. valid on its face until the injured party voids the contract
    d. void on its face until enforceable

14. A 17-year-old divorced man wishes to sell his separate real property. A real estate broker legally:
    a. can accept the listing
    b. cannot accept the listing until the owner is 18 years old
    c. can accept the listing only if the owner has a legal guardian
    d. cannot accept the listing unless the owner's parents consent

15. The Real Estate Transfer Disclosure Statement is signed by the:
    a. buyer only
    b. seller only
    c. seller and agent/broker only
    d. buyer, seller, and agent/broker

Questions 16–20 refer to the completed Exclusive Authorization and Right to Sell form in the appendix of this chapter.

16. Colina Vista Realty is entitled to a commission if the property is sold during the listing period by:
    a. Mr. and Mrs. Seller
    b. Colina Vista Realty
    c. any other real estate company
    d. all of the above

17. If the property is sold during the listing period for $198,000 by Colina Vista Realty, the commission per agreement should be:
    a. $11,880
    b. $12,900
    c. $17,000
    d. nothing, as the home was not sold for the listing price

18. The home has a hidden structural defect that Mr. and Mrs. Seller know about, but fail to tell the listing agent or the ultimate buyers about in the required Real Estate Transfer Disclosure Statement. After the sale, the new owners discover the defect. Per the listing agreement, who is responsible for the cost of correcting the defect?
    a. Colina Vista Realty
    b. Mr. and Mrs. Seller
    c. the arbitrator
    d. the new owners

19. The listing agreement authorizes Colina Vista Realty to do all the following, *except:*
    a. put a for sale sign on the property
    b. install a lockbox containing a key for the use of other agents
    c. require the buyer to pay for all cost for termite work
    d. require the seller to accept arbitration in disputes with the listing agent

20. Prior to signing the listing agreement, Mr. and Mrs. Seller ask Colina Vista Realty Sales Associate Rebecca Salesperson, "What is the prevailing commission rate in our area?" The correct answer is:
    a. "6%."
    b. "Others may charge 7%, but the normal rate is our 6%."
    c. "All commissions are negotiable; there is no fixed rate."
    d. "The real estate commissioner will not allow less than 6%."

Questions 21–25 refer to the completed Real Estate Purchase Contract and Receipt for Deposit form in the appendix of this chapter.

21. When the offer from Mr. and Mrs. Buyer is presented, the seller asks if the buyers are members of a minority race. The broker presenting the offer should correctly respond as follows:
    a. "Yes, I think so."
    b. "I don't know, but I will find out and let you know before you sell."
    c. "By law and my business practice, that is not revelant."
    d. "No, I checked them out per your request."

22. Within the required time, the buyers can only find a loan at 9%. Which of the following is correct?
    a. The buyers must continue with the sale.
    b. The seller can cancel and keep the $1,000 deposit.
    c. The buyers can accept the loan at 9% and reduce the price by $1,000.
    d. The buyer can cancel and receive a refund on the $1,000 deposit.

23. If, through no fault of the sellers, the buyer defaults on the sale per the terms of the contract, the buyers will:
    a. lose the $1,000 deposit
    b. be liable for 3% of the offer price as liquidated damages
    c. owe the broker a commission
    d. be forced via specific performance to complete the sale

24. Which of the following regarding the purchase contract is true?
    a. Buyers will pay for required structural repair work.
    b. Sellers will pay for the buyer's loan fee.
    c. Colina Vista Realty is the buyer's agent.
    d. Any transfer tax will be paid by the sellers.

25. Per the purchase contract, the California sellers agree to sell their principal residence and provide all the following, *except:*
    a. working smoke detectors
    b. pay the buyer's loan fees
    c. transfer disclosure statement
    d. a home protection plan

Appendix

Case Study Using Sample Forms

PART I—LISTING AGREEMENT

Joseph and Sonia Seller have decided to list their home at 123 Main Street, Somewhere, California, for $215,000 with Colina Vista Realty. The completed Exclusive Authorization and Right-To-Sell listing is presented herein. You will need to read this form to answer Questions 16–20 in the review section of this chapter. **The completed portions of this contract are for illustration and discussion purposes only and should not be construed as the legal way to complete this form. All readers may wish to use the services of an attorney when entering into a real estate transaction.**

1. **EXCLUSIVE RIGHT TO SELL:** Joseph B. Seller + Sonia K. Seller ("Seller") hereby employs and grants Colina Vista Realty ("Broker") the exclusive and irrevocable right, commencing on (date) 4/22/XX and expiring at 11:59 P.M. on (date) 7/22/XX ("Listing Period") to sell or exchange the real property in the City of Somewhere, County of Acme, California, described as: Single Family home at 123 main Street ("Property").

2. **TERMS OF SALE:**
   A. **LIST PRICE:** The listing price shall be Two Hundred Fifteen thousand and No/100 ($215,000).
   B. **PERSONAL PROPERTY:** The following items of personal property are included in the above price: Fireplace screen and tools, window coverings, and Garden Shed
   C. **ADDITIONAL TERMS:** None

3. **MULTIPLE LISTING SERVICE:** Information about this listing ☒ will, ☐ will not, be provided to a multiple listing service ("MLS") of Broker's selection and the Property sale, price, terms, and financing will be provided to the MLS for publication, dissemination and use by persons and entities on terms approved by the MLS. Seller authorizes Broker to comply with all applicable MLS rules.

4. **TITLE:** Seller warrants that Seller and no other persons have title to the Property, except as follows: none

5. **COMPENSATION TO BROKER:**
   Notice: The amount or rate of real estate commissions is not fixed by law. They are set by each Broker individually and may be negotiable between Seller and Broker.
   A. Seller agrees to pay to Broker as compensation for services irrespective of agency relationship(s), either ☒ Six percent of the listing price (or if a sales contract is entered into, of the sales price), or ☐ $ _____, AND ___ as follows:
      1. If Broker, Seller, cooperating broker, or any other person, produces a buyer(s) who offers to purchase the Property on the above price and terms, or on any price and terms acceptable to Seller during the Listing Period, or any extension;
      2. If within 90 calendar days after expiration of the Listing Period or any extension, the Property is sold, conveyed, leased, or otherwise transferred to anyone with whom Broker or a cooperating broker has had negotiations, provided that Broker gives Seller, prior to or within **5 calendar days** after expiration of the Listing Period or any extension, a written notice with the name(s) of the prospective purchaser(s);
      3. If, without Broker's prior written consent, the Property is withdrawn from sale, conveyed, leased, rented, otherwise transferred, or made unmarketable by a voluntary act of Seller during the Listing Period, or any extension.
   B. If completion of the sale is prevented by a party to the transaction other than Seller, then compensation due under paragraph 5A shall be payable only if and when Seller collects damages by suit, settlement, or otherwise, and then in an amount equal to the lesser of one-half of the damages recovered or the above compensation, after first deducting title and escrow expenses and the expenses of collection, if any.
   C. In addition, Seller agrees to pay: 50% of escrow Fees and Provide a CLTA Owner's title Policy
   D. Broker is authorized to cooperate with other brokers, and divide with other brokers the above compensation in any manner acceptable to Broker;
   E. Seller hereby irrevocably assigns to Broker the above compensation from Seller's funds and proceeds in escrow.
   F. Seller warrants that Seller has no obligation to pay compensation to any other broker regarding the transfer of the Property except: None

   If the Property is sold to anyone listed above during the time Seller is obligated to compensate another broker: (a) Broker is not entitled to compensation under this Agreement and (b) Broker is not obligated to represent Seller with respect to such transaction.

6. **BROKER'S AND SELLER'S DUTIES:** Broker agrees to exercise reasonable effort and due diligence to achieve the purposes of this Agreement, and is authorized to advertise and market the Property in any medium selected by Broker. Seller agrees to consider offers presented by Broker, and to act in good faith toward accomplishing the sale of the Property. Seller further agrees, regardless of responsibility, to indemnify, defend and hold Broker harmless from all claims, disputes, litigation, judgments and attorney's fees arising from any incorrect information supplied by Seller, whether contained in any document, omitted therefrom, or otherwise, or from any material facts which Seller knows but fails to disclose.

7. **AGENCY RELATIONSHIPS:** Broker shall act as the agent for Seller in any resulting transaction. Depending upon the circumstances, it may be necessary or appropriate for Broker to act as an agent for both Seller and buyer, exchange party, or one or more additional parties ("Buyer"). Broker shall, as soon as practicable, disclose to Seller any election to act as a dual agent representing both Seller and Buyer. If a Buyer is procured directly by Broker or an associate licensee in Broker's firm, Seller hereby consents to Broker acting as a dual agent for Seller and such Buyer. In the event of an exchange, Seller hereby consents to Broker collecting compensation from additional parties for services rendered, provided there is disclosure to all parties of such agency and compensation. Seller understands that Broker may have or obtain listings on other properties, and that potential buyers may consider, make offers on, or purchase through Broker, property the same as or similar to Seller's Property. Seller consents to Broker's representation of sellers and buyers of other properties before, during, and after the expiration of this Agreement.

8. **DEPOSIT:** Broker is authorized to accept and hold on Seller's behalf a deposit to be applied toward the sales price.

Seller and Broker acknowledge receipt of copy of this page, which constitutes Page 1 of **2** Pages.
Seller's Initials (JBS) (SKS) Broker's Initials (RB) (_____)

Exhibit 5.1a (Reprinted with permission, *California Association of Realtors*®. Endorsement not implied.)

Property Address: *123 Main Street, Somewhere, CA 90xxx*

9. **LOCKBOX:**
   A. A lockbox is designed to hold a key to the Property to permit access to the Property by Broker, cooperating brokers, MLS participants, their authorized licensees and representatives, and accompanied prospective buyers.
   B. Broker, cooperating brokers, MLS and Associations/Boards of REALTORS® are **not** insurers against theft, loss, vandalism, or damage attributed to the use of a lockbox. Seller is advised to verify the existence of, or obtain, appropriate insurance through Seller's own insurance broker.
   C. (If checked:) ☒ Seller authorizes Broker to install a lockbox. If Seller does not occupy the Property, Seller shall be responsible for obtaining occupant(s)' written permission for use of a lockbox.
10. **SIGN:** (If checked:) ☒ Seller authorizes Broker to install a FOR SALE/SOLD sign on the Property.
11. **DISPUTE RESOLUTION:**
    A. **MEDIATION:** Seller and Broker agree to mediate any dispute or claim arising between them out of this Agreement, or any resulting transaction, before resorting to arbitration or court action, subject to paragraph 11C below. Mediation fees, if any, shall be divided equally among the parties involved. If any party commences an action based on a dispute or claim to which this paragraph applies, without first attempting to resolve the matter through mediation, then that party shall not be entitled to recover attorney's fees, even if they would otherwise be available to that party in any such action. THIS MEDIATION PROVISION APPLIES WHETHER OR NOT THE ARBITRATION PROVISION IS INITIALED.
    B. **ARBITRATION OF DISPUTES: Seller and Broker agree that any dispute or claim arising between them regarding the obligation to pay compensation under this Agreement, which is not settled through mediation, shall be decided by neutral, binding arbitration, subject to paragraph 11C below. The arbitrator shall be a retired judge or justice, or an attorney with at least five years of residential real estate experience, unless the parties mutually agree to a different arbitrator, who shall render an award in accordance with substantive California Law. In all other respects, the arbitration shall be conducted in accordance with Part III, Title 9 of the California Code of Civil Procedure. Judgment upon the award of the arbitrator(s) may be entered in any court having jurisdiction. The parties shall have the right to discovery in accordance with Code of Civil Procedure §1283.05.**
       "NOTICE: BY INITIALING IN THE SPACE BELOW YOU ARE AGREEING TO HAVE ANY DISPUTE ARISING OUT OF THE MATTERS INCLUDED IN THE 'ARBITRATION OF DISPUTES' PROVISION DECIDED BY NEUTRAL ARBITRATION AS PROVIDED BY CALIFORNIA LAW AND YOU ARE GIVING UP ANY RIGHTS YOU MIGHT POSSESS TO HAVE THE DISPUTE LITIGATED IN A COURT OR JURY TRIAL. BY INITIALING IN THE SPACE BELOW YOU ARE GIVING UP YOUR JUDICIAL RIGHTS TO DISCOVERY AND APPEAL, UNLESS THOSE RIGHTS ARE SPECIFICALLY INCLUDED IN THE 'ARBITRATION OF DISPUTES' PROVISION. IF YOU REFUSE TO SUBMIT TO ARBITRATION AFTER AGREEING TO THIS PROVISION, YOU MAY BE COMPELLED TO ARBITRATE UNDER THE AUTHORITY OF THE CALIFORNIA CODE OF CIVIL PROCEDURE. YOUR AGREEMENT TO THIS ARBITRATION PROVISION IS VOLUNTARY."
       "WE HAVE READ AND UNDERSTAND THE FOREGOING AND AGREE TO SUBMIT DISPUTES ARISING OUT OF THE MATTERS INCLUDED IN THE 'ARBITRATION OF DISPUTES' PROVISION TO NEUTRAL ARBITRATION." Seller's Initials *JBS* / *SKS*   Broker's Initials *RS* / _____
    C. **EXCLUSIONS FROM MEDIATION AND ARBITRATION:** The following matters are excluded from Mediation and Arbitration hereunder: (a) A judicial or non-judicial foreclosure or other action or proceeding to enforce a deed of trust, mortgage, or installment land sale contract as defined in Civil Code §2985; (b) An unlawful detainer action; (c) The filing or enforcement of a mechanic's lien; (d) Any matter which is within the jurisdiction of a probate, small claims, or bankruptcy court; and (e) An action for bodily injury or wrongful death, or for latent or patent defects to which Code of Civil Procedure §337.1 or §337.15 applies. The filing of a court action to enable the recording of a notice of pending action, for order of attachment, receivership, injunction, or other provisional remedies, shall not constitute a violation of the mediation and arbitration provisions.
12. **EQUAL HOUSING OPPORTUNITY:** The Property is offered in compliance with federal, state, and local anti-discrimination laws.
13. **ATTORNEY'S FEES:** In any action, proceeding, or arbitration between Seller and Broker regarding the obligation to pay compensation under this Agreement, the prevailing Seller or Broker shall be entitled to reasonable attorney's fees and costs, except as provided in paragraph 11A.
14. **ADDITIONAL TERMS:** *None* _____

_____
_____

15. **ENTIRE CONTRACT:** All prior discussions, negotiations, and agreements between the parties concerning the subject matter of this Agreement are superseded by this Agreement, which constitutes the entire contract and a complete and exclusive expression of their agreement, and may not be contradicted by evidence of any prior agreement or contemporaneous oral agreement. This Agreement and any supplement, addendum, or modification, including any photocopy or facsimile, may be executed in counterparts.

Seller warrants that Seller is the owner of the Property or has the authority to execute this contract. Seller acknowledges that Seller has read and understands this Agreement, and has received a copy.

Seller *Joseph B. Seller* Date *4/22/xx*   Seller *Sonia K. Seller* Date *4/22/xx*
Address *123 Main Street*   Address *123 Main Street*
City *Somewhere* State *CA* Zip *90xxx*   City *Somewhere* State *CA* Zip *90xxx*

Real Estate Broker (Firm) *Colina Vista Realty*   By (Agent) *Rebecca Selager* Date *4/22/xx*
Address *462 First St. Somewhere, CA*   Telephone *xxx-xxxx* Fax *xxx-xxxx*
90xx

Page 2 of 2 Pages.

BROKER'S COPY
EXCLUSIVE AUTHORIZATION AND RIGHT TO SELL (A-14 PAGE 2 OF 2) REVISED 10/97

Exhibit 5.1b

PART II—REAL ESTATE PURCHASE CONTRACT AND RECEIPT FOR DEPOSIT

After proper negotiations, a buyer is found for the home owned by Mr. and Mrs. Seller. The selling broker then helps the buyers prepare the following Real Estate Purchase Contract and Receipt for Deposit. You will need to read this eight-page form to answer Questions 20–25 in the review section of this chapter.

The completed portions of this contract are for illustration and discussion purposes only and should not be construed as the legal way to complete this form. All readers may wish to use the services of an attorney when entering into a real estate transaction.

Please note that this form is subject to change since the date of publication. All readers are encouraged to use the most current form available.

CALIFORNIA
ASSOCIATION
OF REALTORS®

RESIDENTIAL PURCHASE AGREEMENT
(AND RECEIPT FOR DEPOSIT)
For Use With Single Family Residential Property — Attached or Detached

Date: **May 15 xxxx**, at **Somewhere**, California,
Received From **William R. Buyer and Maria H. Buyer** ("Buyer"),
A Deposit Of **One thousand and No/100** Dollars $ **1,000 —**, toward the
Purchase Price Of **Two Hundred Fifteen thousand and No/100** Dollars $ **215,000 —**
For Purchase Of Property Situated In **Somewhere**, County Of **Acme**,
California, Described As **Single Family home at 123 Main Street** ("Property").

1. **FINANCING:** Obtaining the loans below **is a contingency** of this Agreement. Buyer shall act diligently and in good faith to obtain the designated loans. Obtaining deposit, down payment and closing costs **is not a contingency.**

   A. **BUYER'S DEPOSIT** shall be held uncashed until Acceptance and then deposited within **3 business days** after Acceptance or ☐ _____, ☒ with Escrow Holder, ☐ into Broker's trust account or ☐ _____, by Personal Check ☐ Cashier's Check ☐ Cash or ☐ _____ .... $ **1,000 —**

   B. **INCREASED DEPOSIT** shall be deposited with **escrow holder** within **5** Days After Acceptance, or ☐ _____ .... $ **2,000 —**

   C. **FIRST LOAN IN THE AMOUNT OF** .... $ **172,000 —**
   NEW First Deed of Trust in favor of LENDER, encumbering the Property, securing a note payable at maximum interest of **8.5** % fixed rate, or ____ % initial adjustable rate with a maximum interest rate cap of of ___ %, balance due in **30** years. Buyer shall pay loan fees/points not to exceed **2%** If FHA/VA, Seller shall pay **N/A** % discount points, other fees not allowed to be paid by Buyer, not to exceed $ **N/A**, and the cost of lender required repairs not otherwise provided for in this Agreement, not to exceed $ **N/A**.

   D. **ADDITIONAL FINANCING TERMS:** **none** .... $ **- 0 -**

   ☐ seller financing, (C.A.R. Form SFA-14); ☐ junior or assumed financing, (C.A.R. Form PAA-14, paragraph 5)

   E. **BALANCE OF PURCHASE PRICE** (not including costs of obtaining loans and other closing costs) to be deposited .. $ **40,000 —** with escrow holder within sufficient time to close escrow.

   F. **TOTAL PURCHASE PRICE** .... $ **215,000 —**

   G. **LOAN CONTINGENCY** shall remain in effect until the designated loans are funded (or ☒ **15** Days After Acceptance, by which time Buyer shall give Seller written notice of Buyer's election to cancel this Agreement if Buyer is unable to obtain the designated loans. If Buyer does not give Seller such notice, the contingency of obtaining the designated loans shall be removed by the method specified in paragraph 16B.)

   H. **LOAN APPLICATIONS; PREQUALIFICATION:** For NEW financing, within 5 (or ☐ ____) Days After Acceptance, Buyer shall provide Seller a letter from lender or mortgage loan broker stating that, based on a review of Buyer's written application and credit report, Buyer is prequalified for the NEW loan indicated above. If Buyer fails to provide such letter within that time, Seller may cancel this Agreement in writing.

   I. ☒ **APPRAISAL CONTINGENCY:** (If checked) This Agreement is contingent upon Property appraising at no less than the specified total purchase price. The Appraisal contingency shall remain in effect for the same period as specified for the Loan Contingency in paragraph 1G.

   J. **ALL CASH OFFER:** If this is an all cash offer, Buyer shall, within 5 (or ☐ ____) Days After Acceptance, provide Seller written verification of sufficient funds to close this transaction. Seller may cancel this Agreement in writing within **5 Days After: (1)** time to provide verification expires, if Buyer fails to provide verification; or **(2)** receipt of verification, if Seller reasonably disapproves it.

2. **ESCROW:** Close Of Escrow shall occur **60** Days After Acceptance (or ☐ _____ (date)). Buyer and Seller shall deliver signed escrow instructions consistent with this Agreement ☒ within **7** Days After Acceptance, ☐ at least ____ Days before Close Of Escrow, or ☐ _____. Seller shall deliver possession and occupancy of the Property to Buyer at **5** AM/PM, ☒ on the date of Close Of Escrow, **or** ☐ no later than ____ Days After date of Close Of Escrow, **or** ☐ _____ Property shall be vacant, unless otherwise agreed in writing. If transfer of title and possession do not occur at the same time, Buyer and Seller are advised to (a) consult with their insurance advisors, and (b) enter into a written occupancy agreement. Escrow instructions may include matters required to close this transaction which are not covered by this Agreement. The omission from escrow instructions of any provision in this Agreement shall not constitute a waiver of that provision.

3. **OCCUPANCY:** Buyer ☒ does, ☐ does not, intend to occupy Property as Buyer's primary residence.

4. **ALLOCATION OF COSTS:** (Check boxes which apply. If needed, insert additional instructions in blank lines.)
   TRANSFER FEES:

   A. ☐ Buyer ☒ Seller shall pay County transfer tax or transfer fee. _____
   B. ☐ Buyer ☒ Seller shall pay City transfer tax or transfer fee. _____
   C. ☒ Buyer ☐ Seller shall pay Homeowners' Association transfer fee. _____
   TITLE AND ESCROW COSTS:
   D. ☐ Buyer ☒ Seller shall pay for owner's title insurance policy, issued by **ACE title** company.
   E. ☒ Buyer ☒ Seller shall pay escrow fee. **50/50 split** Escrow holder shall be **Buena Professional Escrow**
   SEWER/SEPTIC/WELL COSTS:
   F. ☐ Buyer ☒ Seller shall pay for sewer connection, if required by Law prior to Close Of Escrow. _____
   G. ☐ Buyer ☐ Seller shall pay to have septic or private sewage disposal system inspected. **N/A**
   H. ☐ Buyer ☐ Seller shall pay to have wells tested for water quality, potability, productivity, and recovery rate. **N/A**
   OTHER COSTS:
   I. ☐ Buyer ☒ Seller shall pay for zone disclosure reports, if any (paragraph 7). _____
   J. ☐ Buyer ☒ Seller shall pay for Smoke Detector installation and/or Water Heater bracing. _____
   Seller, prior to close of escrow, shall provide Buyer a written statement of compliance in accordance with state and local Law, unless exempt.
   K. ☐ Buyer ☒ Seller shall pay the cost of compliance with any other minimum mandatory government retrofit standards and inspections required as a condition of closing escrow under any Law. _____
   L. ☐ Buyer ☒ Seller shall pay the cost of a one-year home warranty plan, issued by **Fidelity Home** with the following optional coverage: **None** . Policy cost not to exceed $ **400**
   PEST CONTROL REPORT:
   M. ☒ Buyer ☐ Seller shall pay for the Pest Control Report ("Report"), which shall be prepared by **Fumigation Inc.**, a registered structural pest control company.
   N. ☐ Buyer ☒ Seller shall pay for work recommended to correct conditions described in the Report as **"Section 1,".**
   O. ☒ Buyer ☐ Seller shall pay for work recommended to correct conditions described in the Report as **"Section 2,"** if requested by Buyer.

   Buyer and Seller acknowledge receipt of copy of this page, which constitutes Page 1 of **6** Pages.
   Buyer's Initials (**WRB**) (**MHB**) Seller's Initials (**JBS**) (**SKS**)

THIS FORM HAS BEEN APPROVED BY THE CALIFORNIA ASSOCIATION OF REALTORS® (C.A.R.). NO REPRESENTATION IS MADE AS TO THE LEGAL VALIDITY OR ADEQUACY OF ANY PROVISION IN ANY SPECIFIC TRANSACTION. A REAL ESTATE BROKER IS THE PERSON QUALIFIED TO ADVISE ON REAL ESTATE TRANSACTIONS. IF YOU DESIRE LEGAL OR TAX ADVICE, CONSULT AN APPROPRIATE PROFESSIONAL.
The copyright laws of the United States (17 U.S. Code) forbid the unauthorized reproduction of this form by any means, including facsimile or computerized formats.
Copyright © 1997, CALIFORNIA ASSOCIATION OF REALTORS®

Published and Distributed by:
REAL ESTATE BUSINESS SERVICES, INC.
a subsidiary of the CALIFORNIA ASSOCIATION OF REALTORS®
525 South Virgil Avenue, Los Angeles, California 90020

OFFICE USE ONLY
Reviewed by Broker
or Designee
Date **5/16/XX**

EQUAL HOUSING OPPORTUNITY

PRINT DATE
R FEB 98

MASTER COPY

RESIDENTIAL PURCHASE AGREEMENT AND RECEIPT FOR DEPOSIT (RPA-14 PAGE 1 OF 5) REVISED 5/97

Exhibit 5.2a (Reprinted with permission, *California Association of Realtors®. Endorsement not implied.*)

5. **PEST CONTROL TERMS:**

A. The Report shall cover the main building and attached structures and, if checked: ☒ detached garages and carports, ☐ detached decks, ☐ the following other structures on the Property: _____

B. If Property is a unit in a condominium, planned development, or residential stock cooperative, the Report shall cover only the separate interest and any exclusive-use areas being transferred, and shall not cover common areas, unless otherwise agreed.

C. If inspection of inaccessible areas is recommended in the Report, Buyer has the option, within 5 Days After receipt of the Report, either to accept and approve the Report by the method specified in paragraph 16B, to request in writing that further inspection be made. If further inspection recommends "Section 1" and/or "Section 2" corrective work, such work, and the cost of inspection, entry, and closing of the inaccessible areas shall be paid for, respectively, by the party designated in paragraph 4N or 4O. If no infestation or infection is found in the inaccessible areas, the cost of the inspection, entry, and closing of those areas shall be paid for by Buyer.

D. If no infestation or infection by wood destroying pests or organisms is found, the Report shall include a written Pest Control Certification. Certification shall be issued prior to Close Of Escrow, unless otherwise agreed in writing.

E. Inspections, corrective work and Pest Control Certification in this paragraph refers only to the presence or absence of wood destroying pests or organisms, and does not include the condition of roof coverings. Read paragraphs 9 and 12 concerning roof coverings.

F. Nothing in paragraph 5 shall relieve Seller of the obligation to repair or replace shower pans and shower enclosures due to leaks, if required by paragraph 9B(3). Water test of shower pans on upper level units may not be performed unless the owners of property below the shower consent.

6. **TRANSFER DISCLOSURE STATEMENT; SUBSEQUENT DISCLOSURES; MELLO-ROOS NOTICE:**

A. Within 5 (or ☐ _____) **Days** After Acceptance, unless exempt, a Real Estate Transfer Disclosure Statement ("TDS") shall be completed and delivered to Buyer, who shall sign and return a copy of it to Seller.

B. In the event Seller, prior to Close Of Escrow, becomes aware of adverse conditions materially affecting the Property, or any material inaccuracy in disclosures, information, or representations previously provided to Buyer (including those made in a TDS) of which Buyer is otherwise unaware, Seller shall promptly provide a subsequent or amended disclosure, in writing, covering those items **except for those conditions and material inaccuracies disclosed in reports obtained by Buyer.**

C. Seller shall make a good faith effort to obtain a disclosure notice from any local agencies which levy a special tax on the Property pursuant to the Mello-Roos Community Facilities Act, and shall promptly deliver to Buyer any such notice made available by those agencies.

D. If the TDS, the Mello-Roos disclosure notice, or a subsequent or amended disclosure is delivered to Buyer after the offer is signed, Buyer shall have the right to terminate this Agreement within **3 days** after delivery in person, or **5 days** after delivery by deposit in the mail, by giving written notice of termination to Seller or Seller's agent.

7. **DISCLOSURES:** Within the time specified in paragraph 16, Seller shall provide to Buyer the following disclosures and information, take the following actions, and disclose facts pertaining to the following conditions. Buyer shall then, within the time specified in paragraph 16, investigate the disclosures and information, and provide written notice to Seller of any item disapproved.

A. **PROPERTY DISCLOSURES:** Earthquake Fault Zones, Seismic Hazard Zones (when available), Special Flood Hazard Areas, State Fire Responsibility Areas, Earthquake Guides, Lead-Based Paint Disclosures, Environmental Hazards Booklet, and Energy Efficiency Booklet (when published), or any other federal, state, or locally designated zone for which disclosure is required by Law.

B. **CONDOMINIUM/COMMON INTEREST SUBDIVISION:** If Property is a unit in a condominium, planned development, or other common interest subdivision, Seller shall request from the Homeowners' Association ("HOA"), and upon receipt provide to Buyer, a statement indicating any current regular dues and assessments; known pending regular or special assessments, claims, or litigation and the location and number of parking and storage spaces; copies of covenants, conditions, and restrictions; articles of incorporation; "by-laws"; other governing documents; most current financial statement distributed; statement regarding limited enforceability of age restrictions, if applicable; current HOA statement showing any unpaid assessments; any other documents required by Law; and the most recent 12 months of HOA minutes for regular and special meetings, if available.

C. **NOTICE OF VIOLATION:** If, prior to Close Of Escrow, Seller receives notice or is made aware of any notice filed or issued against the Property, of violations of city, county, state, or federal building, zoning, fire or health Laws, Seller shall immediately notify Buyer in writing. Buyer shall, within the time specified in paragraph 16, provide written notice to Seller of any items disapproved.

8. **TITLE AND VESTING:**

A. Within the time specified in paragraph 16A, Buyer shall be provided a current preliminary (title) report (which is only an offer by the title insurer to issue a policy of title insurance, and may not contain every item affecting title). Buyer shall, within the time specified in paragraph 16, provide written notice to Seller of any items reasonably disapproved.

B. At Close Of Escrow, Buyer shall receive a grant deed conveying title (or, for stock cooperative, an assignment of stock certificate), including oil, mineral and water rights if currently owned by Seller. Title shall be subject to all encumbrances, easements, covenants, conditions, restrictions, rights, and other matters which are of record or known to Buyer prior to Close Of Escrow, unless disapproved in writing by Buyer within the time specified in paragraph 16. However, title shall not be subject to any liens against the Property, except for those specified in the Agreement. Buyer shall receive an ALTA-R owner's title insurance policy, if reasonably available. If not, Buyer shall receive a standard coverage owner's policy (e.g. CLTA or ALTA with regional exceptions). Buyer shall pay for Lender's title insurance policy. Title shall vest as designated in Buyer's escrow instructions. The title company, at Buyer's request, can provide information about availability, desirability and cost of various title insurance coverages. THE MANNER OF TAKING TITLE MAY HAVE SIGNIFICANT LEGAL AND TAX CONSEQUENCES.

9. **NO WARRANTIES EXCEPT AS SPECIFIED:**

A. **EXCEPT AS SPECIFIED BELOW, AND ELSEWHERE IN THIS AGREEMENT,** Property is sold "AS IS", in its present physical condition.

B. **(IF CHECKED) SELLER WARRANTS THAT AT THE TIME POSSESSION IS MADE AVAILABLE TO BUYER:**

☒ (1) Roof shall be free of leaks KNOWN to Seller or DISCOVERED during escrow.

☒ (2) Built-in appliances (including free-standing oven and range, if included in sale), heating, air conditioning, electrical, water, sewer and pool/spa systems, if any, shall be repaired, if KNOWN by Seller to be inoperative or DISCOVERED to be so during escrow. (Septic/Well systems are **not** covered in this paragraph. Read paragraphs 4G and H.)

☒ (3) Plumbing systems, shower pans and shower enclosures shall be free of leaks KNOWN to Seller or DISCOVERED during escrow.

☒ (4) All fire, safety, and structural defects in chimneys and fireplaces KNOWN to Seller or DISCOVERED during escrow shall be repaired.

☒ (5) All broken or cracked glass, torn existing window and door screens, and broken seals between multi-pane windows, shall be replaced.

☒ (6) All debris and all personal property not included in the sale shall be removed.

☐ (7) _____

C. **PROPERTY MAINTENANCE:** Unless otherwise agreed, Property, including pool, spa, landscaping and grounds, is to be maintained in substantially the same condition as on the date of Acceptance.

D. **PROPERTY IMPROVEMENTS** may not (a) be built according to codes or in compliance with Law, or (b) have had permits issued.

E. **INSPECTIONS AND DISCLOSURES:** Items discovered in Buyer's Inspections which are not covered by paragraph 9B, shall be governed by the procedure in paragraphs 12 and 16. Buyer retains the right to disapprove the condition of the Property based upon items discovered in Buyer's Inspections. Disclosures in the TDS and items discovered in Buyer's Inspections do NOT eliminate Seller's obligations under paragraph 9B, unless specifically agreed in writing. **WHETHER OR NOT SELLER WARRANTS ANY ASPECT OF THE PROPERTY, SELLER IS OBLIGATED TO DISCLOSE KNOWN MATERIAL FACTS AND TO MAKE OTHER DISCLOSURES REQUIRED BY LAW.**

Buyer and Seller acknowledge receipt of copy of this page, which constitutes Page 2 of _6_ Pages.

Buyer's Initials (*WRB*) (*WAB*) Seller's Initials (*JBS*) (*SKS*)

OFFICE USE ONLY
Reviewed by Broker or Designee _____
Date *5/16/XX*

PRINT DATE
R FEB 98

MASTER COPY

RESIDENTIAL PURCHASE AGREEMENT AND RECEIPT FOR DEPOSIT (RPA-14 PAGE 2 OF 5) REVISED 5/97

Exhibit 5.2b

Property Address: _123 Main Street, Somewhere, CA 90XXX_ Date: _5/15/XX_

10. **FIXTURES:** All EXISTING fixtures and fittings that are attached to the Property, or for which special openings have been made, are INCLUDED IN THE PURCHASE PRICE (unless excluded below), and shall be transferred free of liens and "AS IS," unless specifically warranted. Fixtures shall include, but are not limited to, existing electrical, lighting, plumbing and heating fixtures, fireplace inserts, solar systems, built-in appliances, window and door screens, awnings, shutters, window coverings, attached floor coverings, television antennas, satellite dishes and related equipment, private integrated telephone systems, air coolers/conditioners, pool/spa equipment, water softeners (if owned by Seller), security systems/alarms (if owned by Seller), garage door openers/remote controls, attached fireplace equipment, mailbox, in-ground landscaping including trees/shrubs, and

FIXTURES EXCLUDED: _____.

11. **PERSONAL PROPERTY:** The following items of personal property, free of liens and "AS IS," unless specifically warranted, are INCLUDED IN THE PURCHASE PRICE: _Fireplace Screen + Tools and Garden Shed_.

12. **BUYER'S INVESTIGATION OF PROPERTY CONDITION:** Buyer's Acceptance of the condition of the Property is a contingency of this Agreement, as specified in this paragraph and paragraph 16. Buyer shall have the right, at Buyer's expense, to conduct inspections, investigations, tests, surveys, and other studies ("Inspections"), including the right to inspect for lead-based paint and other lead hazards. No Inspections shall be made by any governmental building or zoning inspector or government employee without Seller's prior written consent, unless required by Law. Buyer shall, within the time specified in Paragraph 16, complete these Inspections and notify Seller in writing of any items reasonably disapproved. Seller shall make Property available for all Inspections. Buyer shall: keep Property free and clear of liens; indemnify and hold Seller harmless from all liability, claims, demands, damages and costs; and repair all damages arising from Inspections. Buyer shall carry, or Buyer shall require anyone acting on Buyer's behalf to carry, policies of liability, worker's compensation, and other applicable insurance, defending and protecting Seller from liability for any injuries to persons or property occurring during any work done on the Property at Buyer's direction, prior to Close Of Escrow. Seller is advised that certain protections may be afforded Seller by recording a notice of non-responsibility for work done on the Property at Buyer's direction. At Seller's request Buyer shall give Seller, at no cost, complete copies of all inspection reports obtained by Buyer concerning the Property. Seller shall have water, gas, and electricity on for Buyer's Inspections, and through the date possession is made available to Buyer.

13. **FINAL WALK-THROUGH; VERIFICATION OF CONDITION:** Buyer shall have the right to make a final inspection of the Property within 5 **(or ☐ _____) Days** prior to Close Of Escrow, NOT AS A CONTINGENCY OF THE SALE, but solely to confirm that Repairs have been completed as agreed in writing, and that Seller has complied with Seller's other obligations.

14. **PRORATIONS AND PROPERTY TAXES:** Unless otherwise agreed in writing, real property taxes and assessments, interest, rents, HOA regular dues and regular assessments, premiums on insurance assumed by Buyer, payments on bonds and assessments assumed by Buyer, payments on Mello-Roos and other Special Assessment District bonds and assessments which are now a lien, and payments on HOA bonds and special assessments which have been imposed prior to Close Of Escrow, shall be PAID CURRENT and prorated between Buyer and Seller as of Close Of Escrow, except: _____.
Prorated payments on Mello-Roos and other Special Assessment District bonds and assessments and HOA special assessments that are now a lien but not yet due, shall be assumed by Buyer WITHOUT CREDIT toward the purchase price. Property will be reassessed upon change of ownership. Any supplemental tax bills shall be paid as follows: **(1)** For periods after Close Of Escrow, by Buyer; and, **(2)** For periods prior to Close Of Escrow, by Seller. TAX BILLS ISSUED AFTER CLOSE OF ESCROW SHALL BE HANDLED DIRECTLY BETWEEN BUYER AND SELLER.

15. **SALE OF BUYER'S PROPERTY:**
  A. This Agreement is NOT contingent upon the sale of Buyer's property, unless paragraph 15B is checked.
  OR **B.** ☐ (If checked) This Agreement IS CONTINGENT on the Close Of Escrow of Buyer's property, described as (address) _____
  _____ ("Buyer's Property"), which is
  (if checked) ☐ listed for sale with _____ Company, and/or
  (if checked) ☐ in Escrow No. _____ with _____ Escrow Holder, scheduled to
  Close Escrow on _____ (date). Buyer shall deliver to Seller, within **5 Days** After Seller's request, a copy of the contract for the sale of Buyer's Property, escrow instructions, and all amendments and modifications thereto. If Buyer's Property does not close escrow by the date specified for Close Of Escrow in this paragraph, then either Seller or Buyer may cancel this Agreement in writing.
  (Check ONLY 1 or 2; do NOT check both.) After Acceptance:
  ☐ **(1)** Seller SHALL have the right to continue to offer the Property for sale. If Seller accepts another written offer, Seller shall give Buyer written notice to **(a)** remove this contingency in writing, **(b)** provide written verification of sufficient funds to close escrow on this sale without the sale of Buyer's Property, and **(c)** comply with the following additional requirement(s) _____
  _____
  If Buyer fails to complete those actions within _____ **hours or** _____ **Days** After receipt of such notice, Seller may cancel this Agreement in writing.
  OR ☐ **(2)** Seller SHALL NOT have the right to continue to offer the Property for sale, except for back-up offers.

16. **TIME PERIODS; INSPECTIONS; SATISFACTION/REMOVAL OF CONTINGENCIES; DISAPPROVAL/CANCELLATION RIGHTS:**
  A. TIME PERIODS: The following time periods shall apply, unless changed by mutual **written** agreement:
    (1) SELLER HAS: 5 (or ☒ _15_) Days After Acceptance **(a)** to deliver to Buyer all reports, disclosures, and information for which Seller is responsible under paragraphs 4G, 4H, 4M and 7A; and, **(b)** to request and **2 Days** After receipt to provide to Buyer all reports, disclosures, and information for which Seller is responsible under paragraphs 7B and 8.
    (2) BUYER HAS: (a) 10 (or ☐ _____) Days After Acceptance to complete all Inspections (including, if applicable, Inspections for wood destroying pests or organisms under paragraph 4M and lead-based paint and lead hazards under paragraph 12), investigations and review of reports and other applicable information, with an additional **7 Days** to complete geologic Inspections. **WITHIN THIS TIME,** Buyer must either disapprove in writing any items which are unacceptable to Buyer or remove the contingency associated with such disapproval right, by the active or passive method, as specified below; **(b) 5 (or _____) Days** After receipt of **(i)** each of the items in paragraph 16A(1); and **(ii)** notice of code and legal violations under paragraph 7C, to either disapprove in writing any items which are unacceptable to Buyer, or remove the contingency associated with such disapproval right by the active or passive method as specified below.
    (3) SELLER'S RESPONSE TO BUYER'S DISAPPROVALS: Seller shall have **5 (or ☐ _____) Days** After receipt of Buyer's written notice of items reasonably disapproved to respond in writing. If Seller refuses or is unable to make repairs to, or correct, any items reasonably disapproved by Buyer, or if Seller does not respond within the time period specified, Buyer shall have **5 (or ☐ _____) Days** After receipt of Seller's response, or after the expiration of the time for Seller to respond, whichever occurs first, to cancel this Agreement in writing.
  B. ACTIVE OR PASSIVE REMOVAL OF BUYER'S CONTINGENCIES:
    (1) ☐ **ACTIVE METHOD (APPLIES IF CHECKED):** If Buyer does not give Seller written notice of items reasonably disapproved, removal of contingencies, or cancellation, within the time periods specified, Seller shall have the right to cancel this Agreement by giving written notice to Buyer.
    (2) PASSIVE METHOD (Applies UNLESS Active Method is checked): If Buyer does not give Seller written notice of items reasonably disapproved, or of removal of contingencies or cancellation within the time periods specified, Buyer shall be deemed to have removed the contingency associated with the disapproval right, or waived the contingency and the right to take those actions or to cancel.
  C. EFFECT OF CONTINGENCY REMOVAL: If Buyer removes any contingency or cancellation right by the active or passive method, as applicable, Buyer shall conclusively be deemed to have: **(1)** Completed all Inspections, investigations, and review of reports and other applicable information and disclosures pertaining to that contingency or cancellation right; **(2)** Elected to proceed with the transaction; and, **(3)** Assumed all liability, responsibility, and expense for repairs or corrections pertaining to that contingency or cancellation right, or for inability to obtain financing if the contingency pertains to financing, except for items which Seller has agreed in writing to repair or correct.

Buyer and Seller acknowledge receipt of copy of this page, which constitutes Page 3 of _6_ Pages.
Buyer's Initials (_LRB_) (_MRB_) Seller's Initials (_JB_) (_SKS_)

EQUAL HOUSING OPPORTUNITY

PRINT DATE
R FEB 98

MASTER COPY
RESIDENTIAL PURCHASE AGREEMENT AND RECEIPT FOR DEPOSIT (RPA-14 PAGE 3 OF 5) REVISED 5/97

Exhibit 5.2c

D. **CANCELLATION OF SALE/ESCROW; RETURN OF DEPOSITS:** If Buyer or Seller gives written NOTICE OF CANCELLATION pursuant to rights duly exercised under the terms of this Agreement, Buyer and Seller agree to sign mutual instructions to cancel the sale and escrow and release deposits, less fees and costs, to the party entitled to the funds. Fees and costs may be payable to service providers and vendors for services and products provided during escrow. Release of funds will require mutual, signed release instructions from both Buyer and Seller, judicial decision, or arbitration award. **A party may be subject to a civil penalty of up to $1,000 for refusal to sign such instructions, if no good faith dispute exists as to who is entitled to the deposited funds (Civil Code §1057.3).**

17. **REPAIRS:** Repairs under this Agreement shall be completed prior to Close Of Escrow, unless otherwise agreed in writing. Work to be performed at Seller's expense may be performed by Seller or through others, provided that work complies with applicable laws, including governmental permit, inspection, and approval requirements. Repairs shall be performed in a skillful manner with materials of quality comparable to existing materials. It is understood that exact restoration of appearance or cosmetic items following all Repairs may not be possible.

18. **WITHHOLDING TAXES:** Seller and Buyer agree to execute and deliver any instrument, affidavit, statement, or instruction reasonably necessary to comply with state and federal withholding Laws, if required.(For example, C.A.R. FIRPTA and California compliance Forms AS-14 and AB-11.)

19. **KEYS:** At the time possession is made available to Buyer, Seller shall provide keys and/or means to operate all Property locks, mailboxes, security systems, alarms, and garage door openers. If the Property is a unit in a condominium or subdivision, Buyer may be required to pay a deposit to the HOA to obtain keys to accessible HOA facilities.

20. **LIQUIDATED DAMAGES: If Buyer fails to complete this purchase by reason of any default of Buyer, Seller shall retain, as liquidated damages for breach of contract, the deposit actually paid. However, if the Property is a dwelling with no more four units, one of which Buyer intends to occupy, then the amount retained shall be no more than 3% of the purchase price. Any excess shall be returned to Buyer. Buyer and Seller shall also sign a separate liquidated damages provision for any increased deposit. (C.A.R. Form RID-11 shall fulfill this requirement.)** Buyer's Initials _WRB_ / _MHB_   Seller's Initials _RKS_ / _SKS_

21. **DISPUTE RESOLUTION:**
    A. **MEDIATION:** Buyer and Seller agree to mediate any dispute or claim arising between them out of this Agreement, or any resulting transaction, before resorting to arbitration or court action, subject to paragraphs 21C and D below. Mediation fees, if any, shall be divided equally among the parties involved. If any party commences an action based on a dispute or claim to which this paragraph applies, without first attempting to resolve the matter through mediation, then that party shall not be entitled to recover attorney's fees, even if they would otherwise be available to that party in any such action. THIS MEDIATION PROVISION APPLIES WHETHER OR NOT THE ARBITRATION PROVISION IS INITIALED.
    B. **ARBITRATION OF DISPUTES: Buyer and Seller agree that any dispute or claim in Law or equity arising between them out of this Agreement or any resulting transaction, which is not settled through mediation, shall be decided by neutral, binding arbitration, subject to paragraphs 21C and D below. The arbitrator shall be a retired judge or justice, unless the parties mutually agree to a different arbitrator, who shall render an award in accordance with substantive California Law. In all other respects, the arbitration shall be conducted in accordance with Part III, Title 9 of the California Code of Civil Procedure. Judgment upon the award of the arbitrator(s) may be entered in any court having jurisdiction. The parties shall have the right to discovery in accordance with Code of Civil Procedure §1283.05.**

       "NOTICE: BY INITIALING IN THE SPACE BELOW YOU ARE AGREEING TO HAVE ANY DISPUTE ARISING OUT OF THE MATTERS INCLUDED IN THE 'ARBITRATION OF DISPUTES' PROVISION DECIDED BY NEUTRAL ARBITRATION AS PROVIDED BY CALIFORNIA LAW AND YOU ARE GIVING UP ANY RIGHTS YOU MIGHT POSSESS TO HAVE THE DISPUTE LITIGATED IN A COURT OR JURY TRIAL. BY INITIALING IN THE SPACE BELOW YOU ARE GIVING UP YOUR JUDICIAL RIGHTS TO DISCOVERY AND APPEAL, UNLESS THOSE RIGHTS ARE SPECIFICALLY INCLUDED IN THE 'ARBITRATION OF DISPUTES' PROVISION. IF YOU REFUSE TO SUBMIT TO ARBITRATION AFTER AGREEING TO THIS PROVISION, YOU MAY BE COMPELLED TO ARBITRATE UNDER THE AUTHORITY OF THE CALIFORNIA CODE OF CIVIL PROCEDURE. YOUR AGREEMENT TO THIS ARBITRATION PROVISION IS VOLUNTARY."

       "WE HAVE READ AND UNDERSTAND THE FOREGOING AND AGREE TO SUBMIT DISPUTES ARISING OUT OF THE MATTERS INCLUDED IN THE 'ARBITRATION OF DISPUTES' PROVISION TO NEUTRAL ARBITRATION." Buyer's Initials _WRB_ / _MHB_   Seller's Initials _RKS_ / _SKS_
    C. **EXCLUSIONS FROM MEDIATION AND ARBITRATION:** The following matters are excluded from Mediation and Arbitration hereunder: **(a)** A judicial or non-judicial foreclosure or other action or proceeding to enforce a deed of trust, mortgage, or installment land sale contract as defined in Civil Code §2985; **(b)** An unlawful detainer action; **(c)** The filing or enforcement of a mechanic's lien; **(d)** Any matter which is within the jurisdiction of a probate, small claims, or bankruptcy court; and **(e)** An action for bodily injury or wrongful death, or for latent or patent defects to which Code of Civil Procedure §337.1 or §337.15 applies. The filing of a court action to enable the recording of a notice of pending action, for order of attachment, receivership, injunction, or other provisional remedies, shall not constitute a violation of the mediation and arbitration provisions.
    D. **BROKERS:** Buyer and Seller agree to mediate and arbitrate disputes or claims involving either or both Brokers, provided either or both Brokers shall have agreed to such mediation or arbitration, prior to, or within a reasonable time after the dispute or claim is presented to Brokers. Any election by either or both Brokers to participate in mediation or arbitration shall not result in Brokers being deemed parties to the purchase and sale Agreement.

22. **DEFINITIONS:** As used in this Agreement:
    A. **"Acceptance"** means the time the offer or final counter offer is accepted by the other party, in accordance with paragraph 30 of the Agreement or the terms of the final counter offer.
    B. **"Agreement"** means the terms and conditions of this Residential Purchase Agreement and any counter offer.
    C. **"Days"** means calendar days, unless otherwise required by Law.
    D. **"Days After . ."** means the specified number of calendar days after the occurrence of the event specified, not counting the calendar date on which the specified event occurs.
    E. **"Close Of Escrow"** means the date the grant deed, or other evidence of transfer of title, is recorded.
    F. **"Law"** means any law, code, statute, ordinance, regulation, or rule, which is adopted by a controlling city, county, state or federal legislative or judicial body or agency.
    G. **"Repairs"** means any repairs, alterations, replacements, or modifications, (including pest control work) of the Property.
    H. **"Pest Control Certification"** means a written statement made by a registered structural pest control company that on the date of inspection or re-inspection, the Property is "free" or is "now free" of "evidence of active infestation in the visible and accessible areas".
    I. **Singular and Plural** terms each include the other, when appropriate.

23. **MULTIPLE LISTING SERVICE ("MLS"):** Brokers are authorized to report the terms of this transaction to any MLS, to be published and disseminated to persons authorized to use the information on terms approved by the MLS.

Buyer and Seller acknowledge receipt of copy of this page, which constitutes Page 4 of ___6___ Pages.
Buyer's Initials (_WRB_) (_MHB_) Seller's Initals (_RKS_) (_SKS_)

PRINT DATE
R FEB 98

| OFFICE USE ONLY |
| Reviewed by Broker |
| or Designee ___ |
| Date _5/16/xx_ |

EQUAL HOUSING
OPPORTUNITY

MASTER COPY

RESIDENTIAL PURCHASE AGREEMENT AND RECEIPT FOR DEPOSIT (RPA-14 PAGE 4 OF 5) REVISED 5/97

Exhibit 5.2d

Property Address: _123 Main Street, Somewhere, CA 90XXX_   Date: _5/15/XX_

24. **EQUAL HOUSING OPPORTUNITY:** The Property is sold in compliance with federal, state, and local anti-discrimination Laws.
25. **ATTORNEY'S FEES:** In any action, proceeding, or arbitration between Buyer and Seller arising out of this Agreement, the prevailing Buyer or Seller shall be entitled to reasonable attorney's fees and costs from the non-prevailing Buyer or Seller, except as provided in paragraph 21A.
26. **SELECTION OF SERVICE PROVIDERS:** If Brokers give Buyer or Seller referrals to persons, vendors, or service or product providers ("Providers"), Brokers do not guarantee the performance of any of those Providers. Buyer and Seller may select ANY Providers of their own choosing.
27. **TIME OF ESSENCE; ENTIRE CONTRACT; CHANGES:** Time is of the essence. All understandings between the parties are incorporated in this Agreement. Its terms are intended by the parties as a final, complete, and exclusive expression of their agreement with respect to its subject matter, and may not be contradicted by evidence of any prior agreement or contemporaneous oral agreement. **This Agreement may not be extended, amended, modified, altered, or changed, except in writing signed by Buyer and Seller.**
28. **OTHER TERMS AND CONDITIONS,** including ATTACHED SUPPLEMENTS:
    - ☒ Buyer Inspection Advisory (C.A.R. Form BIA-14) _____
    - ☐ Purchase Agreement Addendum (C.A.R. Form PAA-14, paragraph number(s) _____) _____
    - _____
    - _____
    - _____
    - _____
    - _____

29. **AGENCY CONFIRMATION:** The following agency relationships are hereby confirmed for this transaction:
    Listing Agent: _Colina Vista Realty_____ (Print Firm Name) is the agent of (check one):
    ☒ the Seller exclusively; or ☐ both the Buyer and Seller.
    Selling Agent: _High View Realty_____ (Print Firm Name) (if not same as Listing Agent) is the agent of (check one):
    ☒ the Buyer exclusively; or ☐ the Seller exclusively; or ☐ both the Buyer and Seller.
    Real Estate Brokers are not parties to the Agreement between Buyer and Seller.
30. **OFFER:** This is an offer to purchase the Property on the above terms and conditions. All paragraphs with spaces for initials by Buyer and Seller are incorporated in this Agreement only if initialed by all parties. If at least one but not all parties initial, a counter offer is required until agreement is reached. Unless Acceptance of Offer is signed by Seller, and a signed copy delivered in person, by mail, or facsimile, and personally received by Buyer, or by _____, who is authorized to receive it, by _5/22/XX_ (date), at _5_ AM/PM, the offer shall be deemed revoked and the deposit shall be returned. Buyer has read and acknowledges receipt of a copy of the offer and agrees to the above confirmation of agency relationships. If this offer is accepted and Buyer subsequently defaults, Buyer may be responsible for payment of Brokers' compensation. This Agreement and any supplement, addendum, or modification, including any photocopy or facsimile, may be signed in two or more counterparts, all of which shall constitute one and the same writing.

Buyer and Seller acknowledge and agree that Brokers: (a) Do not decide what price Buyer should pay or Seller should accept; (b) Do not guarantee the condition of the Property; (c) Shall not be responsible for defects that are not known to Broker(s) and are not visually observable in reasonably accessible areas of the Property; (d) Do not guarantee the performance or Repairs of others who have provided services or products to Buyer or Seller; (e) Cannot identify Property boundary lines; (f) Cannot verify inspection reports or representations of others; (g) Cannot provide legal or tax advice; (h) Will not provide other advice or information that exceeds the knowledge, education and experience required to obtain a real estate license. Buyer and Seller agree that they will seek legal, tax, insurance, and other desired assistance from appropriate professionals.

BUYER _William R Buyer_____   BUYER _Maria H. Buyer_____

31. **BROKER COMPENSATION:** Seller agrees to pay compensation for services as follows:
    $6,450 (3%) , to _Colina Vista Realty_____, Broker, and
    $6,450 (3%) , to _High View Realty_____, Broker,
    payable: **(a)** On recordation of the deed or other evidence of title; or **(b)** If completion of sale is prevented by default of Seller, upon Seller's default; or, **(c)** If completion of sale is prevented by default of Buyer, only if and when Seller collects damages from Buyer, by suit or otherwise, and then in an amount equal to one-half of the damages recovered, but not to exceed the above compensation, after first deducting title and escrow expenses and the expenses of collection, if any. Seller hereby irrevocably assigns to Brokers such compensation from Seller's proceeds, and irrevocably instructs Escrow Holder to disburse those funds to Brokers at close of escrow. Commission instructions can be amended or revoked only with the consent of Brokers. In any action, proceeding or arbitration relating to the payment of such compensation, the prevailing party shall be entitled to reasonable attorney's fees and costs, except as provided in paragraph 21A.
32. **ACCEPTANCE OF OFFER:** Seller warrants that Seller is the owner of this Property or has the authority to execute this Agreement. Seller accepts the above offer, agrees to sell the Property on the above terms and conditions, and agrees to the above confirmation of agency relationships. Seller has read and acknowledges receipt of a copy of this Agreement, and authorizes Broker to deliver a signed copy to Buyer.

If checked: ☐ SUBJECT TO ATTACHED COUNTER OFFER, DATED _____ .

SELLER _Joseph B. Seller_____   Date _5/16/XX_
SELLER _Sonia Y. Seller_____   Date _5/16/XX_

WRB/MHB ACKNOWLEDGMENT OF RECEIPT: Buyer or authorized agent acknowledges receipt of signed Acceptance on (date) _5/16/XX_
(Initials)   at _____ AM/PM.

Agency relationships are confirmed as above. Real Estate Brokers are not parties to the Agreement between Buyer and Seller.
Receipt for deposit is acknowledged:
Real Estate Broker (Selling Firm Name) _High View Realty_ By _Sam Whaley_ Date _5/15/XX_
Address _789 Fifth Avenue, Somewhere, CA 90XXX_ Telephone _XXX-XXXX_ Fax _XXX-XXXX_
Real Estate Broker (Listing Firm Name) _Colina Vista Realty_ By _Ralph Smith_ Date _5/16/XX_
Address _462 First Street, Somewhere, CA 90XXX_ Telephone _XXX-XXXX_ Fax _XXX-XXXX_

This form is available for use by the entire real estate industry. It is not intended to identify the user as a REALTOR®. REALTOR® is a registered collective membership mark which may be used only by members of the NATIONAL ASSOCIATION OF REALTORS® who subscribe to its Code of Ethics.
Page 5 of _6_ Pages.

OFFICE USE ONLY
Reviewed by Broker or Designee ___
Date _5/16/XX_

PRINT DATE
R FEB 98
MASTER COPY
RESIDENTIAL PURCHASE AGREEMENT AND RECEIPT FOR DEPOSIT (RPA-14 PAGE 5 OF 5) REVISED 5/97

Exhibit 5.2e

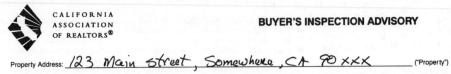

Property Address: _123 Main Street, Somewhere, CA 90xxx_ ("Property")

IMPORTANCE OF PROPERTY INSPECTION: The physical condition of the land and improvements being purchased are not guaranteed by either Seller or Brokers, except as specifically set forth in the purchase agreement. For this reason, Buyer should conduct a thorough inspection of the Property personally and with professionals, who should provide a written report of their inspections. If the professionals recommend further investigation, tests, or inspections, Buyer should contact qualified experts to conduct such additional investigations, tests, or inspections. **Disclosure duties:** The law requires Seller and Brokers to disclose to Buyer all material facts known to them which affect the value or desirability of the Property. In sales involving residential dwellings with no more than four units, Brokers have a duty to make a diligent visual inspection of the accessible areas of the Property, and to disclose the results of that inspection. However, as some Property defects or conditions may not be discoverable from a visual inspection, it is possible neither Seller nor Brokers are aware of them. **Buyer duties:** Buyer has an affirmative duty to exercise reasonable care to protect himself or herself, including discovery and investigation of information and facts which are known to Buyer, or are within the diligent attention and observation of Buyer. **Property inspections:** Brokers do not have expertise, and therefore cannot advise Buyer on many items, such as soil stability, geologic conditions, hazardous substances, structural conditions of the foundation or other improvements, or the condition of the roof, heating, air conditioning, plumbing, electrical, sewer, septic, waste disposal or other systems. The only way to accurately determine the condition of the Property is through an inspection by an appropriate professional selected by Buyer.

YOU ARE ADVISED TO CONDUCT INSPECTIONS OF THE ENTIRE PROPERTY, INCLUDING BUT NOT LIMITED TO THE FOLLOWING:

1. **GENERAL CONDITION OF THE PROPERTY, ITS SYSTEMS AND COMPONENTS:** Foundation, roof, plumbing, heating, air conditioning, electrical, mechanical, security, pool/spa, and other structural and non-structural systems and components, built-in appliances, any personal property included in the sale, and energy efficiency of the Property. (Structural engineers are best suited to determine possible design or construction defects, and whether improvements are structurally sound.)
2. **SQUARE FOOTAGE, AGE, BOUNDARIES:** Square footage, room dimensions, lot size, age of improvements, and boundaries. Any numerical statements regarding these items are APPROXIMATIONS ONLY, and have not been and cannot be verified by Brokers. Fences, hedges, walls, retaining walls, and other natural or constructed barriers or markers do not necessarily identify true Property boundaries. (An appraiser, architect, surveyor, or civil engineer is best suited to determine respectively square footage, dimensions and boundaries of the Property.)
3. **SOIL STABILITY/GEOLOGIC CONDITIONS:** Existence of fill or compacted soil, or expansive or contracting soil, susceptibility to slippage, settling or movement, and the adequacy of drainage. These types of inspections are particularly important for hillside or sloped properties, but the referenced conditions may also exist on flat land. (Geotechnical engineers are best suited to determine such conditions, causes, and remedies.)
4. **ROOF:** Present condition, approximate age, leaks, and remaining useful life. (Roofing contractors are best suited to determine these conditions.)
5. **POOL/SPA:** Whether there are any cracks, or operational problems. (Pool contractors are best suited to determine these conditions.)
6. **WASTE DISPOSAL:** Type, size, adequacy, capacity and condition of sewer and septic systems and components, connection to sewer, and applicable fees.
7. **WATER AND UTILITIES; WELL SYSTEMS AND COMPONENTS:** Water and utility availability, use restrictions, and costs. Adequacy, condition, and performance of well systems and components.
8. **ENVIRONMENTAL HAZARDS:** Potential environmental hazards, including asbestos, lead-based paint and other lead contamination, methane, other gases, fuel, oil or chemical storage tanks, contaminated soil or water, hazardous waste, waste disposal sites, electromagnetic fields, nuclear sources, and other substances, materials, products, or conditions. (For further information, read the booklet "Environmental Hazards: A Guide for Homeowners and Buyers," or consult an appropriate professional.)
9. **EARTHQUAKE AND FLOOD; INSURANCE AVAILABILITY:** Susceptibility of the Property to earthquake hazards and propensity of the Property to flood. These and other conditions may affect the availability and need for certain types of insurance. (Geologist, Geotechnic Engineer and insurance agents are best suited to provide information on these conditions.)
10. **GOVERNMENTAL REQUIREMENTS AND LIMITATIONS:** Permits, inspections, certificates, zoning, other governmental limitations, restrictions, and requirements affecting the current or future use of the Property, its development or size. (Such information is available through appropriate governmental agencies and private information providers. Brokers are not qualified to obtain, review, or interpret any such information.)
11. **RENT AND OCCUPANCY CONTROL:** Some cities and counties impose restrictions which may limit the amount of rent that can be charged, the maximum number of persons who can occupy the Property, and the circumstances in which tenancies can be terminated. (Information about such restrictions can be obtained from local governmental agencies.)
12. **NEIGHBORHOOD, AREA, SUBDIVISION CONDITIONS; PERSONAL FACTORS:** Neighborhood or area conditions, including schools, proximity and adequacy of law enforcement, crime statistics, registered felons or offenders, fire protection, other governmental services, proximity to commercial, industrial or agricultural activities, existing and proposed transportation, construction and development which may affect noise, view, or traffic, airport noise, noise or odor from any source, wild and domestic animals, other nuisances, hazards, or circumstances, facilities and condition of common areas of common interest subdivisions, and possible lack of compliance with any governing documents or Homeowners' Association requirements, conditions and influences of significance to certain cultures and/or religions, and personal needs, requirements and preferences of Buyer.

> Buyer acknowledges and agrees that Brokers: (a) Do not guarantee the condition of the Property; (b) Shall not be responsible for defects that are not known to Broker(s) or are not visually observable in reasonably and normally accessible areas of the Property; (c) Cannot verify information contained in inspection reports or representations made by others; (d) Do not guarantee the performance of others who have provided services or products to Buyer or Seller; (e) Do not guarantee the adequacy or completeness of repairs made by Seller or others; (f) Cannot identify Property boundary lines; and (g) Do not decide what price a buyer should pay or a seller should accept. Buyer agrees to seek desired assistance from appropriate professionals.

YOU ARE STRONGLY ADVISED TO INVESTIGATE THE CONDITION AND SUITABILITY OF ALL ASPECTS OF THE PROPERTY. IF YOU DO NOT DO SO, YOU ARE ACTING AGAINST THE ADVICE OF BROKERS.

By signing below, Buyer acknowledges receipt of a copy of this document. Buyer is encouraged to read it carefully.

William R. Buyer   5/15/xx   _Maria H. Buyer_   5/15/xx
Buyer Signature   Date   Buyer Signature   Date

Buyer(s) (Print Name(s)) _William R. Buyer_   _Maria H. Buyer_

Published and Distributed by:
REAL ESTATE BUSINESS SERVICES, INC.
a subsidiary of the CALIFORNIA ASSOCIATION OF REALTORS®
525 South Virgil Avenue, Los Angeles, California 90020

Page _6_ of _6_ Pages.

OFFICE USE ONLY
Reviewed by Broker
or Designee
Date _5/16/xx_

PRINT DATE
R FEB 98

MASTER COPY
BUYER'S INSPECTION ADVISORY (BIA-14 PAGE 1 OF 1) REVISED 5/97

Exhibit 5.2f

CALIFORNIA
ASSOCIATION
OF REALTORS®

REAL ESTATE TRANSFER DISCLOSURE STATEMENT
(CALIFORNIA CIVIL CODE 1102, ET SEQ.)

THIS DISCLOSURE STATEMENT CONCERNS THE REAL PROPERTY SITUATED IN THE CITY OF _____
_____, COUNTY OF _____, STATE OF CALIFORNIA,
DESCRIBED AS _____.
THIS STATEMENT IS A DISCLOSURE OF THE CONDITION OF THE ABOVE DESCRIBED PROPERTY IN COMPLIANCE
WITH SECTION 1102 OF THE CIVIL CODE AS OF _____, 19 _____. IT IS NOT A WARRANTY
OF ANY KIND BY THE SELLER(S) OR ANY AGENT(S) REPRESENTING ANY PRINCIPAL(S) IN THIS TRANSACTION,
AND IS NOT A SUBSTITUTE FOR ANY INSPECTIONS OR WARRANTIES THE PRINCIPAL(S) MAY WISH TO OBTAIN.

I
COORDINATION WITH OTHER DISCLOSURE FORMS

This Real Estate Transfer Disclosure Statement is made pursuant to Section 1102 of the Civil Code. Other statutes require disclosures, depending upon the details of the particular real estate transaction (for example: special study zone and purchase-money liens on residential property).

Substituted Disclosures: The following disclosures have or will be made in connection with this real estate transfer, and are intended to satisfy the disclosure obligations on this form, where the subject matter is the same:

☐ Inspection reports completed pursuant to the contract of sale or receipt for deposit.

☐ Additional inspection reports or disclosures:_____
_____

II
SELLER'S INFORMATION

The Seller discloses the following information with the knowledge that even though this is not a warranty, prospective Buyers may rely on this information in deciding whether and on what terms to purchase the subject property. Seller hereby authorizes any agent(s) representing any principal(s) in this transaction to provide a copy of this statement to any person or entity in connection with any actual or anticipated sale of the property.

THE FOLLOWING ARE REPRESENTATIONS MADE BY THE SELLER(S) AND ARE NOT THE
REPRESENTATIONS OF THE AGENT(S), IF ANY. THIS INFORMATION IS A DISCLOSURE AND IS NOT
INTENDED TO BE PART OF ANY CONTRACT BETWEEN THE BUYER AND SELLER.

Seller ☐ is ☐ is not occupying the property.

A. The subject property has the items checked below (read across):

☐ Range	☐ Oven	☐ Microwave
☐ Dishwasher	☐ Trash Compactor	☐ Garbage Disposal
☐ Washer/Dryer Hookups		☐ Rain Gutters
☐ Burglar Alarms	☐ Smoke Detector(s)	☐ Fire Alarm
☐ T.V. Antenna	☐ Satellite Dish	☐ Intercom
☐ Central Heating	☐ Central Air Conditioning	☐ Evaporator Cooler(s)
☐ Wall/Window Air Conditioning	☐ Sprinklers	☐ Public Sewer System
☐ Septic Tank	☐ Sump Pump	☐ Water Softener
☐ Patio/Decking	☐ Built-in Barbecue	☐ Gazebo
☐ Sauna		
☐ Hot Tub ☐ Locking Safety Cover*	☐ Pool ☐ Child Resistant Barrier*	☐ Spa ☐ Locking Safety Cover*
☐ Security Gate(s)	☐ Automatic Garage Door Opener(s)*	☐ Number Remote Controls _____
Garage: ☐ Attached	☐ Not Attached	☐ Carport
Pool/Spa Heater: ☐ Gas	☐ Solar	☐ Electric
Water Heater: ☐ Gas	☐ Water Heater Anchored, Braced, or Strapped*	
Water Supply: ☐ City	☐ Well	☐ Private Utility or
Gas Supply: ☐ Utility	☐ Bottled	Other _____
☐ Window Screens	☐ Window Security Bars ☐ Quick Release Mechanism on Bedroom Windows*	

Exhaust Fan(s) in _____ 220 Volt Wiring in _____ Fireplace(s) in _____
☐ Gas Starter _____ ☐ Roof(s): Type: _____ Age: _____ (approx.)
☐ Other: _____

Are there, to the best of your (Seller's) knowledge, any of the above that are not in operating condition? ☐ Yes ☐ No. If yes, then describe. (Attach additional sheets if necessary.): _____
_____

B. Are you (Seller) aware of any significant defects/malfunctions in any of the following? ☐ Yes ☐ No. If yes, check appropriate space(s) below.
☐ Interior Walls ☐ Ceilings ☐ Floors ☐ Exterior Walls ☐ Insulation ☐ Roof(s) ☐ Windows ☐ Doors ☐ Foundation ☐ Slab(s)
☐ Driveways ☐ Sidewalks ☐ Walls/Fences ☐ Electrical Systems ☐ Plumbing/Sewers/Septics ☐ Other Structural Components
(Describe: _____

If any of the above is checked, explain. (Attach additional sheets if necessary): _____
_____
_____

*This garage door opener or child resistant pool barrier may not be in compliance with the safety standards relating to automatic reversing devices as set forth in Chapter 12.5 (commencing with Section 19890) of Part 3 of Division 13 of, or with the pool safety standards of Article 2.5 (commencing with Section 115920) of Chapter 5 of Part 10 of Division 104 of, the Health and Safety Code. The water heater may not be anchored, braced, or strapped in accordance with Section 19211 of the Health and Safety Code. Window security bars may not have quick release mechanisms in compliance with the 1995 Edition of the California Building Standards Code.

Buyer and Seller acknowledge receipt of copy of this page, which constitutes Page 1 of 2 Pages.
Buyer's Initials (_____) (_____)   Seller's Initials (_____) (_____)

Published and Distributed by:
REAL ESTATE BUSINESS SERVICES, INC.
a subsidiary of the CALIFORNIA ASSOCIATION OF REALTORS®
525 South Virgil Avenue, Los Angeles, California 90020

PRINT DATE
R AUG 97

┌─ OFFICE USE ONLY ─┐
│ Reviewed by Broker │
│ or Designee _____ │
│ Date _____ │
└───────────────────┘

EQUAL HOUSING OPPORTUNITY

BROKER'S COPY
REAL ESTATE TRANSFER DISCLOSURE STATEMENT (TDS-14 PAGE 1 OF 2) REVISED 3/97

Exhibit 5.3a (Reprinted with permission, *California Association of Realtors*®. Endorsement not implied.)

Subject Property Address: _____ Date _____

C. Are you (Seller) aware of any of the following:

1. Substances, materials, or products which may be an environmental hazard such as, but not limited to, asbestos, formaldehyde, radon gas, lead-based paint, fuel or chemical storage tanks, and contaminated soil or water on the subject property . . . . ☐ Yes ☐ No
2. Features of the property shared in common with adjoining landowners, such as walls, fences, and driveways, whose use or responsibility for maintenance may have an effect on the subject property . . . . ☐ Yes ☐ No
3. Any encroachments, easements or similar matters that may affect your interest in the subject property . . . . ☐ Yes ☐ No
4. Room additions, structural modifications, or other alterations or repairs made without necessary permits . . . . ☐ Yes ☐ No
5. Room additions, structural modifications, or other alterations or repairs not in compliance with building codes . . . . ☐ Yes ☐ No
6. Fill (compacted or otherwise) on the property or any portion thereof . . . . ☐ Yes ☐ No
7. Any settling from any cause, or slippage, sliding, or other soil problems. . . . . ☐ Yes ☐ No
8. Flooding, drainage or grading problems . . . . ☐ Yes ☐ No
9. Major damage to the property or any of the structures from fire, earthquake, floods, or landslides. . . . . ☐ Yes ☐ No
10. Any zoning violations, nonconforming uses, violations of "setback" requirements. . . . . ☐ Yes ☐ No
11. Neighborhood noise problems or other nuisances . . . . ☐ Yes ☐ No
12. CC&R's or other deed restrictions or obligations. . . . . ☐ Yes ☐ No
13. Homeowners' Association which has any authority over the subject property . . . . ☐ Yes ☐ No
14. Any "common area" (facilities such as pools, tennis courts, walkways, or other areas co-owned in undivided interest with others). . . . . ☐ Yes ☐ No
15. Any notices of abatement or citations against the property. . . . . ☐ Yes ☐ No
16. Any lawsuits by or against the seller threatening to or affecting this real property, including any lawsuits alleging a defect or deficiency in this real property or "common areas" (facilities such as pools, tennis courts, walkways, or other areas, co-owned in undivided interest with others). . . . . ☐ Yes ☐ No

If the answer to any of these is yes, explain. (Attach additional sheets if necessary.): _____
_____
_____

Seller certifies that the information herein is true and correct to the best of the Seller's knowledge as of the date signed by the Seller.

Seller _____ Date _____

Seller _____ Date _____

III
AGENT'S INSPECTION DISCLOSURE
(To be completed only if the Seller is represented by an agent in this transaction.)

THE UNDERSIGNED, BASED ON THE ABOVE INQUIRY OF THE SELLER(S) AS TO THE CONDITION OF THE PROPERTY AND BASED ON A REASONABLY COMPETENT AND DILIGENT VISUAL INSPECTION OF THE ACCESSIBLE AREAS OF THE PROPERTY IN CONJUNCTION WITH THAT INQUIRY, STATES THE FOLLOWING:

☐ Agent notes no items for disclosure.
☐ Agent notes the following items: _____
_____
_____
_____

Agent (Broker Representing Seller)_____ By _____ Date_____
                                    (Please Print)   (Associate Licensee or Broker Signature)

IV
AGENT'S INSPECTION DISCLOSURE
(To be completed only if the agent who has obtained the offer is other than the agent above.)

THE UNDERSIGNED, BASED ON A REASONABLY COMPETENT AND DILIGENT VISUAL INSPECTION OF THE ACCESSIBLE AREAS OF THE PROPERTY, STATES THE FOLLOWING:

☐ Agent notes no items for disclosure.
☐ Agent notes the following items: _____
_____
_____

Agent (Broker Obtaining the Offer)_____ By _____ Date_____
                                   (Please Print)   (Associate Licensee or Broker Signature)

V
BUYER(S) AND SELLER(S) MAY WISH TO OBTAIN PROFESSIONAL ADVICE AND/OR INSPECTIONS OF THE PROPERTY AND TO PROVIDE FOR APPROPRIATE PROVISIONS IN A CONTRACT BETWEEN BUYER AND SELLER(S) WITH RESPECT TO ANY ADVICE/INSPECTIONS/DEFECTS.

I/WE ACKNOWLEDGE RECEIPT OF A COPY OF THIS STATEMENT.

Seller _____ Date _____ Buyer _____ Date _____

Seller _____ Date _____ Buyer _____ Date _____

Agent (Broker Representing Seller)_____ By _____ Date_____
                                                                  (Associate Licensee or Broker Signature)

Agent (Broker Obtaining the Offer) _____ By _____ Date_____
                                                                  (Associate Licensee or Broker Signature)

SECTION 1102.3 OF THE CIVIL CODE PROVIDES A BUYER WITH THE RIGHT TO RESCIND A PURCHASE CONTRACT FOR AT LEAST THREE DAYS AFTER THE DELIVERY OF THIS DISCLOSURE IF DELIVERY OCCURS AFTER THE SIGNING OF AN OFFER TO PURCHASE. IF YOU WISH TO RESCIND THE CONTRACT, YOU MUST ACT WITHIN THE PRESCRIBED PERIOD.

A REAL ESTATE BROKER IS QUALIFIED TO ADVISE ON REAL ESTATE. IF YOU DESIRE LEGAL ADVICE, CONSULT YOUR ATTORNEY.

BROKER'S COPY
REAL ESTATE TRANSFER DISCLOSURE STATEMENT (TDS-14 PAGE 2 OF 2) REVISED 3/97

Exhibit 5.3b

Chapter 6

Practical Real Estate Mathematics

Chapter Preview   This chapter will help you to understand the fundamentals of mathematics as they apply to real estate. Basic concepts of addition subtraction, multiplication, division, fractions, and decimals are briefly reviewed to set a solid foundation for more complicated real estate computations. At the conclusion of the chapter, you will be able to:

1. Solve problems related to investment, discounting notes, appraisal, commissions, interest and loans, cost and selling price, square footage and area calculations, prorations, and documentary transfer taxes

2. Use amortization and other tables to simplify real estate mathematical computations

6.1 REVIEW OF FUNDAMENTALS   The practical application of real estate mathematics often creates apprehension in some people. The use of calculators and the development of helpful tables can do much to alleviate the fear of math. An understanding of the simple formulas presented in this lesson will help students gain confidence in their ability to solve everyday real estate mathematical problems.

The difficulty some people have with mathematics comes from a lack of knowledge or a forgetfulness of some of the basic rules of mathematics, particularly with regard to percentages, decimals, and fractions.

Decimals

Before solving various real estate mathematical problems, it is helpful to review the concept of decimals. A decimal is the period that sets apart the whole number from the fractional part of the number. The position of the decimal in a number determines the value of the number.

All numbers to the right of the decimal are less than one. The first position to the right of the decimal is the "tenth" position; the second is the "hundredth"; the third is the "thousandth"; the fourth is the "ten thousandth"; the fifth is the "hundred thousandth"; and so on.

To the left of the decimal are the whole numbers. The first position is known as the "units" position; the second is the "tens"; the third is the "hundreds"; the fourth is the "thousands"; the fifth is the "ten thousands"; the sixth is the "hundred thousands"; and so on. Table 6.1 may help to clarify the relationships among percentages, decimals, and fractions.

TABLE 6.1

Percentage (%)	Decimal	Fraction
4½	0.045	$^{45}/_{1000}$
6⅔	0.0667	$^{1}/_{15}$
10	0.10	$^{1}/_{10}$
12½	0.125	$^{1}/_{8}$
16⅔	0.1667	$^{1}/_{6}$
25	0.25	$^{1}/_{4}$
33⅓	0.333	$^{1}/_{3}$
50	0.50	$^{1}/_{2}$
66⅔	0.6667	$^{2}/_{3}$
75	0.75	$^{3}/_{4}$
100	1.00	$^{1}/_{1}$

Converting Percentages to Decimals

To remove the percentage sign, simply move the decimal two places to the left to form a usable decimal number. (See Table 6.2.)

TABLE 6.2

8%	converts	.08
25%	converts	.25
9.5%	converts	.095
105%	converts	1.05

Many times an answer will appear as a decimal and you may wish to convert the answer to an answer with a percentage sign (%). To do this, simply reverse the procedure. (See Table 6.3.)

TABLE 6.3

.08	converts to	8%
.25	converts to	25%
.095	converts to	9.5%
1.05	converts to	105%

Addition of Decimal Numbers

When adding numbers with decimals, place figures in a vertical column and make sure each decimal is in a direct vertical line.

EXAMPLE

```
126.06
  5.715
400.8
-------
532.575
```

Subtraction of Decimal Numbers

The same procedure is used to subtract one decimal number from another.

EXAMPLE

```
$18,450.60
-   425.20
----------
$18,025.40
```

Multiplication of Decimal Numbers

Multiply the two numbers in the normal fashion and then mark off as many decimal places in the answer as there are in the two numbers being multiplied.

EXAMPLE

```
   7.064    (multiplicand)
×37.6       (multiplier)
--------
265.6064    (product)
```

Division of Decimal Numbers

In a division problem that contains a decimal in the divisor, it is necessary to remove that decimal before proceeding with the problem. Mentally move the decimal in the dividend the same number of places shown in the divisor. Add zeros to the dividend if the dividend has fewer digits than are needed to carry out the division process. The decimal point in the quotient (answer) will appear directly above the imaginary decimal in the dividend.

EXAMPLE

$$\overset{\displaystyle 6000}{\text{(divisor) }.045\overline{)270.000}}$$

When no decimal appears in the divisor, the decimal in the quotient will appear directly above the decimal in the dividend.

EXAMPLE

$$\overset{\displaystyle 3.02}{24\overline{)72.48}}$$

6.2 VARIABLES Most real estate problems involve three variables—two known and one unknown. It is the student's responsibility to find the unknown variable. The three variables are termed *Paid, Made,* and *Rate (%)*. The relationship among these variables is shown in Figure 6.1.

These basic formulas evolve from the illustration:

Made = Paid × Rate
Paid = Made ÷ Rate
Rate = Made ÷ Paid

In any problem involving these formulas, one quantity will be unknown and you must determine from the given information whether you must multiply or divide the others to compute the third variable.

To assist in this process, Table 6.4 equates various real estate terms with the three terms shown in Figure 6.1.

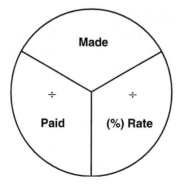

Figure 6.1

TABLE 6.4

Amount Made	Amount Paid	Rate (%)
1. Income (earned per year)	Amount of investment	Percentage return
2. Sales commission	Selling price	Rate of commission
3. Documentary transfer tax	Taxable equity	Transfer tax rate
4. Monthly rent	Investment amount	Rate of return
5. Annual net income	Property value	Capitalization rate
6. Interest	Principal	Rate × Time
7. Discount amount	Loan balance	Rate of discount
8. Area of property	Length	Width

If the terms in the problem relate to those in Table 6.4, substitute the amounts in the problem into any one of the three formulas previously given, depending on what is to be determined.

Investment Problems

To find the amount of money to be invested when the income and rate of return are known:

$$\text{Amount of investment (paid)} = \frac{\text{Income (made)}}{\text{Rate (\% of return)}}$$

To find the rate (%) of return when the income and the amount invested are known:

$$\text{Rate (\%)} = \frac{\text{Income (made)}}{\text{Amount invested (paid)}}$$

To find the income when the amount invested and the rate (%) are known:

$$\text{Income (made)} = \text{Amount invested (paid)} \times \text{Rate (\%)}$$

Sample investment problems using the preceding formulas follow.

Caution: When you are given monthly figures, always convert them to annual figures (for example, $80 per month × 12 = $960 per year).

PROBLEM 1　If an investor wants to earn $50 per month from a savings account and the account pays 5% simple interest, how much must be put in the account?

The given variables are:

Income = $600 per year ($50 × 12 months)
Rate of return = 5%

The unknown variable is the amount of investment. By substituting in the formula, we obtain:

$$\text{Amount} = \frac{\$600}{5\% \text{ or } .05} \qquad 05\overline{)600.00}^{\,12,000}$$

Amount of investment = $12,000

PROBLEM 2　An investor bought a small lot for $45,000. Assume the lot was later listed for sale and sold for $60,000. What is the rate (%) of profit the investor made on this sale?

The given variables are:

Paid = $45,000
Made = $15,000 ($60,000 − $45,000)

The unknown variable is the rate of profit. By substituting in the formula, we obtain:

$$45000\overline{)15000.00}^{\,.33 \text{ or } 33\%}$$

Discounting Notes

PROBLEM 3　A $5,000 note to a private lender is to be paid off in 12 months. The borrower is to pay the $5,000 plus 8% interest on the due date. An investor purchases the note today at a discount rate of 10%. What is the investor's rate of return on the amount invested?

The first step is to determine the amount made.

Paid × Rate = Made

By substituting in the formula, we obtain:
$5000 × .08 = $400 (interest to the lender on due date)
$5000 × .10 = $500 (discount allowed investor)
Made = $900 ($400 + $500)
Paid = $5,000 less 10% or $4,500

The given variables are:

Made = $900
Paid = $4,500

The unknown variable is the rate (%).

Made ÷ Paid = Rate

Substitution results in:

$$\frac{.20 \text{ or } 20\%}{4500 \overline{)900.00}}$$

Rate or percentage of profit = .20, or 20%

Appraisal Problems In appraisal problems, use the formula:

Paid × Rate (%) = Made

Reconstructed, the choices become:

1. Value of property × Capitalization rate = Net income or net loss
2. Value = Made ÷ Rate (capitalization rate)
3. Capitalization rate = Made ÷ Paid (value of property)
4. Income or loss = Paid × Capitalization rate

PROBLEM 4 A triplex nets an income of $500 per month per apartment unit. A prospective investor is interested in purchasing the property, and he or she demands an investment rate (capitalization rate) of 9%. What is the maximum the investor should pay for the triplex?

$500 per unit × 3 units = $1,500 net income per month
$1,500 × 12 months = $18,000 annual net income

The given variables are:

Made = $18,000
Rate = 9%

The unknown variable is the paid. Substitution in the formula results in:

$$\frac{200,000}{.09\overline{)18000.00}}$$

The investor should pay no more than $200,000.

PROBLEM 5   An investor pays $400,000 for an older six-unit apartment house that has a gross income of $550 rent per month per unit with total expenses of $3,600 per year. What capitalization rate (%) will the investor make on the purchase price?

Gross income = 12 months × 550   = $6,600 × 6 units
                                  = $39,600
Less expenses   − 3,600
Net Income (made) $36,000

By substituting in the formula:

$$\frac{.09}{400,000\overline{)36000.00}}$$

The capitalization rate = 9%.

Commission Problems

In commission problems:

Paid figure refers to the selling price.
Rate is the commission rate.
Made is the amount of commission.

PROBLEM 6   A real estate salesperson found a buyer for a $300,000 home. The seller agreed to pay a 6% commission on the sale to the broker. The broker pays the salesperson 40% of the commission. What is the salesperson's commission?

The unknown variable is the made. Substitution in the formula results in:

Paid = $300,000 (selling price)
Rate = 40% of 6%
Made (commission) = Paid (selling price) × Rate

$300,000 $18,000
  × .06   × .40
  $18,000 Total commission $7,200 Salesperson's
                                     commission

The amount of the salesperson's share of the commission is $7,200.

PROBLEM 7 A real estate office listed a parcel of land for $800,000 with an agreed commission of 10%. The broker presents an offer for 10% less than the listed price, which the seller agreed to accept if the broker would reduce the amount of commission by 25%. If the broker agrees to the reduction, what will be the amount of the commission?

The missing variable is the made.

Paid = $800,000 less 10% ($80,000) = $720,000
Rate = 10% less 25% = 7½% or (.075)

Substitution in the formula results in:

Made (commission) = Paid (selling price) × Rate

$800,000	.100	$720,000
− 80,000	−.025	× .075
$720,000	.075	$54,000

The amount of commission = $54,000.

There are a variety of commission splits in actual practice.

A broker could take a listing, make the sale, and receive the entire commission. Possibly, one or more salespersons in a broker's office could be involved; if so, the salespeople would divide the commission with the broker.

A listing may be taken by Broker A and be placed in multiple listing. If the sale was made by Broker B, he or she would split the commission with Broker A's office. One of Broker B's salespersons may make the sale. If so, the salesperson would split the office's share of the commission with Broker B.

Commission splits between multiple listing brokers vary, with 50/50 being the most common. In some cases this split could be 40% to the listing broker's office and 60% to the selling broker's office.

When the listing and the sale are in-house, the splits might be:

20% to the listing salesperson
40% to the salesperson making the sale
40% to the broker

OR

35% to the listing salesperson
35% to the salesperson making the sale
30% to the broker

The amount of the commission split depends on the individual broker's commission schedule. An example of a possible commission split between real estate brokers and salespersons might be as follows: Assume that $70,000 is the sales price for a rural home, and the seller agreed to pay a 6% commission. Then 6% × $70,000 = $4,200 commission. The $4,200 commission might be divided up between brokers and salespeople as shown in Figure 6.2.

Interest and Loan Problems

Interest is the charge for the use of money. The dollar amount of interest is determined by the rate of interest charged and the amount of money borrowed. When borrowing money, the borrower is obligated to pay back the amount borrowed as well as interest per agreed terms between the borrower and the lender.

> Note: In working with interest problems, it is very important to convert monthly figures to annual figures.

To solve interest problems, you will use these terms and formula.

Interest is the charge for the use of money expressed as dollars.
Principal is the amount of money borrowed.
Rate is the percentage of interest charged on the principal.

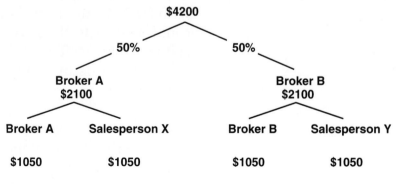

Figure 6.2

Time represents the interval between payments on principal and/or interest. In the formula it is expressed as years or a fraction of a year. Interest = Principal × Rate × Time $(I = P \times R \times T)$

By applying this formula to our standard made, paid, rate formula, the paid figure refers to the amount of the loan or the principal, rate (%) is the rate of interest multiplied by the years or fraction of a year, and made is the amount of interest expressed in money. The following formulas are therefore derived:

$$\text{Amount of loan} = \frac{\text{Amount of interest}}{\text{Rate of interest} \times \text{time}} \text{ or } P = \frac{I}{R \times T}$$

$$\text{Rate of interest} = \frac{\text{Amount of interest}}{\text{Amount of loan} \times \text{time}} \text{ or } R = \frac{I}{P \times T}$$

$$\text{Amount of interest} = \text{Amount of loan} \times \text{Rate of interest} \times \text{Time or } I = P \times R \times T$$

PROBLEM 8 If you borrowed $8,000 for one year and paid $640 interest, what rate of interest did you pay?

The known variables are:

Paid = $8,000
Made = $640 × 1 year = $640 per year

Substitution results in:

$$\text{Rate} = \text{Made} \div \text{Paid or } \frac{I}{P \times T}$$

$$\overset{.08}{\$8000\overline{)640.00}} \quad \text{or} \quad \frac{640}{8000 \times 1}$$

PROBLEM 9 If one month's interest is $45 on a seven-year straight note (interest-only note) and the note calls for interest at 9% per year, what is the amount of the loan?

The known variables are:

Rate = 9%
Made = $45 × 12 months = $540 interest per year

Substitution in the formula results in:

Paid = Made ÷ Rate

$$\begin{array}{r} 6000. \\ .09\overline{)540.00} \end{array}$$ Proof: $\begin{array}{r} \$6{,}000 \text{ Principal} \\ \underline{\times .09} \text{ Rate} \\ \$540.00 \text{ Interest paid for year} \end{array}$

Cost and Selling Price Problems

In dealing with cost problems you are given a selling price and are asked to calculate the profit, or the cost before a fixed profit.

The first step is to consider the cost figure as 100%. Next, add the profit percent to the 100% and then divide the total percentage into the selling price.

PROBLEM 10

A person sold a rural cabin for $60,000, which allowed her to make a 20% profit. What did she pay for the property?

Substitution in the formula results in:

Cost = Selling price ÷ (Profit % + 100%)

$$\text{Cost} = 1.20\overline{)60{,}000.00}^{\,50{,}000}$$

She paid $50,000 for the property.

PROBLEM 11

Another problem arises when the seller receives a given net amount, and you are asked to establish the selling price or amount of the loan.

For instance, you offer your lot for sale asking for a certain net amount. A broker who found a buyer gave you a check for $37,600. The broker had already deducted a 6% commission. What did the lot sell for?

The formula used to solve this problem is:

$$\text{Selling price} = \frac{\text{Net amount received}}{100\% - \text{Commission rate}}$$

Substitution in this formula results in:

Selling price = $37,600 ÷ (100% − 6%) or 94%

$$\text{Selling price} = .94\overline{)37{,}600.00}^{\,40{,}000}$$

6.3 SQUARE FOOTAGE AND AREA CALCULATION

Problems related to square footage are simple. This technique is used when you desire to know the number of square feet in a property. Once you have determined the square footage, you can then refer to an index on residential property to determine the cost per square foot or obtain estimates per square foot from local contractors. The cost per square foot multiplied by the square footage gives an estimated new construction cost of a building.

The basic formula for determining the area of a piece of property is:

Area = Length × Width

In Figure 6.3 we substitute these terms in our basic symbol.

The following formulas can be used:

Area = Length × Width
Length = Area ÷ Width
Width = Area ÷ Length

PROBLEM 12   What would be the depth, or length, of a piece of vacant land containing six acres, with a width, or front footage, of 400 feet on a county road? (Remember there are 43,560 square feet in an acre.)

Convert the piece of property into square feet by multiplying 43,560 by 6 = 261,360 square feet.

Substitution in the formula results in:

Length = Area ÷ Width
Length = 261,360 ÷ 400 = 653.4 feet
Proof: 400 feet × 653.4 feet = 261,360 square feet

If the piece of property you are measuring is irregular in shape, try to make rectangles and triangles of the area given. (The area of a triangle = altitude × base ÷ 2.) An example of this type of computation is given in Problem 13.

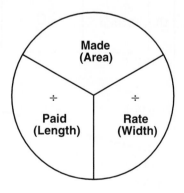

Figure 6.3

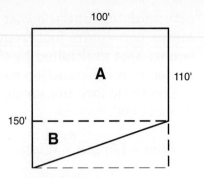

Figure 6.4

PROBLEM 13   Use Figures 6.4 and 6.5 and (a) compute the square footage of the lot, then (b) find the total construction cost of the garage and house. Assume contractors are quoting $30 per square foot for garages and $75 per square foot for homes.

Insert dotted lines in the diagram in order to form a rectangle A and a triangle B.

1. Compute the area in rectangle A as follows: $110 \times 100 = 11,000$ square feet.
2. Compute the area of the triangle B as follows: $40 \times 100 \div 2 = 2,000$ square feet.

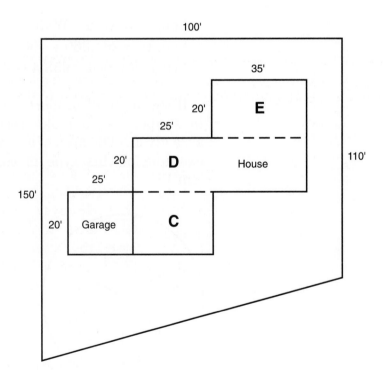

Figure 6.5

Thus the size of the lot is: 11,000 + 2,000 = 13,000 square feet

To figure the area in the house:

1. Place dotted lines as indicated in the diagram, thus forming three rectangles, C, D, E, in the house.
2. Compute the area of each rectangle as follows:
   Rectangle C = 25 × 20 = 500 square feet
   Rectangle D = 60 × 20 = 1,200 square feet
   Rectangle E = 20 × 35 = 700 square feet
   Total = 2,400 square feet in house
3. Compute the area of the garage as follows: 20 × 25 = 500 square feet
4. Compute the costs as follows:
   2,400 square feet × $75 per square foot   = $180,000
   500 square feet × $30 per square foot   =   <u>$ 15,000</u>
                                Total = $195,000

Answers

(a) 13,000 square feet in the lot
(b) $195,000 cost of construction for the total improvements

6.4 PRORATIONS

Ownership of real property entails certain expenses. Some of these expenses are paid in advance, others in arrears. They may be paid for by the seller prior to the sale of the property, or the buyer may assume costs owed by the seller at the close of escrow.

It is only fair that expenses paid in advance should be credited (allocated) to the seller, and the buyer debited (charged); and by the same token, expenses owed by the seller and not paid by the seller prior to the close of escrow, but to be paid later by the buyer, should be debited to the seller and credited to the buyer.

Proration is the act of making an equitable distribution of these expenses in escrow at the close of the sale.

There are four basic steps in proration:

1. Determine the number of days to be prorated.
2. Tabulate the cost per day.
3. Multiply the number of days by the cost per day.

4. Determine whether the amount should be a credit or a debit to the seller or to the buyer.

> **Remember:** For simplicity in determining prorations assume that there are 30 days in a month and 360 days in the year.

Expenses that are normally subject to proration are real property taxes and assessments, interest on loans assumed, hazard insurance, and prepaid rents, if the property is income producing.

PROBLEM 14 Ms. A sells her home on September 1, 2000. She has an existing loan of $100,000 on the house. The interest on the loan is 9%. Buyer B assumes Ms. A's loan with interest paid to August 15, 2000. The buyer also assumes an existing three-year hazard insurance policy for $360 per year, paid by Ms. A until October 15, 2001. Ms. A also neglected to pay her property taxes of $1,800 for the year. What is the interest proration, and who is credited or debited? What is the insurance proration, and who is credited or debited? What is the tax proration, and who is credited or debited?

To figure the proration on the interest:

Step 1. August 15 to September 1 = 15 days

Step 2. $100,000 × 9% ÷ 360 = $25 per day

Step 3. 15 days × $25 per day = $375 interest

Step 4. Credit the buyer and debit the seller

To figure the proration on the insurance policy:

Step 1. September 1, 2000, through October 15, 2001 = 405 days

Step 2. $360 ÷ 360 = $1.00 per day

Step 3. 405 days × $1.00 = $405

Step 4. Credit the seller and debit the buyer

To figure the tax proration:

Step 1. July 1 to September 1 = 60 days

Step 2. $1,800 ÷ 360 = $5.00 per day

Step 3. 60 days × $5.00 = $300

Step 4. Debit the seller and credit the buyer

> **Note:** A general rule to use in proration is as follows: When expenses are paid beyond escrow, credit the seller and debit the buyer. When expenses are paid short of escrow, debit the seller and credit the buyer.

6.5 DOCUMENTARY TRANSFER TAX

When real property is transferred, state law allows the county recorder to apply a documentary transfer tax. The amount of the tax is placed on the deed and is computed based on the following schedule:

1. $1.10 for $1,000 of value transferred, or $0.55 for every $500 or fraction thereof.
2. When the terms of the sale are all cash, the documentary transfer tax is paid on the entire sales price. A new loan by the buyer is treated the same as an all-cash sale.
3. When the buyer assumes the seller's existing loan, the amount of the loan on property is exempt and is subtracted from the total selling price, and the tax is computed only on the equity amount. The transfer tax can be paid by either the buyer or seller, but custom usually has the seller pay the tax.

In some areas, cities are allowed to levy a real estate transfer tax on top of this statewide documentary tax. These transfer taxes are not standardized and will vary from city to city and are not presented in this book.

PROBLEM 15

A home is sold for $210,000. The buyer puts some cash down and obtains new financing for the balance of the sales price. What is the documentary transfer tax?

$$\frac{\$210,000}{1,000} = 210 \times \$1.10 = \$231 \text{ Documentary transfer tax}$$

PROBLEM 16

A one-bedroom condo is sold for $87,500, but in this case the buyer assumes the seller's existing $50,000 loan. What is the documentary transfer tax?

$87,500 Sales price
$- 50,000$ Existing loan assumed
$37,500 Equity transferred

$$\frac{\$37,500}{1,000} = 37.5 \times \$1.10 = \$41.25 \text{ Documentary transfer tax}$$

6.6 USE OF FINANCIAL TABLES

In order to facilitate mathematical computations, shortcut financial tables have been devised.

Interest Computation

We previously discussed how to compute the amount of interest to be paid using formula $I = P \times R \times T$. Also, remember it was stressed that computations are usually based on a 30-day month and 360-day year.

Let's explore an example using both the conventional method and the use of an interest table. (See Table 6.5)

TABLE 6.5 Interest Table Figured on $1,000 360 Days to the Year

Days	5%	6%	7%	8%	9%	10%
1	0.1389	0.1667	0.1944	0.2222	0.2500	0.2778
2	0.2778	0.3333	0.3889	0.4444	0.5000	0.5556
3	0.4167	0.5000	0.5833	0.6666	0.7500	0.8334
4	0.5556	0.6667	0.7778	0.8888	1.0000	1.1112
5	0.6944	0.8333	0.9722	1.1111	1.2500	1.3890
6	0.8333	1.0000	0.1667	1.3333	1.5000	1.6668
7	0.9722	1.1667	1.3611	1.5555	1.7500	1.9446
8	1.1111	1.3333	1.5556	1.7777	2.0000	2.2224
9	1.2500	1.5000	1.7500	2.0000	2.2500	2.5002
10	1.3889	1.6667	1.9444	2.2222	2.5000	2.7780
11	1.5278	1.8333	2.1389	2.4444	2.7500	3.0558
12	1.6667	2.0000	2.3333	2.6666	3.0000	3.3336
13	1.8056	2.1667	2.5278	2.8888	3.2500	3.6114
14	1.9444	2.3333	2.7222	3.1111	3.5000	3.8892
15	2.0833	2.5000	2.9167	3.3333	3.7500	4.1670
16	2.2222	2.6667	3.1111	3.5555	4.0000	4.4448
17	2.3611	2.8333	3.3055	3.7777	4.2500	4.7226
18	2.5000	3.0000	3.5000	4.0000	4.5000	5.0004
19	2.6389	3.1667	3.6944	4.2222	4.7500	5.2782
20	2.7778	3.3333	3.8889	4.4444	5.0000	5.5560
21	2.9167	3.5000	4.0833	4.6666	5.2500	5.8338
22	3.0556	3.6667	4.2778	4.8888	5.5000	6.1116
23	3.1944	3.8333	4.4722	5.1111	5.7500	6.3894
24	3.2222	4.0000	4.6667	5.3333	6.0000	6.6672
25	3.4722	4.1667	4.8611	5.5555	6.2500	6.9450
26	3.6111	4.3333	5.0555	5.7777	6.5000	7.2228
27	3.7500	4.5000	5.2500	6.0000	6.7500	7.5006
28	3.8889	4.6667	5.4444	6.2222	7.0000	7.7784
29	4.0278	4.8333	5.6389	6.4444	7.2500	8.0562
30	4.1667	5.0000	5.8333	6.6666	7.5000	8.3340
31st day						

PROBLEM 17 What is the interest on a $6,500 loan for one year, three months, and 20 days at 9% interest?

Conventional Method $P \times R \times T = I$

Principal is $6,500
Rate is 9%
Time is 470 days (1 year + 3 months + 20 days)

Thus:

$$\$6{,}500 \times .09 \times 1.3056 \ \left(\frac{470}{360}\right) = \begin{array}{l} \$763.75 \text{ (approximate)} \\ \$763.78 \text{ (actual)} \end{array}$$

Use of Interest Table 1 year and 3 months = 15 months

Under the 9% column in Table 6.5, the 30-day factor = 7.5000

15 months × 7.5000 = 112.50 + the 20-day factor of 5.00 = 117.50

$117.50 × 6.5 (number of thousands in $6,500) = $763.75

Amortization Tables Amortization tables are used to compute monthly payments for various loan amounts at various interest rates and terms. A typical table showing various rates of interest and length of loans (called term) is shown in Table 6.6.

A typical table shows along one axis a list of various loan terms expressed in years and along the other axis various amounts of interest. At the intersection of any two axes in the table itself is found the monthly payment to pay off $1,000 in dollars and cents at various interest rates.

TABLE 6.6 **Table of Monthly Payments to Amortize $1,000 Loan**

Term of Years	6%	7%	8%	9%	10%	11%	12%
10	11.11	11.62	12.14	12.67	13.22	13.78	14.35
15	8.44	8.99	9.56	10.15	10.75	11.37	12.00
20	7.17	7.76	8.37	9.00	9.66	10.32	11.01
25	6.45	7.07	7.72	8.40	9.09	9.80	10.53
30	6.00	6.66	7.34	8.05	8.78	9.52	10.29
40	5.51	6.22	6.96	7.71	8.49	9.28	10.09

PROBLEM 18   A $100,000 loan for 30 years at 10% interest will have what monthly payment? To solve this problem by using an amortization table, use the following procedure:

Go to the 10% interest column in Table 6.6, and follow it down to the 30-year line. There you will find the factor 8.78. This means $8.78 per month will pay off $1,000 in 30 years. Our loan amount is $100,000; therefore:

$$\frac{\$100,000}{\$1,000} = 100$$

Thus, $100 \times \$8.78 = \$878$ per month, which will pay off a $100,000 loan at 10% in 30 years.

PROBLEM 19   If an individual made payments of $1,234.60 per month including 9% on a fully amortized 30-year loan, what was the original amount of the loan?

In Table 6.6, the point where the 30-year line intersects with the 9% interest line is $8.05 for a $1,000 loan.

$1,234.60 ÷ 8.05 = 153.37 × 1,000 = $153,366 loan
(approximate)

PROBLEM 20   If you borrowed $48,000 using a fully amortized home equity loan and were to make payments of $495.45, including 11% interest, how many years would it take to pay off the loan?

Solution:
Reduce $495.45 to the amount of each payment per $1,000 as follows:

$495.45 ÷ 48 = $10.32

Using the 11% interest column in Table 6.6, locate the amount $10.32. This amount falls on the 20-year loan term line. It will take approximately 20 years to pay off the $48,000 loan.

PROBLEM 21   If an individual borrowed $76,000 using a fully amortized second home loan, payable $782.04 per month including interest, for a period of 30 years, what would be the rate of interest?

<u>Solution</u>:
Divide $782.04 by 76 to determine the amount of each payment per $1,000:

$782.04 ÷ 76 = $10.29

Using Table 6.6, the intersection of the 30-year line and the $10.29 = 12% interest rate.

CHAPTER SUMMARY

In this chapter we have laid the foundation for real estate mathematics by discussing the basic computations using decimals and fractions when adding, subtracting, multiplying, and dividing.

In most real estate transactions there are three variables—two of these will be given and you will be asked to solve for the third. Three formulas can be used to solve many real estate problems.

Made = Paid × Rate (%)
Rate = Made ÷ Paid
Paid = Made ÷ Rate

In this chapter problems related to investments, discounting notes, appraisal, commissions, interest and loans, cost and selling price problems, and square footage and area problems were presented. Prorations and the documentary transfer taxes were computed.

As an aid to rapid calculation, interest tables, amortization tables, and financial pocket calculators can reduce the time needed to determine a correct answer.

IMPORTANT TERMS AND CONCEPTS

Amortization table	Documentary transfer tax
Capitalization rate	Interest = Principal × Rate × Time
Commission split	Principal
Decimals	Proration

PRACTICAL APPLICATION

1. You are thinking about buying a property that is listed for $300,000. The seller has owned the property for three years and you are curious as to what the seller originally paid for the property. The seller's deed in the county recorder's office shows a Documentary Transfer Tax of $244.75 based on an all-cash sale price. How much did the seller pay for the property? If you buy the property for $300,000, not counting closing cost, what percentage profit will the seller make?

2. The N ½, and the NW ¼ of the SW ¼ of Section 9 are sold for $5,000 per acre. The commission rate is 10% with Broker A getting 50% and Broker B 50%. You work as a salesperson for Broker B who agrees to give you 60% for your sales effort. How much commission did you earn?

3. A 2,000-square-foot home with a 500-square-foot garage can be built for $80 per square foot for the home and $30 per square foot for the garage. Other improvements, including the land, will cost $60,000. If the contractor wishes to resell the home for a 20% profit, what should be the resale price?

REVIEWING YOUR UNDERSTANDING

Note: Some of the problems will require use of the tables presented in Chapter 6.

1. An investor is thinking about purchasing an older four-unit apartment. Each unit rented for $600 per month, with a vacancy factor of 5% and operating expenses of $8,000 annually. To realize a capitalization rate of 10%, how much should the investor pay for the property?
   a. $127,500
   b. $105,000
   c. $179,300
   d. $193,600

2. Ms. B sold her vacant lot for $63,000. This was 20% more than she paid. The commission to the broker and other selling costs amounted to 6% of the selling price. How much was her profit?
   a. $12,600
   b. $6,720
   c. $15,250
   d. $5,250

3. Mr. A wishes to place a lump sum into a savings account that will pay 6% interest. He hopes to earn $150 in monthly interest. To realize this monthly interest income, how much must he deposit?
   a. $15,000
   b. $9,000
   c. $25,000
   d. $30,000

4. Ms. Jones purchased a small home for $70,000; she assumed an existing loan for $40,000. The seller agrees to pay the documentary transfer tax. What is the tax?
   a. $77.00
   b. $33.00
   c. $45.00
   d. $154.00

5. Mr. and Mrs. Chu paid their annual property taxes of $720. They sold their home on April 1. On the settlement sheet, what entry would be made?
   a. Debit the seller $180
   b. Credit the seller $240
   c. Credit the buyer $180
   d. Credit the seller $180

6. Mr. Brown sold his rural cabin for $60,000. He purchased it one year ago for $40,000. What percentage gross profit did he realize on the sale?
   a. 66½%
   b. 50%
   c. 33⅓%
   d. 48%

7. Broker Santos listed a home and the seller agreed to pay a 6% commission. If the commission amounted to $18,000, what was the listing price?
   a. $108,000
   b. $195,000
   c. $300,000
   d. $405,000

8. If you were to borrow $42,000 and make fully amortized payments for 15 years including 9% interest, using the amortization table what would be your monthly payments?

   a. $426.30

   b. $10.15

   c. $375.20

   d. $315.00

9. If you owned a four-acre parcel of land and wished to divide it into eight equal lots each 400 feet deep, what would be the width of each lot?

   a. 55.40 feet

   b. 54.45 feet

   c. 435.6 feet

   d. 45.54 feet

10. A payment of $840 per month principal and interest is made on a $66,000 loan, which includes interest at 10%. How much of the payment is principal the first month?

   a. $550

   b. $100

   c. $95

   d. $290

11. A 1,920-square-foot home can be built for $80 per square foot. The 425-square-foot garage can be built for $29 per square foot. The 8,000-square-foot lot sells for $15 per square foot. What will the entire property cost?

   a. $285,925

   b. $244,325

   c. $237,600

   d. $226,890

12. A $425,000 amortized loan at 10% interest, payable at $3,861.98 per month, will take approximately how long to pay off?

   a. 15 years

   b. 20 years

   c. 25 years

   d. 30 years

13. A commercial property generates $60,000 net income, and prevailing capitalization rates in the market are 9.75%. What is the maximum price that should be paid for this property? (Round answer to the nearest $1,000.)

   a. $600,000

   b. $605,000

   c. $610,000

   d. $615,000

14. Broker A employs Salesperson B under the following terms: In-house sales shall be split 20/40/40. Salesperson B, who did not list the property, finds a buyer for Broker A's listing at a price of $179,500. The seller agrees to pay a 7% commission. What will be Salesperson B's share?
    a. $12,250
    b. $7,350
    c. $5,026
    d. $2,450

15. A buyer offers to purchase a home for $225,000 and applies for a 90% loan at 10% interest-only payments, all due in 30 years. If granted, what will be the monthly loan payments?
    a. $1,975.50
    b. $1,875.00
    c. $1,777.95
    d. $1,687.50

16. You are trying to figure out what a person paid for a home. The deed in the courthouse shows a county documentary transfer tax of $206.25 based on the full cash price. The estimated purchase price of the home is:
    a. $187,500
    b. $206,250
    c. $226,875
    d. $319,680

17. A one-fifth-acre parcel sold for $13 per square foot. The commission was 9%. The salesperson received a 50% split. How much did the salesperson receive? (Round answer to nearest dollar.)
    a. $6,371
    b. $5,097
    c. $4,113
    d. $3,987

18. Escrow closed 9/10/99. The buyer's first payment on the $150,000 purchase money loan at 9% amortized for 30 years is due 10/1/99. The lender wants 20 days' worth of interest paid by the buyer in escrow as a closing cost. The interest on the buyer's closing statement is:
    a. $750 and will show as a credit
    b. $750 and will show as a debit
    c. $805 and will show as a credit
    d. $805 and will show as a debit

19. A buyer purchases a home for $127,000, putting 10% down and obtaining a new first loan for 80% at 9% amortized for 30 years. The seller carries a 10% second loan at 10% amortized for 20 years. The buyer's total monthly loan payments will be approximately:
    a. $1,217
    b. $1,146
    c. $941
    d. $893

20. A large apartment building loan of $2,500,000 at 9% amortized for 30 years will have how much interest allocated in the first payment?

  a. $225,000

  b. $20,125

  c. $19,375

  d. $18,750

Chapter 7

Introduction to Real Estate Finance

Chapter Preview   This chapter stresses the legal aspects of real estate finance. At the conclusion of the chapter, you will be able to:

1. Describe two types of promissory notes and then explain adjustable rate loans

2. Explain deeds of trust (trust deeds) and installment sales contracts, and describe the foreclosure process (trustee's sale)

3. Define acceleration, alienation, subordination, and prepayment penalty clauses

4. Outline the principles of the Real Property Loan Law and truth-in-lending regulations

7.1 REAL ESTATE FINANCING INSTRUMENTS   Access to money and credit is the key factor in most real estate transactions. Real estate is expensive, and few people ever accumulate enough savings to pay all cash for property. Therefore, the completion of a real estate sale hinges upon the buyer's ability to obtain financing. Even people who have sufficient funds rarely pay cash for real estate. Income tax deductions and an investment concept called leverage (see this chapter's appendix) in some cases favor purchasing real estate with borrowed funds. Thus, whether by necessity or by choice, financing is essential for most real estate transactions.

Real Estate Financing Process

Real estate financing usually involves five phases: (1) application, (2) analysis, (3) processing, (4) closing, and (5) servicing. (See Figure 7.1.)

The lending process begins by having the prospective borrower complete a lender's loan application form. A loan application form requests information about the borrower's financial status, such as level and consistency of income, personal assets, existing debts, and current expenses. The loan application form also asks for data concerning the property, including its location, its age, and the size of the lot and any existing improvements.

Once the application is completed, the lender reviews the form and uses it as a screening device to determine if the prospective borrower and the subject property appear to meet the lender's requirements. If it becomes obvious that the borrower or the property are unacceptable for a loan, the lender informs the applicant. If it appears that both the borrower and the property might be acceptable, the analysis phase begins.

Analysis involves an in-depth appraisal of the property and a professionally compiled credit report on the prospective borrower. After the appraisal and credit report are completed, and assuming that both are favorable, the lender then presents the terms and cost of financing to the borrower. The borrower may accept, reject, or attempt to negotiate the financing terms with the lender. Assuming that an agreement is reached, the processing phase begins.

Processing involves drawing up loan papers, preparing disclosure forms regarding loan costs, and issuing instructions for the escrow and title insurance company. Each lender establishes its own processing pattern in view of its special in-house needs.

Once the loan package has been processed, the closing phase begins. Closing the loan involves signing all loan papers and then, in conjunction with the other terms of the

REAL ESTATE FINANCING PROCESS

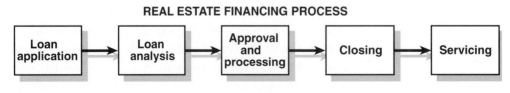

Figure 7.1

sale, transferring the property. In Southern California, an independent escrow company, the escrow department of a title company, or, in some cases, the lender handles the entire escrow. In much of northern California, after the loan papers have been signed, they are usually forwarded to the escrow department of a title insurance company, which closes the sale.

After the title has been transferred and the escrow is closed, the loan servicing phase begins. Loan servicing refers to the record-keeping process once the loan has been placed. Many lenders do their own servicing, while others pay independent mortgage companies to handle the paperwork. The goal of loan servicing is to see that the lender makes the expected yield on the loan by promptly collecting and processing the loan payments with minimum cost.

Promissory Notes

When money is borrowed to purchase real estate, the borrower agrees to repay the loan by signing a *promissory* note, which outlines the terms of repayment and sets the due date. The promissory note is legal evidence that a debt is owed. The two types of promissory notes in general use are the *straight* note and the *installment* note.

Straight Note

The straight note is frequently referred to as an "interest-only" note. Under a straight note the borrower agrees to pay the interest, usually monthly, and to pay the entire principal in a lump sum on the due date. For example, if you borrow $100,000 for 30 years at a 10% interest rate using a straight note, the monthly payments would be $833.33 per month. The $833.33 payments cover just the monthly interest. Thus, 30 years hence, on the due date, you must pay back the entire $100,000 principal. In other words, the payments were only large enough to cover the monthly interest and did not reduce the $100,000 principal. (Proof: $100,000 × 10% = $10,000 ÷ 12 months = $833.33 per month.)

Installment Note

The second and by far the most common type of real estate promissory note is the installment note. *An installment note requires payments that include both principal and interest.* If you borrow $100,000 for 30 years at 10% interest payable at $877.57 per month including both principal and interest, you will find that at the end of 30 years the entire debt is liquidated. Each monthly payment of $877.57 includes not only the monthly interest due, but also reduces a portion of the $100,000 principal. By the time the due date arrives 30 years hence, the entire principal has been paid back. *An installment loan that includes principal and interest of equal installment payments that liquidate the debt is called a fully amortized loan.* Under a fully amortized loan there is no large balloon payment on the due date of the loan as the loan is completely paid off.

One variation of the installment note is to have monthly payments that are large enough to pay the monthly interest and reduce some of the principal, but the monthly principal portion is not sufficient to entirely liquidate the debt by the due date. Thus, on the due date the remaining unpaid principal must be paid in a lump sum, often referred to as a *balloon payment.* (Any payment more than double the normal amount is called a balloon payment.) One hundred thousand dollars for 30 years at 10% interest, payable at $850 per month, would require a balloon payment of $62,325.20 on the due date. Why? Because the $850 per month was enough to cover the monthly interest ($833.33), but it was not enough to cover the monthly interest and all of the monthly principal (that would have taken $877.57 per month). Thus, the difference over the 30-year life of the loan comes to $62,325.20, which must be paid on the due date in the form of a balloon payment. Loan payments and balloon payments can be calculated using financial tables or financial calculators. Figure 7.2 is an example of an installment note.

Adjustable Rate Loans

Most real estate lenders will allow a borrower to choose either a fixed interest rate or an adjustable rate loan. The *fixed interest rate* is the traditional real estate loan where the interest rate does not change over the life of the loan. Under the *adjustable rate* plan, the rate may move up or down. Therefore, your monthly payment may decrease or increase over the life of the loan.

HOW DOES IT WORK?

Adjustable rate loans, usually called adjustable rate mortgages (ARMs), have the following characteristics:

1. They are usually offered at a lower initial interest rate than traditional fixed interest rate loans.
2. Once the initial interest rate is established, the rate is tied to some neutral index, which is beyond the control of the lender or the borrower.
3. The index is usually a government index. Examples are: One-year Treasury Spot index, the Treasury 12-month Average index, or the 11th District Cost-of-

Do Not Destroy This Original Note: When paid the Original Note, together with the Deed of Trust securing same, must be surrendered to Trustee for cancellation and retention before reconveyance will be made.

NOTE SECURED BY DEED OF TRUST

(INSTALLMENT - INTEREST INCLUDED)

$__________ ____________________, California, ________________, 19___

In installments as herein stated, for value received, I promise to pay to

or order at ____________________________________
the sum of ________________________________ DOLLARS,
with interest from ________________________ on unpaid principal at the rate of
__________________ per cent per annum; principal and interest payable in installments of
____________________________________ Dollars
or more on the ____________ day of each ____________ month, beginning on the
__________ day of ____________, 19___ ________________________
__________________ and continuing until said principal and interest have been paid.

Each payment shall be credited first on interest then due and the remainder on principal; and interest shall thereupon cease upon the principal so credited. In the event of any default in the payment of principal or interest as herein provided all sums so due including interest, shall bear interest at the rate set forth above, but such unpaid interest so compounded shall not exceed an amount equal to simple interest on the unpaid principal at the maximum rate permitted by law. In the event of any default in the payment of any installment of principal or interest when due the whole sum of principal and interest shall become immediately due at the option of the holder of this note. Principal and interest shall be payable in lawful money of the United States. If an action is instituted on this note, I promise to pay such sum as the Court may fix as attorney's fees. This note is secured by a DEED OF TRUST to CONTINENTAL LAWYERS TITLE COMPANY, a corporation, as Trustee.

____________________ ____________________

____________________ ____________________

TT-221 (Rev 10/88)

THIS FORM FURNISHED BY CONTINENTAL LAWYERS TITLE COMPANY

DO NOT DESTROY THIS NOTE

Figure 7.2

Funds index. Other indexes used are tied to certificate of deposit (CD) rates, prime rates, or even a European rate known as the London Interbank Offered Rate (LIBOR). The distance between the actual rate paid by the borrower and the index is called the *margin.* A typical margin is 2% to 3%.

4. Although not required, most lenders place a cap on how high the rate can climb. A typical cap is 5% or 6%; therefore, if the initial interest rate is 8%, the maximum it can rise to is 13% or 14%.

5. The adjustment period can vary, with some lenders adjusting the rate at either six-month, one-year, or three-year intervals.

6. The maximum increase or decrease per period is established in the lender's contract, with a maximum change of 1% per adjustment period being typical.

7. If the interest rate increases because of a change in the index, in some cases the borrower may have the option of: (a) increasing the monthly payment so the term of the loan remains the same, or (b) maintaining the same monthly payment and increasing the term of the loan. Usually, the maximum term to which a 30-year loan may be extended is 40 years. Once a 40-year term is reached, any increase in interest rate must increase the monthly payment. If the interest rate drops below the initial rate, the borrower can continue the existing payments (which will shorten the term) or decrease the monthly payments. However, in recent years fewer lenders are offering this feature.

8. The borrower must be notified at least 25 days prior to a change in rate.

9. Adjustable rate mortgages are sometimes assumable in that the ARM loan may not have an alienation (due-on-sale) clause.

10. Some ARMs may be negative amortized loans. This means the payments may not cover the annual interest. The unpaid interest is added to the principal, making the loan larger. This can cause some problems in later years.

11. Many lenders offer a convertible feature that allows the borrower to convert an ARM loan to a fixed interest rate loan or a fixed rate loan to an ARM. The conversion is only offered during a certain "window period," usually from the beginning of the second year through the end of the fifth year. The borrower may be required to meet

credit standards at the time of the conversion and is usually required to pay extra fees.

Other Alternative Types of Real Estate Loans

Other experimental types of loans include names like FLIP (flexible payment mortgage), GPM (graduated payment mortgage), and SAM (shared appreciation mortgage), plus many other loans called "alphabet soup" financing. The details of these alternative loan types can be found in a textbook on real estate finance, such as *California Real Estate Finance,* 6th ed., by Robert J. Bond, Alfred Gavello, and Carden Young (Upper Saddle River, N.J.: Prentice Hall, 1998).

PURPOSE OF ADJUSTABLE RATE AND OTHER ALTERNATIVE LOANS

Alternative real estate loans have been recommended by financial experts and real estate economists for many years. Here are some of the reasons.

Institutional lenders have a constant problem with cycles of tight and loose money. This unsteady flow of funds is disruptive to their operations and the housing industry. When money is tight, it flows out of saving institutions because depositors can obtain higher yields elsewhere.

Advocates of alternative loans say that this problem can be reduced by using adjustable rate mortgages. If money gets tight and interest rates rise, the savings institutions should be allowed to increase the rate they pay their depositors in order to prevent an outflow of savings. However, in order to pay higher interest on savings accounts, lenders must receive a higher interest rate on their existing loans. With an adjustable rate mortgage, lenders could increase interest rates on their existing loans when they increase the savings rate.

Another problem facing lending institutions deals with old, low fixed interest rate loans currently on the lender's books. If the current cost of money exceeds the interest rates on these older loans, the institutions are losing money on these loans. That means that the interest rate on new loans must be increased to compensate for the loss on these old loans. In effect, new borrowers are subsidizing the old borrowers. If all the borrowers were on an adjustable rate, this subsidizing process would not be as severe. Those who are opposed to alternative loans argue that lenders are merely shifting the risk of rising interest rates to the borrower.

Adjustable rate mortgages are not new. They have been used for many years in Canada and in some European countries. In California, the Cal-Vet loan program has been using adjustable rates since the program was started over 70 years ago.

Deeds of Trust To give added insurance that a borrower will repay the loan, lenders require collateral or security for the loan. To give something as security for a loan without giving possession is called *hypothecation*. A real estate lender's most logical security is real property owned or about to be acquired by the borrower. To secure an interest in the borrower's real property, lenders in California use a deed of trust (also called a trust deed).

A deed of trust is a three-party instrument consisting of a borrower (*trustor*), a lender (*beneficiary*), and a neutral third party (*trustee*). Under a deed of trust (trust deed), the trustor deeds legal title (sometimes called "naked") to the trustee, who keeps the title as security until the promissory note is repaid. Once the debt is repaid, the beneficiary (lender) orders the trustee to reconvey the title back to the trustor (borrower). If the trustor should default on the loan, the beneficiary can order the trustee to hold a trustee's sale and sell the property to obtain the cash needed to pay the loan. Figure 7.3 illustrates how title is passed between a trustor and trustee in a deed of trust and a deed of reconveyance.

In other states, frequently a mortgage is used to secure a real estate loan instead of a deed of trust. But in California, mortgages are rare—most lenders insist on deeds of trust instead. Why? Because in most cases, deeds of trust favor the lender over the borrower. If the borrower should default under a deed of trust, the lender can order the trustee to sell the property without a court proceeding, and it can be accomplished in approximately four months. Once the sale takes place, the borrower loses all rights to redeem the property.

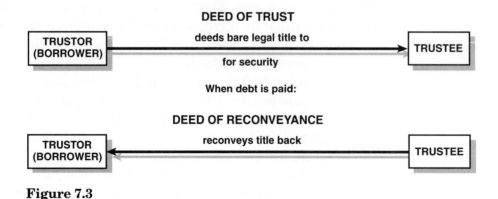

DEED OF TRUST

TRUSTOR (BORROWER) — deeds bare legal title to / for security → TRUSTEE

When debt is paid:

DEED OF RECONVEYANCE

TRUSTOR (BORROWER) ← reconveys title back — TRUSTEE

Figure 7.3

Foreclosure under a mortgage usually requires a court proceeding and can take up to one year. After the foreclosure takes place, the borrower has a one-year right of redemption. In short, most California real estate lenders prefer to use deeds of trust rather than mortgages as security instruments because foreclosure is quicker and cheaper with a deed of trust. Figure 7.4 is an example of a standard form deed of trust.

Special Clauses

In addition to repayment terms, many real estate financing instruments contain special clauses or loan conditions that the borrower and lender agree to honor. Two common clauses that appear in most promissory notes and deeds of trust are:

1. *Acceleration clause.* A clause that gives the lender the right to call all sums immediately due and payable upon the happening of certain events, such as nonpayment of monthly obligations, nonpayment of real property taxes, or willful destruction of the subject property.

2. *Alienation (due-on-sale) clause.* A specific type of acceleration clause that gives the lender the right to call the loan due and payable if the borrower conveys legal title to a new owner. After a period of controversy, the due-on-sale issue is now settled. Per federal law, effective October 15, 1985, all-due-on sale clauses are enforceable, except for transfers between spouses and family trusts.

Other major clauses, although not as common, that occasionally appear in promissory notes and deeds of trust include:

3. *Subordination clause.* A clause where the holder of the first deed of trust agrees to become a junior lien (second) to pave the way for a new first. This is most common when the holder of the first loan on vacant land agrees to allow a new construction loan to be put on record as a first deed of trust.

4. *Prepayment penalty clause.* A clause that allows a lender to charge the borrower a penalty if the loan is paid before the scheduled due date. A typical prepayment penalty is six months' interest on the amount prepaid which exceeds 20% of the original principal amount of the loan. Example: $100,000 original loan at 10% interest. Assume that two years later the loan balance is $98,000. If

AND WHEN RECORDED MAIL TO

Name

Address

City &
State

TT-272 (Rev. 7/94) Ω

SPACE ABOVE THIS LINE FOR RECORDER'S USE

DEED OF TRUST AND ASSIGNMENT OF RENTS AND REQUEST FOR SPECIAL NOTICE

APN. No.   **Title No.**   **Escrow No.**

This Deed of Trust, made this   day of   , between
herein called **Trustor**,
whose address is   and
, herein called **Beneficiary**,
whose address is
and **Continental Lawyers Title Company,** a California corporation, herein called **Trustee,**
Witnesseth: THAT TRUSTOR IRREVOCABLY GRANTS, TRANSFERS AND ASSIGNS to TRUSTEE IN TRUST, WITH POWER OF SALE, that property in   County, California, described as:

TOGETHER WITH the rents, issues and profits thereof, SUBJECT HOWEVER, to the right, power and authority given to and conferred upon Beneficiary by paragraph (11) of the provisions set forth below to collect and apply such rents, issues and profits.
For the Purpose of Securing: 1. Performance of each agreement of Trustor incorporated by reference or contained herein. 2. Payment of the indebtedness evidenced by one promissory note of even date herewith, and any extension of renewal thereof, in the principal sum of

$ executed by Trustor in favor of beneficiary or order. 3. Payment of such further sums as the then record owner of such property hereafter may borrow from Beneficiary, when evidenced by another note (or notes) reciting it is so secured.

To Protect the Security of This Deed of Trust, Trustor Agrees:

(1) That Trustor will observe and perform said provisions; and that the references to property, obligations, and parties in said provisions shall be construed to refer to the property, obligations, and parties set forth in this Deed of Trust.

(2) To keep said property in good condition and repair; not to remove or demolish any building thereon; to complete or restore promptly and in good and workmanlike manner any building which may be constructed, damaged or destroyed thereon and to pay when due all claims for labor performed and materials furnished therefor; to comply with all laws affecting said property or requiring any alterations or improvements to be made thereon, not to commit or permit waste thereof; not to commit, suffer or permit any act upon said property in violations of law; to cultivate, irrigate, fertilize, fumigate, prune and do all other acts which from the character or use of said property may be reasonably necessary, the specific enumerations herein not excluding the general.

(3) To provide, maintain and deliver to Beneficiary fire insurance satisfactory to and with loss payable to Beneficiary. The amount collected under any fire or other insurance policy may be applied by Beneficiary upon any indebtedness secured hereby and in such order as Beneficiary may determine, or at option of Beneficiary the entire amount so collected or any part thereof may be released to Trustor. Such application or release shall not cure or waive any default or notice of default hereunder or invalidate any act done pursuant to such notice.

(4) To appear in and defend any action or proceeding purporting to affect the security hereof or the rights or powers of Beneficiary or Trustee; and to pay all costs and expenses, including cost of evidence of title and attorney's fees in a reasonable sum, in any such action or proceeding in which Beneficiary or Trustee may appear, and in any suit brought by Beneficiary to foreclose this Deed.

(5) To pay: at least ten days before delinquency all taxes and assessments affecting said property, including assessments on appurtenant water stock; when due, all incumbrances, charges and liens, with interest, on said property or any part thereof, which appear to be prior or superior hereto; all costs, fees and expenses of this Trust.

Should Trustor fail to make any payment or to do any act as herein provided, then Beneficiary or Trustee, but without obligation so to do and without notice to or demand upon Trustor and without releasing Trustor from any obligation hereof, may: make or do the same in such manner and to such extent as either may deem necessary to protect the security hereof. Beneficiary or Trustee being authorized to enter upon said property for such purposes; appear in and defend any action or proceeding purporting to affect the security hereof or the rights or powers of Beneficiary or Trustee; pay, purchase, contest or compromise any encumbrance, charge or lien which in the judgment of either appears to be prior or superior hereto; and, in exercising any such powers, pay necessary expenses, employ counsel and pay his reasonable fees.

(6) To pay immediately and without demand all sums so expended by Beneficiary or Trustee, with interest from date of expenditure at the amount allowed by law in effect at the date hereof, and to pay for any statement provided for by law in effect at the date hereof regarding the obligation secured hereby any amount demanded by the Beneficiary not to exceed the maximum allowed by law at the time when said statement is demanded.

(7) That any award of damages in connection with any condemnation for public use of or injury to said property or any part thereof is hereby assigned and shall be paid to Beneficiary, who may apply or release such monies received by him in the same manner and with the same effect as above provided for disposition of proceeds of fire or other insurance.

(8) That by accepting payment of any sum secured hereby after its due date, Beneficiary does not waive his right either to require prompt payment when due of all other sums so secured or to declare default for failure so to pay.

(9) That at any time or from time to time, without liability therefor and without notice, upon written request of Beneficiary and presentation of this Deed and said note for endorsement, and without affecting the personal liability of any person for payment of the indebtedness secured hereby, Trustee may: reconvey any part of said property; consent to the making of any map or plat thereof; join in granting any easement thereon; or join in any extension agreement or any agreement subordinating the lien or charge hereof.

(10) That upon written request of Beneficiary stating that all sums secured hereby have been paid, and upon surrender of this Deed and said note to Trustee for cancellation and retention and upon payment of its fees, Trustee shall reconvey, without warranty, the property then held hereunder. The recitals in

Figure 7.4a

such reconveyance of any matters or facts shall be conclusive proof of the truthfulness thereof. the grantee in such reconveyance may be described as "The person or persons legally entitled thereto" Five years after issuance of such full reconveyance, Trustee may destroy said note and this Deed (unless directed in such request to retain them).

(11) That as additional security, Trustor hereby gives to and confers upon Beneficiary the right, power and authority, during the continuance of these Trusts, to collect the rents, issues and profits of said property, reserving unto Trustor the right, prior to any default by Trustor in payment of any indebtness secured hereby or in performance of any agreement hereunder, to collect and retain such rents, issues and profits as they become due and payable. Upon any such default, Beneficiary may at any time without notice, either in person, by agent, or by a receiver to be appointed by a court, and without regard to the adequacy of any security for the indebtness hereby secured, enter upon and take possession of said property or any part thereof, in his own name sue for or otherwise collect such rents, issues and profits, including those past due and unpaid, and apply the same, less costs and expenses of operation and collection, including reasonable attorney's fees, upon any indebtness secured hereby, and in such order as Beneficiary may determine. The entering upon and taking possession of said property, the collection of such rents, issues and profits and the application thereof as aforesaid, shall not cure or waive any default or notice of default hereunder or invalidate any act done pursuant to such notice.

(12) That upon Default by Trustor in payment of any indebtedness secured hereby or in performance of any agreement hereunder, Beneficiary may declare all sums secured hereby immediately due and payable by delivery to Trustee of written declaration of default and demand for sale and of written notice of default and of election to cause to be sold said property, which notice Trustee shall cause to be filed for record. Beneficiary also shall deposit with Trustee this Deed, said note and all documents evidencing expenditures secured hereby.

After the lapse of such time as may then be required by law following the recordation of said notice of default, and notice of sale having been given as then required by law, Trustee without demand on Trustor, shall sell said property at the time and place fixed by it in said notice of sale, either as a whole or in separate parcels, and in such order as it may determine, at public auction to the highest bidder for cash in lawful money of the United States, payable at time of sale. Trustee may postpone sale of all or any portion of said property by public announcement at such time and place of sale, and from time to time thereafter may postpone sale by public announcement at the time fixed by the preceding postponement. Trustee shall deliver to such purchaser its deed conveying the property so sold, but without any covenant or warranty, express or implied. The recitals in such deed of any matters or facts shall be conclusive proof of the truthfulness thereof. Any person, including Trustor, Trustee, or Beneficiary as hereinafter defined, may purchase at such sale.

After deducting all costs, fees and expenses of Trustee, and of this Trust, including cost of evidence of title in connection with sale, Trustee shall apply the proceeds of sale to payment of all sums expended under the terms hereof, not then repaid, with accrued interest at the amount allowed by law in effect at the date hereof; all other sums then secured hereby; and the remainder, if any, to the person or persons legally entitled thereto.

(13) Beneficiary, or any successor in ownership of any indebtedness secured hereby, may from time to time, by instrument in writing, substitute a successor or successors to any Trustee named herein or acting hereunder, which instrument, executed by the Beneficiary and duly acknowledged and recorded in the office of the recorder of the county or counties where said property is situated, shall be conclusive proof of proper substitution of such successor Trustee or Trustees, who shall, without conveyance from the Trustee predecessor, succeed to all its title, estate, rights, powers and duties. Said instrument must contain the name of the original Trustor, Trustee and Beneficiary hereunder, the book and page where this Deed is recorded and the name and address of the new Trustee.

(14) That this Deed applies to, inures to the benefit of, and binds all parties hereto, their heirs, legatees, devisees, administrators, executors, successors and assigns. The term Beneficiary shall mean the owner and holder, including pledgees, of the note secured hereby whether or not named as Beneficiary herein. In this Deed, whenever the context so requires, the masculine gender includes the feminine and/or neuter, and the singular number includes the plural.

(15) That Trustee accepts this Trust when this Deed, duly executed and acknowledged, is made a public record as provided by law. Trustee is not obligated to notify any party hereto of pending sale under any other Deed of Trust or of any action or proceeding in which Trustor, Beneficiary or Trustee shall be a party unless brought by Trustee.

The undersigned Trustor requests that a copy of any Notice of Default and of any Notice of Sale hereunder be mailed to him at his address hereinbefore set forth.

In accordance with Section 2924b, Civil Code, request is hereby made by the undersigned TRUSTOR that a copy of any notice of Default and a copy of any Notice of Sale under Deed of Trust recorded on _____ as Instrument No. _____

in Book _____ , Page _____ , of Official Records in the Office of the County Recorder of _____

as affecting above described property, executed by _____ as Trustor in which

is named _____ as Beneficiary, and _____ as Trustee,

be mailed to _____

whose address is _____

NOTICE: A copy of any Notice of Default and of any Notice of Sale will be sent to the address contained in this recorded request. If your address changes, a new request must be recorded.

Dated: _____

_____   _____

_____   _____

State of California

County of _____ } **ss.**

On_____ before me, _____ (here insert name) Notary Public,

personally appeared _____ , personally known to me

(or proved to me on the basis of satisfactory evidence) to be the person(s) whose name(s) is/are subscribed to the within instrument and acknowledged to me all that he/she/they executed the same in his/her/their authorized capacity(ies), and that by his/her/their signature(s) on the instrument the person(s), or the entity upon behalf of which the person(s) acted, executed the instrument. WITNESS my hand and official seal.

Signature _____

affix seal within border

CLT **Continental Lawyers Title Company**   Subsidiary of Lawyers Title Insurance Corporation

Figure 7.4b

the borrower pays the loan off, the penalty may be as follows:

Step 1: $100,000   Original loan amount × 20% = $20,000

Step 2: $98,000   Existing loan balance
          −20,000   Allowed to be paid
                    without penalty per Step 1
          $78,000   Subject to prepayment penalty
            ×10%   Interest rate
           $7,800   One year's interest

$7,800 ÷ 2 = $3,900 Six months' interest as prepayment penalty

However, penalties do vary with the lender. In today's real estate market most loans have no prepayment penalty. California regulations prohibit lenders from charging a prepayment penalty on owner-occupied home loans if the loan has been on the lender's books for more than five years. But if the lender is supervised by a federal agency, this California regulation will not apply. There is no prepayment penalty on FHA-insured or VA-guaranteed home loans. Technically, the Cal-Vet program has a prepayment penalty if the veteran pays off the loan in the first five years. However, Cal-Vet frequently only enforces the penalty if the loan is paid off in the first two years.

A financing instrument may contain several other special clauses depending upon the operating policies of the lender. Borrowers should carefully read all documents to make certain that they completely understand what all clauses mean. This will help to maintain harmony between the lender and the borrower during the life of the loan.

Junior Deed of Trust   Any trust deed other than a first is called a "junior deed of trust" or a "junior loan or lien." When a buyer does not have enough cash down payment to cover the gap between the sales price and the first deed of trust loan, a *junior* (or second) *deed of trust* loan is frequently carried back by the seller.

EXAMPLE.   Sales price $190,000; buyer has $30,000 cash down payment and is willing to assume the seller's existing first deed of trust bank loan of $150,000. Therefore, $150,000 + 30,000 = $180,000. The buyer is short $10,000. To cover the gap the seller agrees to carry back a $10,000

promissory note secured by a second deed of trust. This can be illustrated as follows:

$190,000   Sales price
−150,000   First deed of trust
$40,000   Required to close the sale (excluding closing costs)
−30,000   Cash down payment
$10,000   Size of second deed of trust

Homeowner equity loans are another common example of the use of junior (second) deeds of trust. Many banks and finance companies advertise their home equity loan programs, where the lender grants a loan based on the homeowner's increase in equity caused by appreciation of property values or earlier loan pay down. Home equity loans are usually secured by junior deeds of trust. Because junior trust deeds are less secure than first trust deeds, lenders usually demand a higher interest rate on home equity loans.

Taking Over a Seller's Existing Loan

The placement of a new real estate loan from an institutional lender requires the payment of loan fees, appraisal fees, credit report charges, and other loan closing costs.

In addition, the interest rate paid by the buyer is at the current prevailing market rate. If a buyer has enough cash down payment and if legally possible, it is usually cheaper to take over the seller's existing loan, rather than obtain a new loan. Many of the loan costs are avoided, and in some cases the interest rate on the seller's loan is less than the prevailing interest rates on new real estate loans.

There are two ways a buyer can take over a seller's existing loan. A buyer can *assume* a seller's existing loan, or a buyer can *purchase subject to* a seller's existing loan. When a buyer *assumes* a seller's existing loan, the buyer agrees to take over the payments and to become personally liable for the debt. But when a buyer *purchases subject to* the existing loan, the buyer agrees to take over the payments, but not the primary liability for the debt; the seller remains personally liable. This distinction becomes important if a lender should foreclose and sue for a deficiency judgment.

A *deficiency judgment* is where a lender sues a borrower after a foreclosure, when the proceeds from a foreclosure are not enough to cover the outstanding loan amount. An example would be: A real estate lender is owed $100,000;

there is a default on the loan and the lender sells the property in foreclosure sale for $90,000. The amount owed was $100,000; the proceeds from the foreclosure were only $90,000; therefore, the deficiency is $10,000.

If the lender is allowed to sue for the $10,000 deficiency, the question arises, "Who shall be sued?" The answer is, "Whoever is personally liable for the debt." If a buyer has *assumed* a seller's existing loan, the action would be brought against the buyer as he or she is personally liable. On the other hand, if a buyer *purchased subject to* a seller's existing loan, the seller is still primarily liable and the deficiency action would be brought against the seller. Deficiency judgments on owner-occupied residential dwellings are difficult to obtain in California because of special laws protecting homeowners. But deficiency judgments are obtainable on FHA-insured and VA-guaranteed home loans, because these are federally backed loans and federal law supersedes state anti-deficiency laws.

Installment Sales Contracts (Land Contracts)

Another real estate financing instrument is an installment sales contract, also called a contract of sale, or agreement of sale or land contract. An *installment sales contract* is an agreement between the seller, called the *vendor,* and the buyer, called the *vendee,* where the buyer is given possession and use of the property. In exchange for possession and use, the buyer agrees to make regular payments to the seller. Legal title to the property remains with the seller until an agreed amount has been paid, at which time the seller formally deeds title to the buyer. In essence, under an installment sales contract, the seller becomes the lender. Outside lending institutions, such as banks or mortgage companies, are not needed in such a transaction.

The lack of immediate title poses some risks for the buyer. If the seller should die, become bankrupt, or incompetent, or encumber the title during the contract, the buyer could become involved in legal entanglements.

Recent court cases have greatly restricted the ease by which a seller can remove a buyer if he or she defaults on the payments. A long, expensive court action may be needed to remove a defaulted buyer from possession. In light of the disadvantage for both the buyer and seller, installment sales contracts are no longer popular in California. They are still used on a regular basis in other states.

7.2 FORECLOSURE PROCESS—TRUSTEE'S SALE

Borrowers default on repayment of loans for a variety of reasons, usually because of events beyond their control. Financial reversals such as loss of a business or job probably head the list, but other circumstances are closely related: death, disability, bankruptcy, dissolution of marriage, drop in property values, and poor budgeting. When a borrower defaults on a real estate loan, unless arrangements can be made with the lender to work out a satisfactory schedule for repayment, foreclosure takes place. However, most lenders try to avoid foreclosure whenever possible and use it only as a last resort. Lenders are in the business of lending money and do not want to become involved in owning and managing real estate.

A borrower can be in default for reasons other than nonpayment. There could be a violation of other terms listed on the trust deed, such as failure to maintain the property or failure to pay property taxes and fire insurance. Regardless of the violation, lenders in California must follow a prescribed procedure in order to take title from a delinquent debtor. Here is a summary of the process, which is also illustrated in Figure 7.5.

Trustee's Sale

Virtually all trust deeds contain a power-of-sale clause, which empowers the trustee, in the event of default by the trustor, to sell the property at public auction. Although the provisions of the power-of-sale clause are a matter of contract and may vary from instrument to instrument, there are laws that specifically regulate foreclosure through trustee's sale. The statutory requirements are as follows:

1. *Notice of default.* After the beneficiary is reasonably certain that a trustor is unable to make good on the loan, the beneficiary orders the trustee to record a notice of default in the county where the property is located. This begins a reinstatement period. The notice must contain a correct legal description of the property, name of trustor, nature of the breach, and a statement to the effect that

TRUSTEE'S SALE (FORECLOSURE)

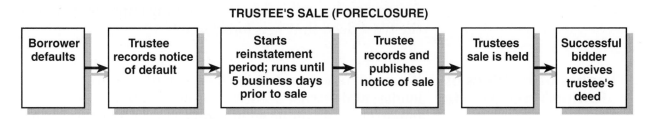

Figure 7.5

the party executing the notice of default has elected to sell the property in order to satisfy the obligation.

Within 10 days after filing the notice of default, a copy must be sent by registered or certified mail to the borrower, junior lienholders, and to anyone whose "request for notice" appears on record.

During this reinstatement period, which runs until five days before the date of sale, the trustor (borrower) may reinstate the loan by paying all delinquent installments. The trustor must also pay foreclosure costs and trustee's fees. This is referred to as the right of reinstatement.

2. *Notice of sale.* In addition to recording a notice of default, a trustee must also record a notice of sale. This notice of sale is filed if the borrower fails to reinstate the loan.

The notice must contain a correct identification of the property, such as the street address or legal description. It must be published in a newspaper of general circulation in the county or jurisdiction in which the property is located. The publication must appear at least once a week for three consecutive calendar weeks. Moreover, the notice must also be posted in a public place, such as a courthouse, and also in some conspicuous place on the property, such as the front door. The sale must be held in a public place, during business hours, on a weekday (Monday through Friday).

3. *Final sale.* Any person, including the trustor and beneficiary, may bid on the property via public auction. All bids must be in cash or its equivalent. However, the lender foreclosing can submit the amount owed the lender as a bid in lieu of cash.

A trustee's deed is issued to the highest bidder. Any surplus funds, that is, funds remaining after paying off the lender, foreclosure costs, and junior liens if any, are given to the trustor.

No right of redemption exists after a trustee's sale. The purchaser acquires all rights held by the former owner, becoming the successor in interest, and is entitled to immediate possession, subject to those having superior rights over the trust deed that was foreclosed.

Rights of Holders of Junior Trust Deeds

When a trustee's sale is held on behalf of a first trust deed lender, junior trust deeds can be eliminated. Therefore, it is important to examine what rights a junior trust deed holder has in the foreclosure process.

Assume that a homeowner has a first and a second trust deed loan against the property and is in default on the loans. If the first trust deed lender begins to foreclose, the second trust deed lender can step in and make the payments due on the first loan. This will stop the first lender from foreclosing. *The second trust deed lender then adds the payments made on the first trust deed loan to the balance the borrower owes on the second trust deed loan.* The holder of the second trust deed loan then demands repayment from the borrower. If the borrower fails to repay, the holder of the second trust deed then forecloses under the trustee sale provisions of the second trust deed. The successful bidder at the trustee's sale becomes the owner of the property, subject to the first trust deed—that is, takes over the property and is required to make all future payments on the first trust deed loan. In short, a holder of a junior trust deed can stop the first from foreclosing on the first trust deed. This in turn will keep the second trust deed from being eliminated. The holder of the second trust deed will get either title to the property as the lone bidder at the trustee's sale, or cash from a third party who is the successful bidder at the trustee's sale on the second trust deed.

How does a holder of a second trust deed know when a borrower has defaulted on the first trust deed? The law requires that senior trust deed holders must send a certified copy of any notice of default and sale to all holders of junior trust deeds. To be doubly sure, a holder of a junior trust deed may also wish to record an instrument called a *request for copy of notice of default.* This places on public record a notice to the senior trust deed holder that the junior trust deed holder wishes to be informed when a default is declared on the first loan.

7.3 TRUTH-IN-LENDING, EQUAL CREDIT OPPORTUNITY, AND REAL ESTATE SETTLEMENT PROCEDURES ACT

Many years ago, Congress passed the *Truth-in-Lending Law,* also called Regulation Z. The purpose of the law is to help borrowers understand how much it is costing to borrow money. The law requires all lenders to show loan costs in the same way. This allows borrowers to compare one lender's cost against the other.

The law requires lenders to quote the cost of borrowing, using what is called an *annual percentage rate* (APR). The APR is not an interest rate, but rather a percentage rate that reflects the effective interest rate on the loan, including other prepaid financing charges such as loan fees, prepaid interest, and tax service fees.

Regulation Z requires a lender to give the borrower a disclosure statement showing a complete breakdown of all loan costs, plus other loan information. The law also provides that certain loans are rescindable within three business days. This means that borrowers have three days after they agree to a loan to cancel it if they wish. Generally, the rescindable right applies only to loans to refinance a borrower's home and to certain types of junior deeds of trust, including home improvement loans. First deeds of trust to purchase a home do not carry a three-day right to rescind, nor do loans carried back by a seller of real estate.

Real Estate Advertisements

Real estate advertisements must comply with Regulation Z. If one financial term such as *interest rate* or *no money down* is mentioned, all financing terms—interest rate, monthly payments, length of loan, and so on, must be stated in the ad. There are severe penalties for people who advertise real estate loan terms incorrectly.

Equal Credit Opportunity Act

The Equal Credit Opportunity Act prohibits lenders from discrimination on the basis of race, color, religion, national origin, age, sex, family size, or handicap, marital status, or on the grounds of receipt of income from a public assistance program.

Some of the basic provisions of the act are:

1. A lender cannot ask if the borrower is divorced or widowed. The lender may ask if the borrower is married, unmarried, or separated. For purposes of the law, unmarried means single, divorced, or widowed.
2. A lender cannot ask about receiving alimony or child support unless the borrower is first notified that it need not be revealed. However, the lender may ask about obligations to pay alimony or child support.
3. A lender cannot ask about birth control practices or childbearing intentions or capabilities.
4. A lender must notify every borrower within 30 days of what action has been taken on his or her loan application. In case of disapproval, the reason must be given if requested.
5. If the borrower requests, the lender must consider information provided by the borrower indicating that a bad history of a joint account does not reflect on his or her credit.

In short, the Equal Credit Opportunity Act assures that all qualified persons shall have equal access to credit. This law has been especially helpful in assuring women that they shall not be discriminated against because of their sex.

Real Estate Settlement Procedures Act

The Real Estate Settlement Procedures Act (RESPA) is a federal law that requires certain forms be provided regarding closing costs. The law applies whenever a person purchases an owner-occupied residence, using funds obtained from institutional lenders which are regulated by a federal agency. Virtually all banks, savings and loan associations, and most other lenders fall directly or indirectly under RESPA's rules. The one major exception would be real estate loans made by private parties.

RESPA rules require the lender to furnish the borrower with a special information booklet and a good faith estimate of closing costs three days from the time the prospective borrower files an application for a real estate loan. RESPA rules prohibit any kickbacks or unearned fees from being listed as closing costs. The law states that only valid, earned, closing costs shall be charged the buyer or seller. Any violators can be punished by up to one year in jail and/or a $10,000 fine.

Most of the burden for implementing RESPA falls upon the real estate lender. However, escrow agents are also involved. RESPA requires the use of a Uniform Settlement Statement (HUD-1) which must itemize all final closing charges. Upon request, the escrow agent must let the borrower-buyer inspect the Uniform Settlement Statement one day before the close of escrow. In addition, the escrow officer must see that all parties receive a copy of the Uniform Settlement Statement after the close of escrow.

7.4 REAL PROPERTY LOAN LAW

Another consumer-oriented law is the Real Property Loan Law found in Sections 10240–48 of the California Business and Professions Code (Article 7). This segment of the law is commonly called the "Mortgage Loan Broker Law." The purpose of this law is to protect borrowers who use the services of mortgage loan brokers. The law requires mortgage brokers to give a loan disclosure statement to all borrowers before they become obligated for the loan. The disclosure statement itemizes all closing costs, loan expenses, and commissions to be paid, thereby showing the borrower how much he or she will net from the loan.

Exceptions to the Mortgage Loan Broker Law

It is easier to state which lenders and what transactions are *not* covered by the law than to list those that are. As of January 1999, the following are exempt from the Real Property Loan Law:

1. Regulated institutional lenders, such as banks, savings and loan associations, credit unions, and finance companies
2. Purchase money transactions where a seller carries back the loan as part of the sale price. However, if a seller carries back the loan for more than seven transactions in one year, the Mortgage Loan Broker Law does apply.
3. Loans secured by first trust deeds when the principal amount is $30,000 or more
4. Loans secured by junior trust deeds when the principal amount is $20,000 or more

Maximum Commissions

Mortgage loan brokers are limited in the percentage amount of commissions that they may charge, as shown in Table 7.1.

As is evident in Table 7.1, the shorter the term of the loan, the less commission the broker may charge as a percentage of the face amount of the loan. On loans of $30,000 and over for first liens, and $20,000 for junior liens, the broker may charge as much as the borrower agrees to pay. Even for loans covered by the law, however, competition frequently keeps rates below the maximum allowed.

Other Costs and Expenses

Under transactions covered by the Real Property Loan Law, brokers are also limited in the amount of costs and expenses, other than commissions, that they may charge a borrower for arranging the loan. Such costs and expenses may not exceed 5% of the amount of the loan. However, if 5% of the loan is less than $390, the broker may charge up to that amount, provided that the charges do not exceed

TABLE 7.1 Maximum Commission as a Percentage

	Less than two years	*Two years but less than three*	*Three years and over*	*Exempt transactions*
Type and Length of Loan				
First Trust Deeds	5%	5%	10%	**Loans of $30,000 and over**
Junior Trust Deeds	5%	10%	15%	**Loans of $20,000 and over**

actual costs and expenses paid, incurred, or reasonably earned by the broker.

Regardless of the size of the loan, the borrower cannot be charged more than $700 for miscellaneous costs and expenses, excluding commission, title and recording fees, as of January 1999.

Balloon Payments A balloon payment is prohibited if (1) the term of the loan is for six years or less, and (2) the loan is secured by the dwelling place of the borrower. Again, this provision does not apply to loans carried by sellers.

Insurance A borrower is not required to purchase credit life or disability insurance as a condition for obtaining the loan. However, the lender may insist, for self-protection, that fire and hazard insurance be obtained on the property until the loan has been repaid. If licensed to sell such insurance, the mortgage broker may act as the agent for the borrower, but the borrower is not obligated to purchase the insurance coverage through the mortgage loan broker.

Miscellaneous Provisions Mortgage brokers are prohibited from charging loan servicing or collection fees to be paid by the borrower. Late charges, if any, may not exceed $5 or 10% of the principal and interest part of an installment payment, whichever is greater. If the installment payment is made within 10 days of its due date, however, no late charge can be assessed.

In case of early repayment of the loan, there can be no prepayment penalty against the borrower when the loan is over seven years old. During the first seven years, a borrower is allowed to pay up to 20% of the remaining principal balance of the loan during any 12-month period without a penalty. The remaining balance may then be subjected to a maximum prepayment penalty of six months' unearned interest. Mortgage brokers must keep copies of all loan papers for at least four years.

CHAPTER SUMMARY The financing of real estate usually involves a five-phase process consisting of the loan application, analysis, processing, closing, and servicing phases. In California, the major instruments of finance are promissory notes and deeds of trust (trust deeds). Promissory notes can be straight notes, which contain interest-only payments, or installment notes, which have payments of principal and interest. The most common promissory note is the fully amortized installment note. In addition to fixed interest rate loans, adjustable rate loans are also popular.

Real estate loans in California are secured by deeds of trust, also called trust deeds. A deed of trust is a three-party instrument consisting of a trustor (borrower), trustee (title holder), and a beneficiary (lender). Upon repayment of the loan, the trustee reconveys title back to the trustor. If the trustor (borrower) should default on the loan, the trustee forecloses on the property under what is called a trustee's sale.

Many promissory notes and deeds of trust contain special clauses that outline the duties and responsibilities of the borrower. Acceleration and alienation (due-on-sale) are most common. Subordination and prepayment penalty clauses also exist. Junior deeds of trust are used in many real estate transactions when the buyer does not have enough money to cover the gap between the sales price and the first loan. Installment sales contracts are no longer popular for the purchase and financing of real estate.

The Truth-in-Lending Act, the Equal Credit Opportunity Act, and the Real Estate Settlement Procedures Act (RESPA) are examples of federal laws designed to assure the proper disclosure and equal treatment of prospective real estate borrowers. The Real Property Loan Law is a California law that requires full disclosure when a borrower procures a loan through a mortgage loan broker. This law also regulates maximum commissions and closing costs that can be charged to the borrower. The Real Property Loan Law does not apply to first deed of trust loans of $30,000 or more or second deed of trust loans of $20,000 or more.

IMPORTANT TERMS AND CONCEPTS

Acceleration clause

Adjustable rate loan

Alienation (due-on-sale) clause

Annual percentage rate (APR)

Balloon payment

Beneficiary

Deed of trust

Equal Credit Opportunity Act

Installment note

Installment sales contract

Junior deed of trust

Leverage

Prepayment penalty

Real Property Loan Act

RESPA

Straight note

Trustee

Trustee's sale

Truth-in-Lending Act

Trustor

Usury law

1. A homeowner has a $200,000 interest-only ARM loan with a current interest rate of 6% with a 2% margin over the 11th District Cost-of-Funds Index with a cap rate of 11%. What are the current monthly loan payments? With an annual maximum increase of 2% per year, under a worse-case circumstance, what will be the maximum monthly loan payments for the second, third, and fourth years?

2. An owner is in financial trouble and is behind $2,000 in payments on a $175,000 home loan. The lender files a notice of default and begins to foreclose. To date foreclosure costs total $1,000, plus the $2,000 back payments. Explain what the owner must do to save the home.

3. Using the services of a mortgage loan broker, a homeowner borrows a $15,000 junior loan for a 10-year period to pay off consumer debts. Assuming the loan broker charges the maximum commission and fees allowed by law, how much will the homeowner net after paying these fees?

REVIEWING YOUR UNDERSTANDING

1. A fully amortized promissory note with equal payments to liquidate the debt would be:
   a. a straight note
   b. a principal plus interest note
   c. a conventional note
   d. an installment note

2. Sales price $120,000; $30,000 cash down; seller carries $90,000 loan; seller continues to pay on existing $50,000 bank loan against the property. The seller carry loan is:
   a. a first deed of trust
   b. a senior lien
   c. a wraparound deed of trust
   d. an institutional loan

3. Under a deed of trust (trust deed. the lender is the:
   a. beneficiary
   b. trustee
   c. trustor
   d. mortgagor

4. A due-on-sale clause is correctly called:
   a. a subordination clause
   b. an alienation clause
   c. an escalation clause
   d. a prepayment clause

5. Which real estate sale will make use of a junior lien?
   a. all-cash sale
   b. buyer puts 20% down payment, obtains an 80% loan
   c. seller carries the first deed of trust
   d. buyer puts 10% percent down payment, obtains 80% loan, seller carries a 10% second deed of trust

6. Under which financing instrument is the seller known as the vendor?
   a. installment sales contract
   b. contract of sale
   c. agreement of sale
   d. all of the above

7. Once a trustee records a notice of default, how much time does the borrower have to make up the delinquencies and stop the foreclosure?
   a. 5 days prior to sale
   b. 90 days prior to sale
   c. 21 days prior to sale
   d. 180 days prior to sale

8. The law that requires a lender to quote the cost of borrowing as an annual percentage rate is:
   a. Real Estate Settlement Procedures Act (RESPA)
   b. Truth-in-Lending Act
   c. Equal Credit Opportunity Act
   d. Fair Credit Reporting Act

9. Under the Real Property Loan Law, the maximum commission a mortgage broker can charge for a $19,000 junior trust deed loan, payable in 37 equal installments, is:
   a. $2,850
   b. $1,900
   c. $950
   d. no maximum commission

10. Regarding question 9, what would be the maximum amount the borrower can be charged for actual fees and expenses, excluding commission, title, and recording fees?
    a. $700
    b. $950
    c. $390
    d. no maximum amount

11. A $100,000 note at 9.5% interest, payable $791.67 per month, is what kind of note?
    a. principal and interest included
    b. fully amortized
    c. accommodation
    d. straight

12. In a normal sale using a grant deed and deed of trust, the buyer is the:
    a. grantee and trustee
    b. grantor and trustor
    c. grantee and trustor
    d. grantor and trustee

13. A clause where the holder of the first loan agrees to become a second in favor of a new construction loan is:
    a. prepayment penalty
    b. alienation
    c. subordination
    d. subject to

14. Under an adjustable rate mortgage (ARM), the distance between the actual rate paid by the borrower and the index is called the:
    a. cap
    b. margin
    c. term
    d. adjustment

15. The maximum interest rate on an ARM loan is called the:
    a. cap
    b. margin
    c. term
    d. adjustment

16. Giving something as security for a loan without giving up possession is called:
    a. pledging
    b. granting
    c. hypothecating
    d. vesting

17. If a lender calls a loan due and payable because the borrower is willfully destroying the property, the lender is exercising which clause?
    a. alienation
    b. acceleration
    c. subservient
    d. subordination

18. Which law requires a lender to give a borrower a good faith estimate of closing costs and also requires a HUD-1 closing statement?
    a. Regulation Z
    b. Equal Credit Opportunity Act
    c. Truth in Lending Law
    d. RESPA

19. A buyer purchases subject to a seller's existing loan. Later a foreclosure occurs and the lender sues for a deficiency judgment. Who has prime liability?
    a. buyer
    b. seller
    c. lender
    d. beneficiary

20. For nonexempt lenders, the maximum interest that can be charged under California usury law is:

a. 10%

b. 5% above the Federal Reserve discount rate

c. 10% or 5% above the Federal Reserve discount rate, whichever is greater

d. 10% or 5% above the Federal Reserve discount rate, whichever is the lesser

APPENDIX A
Wraparound Deed of Trust

A wraparound deed of trust, also called all-inclusive trust deed (AITD), is a financing device used to increase the lender's yield upon the sale of real property and to make it easier for the buyer to finance the purchase.

> **EXAMPLE.** An owner has a $200,000 property with an existing loan of $100,000 at 7% interest, payable at $800 per month. The owner sells for $200,000, the buyer puts down $50,000 cash, and the seller carries a wraparound deed of trust for $150,000 at 10%, payable at $1,100 per month. The buyer makes the $1,100 payments to the seller on the $150,000 wraparound loan, and the seller then makes the $800 payments on the $100,000 underlying loan, keeping the $300 difference ($1,100 − $800 = $300).

The seller's yield is increased because the seller receives 10% on $150,000, but pays only 7% interest on $100,000.

The buyer does not assume the seller's existing loan, but rather makes payments only on the wraparound deed of trust (AITD). The seller is responsible for all existing loans. By having the seller carry a wraparound deed of trust, the buyer avoids the new loan fees charged by institutional lenders.

A wraparound deed of trust is a complicated financing device that should be used only if all parties understand its details. Also, adequate provisions should be inserted to protect the buyer's interest in case the seller fails to make the payments on the underlying loan(s) after receiving the buyer's payment on the wraparound deed of trust. Many existing real estate loans may have enforceable due-on-sale clauses which prohibit the use of a wraparound deed of trust. A wraparound deed of trust can also be used to refinance a property—a lender makes a new wraparound loan and the lender agrees to make payments on the underlying existing loan(s).

APPENDIX B
Leverage

Leverage can be described as using a small amount of your money (equity capital) and a large amount of someone else's money (borrowed capital) to buy real estate. Leverage can be advantageous if the property increases in value.

For example, assume that you can purchase a home for $100,000 and resell it later for $150,000. If you pay $100,000 all cash and sell the property for $150,000, you would realize a $50,000 gain or a 50% return on your investment.

All-cash Transaction

$150,000	Resale price		
−100,000	Purchase price	$50,000 Gain	= 50%
$50,000	Gain	$100,000 Investment	

On the other hand, if you could obtain a $90,000 real estate loan, you would need to invest only $10,000 as a down payment. If you resell the property for $150,000 and pay off the $90,000 loan, you would have a $50,000 gain or a 500% return on your investment.

Leverage Transaction

$100,000	Purchase price	$150,000	Resale price
−90,000	Loan	−90,000	Loan
$10,000	Down payment (investment)	$60,000	
		−10,000	Down payment
		$50,000	Gain

$50,000	Gain
$10,000	Investment = 500%

Of course the percentage return will be reduced by income taxes paid, closing costs, and interest paid on the loan, but they have been omitted in order to stress the impact of leverage. However, leverage is rosy only if property values increase. If property values decrease, look out! See the following section on pitfalls.

PITFALLS

Leverage can work in reverse if the value of the property declines. Let us see what happens if the property in our example has declined in value by 10% upon resale.

All-cash Transaction

$100,100	Purchase price		
−90,000	Resale price	$10,000 Loss	= −10% Loss on investment
(10,000)	Loss on resale	$100,000 invested	

Leverage Transaction

$90,000	Resale price	0 Gain	= −100% Loss on investment
−90,000	Loan	$10,000 Invested	
0	Gain		

If you paid $100,000 all cash, your loss is 10%. But if you paid $100,000 by borrowing $90,000 and putting $10,000 as down payment and the property resold for only $90,000, you were just able to repay the lender, and you lost all of your $10,000 down payment! If the property were to decline in value more than 10%, you would now owe more than what the property is worth. If this becomes the case and the buyer "walks away" from the property and the lender forecloses, the buyer's credit rating is destroyed. In addition, any difference between the loan amount and what the lender receives from the resale of the property could result in an income tax liability for the former owner.

EXAMPLE

$90,000	Loan balance owed at the time of foreclosure
−70,000	Resale price lender receives for the property after foreclosure
$20,000	Difference is known as "debt forgiveness" and could be taxable to the former owner as income (see a tax expert for details).

Chapter 8

Part I: Real Estate Lenders

Chapter Preview, Part I

This chapter has been divided into two parts. Part I covers the principal types of real estate lenders found in California. Part II discusses government's role in real estate financing, stressing the main points of the Federal Housing Administration (FHA), Department of Veterans Affairs (VA), and the California Department of Veteran's Affairs (Cal-Vet) programs. At the conclusion of Part I of the chapter, you will be able to:

1. Compute the multipliers and ratios used by many real estate lenders to qualify borrowers

2. List three institutional and noninstitutional real estate lenders

3. Describe how private mortgage insurance has changed real estate lending practices in California

8.1 QUALIFYING FOR A REAL ESTATE LOAN

When qualifying a borrower, a lender tries to determine if a borrower will make his or her loan payments in the future. To make this determination, a loan officer analyzes two major characteristics:

1. *Capacity to pay.* To determine capacity to pay, these questions must be asked: Does the borrower make enough

189

money to make the payments? And if so, is it a stable source of income? Does the borrower have enough cash to buy this property? What other assets does the borrower have? The answers to these questions all affect the borrower's capacity to pay.

2. *Desire to pay.* The desire to pay is the other major factor a lender must analyze. A person may have the capacity to pay but lack the desire to do so. The desire to pay is just as important, but it is more difficult to measure. The desire to pay is generally reflected by the past credit history of a borrower.

Old Rule of Thumb Is Inadequate

"A home should not cost more than 2½ times a buyer's (borrower's) gross income." This old lender's rule is inadequate. The rule ignores the real issue—the buyer's ability to pay the monthly housing payment. This rule also ignores the issue of a buyer's personal debts. Isn't a buyer who is free of debt able to pay more for housing than a buyer heavily in debt? Many lenders today recognize that the 2½ times the gross income rule is riddled with errors and pitfalls.

Use of Multipliers and Ratios

Most lenders qualify borrowers by using income multipliers or ratios. The ratios can vary from lender to lender; however, the traditional 4:1 multiplier has been used by conservative real estate lenders for many years.

A 4:1 multiplier simply means that the monthly income of the borrower should be approximately four times the monthly housing payment. Thus, if the monthly housing payment (principal + interest + monthly taxes and insurance) will be $1,000, four times this amount ($1,000 × 4) or $4,000, should be the borrower's gross monthly income. When converted to a ratio, the 4:1 multiplier means that a borrower's monthly housing payment should not be much more than 25% of the borrower's gross monthly income. Gross income must include all the stable income of the borrower and co-borrowers, such as a spouse's income, alimony payments, and public assistance payments, as well as regular wages, commissions, and salaries.

Trend Toward More Liberal Ratios

Recently there has been a move toward use of 3.5:1 multipliers. This means that the borrower's monthly housing payments should not exceed approximately 30% of the borrower's gross income. Lenders recognize that because of higher costs for homes in California, more of a borrower's income must be used to cover housing payments. Therefore, if a borrower's monthly housing payment (principal + interest + monthly taxes and insurance) will be $1,000, three and one-half times this amount, or $3,500, should be the borrower's gross monthly income. Contrast this $3,500 with the $4,000 required when a lender uses the 4:1 multiplier and you can see that the lower the ratio, the less gross income is needed to qualify for a real estate loan.

Debts The lender must also consider a borrower's debts in order to determine the capacity to pay. A borrower's debts may be short term or long term.

Short-term debts usually are ignored, and long-term debts are counted. The definition of long- versus short-term debts can vary depending upon the lender. However, many lenders consider long-term debts to be obligations that exist for six months or more.

When considering debts, conventional lenders traditionally have used the following guidelines: The monthly housing payment + long-term debts = total monthly expenses. The total monthly expenses should not exceed 33% to 38% of the borrower's gross monthly income.

EXAMPLE. $1,000 monthly housing expense + $250 long-term monthly debts = $1,250 × 3 = $3,750, the gross monthly income required from the borrowers.

Summary of Qualifying Guidelines 1. (Principal + interest + monthly taxes and insurance)

$$\frac{\text{Monthly housing payments}}{\text{Gross monthly income}} = \text{Percentage \%}$$

This rate should not exceed 25% to 30%, with 28% required by most lenders.

2. (Monthly housing payments + long-term monthly debts)

$$\frac{\text{Total monthly expenses}}{\text{Gross monthly income}} = \text{Percentage \%}$$

This ratio should not exceed 33% to 38%, with 36% required by most lenders.

Most real estate lenders require that the borrower(s) must qualify under both these tests. Some borrowers can qualify on the first test, but not on the second, because they are too heavily in debt. These guidelines can vary from lender to lender; thus, consumers and real estate agents should contact local lenders to obtain specific guidelines. (See the case study on qualifying for a home loan in the appendix of this chapter.)

8.2 INSTITUTIONAL LENDERS

An institutional lender is a financial depository that gathers funds received from clients and depositors and then invests these funds. As indicated in Figure 8.1, California has three major types of institutional lenders: commercial banks, savings banks (formerly called savings and loan associations), and life insurance companies. All three of these institutions pour billions of dollars into California real estate loans. Before studying institutional lenders, it is helpful to review the characteristics of the California mortgage market and the concept of savings forming the pool for borrowing.

The California Mortgage Market

The characteristics of the California mortgage market can be summarized as follows:

1. *Usually high demand.* Because of its large economy, California traditionally has needed large amounts of mortgage funds. However, in periods of recession and economic slowdown, the demand for real estate loans declines.
2. *Population growth.* California is the most populous state. High population means high demand for housing to either own or rent.
3. *Financial institutions.* California has many of the nation's largest commercial and savings banks.
4. *Loan correspondents.* California has many experienced mortgage companies that represent out-of-state life

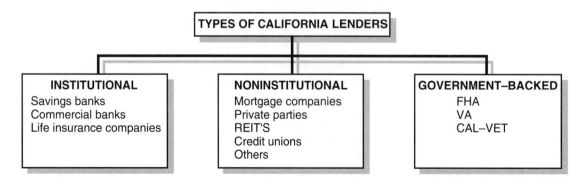

Figure 8.1

insurance companies and other lenders that, in boom times, are eager to invest in California real estate loans.

5. *Title and escrow companies.* Title insurance and escrow companies originated in California. Many of the nation's largest are in California and provide fast and efficient service for real estate lenders.

6. *Use of deeds of trust.* The deed of trust (trust deed) is used rather than the mortgage instruments for securing real estate loans. Deeds of trust give lenders more flexibility than mortgages.

7. *Active secondary market.* Existing real estate loans are sold to out-of-state lenders. These include mutual savings banks, which are not located in California but still make the capital available through secondary purchases.

Savings Form the Pool for Borrowing

Profits and income can be taxed, spent, or saved. For most people taxes are taken out first, and the remainder is then used for consumer or business expenditures. If any funds remain after expenditures, they are saved (or invested, which is a form of saving).

Sometimes we spend more than we earn, and we need to borrow to cover the excess spending. Where do the funds come from when we borrow? (Answer: someone else's savings.) If all income was taxed or spent, there wouldn't be any savings left over to borrow, and it would be impossible to obtain a loan. Thus, it can be said that all private funds for loans, including real estate loans, can be traced back to some form of savings. With this background, let us turn our attention to the characteristics of institutional real estate lenders.

Commercial Banks

Commercial banks operate under a license or charter from either the state or the federal government. As far as real estate loans are concerned, there is little difference between a state and a national bank.

In recent years commercial banks have been a powerful source for home loans, be it for purchase or refinance. Commercial banks also specialize in short-term construction financing, where the builder or developer has a "take-out" commitment from some other lender—most often an insurance company or a savings bank—for the permanent mortgage loan. Large commercial banks play a major role in financing business and commercial properties, whereas some smaller banks deal exclusively with home loans.

Bankers may make conventional real estate loans up to 90% of appraised value, for as long as 30 years, on single-family dwellings. Many banks will require private mortgage insurance on loans whose loan-to-value ratio is in excess of 80%. Bankers are sometimes authorized to grant FHA-insured and VA-guaranteed loans. Bankers are active seekers of home improvement and home equity loans.

Savings Banks (Formerly Called Savings and Loans)

A savings bank is a financial institution that accepts savings from the public and invests these savings mainly in real estate trust deeds and mortgages. The majority of savings bank loans are in residential properties, mostly single-family dwellings. A savings bank is also classified as either a state-chartered or a federally chartered institution. As far as real estate lending is concerned, there is little difference.

Under certain conditions 90% to 95% loan-to-value ratio loans are obtainable at some savings banks if they are covered by private mortgage insurance. Most savings banks limit their loans to 30 years. Their prime real estate loan is on a single-family, owner-occupied dwelling, but in a favorable market, savings banks will also grant mobile home loans and apartment loans. Combination loans that unite home construction and long-term, take-out financing in one package are common.

The Savings and Loan Crisis*

What happened? Why did we have a savings and loan crisis? Why did Congress need to pass the bailout legislation known as the Financial Institutions Reform Recovery and Enforcement Act of 1989 (FIRREA)? Did deregulations fail? Were savings and loan managers asleep at the wheel? Or worse yet—were they crooks? Was the problem caused by an unexpected economic recession? Economists and politicians will be debating this issue for many years to come. Finger pointing will prevail, but in the end the U.S. taxpayer will foot most of the bill. Here are the key government agencies involved in the bailout process.

1. Office of Thrift Supervision (OTS)
   This is the arm of the U.S. Treasury. It was created by FIRREA to replace the Federal Home Loan Bank Board as the chief regulator of all savings associations whose deposits are federally insured. It is the OTS that reports the popular "11th District Cost-of-Funds" index used to adjust interest rates on many ARM loans.
2. Savings Association Insurance Fund (SAIF)

*California Real Estate Finance, 6th ed. by R. J. Bond, A. Gavello, and C. Young (Upper Saddle River, NJ: Prentice Hall, 1998).

This is the agency created by FIRREA to replace the Federal Savings and Loan Insurance Corporation (FSLIC) that became insolvent in 1988. Managed by the Federal Deposit Insurance Corporation, this fund collects premiums to generate the funds to insure accounts at savings banks.

3. Federal Housing Finance Board (FHFB)

   This agency oversees mortgage lending by the 12 regional Federal Home Loan Banks. The regulatory function was previously performed by the now defunct Federal Home Loan Bank Board. Savings associations that fail to meet so-called "Qualified Thrift Lender" (QTL) requirements are not able to borrow or access funds from any of the Federal Home Loan Banks. If an institution is in serious trouble, this agency may declare it to be insolvent.

4. Resolution Trust Corporation (RTC)

   The RTC was extensively involved in managing and selling real estate, securities, and other assets of failed savings institutions. Controversy revolves around the speed and methods the RTC used to unload these assets and what impact they had on local real estate markets. This agency has recently been abolished and its function taken up by other government agencies.

5. Federal Deposit Insurance Corporation (FDIC)

   This familiar agency insures deposits of up to $100,000 per account for commercial and savings banks, and manages the Savings Association Insurance Fund.

6. Federal Reserve Bank Board (FRB)

   The Federal Reserve has control over the monetary policy of the United States, including the reserve and lending requirements of commercial and savings banks.

   Although the savings and loan crisis has been painful and complicated, it should be remembered that not all savings and loans failed. Many are soundly managed and are strong and profitable. Real estate borrowers can look forward to working with many savings and loan banks that are ready and willing to help people acquire real estate.

Life Insurance Companies

Life insurance companies are another important source for real estate financing, particularly for large commercial and industrial properties such as shopping centers, office buildings, and warehouses. They also provide a significant amount of money for new housing subdivisions.

In general, life insurance companies have broad lending powers.

Loan-to-value ratios are usually on the conservative side, generally in the 66⅔% to 75% range for conventional financing, commonly with 30-year terms. Historically, insurance companies have preferred to grant large commercial and industrial real estate loans, but only if they are occupied by owners and tenants who have excellent credit and good company balance sheets.

"Loan correspondents," such as mortgage companies, are widely used as agents of insurance companies. In this way the insurance company is relieved of the burden of originating and processing loans, as well as some administrative and service functions.

8.3 NONINSTITUTIONAL LENDERS

Institutional lenders such as commercial banks, savings banks, and life insurance companies are highly regulated by state and federal agencies. Noninstitutional lenders are lenders whose real estate activities are not as strictly regulated. Major noninstitutional lenders include mortgage companies, private parties, real estate investment trusts, credit unions, and pension funds.

Mortgage Companies

Mortgage companies are a major type of noninstitutional real estate lender. When a mortgage company represents a life insurance company, commercial bank, savings bank, or other lender, it is called a *mortgage or loan correspondent*. It "corresponds" on behalf of its principal(s) in dealing with prospective borrowers. The mortgage correspondent is paid a fee in exchange for originating, processing, closing, and servicing loans. A loan correspondent serves a valuable function in the field of real estate financing for lenders whose headquarters or principal offices are located great distances from the properties on which they make loans.

Rules Regarding Mortgage Companies

Mortgage companies that do not use their own funds are subject in their lending activities to the same restrictions that govern their principal(s). Thus, if a California mortgage correspondent or banker represents an Eastern life insurance company, the correspondent would have the same loan-to-value limitations placed on its loans as the insurance company.

Mortgage companies have some special restrictions placed upon them. In California, they must be licensed and state approved. Even though they may not be lending money belonging to third parties, they are subject to the

Real Property Loan Law when they make loans that are not specifically exempt under that law. They are also subject to some lending and other business regulations.

Mortgage Banker versus Mortgage Broker

A mortgage company could be a mortgage banker or a mortgage broker, or both. Mortgage bankers lend their own money and then either resell the loan to another lender or keep the loan for an investment. Mortgage brokers do not lend their own money; rather, they find a lender and a borrower and get a fee for bringing them together.

MAJOR PLAYER

Mortgage companies have become a dominant force in the California real estate market. In some areas, mortgage companies place more home loans than do institutional lenders. Many traditional real estate brokerage offices have added a mortgage brokerage division to give buyers a "one stop shopping center" option of both buying and financing the purchase at the same office.

Private Lenders

Private lenders are individuals who invest their savings in real estate loans. Private persons can invest directly by granting loans to borrowers, or they can invest indirectly by turning to mortgage brokers who find borrowers for the private lender. Sellers frequently become private lenders when they carry back trust deeds in order to facilitate the sale of their property.

The prime motivation of private lenders is to earn a high yield, with some degree of safety. Some private lenders are becoming investors by entering into partnership with young home buyers in equity-share programs for the purchasing and financing of homes.

On seller carry loans on 1 to 4 residential units, a *Seller Financial Disclosure Statement* is required. This disclosure statement gives both the buyer-borrower and seller-lender an extensive breakdown of the major financial terms in the seller carry loan. Most real estate brokers have preprinted forms that satisfy this disclosure requirement.

CHARACTERISTICS OF PRIVATE LENDERS

Private lenders generally have some common characteristics, regardless of whether the loan is made directly by the individual, or indirectly through a loan broker:

1. Most private lenders operate in the second trust deed market. Frequently these loans are seller carry-back seconds that thereafter are sold to investors, usually at a discount, when the seller needs cash.

2. Most loans are on single-family dwellings because this type of property is most familiar to the typical private investor, and also because the size of the loan is usually small.

3. The term of a private loan is usually short and often calls for a balloon payment. Three to six years are the most common maturities.

SPECIAL INTEREST TOPIC

Investing in Trust Deeds

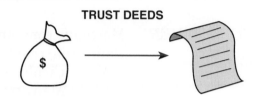

TRUST DEEDS

Some private investors prefer to purchase existing notes and trust deeds instead of granting a loan directly to a borrower. These investors search for a sale where the seller carries back the paper. They then attempt to purchase existing seller carry loans at a discount. Many times the seller is willing to sell the note for cash rather than wait several years for the buyer to pay off the loan.

The investor usually buys the note at a discount, which increases the investor's yield to a rate higher than the amount of interest on the face of the note. The size of the discount varies with the quality of the borrowers, the equity in the property, and current money market conditions. Some mortgage brokers earn commissions by bringing buyers and sellers of notes together.

Here are two legal terms regarding the selling of existing notes and trust deeds.

1. *Negotiable Instrument.* A promissory note that is a written promise or order to pay an amount of money at a definite time or on demand. Negotiable instruments are allowed to be freely sold.

2. *Holder in Due Course.* A person who in good faith has purchased a note for value without any knowledge regarding defects or past due payments. A person who purchased a note as a holder in due course has some superior rights if the borrower on the note refuses to pay based on certain disputes with the former owner of the note.

Real Estate Investment Trusts

The *real estate investment trust* (or REIT) is a creature of the federal tax law. It was created in 1960 with the goal of encouraging small investors to pool their resources with others in order to raise venture capital for real estate transactions. It has been called the "mutual funds" of the real estate business. Just as mutual funds invest in a diversified portfolio of corporate stocks and bonds, REITs invest in a diversified portfolio of real estate and mortgage investments.

To qualify as a trust, there are many tests that must be met, such as the requirement that at least 95% of the REIT's ordinary income be distributed to the investors to qualify for favorable tax treatment. The legal ramifications of REITs are beyond the scope of this course; anyone interested in forming or participating in REITs should seek legal counsel.

Credit Unions

A *credit union* is a mutual, voluntary, cooperative organization of people who agree to save their money together in order to provide money for loans to each other. There are many credit unions throughout the United States, and their numbers are growing rapidly. For the most part, credit union lending in the field of real estate has been short term, but law changes now allow long-term real estate loans.

Syndicates, pension funds, trust funds, and various types of endowment funds are also noninstitutional real estate lenders. But their lending practices are beyond the scope of this course.

8.4 PRIVATE MORTGAGE INSURANCE

What is *private mortgage insurance?* It is insurance that is used to guarantee lenders the payment of the upper portion of a conventional loan if a borrower defaults and a deficiency occurs at the foreclosure sale. Private mortgage insurance, formerly called Mortgage Guaranty Insurance, is sold by private insurance companies, and in the lending business this is referred to as PMI.

The private mortgage system stimulates the housing market by allowing buyers with smaller down payments to qualify for a loan. Lenders who normally want buyer-borrower to put at least 20% cash down will allow qualified buyer-borrowers to put less down, if they purchase private mortgage insurance.

Coverage and Cost of Private Mortgage Insurance

Private mortgage insurance is available on 1 to 4 unit dwellings. It generally covers the top 20% to 25% of the loan amount, based on the value of the property. For example, if a home sold for $180,000 and the loan was 90%, the loan would be $180,000 \times 90\% = \$162,000$ loan. The private mortgage insurance coverage would be $20\% \times \$162,000$ loan $= \$32,400$ of insurance coverage to the lender.

The initial insurance premium fee varies with PMI companies, but it is usually paid by the borrower. In addition, there is an annual premium that is divided by 12 and added to the borrower's monthly payment. There are also plans whereby you can pay one fee at the time of closing and no annual premium. Recent laws allow the borrower to cancel the PMI once the homeowner achieves a 20% or more equity.

CHAPTER SUMMARY, PART I

Real estate lenders are concerned about a borrower's ability to repay a loan. To screen loan applicants, lenders use qualifying ratios coupled with an examination of the borrower's credit history and net worth.

Real estate lenders can be divided into three categories: (1) institutional lenders, (2) noninstitutional lenders, and (3) government-backed programs. Institutional real estate lenders are commercial banks, savings and loan associations (savings banks), and life insurance companies.

Noninstitutional real estate lenders include mortgage companies, private lenders, REITs, credit unions, and pension funds. Government-backed programs include FHA, VA, and Cal-Vet.

Private mortgage insurance (PMI) is used to guarantee a lender the payment of the upper portion of a loan if a borrower should default and a foreclosure sale does not generate enough money to cover the loan. PMI allows lenders to grant higher loans, thereby requiring less down payment.

IMPORTANT TERMS AND CONCEPTS

Commercial banks

Credit unions

Institutional lenders

Life insurance companies

Loan qualification ratios

Mortgage banker

Mortgage broker

Mortgage companies

Noninstitutional lenders

Private lenders

Private mortgage insurance (PMI)

Real estate investment trust (REIT)

Savings banks (Savings and Loan Associations)

PRACTICAL APPLICATION

1. A borrower earns $3,000 gross income per month and has $300 in long-term monthly debts. The lender's maximum qualifying ratios are 28% and 36%. Assuming good credit, what is the maximum monthly housing payment this borrower is qualified to pay?

2. Economists state that people can do only two things with their after-tax income and profits. What are these two things? Then explain how the real estate market is affected by these two choices.

3. Recent stories have surfaced about borrowers being overcharged for their PMI coverage. A new law requires the PMI insurers to cancel the PMI coverage once a loan amount is reduced to 80% or less of the value of the home. Assume that a loan balance is $180,000 and represents 80% or less of the value of the home. If the annual PMI charge is .0025 of the loan amount ($\frac{1}{4}$ of 1%), how much will a borrower's loan payment be reduced by canceling the PMI?

REVIEWING YOUR UNDERSTANDING

1. A borrower's total monthly housing payments will be $1,000. The borrower's other long-term debts are $300 per month. The borrower's gross monthly income is $3,600. What are the borrower's qualifying ratios?
   a. 25% and 33.3%
   b. 27.8% and 36.1%
   c. 30% and 38.9%
   d. 31.2% and 37.3%

2. Which of the following is a noninstitutional lender?
   a. commercial bank
   b. life insurance company
   c. pension fund
   d. savings and loan association

3. The government agency that insures savings accounts at approved institutions is the:
   a. RTC
   b. FSLIC
   c. FRB
   d. FDIC

4 Which real estate lender frequently acts as a loan correspondent for other lenders?
   a. pension funds
   b. mortgage companies
   c. real estate investment trusts
   d. private lenders

5. The use of private mortgage guaranty insurance permits lenders to make up to what percent loans on owner-occupied homes?
   a. 80%
   b. 90%
   c. 95%
   d. 100%

6. Which of the following statements is false?
   a. The higher the qualifying ratios, the more income a borrower needs to qualify for a real estate loan.
   b. Savings form the pool for borrowing.
   c. Life insurance companies specialize in making individual homeowner loans.
   d. Private lenders, who grant hard money loans to private individuals, are not exempt from usury laws.

7. A person who purchases a note for value at good faith without prior notice of a default or defect is a:
   a. holder in due course
   b. negotiable buyer
   c. mortgage broker
   d. loan correspondent

8. Lender that makes hard money loans by lending its own money:
   a. seller, through seller carry loans
   b. mortgage broker
   c. mortgage banker
   d. purchaser of existing trust deeds

9. Lender that tends to use the lowest loan-to-value ratios:
   a. savings bank
   b. commercial bank
   c. mortgage company
   d. life insurance company

10. In the financing of the sale of a home, which lender is required to complete a Seller Financial Disclosure Statement?
    a. owner carry lender
    b. credit union
    c. savings banks
    d. commercial banks

Part II: FHA, VA, Cal-Vet Loans, and the Secondary Mortgage Market

Chapter Preview, Part II

Chapter 8, Part II, focuses on specific government programs designed to help people acquire their own home. Three programs presented in detail are the Federal Housing Administration (FHA), the Department of Veterans' Affairs (VA), and the California Department of Veteran Affairs (Cal-Vet). In addition, the purpose and function of the secondary mortgage market is discussed. At the conclusion of Part II, you will be able to:

1. *Discuss the main characteristics of FHA-insured, VA-guaranteed, and Cal-Vet loans*

2. *Define the secondary mortgage market and discuss the role played by government agencies in this market*

8.5 GOVERNMENT ROLE IN REAL ESTATE FINANCING

Government has become heavily involved in helping Americans acquire decent housing. There are many government housing programs, but in this text only FHA-insured, VA-guaranteed, and Cal-Vet loan programs are discussed.

Federal Housing Administration (FHA)

The FHA, a part of the Department of Housing and Urban Development (HUD), was established in 1934 to improve the construction and the financing of housing. Since its creation, the FHA has had a major influence on real estate financing. Some of today's loan features that are taken for granted were initiated by the FHA.

The FHA is not a lender—*it does not make loans.* Approved lenders such as mortgage companies, insurance companies, and banks make the loans. However, the loans must be granted under FHA guidelines. Once the loan is granted, if the borrower defaults on the loan, FHA insures the lender against foreclosure loss.

The FHA collects a fee for this insurance, which is called *Mortgage Insurance Premium* (MIP). The MIP fees are paid up front in cash or financed as part of the loan.

This insurance should not be confused with credit life insurance. An FHA mortgage insurance policy does not insure the borrower's life. A mortgage insurance policy is used by FHA to reimburse a lender if the borrower defaults on mortgage payments, and the foreclosure results in a loss for the insured lender.

ADVANTAGES OF FHA LOANS

1. *Low down payment.* The main advantage of an FHA-insured loan is the low down payment. It used to be that FHA interest rates were set below the conventional rates. But deregulation now allows the FHA interest rate to float with the market. Therefore, sellers are no longer required to pay discount points to increase the lender's yield. Any loan fees or points charged by the lender are an item of negotiation and can be paid by either the buyer or seller.

2. *No prepayment penalty.* An FHA-insured loan does not allow a prepayment penalty.

3. *Under some circumstances, FHA-insured loans are assumable.* FHA-insured loans do not allow alienation clauses (due-on-sale clauses). This makes it possible to buy property, and, with FHA approval, take over the seller's existing FHA-insured loan. At one time, all FHA-insured loans were assumable without requiring a credit and/or income check. But, beginning with FHA-insured loans originating as of December 15, 1989, all assumptions must be approved by FHA. In addition, nonowner-occupied assumptions are prohibited on FHA-insured loans as of the same date. Under some circumstances, FHA-insured loans dated before December 15, 1989, can still be taken over without formal FHA approval. See a qualified loan representative for details.

4. *All cash to the seller.* New FHA-insured loans cash out the seller. In today's up and down real estate market, many sellers must carry a second in order to help finance a conventional loan for a buyer. Under FHA terms, the high loan-to-value ratio gives the seller all cash.

5. *Minimum property standards.* FHA will not allow a lender to grant a loan unless the property meets FHA housing standards, which in some cases are more stringent than what some conventional lenders allow.

DISADVANTAGES OF FHA LOANS

1. *Low loan amounts.* As a result of high home prices in many areas of California, the FHA program is not practical because of the cap that FHA sets on its maximum loan amount allowed (see FHA Loan Amounts later).

2. *Red tape and processing time.* The FHA is a large federal agency; therefore, you may experience the problem of dealing with a bureaucracy. However, some FHA-insured lenders have preapproval rights that can speed up the FHA process.

3. *Repairs on existing property.* The FHA-appointed appraiser also checks for repairs that he or she feels are necessary. FHA will then require that these repairs be made before the property is approved. Sellers may not wish to make these repairs and may refuse to sell to an FHA-insured buyer.

Federal Housing Administration Programs

Here are some general rules that apply to all FHA homeowner programs:

1. FHA will approve loans on 1 to 4 residential dwellings, units in planned unit developments (PUDs), condominiums, and mobile homes.

2. The maximum loan fee is 1% of the loan amount, and the buyer normally pays this fee.

3. The maximum term is 30 years or three-quarters of the remaining economic life of the property, whichever is less.

4. FHA requires that monthly payments include principal, interest, and $\frac{1}{12}$ of the annual property taxes and hazard insurance premium.

5. There is no maximum purchase price. The buyer can pay more than the FHA appraisal. However, the loan is based on the FHA appraisal if it is lower than the sales price.

6. The interest rates on FHA-backed loans now float with the market instead of being fixed by FHA.

7. FHA appraisals are good for six months on existing property; one year on new construction.

8. FHA requires a certification that the property has no evidence of termite infestation or other structural pest problems. Certification must be obtained from a licensed structural pest control company.

How to Calculate FHA-Insured Loan Amounts

FHA calculates the loan amount based on the home's sales price or the FHA approved appraisal, whichever is less. The mathematics work as follows:

Take the lesser of the sales price or the appraisal then apply the following formulas:

Sales price/appraisal value above $125,000, the maximum loan-to-value ratio is 97.15%.
Sales price/appraisal value $50,000 to $125,000, the maximum loan-to-value ratio is 97.65%.
Sales price/appraisal value less than $50,000, the maximum loan-to-value ratio is 98.75%.

FHA then sets a ceiling on the maximum loan allowed based on the median home prices in various geographic areas. The dollar amounts can change each year depending on the trend in home prices. Of California's 58 counties, the following 15 counties are considered especially high-cost areas and are allowed the largest FHA loan amounts in the continental United States: Alameda, Contra Costa, Los Angeles, Marin, Monterey, Orange, San Diego, San Francisco, San Joaquin, Sam Mateo, Santa Barbara, Santa Clara, Santa Cruz, Sonoma, and Ventura counties. In the remaining 33 California counties the maximum FHA loan amounts will be less. Because the amounts vary each year and from California county to county, dollar amounts are not quoted here. For the maximum FHA approved loan amount for your area, contact any local FHA approved lender. You can also log on the HUD's website at www.hud.gov and get the latest quote for your county.

Required Cash Investment

FHA requires a minimum 3% cash investment based on the sales price or appraisal, whichever is less. This 3% cash investment can come from an approved gift, and need not be the FHA buyer's own personal money. In that the FHA loan-to-value ratios, as noted above, range from 97.15% to 98.75%, this means that the required 3% cash investment is greater than the simple down payment as measured by price less loan amount.

Examples:			
Price =	100%	100%	100%
Loan =	97.15%	97.65%	98.75%
Down Payment	2.85%	2.35%	1.25%

Therefore, with a 3% required cash investment, this means that the buyer will be paying for some of the closing cost. If the buyer pays no more than the required 3% cash investment, then the remaining closing cost after applying the 3% rule, must be payed by the seller or some other party. The buyer can finance the required Mortgage Insurance Premium (MIP) by increasing the loan amount.

Under recent FHA rules, only the seller, not the buyer must pay for the following closing costs: tax service fee, loan document fee, processing fee, flood certification fee, termite costs, if any. The payment of all other non-recurring closing costs is negotiable between the seller and the buyer. See Chapter 10, The Role of Escrow and Title Insurance Companies, for a complete discussion of the difference between recurring and non-recurring closing costs.

FHA Programs

The National Housing Act of 1934 created the Federal Housing Administration. The act has eleven subdivisions, or "Titles," with further subdivisions called "Sections." This chapter deals only with Section 203b, because this is the most important section for the average home buyer or real estate agent.

SECTION 203B

Under the 203b program:

1. Anyone who is financially qualified is eligible.
2. Loans are available on properties from one to four units.

3. The maximum FHA loan amounts vary from region to region, with high cost areas of California allowed larger loan amounts than lower cost areas within the state.

4. Although a buyer's credit history is important, it does not need to be perfect.

5. The buyer must make a minimum cash investment of 3%, but this can come from an approved gift from family members and certain non-profit groups.

6. Mortgage Insurance Premium (MIP) must be obtained and can be purchased up front, or financed as part of the loan. The MIP added to the loan is allowed to exceed maximum FHA loan limits.

7. FHA permits a borrower to carry more debt than most conventional lenders will allow.

EXAMPLE

A buyer wishes to purchase a home under the FHA 203b program. The buyer agrees to pay $180,000 and the FHA approved appraisal come in at $182,000. Assume that the non-recurring closing cost come to $4,000. What is the maximum FHA loan account? What is the minimum cash the buyer must invest?

Step #1 - Lesser of price or appraisal is $180,000 x 97.15% = $174,870 or maximum loan for the area, whichever is less, plus any amount for MIP.

Step #2 - Lesser of price or appraisal is $180,000 x 3% = $5,400 minimum cash investment required from the buyer. If more cash is needed to pay for closing costs, the buyer can add more money, or the seller or some other party can agree to pay the remaining closing costs. This will be determined on a case by case basis.

Department of Veterans Affairs (VA or G.I.) Loans

In 1944, Congress passed the G.I. Bill of Rights to provide benefits to veterans, including provisions for making real estate loans.

Like the FHA, the VA is not a lender. However, if no approved private lender is located in the area, the VA will make direct loans under certain conditions. One difference between the FHA and VA is that the Department of Veterans Affairs *guarantees* a portion of the loan, while the Federal Housing Administration *insures* the loan.

Currently (as of January 1999), the maximum guarantee on a VA loan to a lender is $50,750 or 50% of the loan amount, whichever is less. For homes priced less than $144,000, $36,000 is the maximum guarantee. Whether a loan is insured or guaranteed is important only if foreclosure takes place. In the case of a foreclosure, the VA has two options:

1. It can pay the lender the balance on the loan and take back the property.
2. It can let the lender keep the property and pay it the amount of the guarantee.

If a foreclosure occurs under the FHA program, the lender is always paid off and the property is taken back by the FHA.

ADVANTAGES AND DISADVANTAGES OF VA (G.I.) LOANS

Advantages of VA Loans

1. *No down payment.* The VA does not require a borrower to make any down payment on loans up to $203,000 (as of January 1999) if the borrower pays the VA appraised value for the property.

2. *Lower interest rate.* Because of the VA guarantee, lenders usually charge less interest than the going conventional rates.

3. *No prepayment penalty.*

Disadvantages of VA Loans

1. *Creditworthiness qualification for assumptions.* Effective March 1, 1988, VA loans are no longer automatically assumable. VA requires a creditworthiness qualification before an existing loan can be taken over by a new buyer. The fee can be as high as $500.

2. *Seller may need to pay discount points.* The VA point system is explained later.

3. *Red tape and processing time.* Processing time, inflexibility, and paperwork occasionally are problems in dealing with a large government agency.

Who Is Eligible for VA Loans?

To be eligible, the veteran must have a discharge or release that is not dishonorable and have served a minimum number of days depending upon the time period in the service. The usual minimum is 181 days of active duty. National Guard and other military reserves who have served at least six years are also eligible.

Those who served less than the required time but were released or discharged because of a service-connected disability are also eligible for VA loans. In addition, many other classifications of veterans may be eligible for a VA-guaranteed loan depending upon the circumstances. Also, a veteran can use his or her VA loan more than once.

General Information on VA Loans

1. *Type of property.* The VA will guarantee loans on properties of from one to four units and on units in planned unit developments (PUDs), condominiums, and mobile homes.

2. *Interest rate.* Within VA guidelines, the interest rate is negotiable between the veteran and the lender.

3. *Loan fee.* The amount of the loan origination fee paid by the borrower is negotiable. Prior to a 1993 law change, the loan fee could only be 1% of the loan amount.

4. *Funding fee.* A separate fee on top of the loan fee is paid by the borrower for granting the loan. This fund fee usually varies from 1% to 2% of the loan amount.

5. *Term of loan.* The maximum term is 30 years.

6. *Down payment.* The VA does not require a down payment on loans up to $203,000. The veteran is frequently

allowed to borrow the full amount of the purchase price. What happens if the VA appraisal is less than the purchase price? The loan amount cannot exceed the appraisal. The difference between the purchase price and the appraisal has to be paid by the borrower in cash.

7. *Maximum loan.* There is no maximum loan amount on a VA loan. This does not mean you can obtain a no-down payment VA loan in any amount. Since the VA guarantees only a portion of the loan, lenders limit the amount they will lend on VA loans. Many lenders will not lend more than four times the guarantee. Thus, a $50,750 guarantee × 4 = $203,000, the maximum VA loan. VA regulations change from time to time regarding loans in excess of $203,000 and secondary financing. Check with your local VA lender.

8. *Occupying the property.* The veteran must occupy the property. The VA does not have a program for veterans who do not intend to occupy the property.

9. *Monthly payments.* Included are principal, interest, and $\frac{1}{12}$ the annual property taxes and hazard insurance premiums.

10. *Appraisal.* The VA appraisal is called "certificate of reasonable value" (CRV). To the VA, reasonable value means current market value.

11. *Structural pest control report.* The VA requires that a report be obtained from a licensed structural pest control company. Any required work must be done, and the veteran must certify that the work has been done satisfactorily.

Calculating Discount Points for VA Loans

Under VA terms, a lender and the veteran negotiate the interest rate. If this negotiated rate is not sufficient to cope with today's cost of overhead and profit, a lender simply refuses to grant a loan under VA terms. This could cause the sale to fall through. Under these circumstances a motivated seller might be willing to pay a discount fee to increase the lender's yield, thereby encouraging the lender to grant a VA loan and allow the sale to close.

EXAMPLE. Assume home sales price and appraisal is $203,000, and the maximum VA-insured loan available is $203,000. Also assume the negotiated VA interest rate that the veteran qualifies for is 8%, but lenders can get 9% interest on nongovernment-backed real estate loans. To entice the lender to make the VA-backed loan at 8%, the seller agrees to pay the 1% difference. This fee is called a "mortgage discount," or points.

*At one time, the rule was one point equals $\frac{1}{8}$ of 1%.

As a rule of thumb, points are calculated as follows: each 1% of discount (1 point) is equal to one-sixth of 1% interest.* For a lender to increase the yield on a loan by 1%, it is necessary for the lender to charge 6% or six points of the loan amount, which is deducted from the seller's net proceeds from the sale. Once again it should be stressed that the seller is made aware of this before accepting the buyer's offer to purchase the home.

Thus, in our example:

$9\% - 8\% = 1\% = 6/6 = 6$ points or .06 of the loan amount

Therefore:

$203,000 loan amount $\times$ .06 = $12,180 discount fee the seller must pay the lender, up front, from the seller's sale proceeds.

The 1% difference in the previous example is used for simplicity's sake to explain VA discount points. In the real world, the interest rate spread between the VA and conventional rate may be only $\frac{1}{8}\%$–$\frac{1}{4}\%$, resulting in only 1 to 2 discount points to be paid by the seller.

In an active market where there are numerous buyers, sellers tend not to sell to VA buyers who require the payment of discount points. But in a slow market, a seller may be more than willing to pay discount points just to get rid of the property.

Cal-Vet Loans   The Cal-Vet program is administered by the State of California, Department of Veterans Affairs, Division of Farms and Home Purchases. The veteran (buyer) normally deals directly with this agency, although recent rules allow a mortgage loan broker to start the loan process on behalf of the buyer. There is no other lender involved; the state makes the loan directly to the veteran. This money is obtained from the sale of State Veteran Bonds.

Who Is Eligible   To Qualify, a veteran must meet these requirements.
for Cal-Vet Loans?   **1.** 90 days' active duty.
2. Honorable discharge, or if still on active duty, a State ment of Service, verifying their status.
3. The veteran must be buying a California home or farm.

Both peace and war time veterans are eligible for a Cal-Vet loan. But if loan funds are limited, a preference is given to war time veterans. The highest priority is given to service connected disabled war veterans. Unremarried surviving spouses of an eligible veteran may also be qualified for a Cal-Vet loan. A Cal-Vet loan may be used more than once, as long as the previous Cal-Vet loan has been paid in full, or awarded in a divorce to a non veteran spouse.

General Information About Cal-Vet Loans

1. *Property* Cal-Vet has generally the same property standards as FHA and VA. The property must be a single-family dwelling or a unit in a planned unit development, condominium, or mobile home. Certain farm loans are also approved. Cal-Vet requires both a structural pest control report and a roof inspection.

2. *Maximum loan.* The maximum home loan (as of January 1999) is $250,000. For a farm the maximum loan is $300,000.

3. *Down payment.* The Cal-Vet down payment has recently been lowered to 2% of the sales price or appraisal, which ever is lower. Previously, Cal-Vet requires 5% down, but in an effort to make the program more competitive, as of January 1999, the minimum down payment has been reduced to 2%.

4. *Term of loan.* Legal maximum is 40 years, but most loans are approved for a term of 30 years.

5. *Interest rate.* The interest rate is variable. The rate is checked periodically to determine if a change is necessary. The cost of the bonds and of running the program determine the interest rate.

6. *Secondary financing.* This is permitted under special circumstances. However, the provisions are too complex to be covered in this text.

7. *Prepayment penalty.* Technically, if the loan is paid off within five years, the penalty is six months' interest on the original loan amount. There is no penalty after five years. As an agency policy, Cal-Vet frequently only charges a prepayment penalty if the loan is paid off in two years, even though the regulations state five years. But Cal-Vet does reserve the right to invoke the five-year rule at any time.

8. *Occupancy.* The veteran must occupy the property.

9. *Monthly payments.* Principal and interest, and $\frac{1}{12}$ the annual property taxes, hazard insurance, disability, and life insurance premiums are included in monthly loan payments.

10. *Title to property.* When a property is being financed with a Cal-Vet loan, title is first conveyed to the Department of Veterans Affairs by the seller. The department then sells the property to the veteran under a

land contract of sale. The department continues to hold title until the veteran has paid the loan in full.

ADVANTAGES AND DISADVANTAGES OF CAL-VET LOANS

The main advantage of Cal-Vet loans are low interest rate, low down payment, inexpensive life and hazard insurance, and low closing costs.

In the past, the main disadvantage has been the long time it took to process a Cal-Vet loan. But recent changes by the California Department of Veterans affairs have attempted to address this issue. Cal-Vet now has several district offices through out the state, with trained personnel to give you the latest information and the help you need to prepare the required forms for faster loan processing. In addition, many mortgage brokers have completed Cal-Vet loan processing seminars and are equipped to help a veteran process a loan. If a private mortgage loan broker is used, the seller and buyer must pay the broker's fee, it cannot be financed as part of a Cal-Vet loan. For more information, as of January 1999, the toll free Cal-Vet number is 1-800-952-5626 and their website is www.ns.net/cadva/.

TABLE 8.1   Comparison of Government-Backed Loans as of January 1999

	Federal Housing Administration	*Department of Veterans Affairs (VA)*	*Cal-Vet*
Purpose of loan	1–4 units	1–4 units	home or farm
Eligibility	any U.S. resident	U.S. veteran	U.S. veteran
Maximum purchase price	none	none	none
Maximum loan	Varies by Geographic area	none by DVA; but restricts the guarantee	$250,000 $300,000 farms
Down payment	3% minimum cash investment	none, but loan limited to CRV	2% of sale price or appraisal whichever is less
Maximum term	usually 30 years	usually 30 years	legally 40 years but usually 30 years
Interest rate	market rate	negotiated rate	variable rate
Prepayment penalty	none	none	6 months' interest if paid during first 5 years on original loan amount

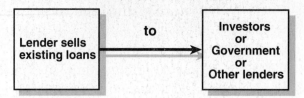

Figure 8.2

8.6 SECONDARY MORTGAGE MARKET

The secondary mortgage market is a market where existing real estate loans are bought and sold—in other words, lenders sell their loans to other lenders and investors. The secondary mortgage market should not be confused with secondary financing. Secondary financing is a loan secured by a second or junior deed of trust, whereas a secondary market is the sale of an existing loan by one lender to another lender or investor. (See Figure 8.2.)

Purpose of the Secondary Mortgage Market

FLOW OF MONEY

Why do lenders need a secondary mortgage market? Why don't they just make a loan and keep it? That would be fine if every lender always had a perfect balance between the demand for loans and its supply of money. However, in the real world, this balance rarely exists. For example, a lender in California may have a greater demand for loans than it can meet. Another lender in Texas might have the opposite problem—surplus funds because of lack of demand in Texas. The solution to this problem is to have the Texas lender buy loans from the California lender. Both would be satisfying their needs. The Texas lender would be putting idle money to work and the California lender would obtain additional funds to use to make new loans. Thus, one of the main purposes of the secondary market is to shift mortgage funds to areas where they are needed.

STABILIZE THE MORTGAGE MARKET

The mortgage market is never static. Instead, it moves through cycles of tight and loose money. The market can be stabilized by providing funds to buy loans during tight money periods and providing loans to be purchased during loose money periods. Three main organizations designed to help stabilize the mortgage market are:

1. Federal National Mortgage Association
2. Federal Home Loan Mortgage Corporation
3. Government National Mortgage Association

Federal National Mortgage Association

The Federal National Mortgage Association is usually called by its nickname "Fannie Mae." Established in 1938 by the U.S. Congress, its main job is to provide a secondary market for mortgages. Fannie Mae remained a part of the federal government until 1968, when it became a private corporation. Its main function today is still to maintain a secondary market.

In order to maintain a secondary market, Fannie Mae buys and sells mortgages. Where does it get the money to do this? It borrows money in the capital market by selling notes and bonds. Fannie Mae can usually obtain a more favorable rate than another corporate borrower because its obligations carry the indirect backing of the U.S. government.

What type of loans can Fannie Mae buy and sell? Fannie Mae will purchase government-backed and conventional loans on one- to four-unit dwellings, units in planned unit developments, and condominiums. Fannie Mae buys conventional loans only if the loans have been issued using Fannie Mae guidelines. Once purchased, the loans are either held as an investment or resold to other lenders and investors.

Federal Home Loan Mortgage Corporation

The Federal Home Loan Mortgage Corporation, known as "Freddie Mac," was created in 1970 under the Emergency Home Finance Act. The main function of Freddie Mac was to provide a secondary mortgage market for the savings and loan associations. However, today it also deals with other institutional lenders.

Freddie Mac buys FHA, VA, and conventional loans. It purchases conventional loans on one- to four-unit buildings, units in planned unit developments, and condominiums. Freddie Mac and Fannie Mae usually have identical loan applications, maximum loan amounts, appraisal standards, and borrower loan qualification guidelines.

Government National Mortgage Association

The Government National Mortgage Association also has a nickname, "Ginnie Mae," and is a wholly owned corporation of the U.S. government. It was created in 1968 when Fannie Mae became a private corporation. At the time, Fannie Mae was relieved of two of its duties, which were given to Ginnie Mae. These were:

1. The management and liquidation of certain mortgages previously acquired by the U.S. government

2. Special assistance functions, including the development of a mortgage-backed security program

By directly and indirectly providing low interest rate loans, Ginnie Mae encourages people to buy new homes. The increased demand for new homes results in more work and jobs for the construction industry.

The real impact of Ginnie Mae is in its mortgage-backed security program. This program was established to attract additional money into the housing market. The mortgage-backed security was created to make investing in mortgages as simple as buying stocks and bonds. Under this mortgage program, an investor will purchase a pool of mortgages and receive a certificate. There is no need to examine each mortgage. All the time-consuming paperwork is eliminated. Since Ginnie Mae is a federal corporation, its guarantee is backed by the "full faith and credit" of the U.S. government.

In short, the Ginnie Mae programs in the secondary mortgage market have added to the funds made available for real estate borrowers.

Special First-Time Home Buyer Programs

The Federal National Mortgage Association (Fannie Mae) has a first-time home buyer program called the *Community Home Buyer's Program.* This program requires only 5% down payment and has less rigid income qualifying ratios. Two percent of the required 5% down payment can be a gift from a relative, thus the buyer only has to put 3% down from his or her own funds. To qualify, the borrower's income cannot exceed 115% to 120% of the median income in the area.

Some local lenders, in an effort to place loans throughout the communities they serve, have their own first-time home buyer programs. Many of these lower cost programs are for people who purchase in designated zip codes and U.S. census tracts.

Real Estate Loan Jargon

Real estate lenders speak a language of their own. Here are some key terms regarding real estate loans:

Conventional loans. Any nongovernment-backed loan.
Conforming loans. Loans that meet the guidelines of Fannie Mae or Freddie Mac.
Nonconforming loans. Loans that do not meet the guidelines of Fannie Mae or Freddie Mac.

Jumbo loans. Loans that exceed the loan limits of Fannie Mae or Freddie Mac.

Portfolio loans. Loans that will not be sold in the secondary mortgage market, but will be held by the lender as an investment.

CHAPTER SUMMARY, PART II

Government has taken an active role in the field of real estate finance. On the federal level, the Federal Housing Administration (FHA) has several programs. The 203b program is the most popular. The Department of Veterans Affairs (VA) has a no-down-payment program for qualified veterans. The State of California's Cal-Vet loan program has been a huge success, with demand usually exceeding the supply of loans available. The extremely low interest rate paid by the California veteran is the main attraction.

The secondary mortgage market consists of real estate lenders who sell existing mortgages to other real estate lenders. The main purpose of the secondary mortgage market is to help strike a balance between the demand for real estate loans and the supply of money available for real estate loans. The Federal National Mortgage Association, the Federal Home Loan Mortgage Corporation, and the Government National Mortgage Association all participate in this secondary mortgage market.

IMPORTANT TERMS AND CONCEPTS

Cal-Vet loans

Department of Veterans Affairs (VA)

Discount points

Federal Home Loan Mortgage Corporation (Freddie Mac)

Federal Housing Administration (FHA)

Federal National Mortgage Association (Fannie Mae)

Government National Mortgage Association (Ginnie Mae)

Secondary mortgage market

203b Program (FHA)

PRACTICAL APPLICATION

1. A buyer agrees to purchase a home using the FHA 203b program. The price and FHA approved appraisal is $150,000 and the seller agrees to pay all closing cost above the buyer's minimum cash investment. Based only on this information, how much cash will the buyer be required to invest to close escrow?

2. Referring to Question #1, assume the buyer used the VA program and paid a 1% loan fee, plus a 1.5% funding fee and $500 in other closing cost. Based only on this information, how much cash will the buyer/veteran need to close escrow?

3. Referring to Question #1 above, assume the buyer used the Cal-Vet program, paid the down payment and $700 in closing cost, with the seller agreeing to pay all other remaining cost. Based only on this information, how much cash will the buyer/veteran need to close escrow?

REVIEWING YOUR UNDERSTANDING

1. Assuming the county qualifies, and with no loan increase for MIP, with an approved FHA price/appraisal of $180,000, what is the maximum FHA-insured amount?
   a. $180,000
   b. $177,750
   c. $174,870
   d. $173,925

2. Of the following government programs, which usually has the lowest interest rate?
   a. Cal-Vet
   b. VA
   c. FHA
   d. Fannie Mae

3. If the maximum VA-negotiated interest rate the veteran is able to pay is 8.5%, but a lender wishes a rate of 9%, how many points difference are there between these two rates?
   a. ½ point
   b. 3 points
   c. 5 points
   d. 6 points

4. Which statement is true about a VA-guaranteed loan?
   a. The buyer must pay the discount points if any.
   b. The down payment requirement is 3% of the first $25,000 and 5% of the remainder.
   c. The maximum loan amount for a home is $60,000.
   d. The veteran can use a VA loan more than once.

5. The least down payment for a $150,000 appraised home would be from:
   a. FHA
   b. VA
   c. Cal-Vet
   d. Fannie Mae

6. During a Cal-Vet loan, title to the real property rests with the:
   a. institutional lender
   b. borrower
   c. Department of Veterans Affairs
   d. buyer

7. A secondary mortgage market is where:
   a. second loans are placed against real estate
   b. existing real estate loans are bought and sold
   c. an insurance company guarantees the loan payments
   d. mortgage brokers arrange loans to borrowers

8. "Fannie Mae" refers to:
   a. Government National Mortgage Association
   b. Federal National Mortgage Association
   c. Federal Home Loan Mortgage Corporation
   d. Department of Veterans Affairs

9. A loan that meets Fannie Mae and Freddie Mac guidelines is known as a:
   a. jumbo loan
   b. portfolio loan
   c. conventional loan
   d. conforming loan

10. When a seller carries back a junior loan, this is best described as:
    a. secondary financing
    b. the secondary mortgage market
    c. a second deed of trust
    d. investing in a second trust deed

Appendix

Case Study—Qualifying for a Home Loan

As a general rule of thumb, there are two percentages to be aware of: 28% and 36%.

1. No more than 28% of your gross monthly income should be used for your total monthly house payment, consisting of principal, interest, taxes, insurance, and, if need be, association dues and private mortgage insurance.

$$\frac{\text{Total monthly house payment}}{\text{Gross monthly income}} = \text{No more than 28\%}$$

2. No more than 36% of your gross monthly income should be used for your total monthly credit obligations (monthly house payments, plus all other monthly credit obligations such as car loans, credit cards, and so on that have six months or more to run).

$$\frac{\text{Total monthly credit obligations}}{\text{Gross monthly income}} = \text{No more than 36\%}$$

Mr. and Mrs. Buyer wish to purchase a $180,000 home. Mr. Buyer has a yearly salary of $33,000, and Mrs. Buyer earns $34,000 per year. They have both been on their jobs for over four years. Their monthly bills are as follows: car payments, three years to go at $375, furniture payment $125 for 13 months, and a student loan of $75 with four months remaining. If they buy the home, their annual property taxes will be $2,100 and a home owner's insurance policy will run $504 per year. There will be no requirement to pay homeowner association dues.

A local lender is willing to make a $162,000 (90%) loan at 8.5% for 30 years, payable at $1,245 per month, plus $38 per month for private mortgage insurance. Assuming that the buyers have the required cash down payment and have a good credit history, do they have the income to qualify for this loan? Do they meet the 28% and 36% ratios?

After you have done your computations, check your answer by turning to the section titled "Answers to Reviewing Your Understanding" toward the end of the book.

Chapter 9
Real Estate Appraisal

Chapter Preview

An appraisal is an essential part of a real estate transaction. Many times the decision to buy, sell, or grant a loan on real estate hinges upon a real estate appraiser's estimate of a property's value. At the conclusion of the chapter, you will be able to:

1. Define appraisal and list four elements and forces that influence value

2. Distinguish between utility value and market value

3. Define depreciation; outline the causes of depreciation; and then describe how to calculate depreciation

4. Discuss the three approaches or methods used to determine value; outline the steps in each approach; define gross multipliers

9.1 APPRAISAL CONCEPTS

An appraisal is defined as an estimate or an opinion of value. Real estate appraisals are needed to:

1. Set sales prices on property
2. Estimate real estate loan values
3. Determine values for real property taxes
4. Help set premiums on fire insurance policies

Other reasons include determining estate taxes and values for government acquisition. Real estate appraisal is not an exact science; therefore, the accuracy of an appraisal is related to the skill, experience, and judgment of the appraiser.

Real Estate Appraisal License Requirements

Any appraisal for a real estate transaction involving federal insurance or assistance must be done by a licensed or certified appraiser. This includes an appraisal for any lender whose deposits are insured, or are regulated by, a federal agency. For these appraisals, the appraiser must have a special license or certificate issued by the California Office of Real Estate Appraisers. It is important to stress that a real estate license alone does not qualify. The appraisal license or certification is completely different from a real estate license. The basic appraisal categories of license or certification are, as of January 1999:

1. Licensed: Allowed to appraise noncomplex 1 to 4 unit residential properties up to $1 million. On non-residential transactions the dollar limit is only $250,000.
2. Certified (Residential): Allowed to appraise all 1 to 4 unit residential properties regardless of the value. On non-residential transactions the dollar limit is $250,000.
3. Certified (General): Allowed to appraise any real estate regardless of type or value.

All appraisers must take a minimum number of hours of real estate appraisal and related educational courses:

Licensed = 90 hours
Certified-Residential = 120 hours
Certified-General = 180 hours

Minimum on-the-job experience requirements are as follows:

Licensed = 2,000 hours
Certified-Residential = 2,500 hours
Certified-General = 3,000 hours, and at least 1,500 hours must be with non-residential properties

After meeting these requirements, an examination must be passed, and then an appraisal license or certification is issued for a four-year period. To renew the license, 40 hours of approved continuing education courses must be taken. For people who may have the education, but not the experience, upon passing the examination a training license is issued for the least complicated appraisals. No training license exists at the higher certification level.

Professional Designations

In addition to a state-issued license or certificate, there are several professional real estate appraisal organizations in the United States that issue highly prized professional designations. Two of the largest appraisal trade associations are the American Institute of Real Estate Appraisers (AREAWAY), which issues the widely recognized designation MAI (Member of the Appraisal Institute), and the Society of Real Estate Appraisers, which issues the designation SRPA.

Market Value

The purpose of an appraisal is to determine a value for a property. Although there are various types of value—sales value, loan value, tax value, and insurance value—two major categories of value are *value in use* (utility value) and *market value.*

Value in use refers to the value of a particular property to a particular owner or user of real estate. The value of property to a particular owner may be emotional, as well as economic; thus, value in use is also known as *subjective value.* For example, the value that you place in a property that has been in your family for over 100 years might be different than what an outside buyer might view as value.

On the other hand, *market value* is value in exchange as determined by supply and demand in the open real estate market. Market value is also referred to as *objective value.* Between utility and market value, without question, most appraisals are for the purpose of establishing market value. Market value can be briefly defined as "the highest price in terms of money for which a property would sell in the open market, the seller not being obligated to sell, the buyer not being obligated to buy, allowing a reasonable length of time to effect the sale." This also assumes that both the buyer and seller are fully knowledgeable persons. In short, when a buyer or seller asks the question, "What is the property worth?" they are asking for an estimate or opinion of the market value as of a certain date.

Market Value versus Price Paid

Price paid may or may not be the same as market value. A person could pay a price of $200,000 for a home that has a market value of $180,000, or just the opposite—pay a price of $180,000 for a home with a market value appraisal of $200,000. On the other hand, a person may pay $200,000 for a home valued at $200,000. The key point is this: Price trends establish market values, but for any single sale, the price paid may be equal to, higher, or lower than market value.

Essential Elements of Value

For property to have value, four elements or characteristics must be present. These are: (1) utility, (2) scarcity, (3) demand, and (4) transferability.

Utility refers to usefulness—the more useful a property, the greater its potential value. Scarcity means lack of abundance. When utility exists, the more scarce an item, the greater its value.

Demand refers to the desire to own real estate, coupled with the financial ability to buy. Assuming a scarce number of properties for sale, the greater the number of ready, willing, and able buyers (demand) the greater the likelihood that the property offered for sale will increase in value.

Transferability refers to the ability to transfer identifiable ownership. A beautiful home on the California coast may be a scarce commodity, with great utility and high demand. But if the property's title is clouded and uncertain, not many people will be willing to buy this home. The clearer the title, the more valuable the property. When a title is clouded, the property is less valuable.

Utility, scarcity, demand, and transferability are the essential elements that create value. If all are present in a favorable combination, a property's value may increase. If one or more elements are missing, a property's value may be stagnant or even decline. (See Figure 9.1.)

Four Forces That Influence Value

Once a property's value has been established, there are four forces that can change its value. These forces are:

1. *Social forces,* such as changes in population, marriage trends, family size, and attitudes toward education, recreation, and lifestyles
2. *Economic forces,* which include changes in income levels, employment opportunities, the cost of money and credit, taxes, and the availability of energy and natural resources

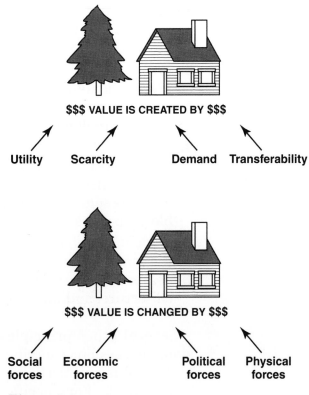

Figure 9.1

3. *Political forces,* such as changes in zoning, building codes, construction moratoriums, government housing programs, and pro-growth or no-growth government philosophy

4. *Physical forces* that affect the physical aspects of the property, such as size and shape of the parcel, the location, climate, and soil conditions

These four forces continually bombard every parcel of real estate and cause values to shift either positively or negatively. Which of these forces is the single most important? There is no simple answer! This is where the skill, experience, and judgment of an appraiser come in. However, there is an old saying that states, "The three most important factors of value are location, location, location."

Basic Principles of Valuation

Appraisal theory and practice are based upon several principles or assumptions:

1. *Principle of highest and best use.* The best use of land is that use which produces the greatest net return to the land.

2. *Principle of change.* Real estate values are constantly changing as a result of social, economic, political, and physical forces within a region, city, and neighborhood.

3. *Principle of supply and demand.* The interaction of supply and demand causes real estate values to change. For example, assuming a fixed supply of homes for sale, an increase in demand should cause prices to increase.

4. *Principle of substitution.* The value of a property tends to be influenced by the price of acquiring an equally desirable substitute property. For example, the value of Property A is somewhat determined by the value of comparable properties B, C, and D.

5. *Principle of conformity.* In a residential neighborhood, the maximum value will be found where there is a high degree of conformity, such as homes of similar design, architecture, and upkeep.

Several other principles are the principles of progression, regression, contribution, anticipation, competition, and surplus productivity. But these are beyond the scope of this book. For specific details, consult any appraisal textbook.

What needs to be emphasized here is that all the principles mentioned previously form the theoretical foundation upon which real estate appraisers rely to estimate value.

9.2 DEPRECIATION

Depreciation is defined as a loss in value from any cause. Depreciation is usually measured as the difference between the new replacement cost of a building or improvement, and its value as of the date of the appraisal. If an existing building (excluding land) is appraised at $150,000, but its replacement cost if it were destroyed and needed to be rebuilt is calculated to be $200,000, the $50,000 difference ($200,000 less $150,000) is the amount of the depreciation.

Causes of Depreciation

The causes or reasons for a loss in real estate value can be grouped into three categories.

1. *Physical deterioration.* A loss in value caused by (a) wear and tear from use; (b) deferred maintenance, lack of upkeep; (c) damage by termites, dry rot, and so on; and (d) weather conditions. A rundown home, in need of paint and repairs, is an example of depreciation caused by physical deterioration.

2. *Functional obsolescence.* A loss in value caused by (a) unpopular floor plan and layout; (b) lack of updated, modern appliances and equipment; and (c) poor or unpopular architectural design and style. A three-bedroom, one-bath home with a wall heater and single-car garage is an example of depreciation caused by functional obsolescence. Why? Because most buyers of three-bedroom homes prefer one and one-half or two bathrooms, a two-car garage, and a forced-air heating system. Therefore, all other things being equal, the three-bedroom, one-bath home noted earlier will usually sell at a lower price.

3. *Economic and social obsolescence.* A loss in value resulting from (a) zoning and other government actions, (b) misplaced improvements, such as a home built next to an all-night service station, and (c) a drop in demand for real estate, or overbuilding, creating an excessive supply of homes. An example of economic obsolescence would be a neighborhood street, recently declared a truck route, whose increased traffic brings noise and fumes into the area. This could cause home values to decline. In short, economic obsolescence is caused by factors outside the boundaries of the property—items beyond the control of the owners.

Curable versus Incurable Depreciation

Physical deterioration and functional obsolescence can be classified as curable or incurable. *Curable* means that if repairs and/or remodeling are undertaken, the expense incurred will be less than the value added to the property. If you spend $15,000 to repair your home and in the process this adds $18,000 in value, this is considered curable.

Incurable depreciation means the cost to repair or remodel exceeds the value added to the property. If you pay $15,000 to repair your home and in the process only add $10,000 in value, this is considered incurable. Physical deterioration and functional obsolescence can be classified as curable or incurable per the guidelines noted earlier. However, economic obsolescence is almost always considered incurable, because the loss in value is caused by negative factors outside the property's boundaries. Therefore, it is assumed that these negative factors are beyond the control of any single property owner.

Accrued Depreciation versus Recapture for Depreciation

Accrued depreciation is the loss in value that has already occurred in a building. Recapture for depreciation (sometimes called accrual for depreciation) is an estimate for depreciation that will occur in the future. Accrued (past) depreciation is used in an appraisal technique called the cost approach. A recapture for depreciation is used in an appraisal technique called the income approach. These approaches to value are discussed in the next section of this chapter.

An Additional Word About Depreciation

Depreciation for appraisal purposes is different from depreciation for income tax purposes. The appraiser looks at depreciation as being an actual decline in value. An accountant, for income tax purposes, uses *book depreciation* as a basis for an income tax deduction. The two concepts are not the same. The accountant uses a theoretical figure allowed by the Internal Revenue Service, whereas an appraiser uses economic analysis to arrive at an actual decline in value.

Appreciation is an increase in value that can result from inflation or from the interaction of supply and demand forces. All real estate improvements suffer some form of depreciation, but simultaneously many properties are appreciating. The question then becomes: Is the rate of appreciation exceeding the rate of depreciation? If so, overall value of the property increases. But if the rate of depreciation is exceeding appreciation, the overall value of the property decreases.

9.3 APPRAISAL METHODS

When an appraiser is hired, the appraiser's estimate of value is submitted as a report. Three common types of - appraisal reports are:

1. Restricted appraisal report
2. Summary appraisal report
3. Self-contained appraisal report

The restricted form is the least comprehensive report. It is used when a client is familiar with the area and therefore does not need appraisal details. It requires a prominent disclaimer that the appraisal is limited in scope. This is the least expensive type of report and formerly was referred to as a letter form report.

The summary report is most commonly used by real estate lenders when appraising property for loan purposes. The short-form report consists of check sheets and spaces to be filled in by the appraiser. In recent years there has been a tendency to standardize the short-form report using guidelines established by government-backed agencies that operate in the secondary mortgage market. This report was formerly referred to as a short form report. (See Figure 9.2.)

The self-contained report is the most comprehensive and expensive appraisal report. It is a complete documentation of the entire appraisal process, including computation, maps, photographs, and detailed analysis. This report is used in court cases, condemnation proceedings, and for expensive commercial and industrial properties. Because of its size, detail, and cost, a self-contained appraisal report is not commonly used in the home market. A self-contained report was formerly referred to as a narrative report.

Appraisal Process

As in many other professional occupations, real estate appraisers have developed a system for conducting their work. The appraisal of real estate can be viewed as a series of steps, with each step logically following the preceding, until a final estimate of value is reached. Figure 9.3 is a flow chart of the real estate appraisal process.

As shown in Figure 9.3, the appraiser starts with a definition of the problem. What is the reason for the appraisal? Why does the client need the appraisal? Then the needed data are gathered and classified. The data are run through three approaches or techniques of analysis called the *cost, market (comparable sales),* and *income approaches.* A separate value is arrived at under each approach, and then these three values are correlated, or reconciled. From this reconciliation process, one final estimate of value is given to the client. It must be stressed that reconciliation is not the averaging of the results from the three approaches, but rather a weighted blend based on what is most appropriate for the property.

Although this appraisal process has its roots in scientific analysis, the appraisal of real estate is still somewhat judgmental. Therefore, the accuracy of the appraisal depends not only on the data gathered, but also on the judgment, skill, and experience of the person doing the appraisal.

Three Approaches to Value

COST APPROACH TO VALUE

The cost approach to value comprises four basic steps:

1. *Estimate the value of the land.* Compare recent lot sales prices.
2. *Estimate the current replacement costs of the improvements.* Building square footage × cost per square foot; also estimate price of fencing, cement work, landscaping.

UNIFORM RESIDENTIAL APPRAISAL REPORT   File No.

Property Description

SUBJECT		
Property Address	City	State Zip Code
Legal Description		County
Assessor's Parcel No.	Tax Year R.E. Taxes $	Special Assessments $
Borrower	Current Owner	Occupant: ☐ Owner ☐ Tenant ☐ Vacant
Property rights appraised ☐ Fee Simple ☐ Leasehold	Project Type ☐ PUD ☐ Condominium (HUD/VA only)	HOA $ _____ /Mo.
Neighborhood or Project Name	Map Reference	Census Tract
Sale Price $ Date of Sale	Description and $ amount of loan charges/concessions to be paid by seller	
Lender/Client	Address	
Appraiser	Address	

NEIGHBORHOOD

Location	☐ Urban	☐ Suburban	☐ Rural
Built up	☐ Over 75%	☐ 25-75%	☐ Under 25%
Growth rate	☐ Rapid	☐ Stable	☐ Slow
Property values	☐ Increasing	☐ Stable	☐ Declining
Demand/supply	☐ Shortage	☐ In balance	☐ Over supply
Marketing time	☐ Under 3 mos.	☐ 3-6 mos.	☐ Over 6 mos.

Predominant occupancy
☐ Owner
☐ Tenant
☐ Vacant (0-5%)
☐ Vac.(over 5%)

Single family housing
PRICE $(000)   AGE (yrs)
Low
High
Predominant

Present land use %
One family _____
2-4 family _____
Multi-family _____
Commercial _____

Land use change
☐ Not likely ☐ Likely
☐ In process
To: _____

Note: Race and the racial composition of the neighborhood are not appraisal factors.

Neighborhood boundaries and characteristics: _____

Factors that affect the marketability of the properties in the neighborhood (proximity to employment and amenities, employment stability, appeal to market, etc.): _____

Market conditions in the subject neighborhood (including support for the above conclusions related to the trend of property values, demand/supply, and marketing time -- such as data on competitive properties for sale in the neighborhood, description of the prevalence of sales and financing concessions, etc.): _____

PUD

Project Information for PUDs   (If applicable) - - Is the developer/builder in control of the Home Owners' Association (HOA)?   ☐ Yes ☐ No
Approximate total number of units in the subject project _____   Approximate total number of units for sale in the subject project _____
Describe common elements and recreational facilities: _____

SITE

Dimensions		Topography
Site area	Corner Lot ☐ Yes ☐ No	Size
Specific zoning classification and description		Shape
Zoning compliance ☐ Legal ☐ Legal nonconforming (Grandfathered use) ☐ Illegal ☐ No zoning		Drainage
Highest & best use as improved: ☐ Present use ☐ Other use (explain)		View

Utilities	Public	Other	Off-site Improvements	Type	Public	Private	
Electricity	☐		Street		☐	☐	Landscaping
Gas	☐		Curb/gutter		☐	☐	Driveway Surface
Water	☐		Sidewalk		☐	☐	Apparent easements
Sanitary sewer	☐		Street lights		☐	☐	FEMA Special Flood Hazard Area ☐ Yes ☐ No
Storm sewer	☐		Alley		☐	☐	FEMA Zone Map Date
							FEMA Map No.

Comments (apparent adverse easements, encroachments, special assessments, slide areas, illegal or legal nonconforming zoning use, etc.): _____

DESCRIPTION OF IMPROVEMENTS

GENERAL DESCRIPTION	EXTERIOR DESCRIPTION	FOUNDATION	BASEMENT	INSULATION
No. of Units	Foundation	Slab	Area Sq. Ft.	Roof ☐
No. of Stories	Exterior Walls	Crawl Space	% Finished	Ceiling ☐
Type (Det./Att.)	Roof Surface	Basement	Ceiling	Walls ☐
Design (Style)	Gutters & Dwnspts.	Sump Pump	Walls	Floor ☐
Existing/Proposed	Window Type	Dampness	Floor	None ☐
Age (Yrs.)	Storm/Screens	Settlement	Outside Entry	Unknown ☐
Effective Age (Yrs.)	Manufactured House	Infestation		

ROOMS	Foyer	Living	Dining	Kitchen	Den	Family Rm.	Rec. Rm.	Bedrooms	# Baths	Laundry	Other	Area Sq. Ft.
Basement												
Level 1												
Level 2												

Finished area **above** grade contains: Rooms;   Bedroom(s);   Bath(s);   Square Feet of Gross Living Area

INTERIOR	Materials/Condition	HEATING	KITCHEN EQUIP.	ATTIC	AMENITIES	CAR STORAGE:
Floors		Type	Refrigerator ☐	None ☐	Fireplace(s) # ___ ☐	None ☐
Walls		Fuel	Range/Oven ☐	Stairs ☐	Patio ☐	Garage # of cars
Trim/Finish		Condition	Disposal ☐	Drop Stair ☐	Deck ☐	Attached ☐
Bath Floor		COOLING	Dishwasher ☐	Scuttle ☐	Porch ☐	Detached ☐
Bath Wainscot		Central	Fan/Hood ☐	Floor ☐	Fence ☐	Built-In ☐
Doors		Other	Microwave ☐	Heated ☐	Pool ☐	Carport ☐
		Condition	Washer/Dryer ☐	Finished ☐		Driveway ☐

Additional features (special energy efficient items, etc.): _____

COMMENTS

Condition of the improvements, depreciation (physical, functional, and external), repairs needed, quality of construction, remodeling/additions, etc.: _____

Adverse environmental conditions (such as, but not limited to, hazardous wastes, toxic substances, etc.) present in the improvements, on the site, or in the immediate vicinity of the subject property.: _____

Freddie Mac Form 70 6/93   PAGE 1 OF 2   Fannie Mae Form 1004 6/93

Figure 9.2a

UNIFORM RESIDENTIAL APPRAISAL REPORT

File No.

Valuation Section

COST APPROACH			
ESTIMATED SITE VALUE		= $	
ESTIMATED REPRODUCTION COST-NEW-OF IMPROVEMENTS:			
Dwelling _____ Sq. Ft. @$ _____		= $ _____	
_____ Sq. Ft. @$ _____		= _____	
		= _____	
Garage/Carport _____ Sq. Ft. @$ _____		= _____	
Total Estimated Cost New		= $ _____	
Less Physical Functional External			
Depreciation _____		= $ _____	
Depreciated Value of Improvements		= $ _____	
"As-is" Value of Site Improvements		= $ _____	
INDICATED VALUE BY COST APPROACH		= $ _____	

Comments on Cost Approach (such as, source of cost estimate, site value, square foot calculation and for HUD, VA and FmHA, the estimated remaining economic life of the property):

ITEM	SUBJECT	COMPARABLE NO. 1	COMPARABLE NO. 2	COMPARABLE NO. 3
Address				
Proximity to Subject				
Sales Price	$	$	$	$
Price/Gross Living Area	$ ⌀	$ ⌀	$ ⌀	$ ⌀
Data and/or Verification Source				

VALUE ADJUSTMENTS	DESCRIPTION	DESCRIPTION	+(−)$ Adjust.	DESCRIPTION	+(−)$ Adjust.	DESCRIPTION	+(−)$ Adjust.
Sales or Financing Concessions							
Date of Sale/Time							
Location							
Leasehold/Fee Simple							
Site							
View							
Design and Appeal							
Quality of Construction							
Age							
Condition							
Above Grade Total Bdrms Baths							
Room Count							
Gross Living Area Sq. Ft.							
Basement & Finished Rooms Below Grade							
Functional Utility							
Heating/Cooling							
Energy Efficient Items							
Garage/Carport							
Porch, Patio, Deck, Fireplace(s), etc.							
Fence, Pool, etc.							
Net Adj. (total)		+ − $		+ − $		+ − $	
Adjusted Sales Price of Comparable		$		$		$	

Comments on Sales Comparison (including the subject property's compatibility to the neighborhood, etc.): _____

ITEM	SUBJECT	COMPARABLE NO. 1	COMPARABLE NO. 2	COMPARABLE NO. 3
Date, Price and Data Source, for prior sales within year of appraisal				

Analysis of any current agreement of sale, option, or listing of subject property and analysis of any prior sales of subject and comparables within one year of the date of appraisal:

INDICATED VALUE BY SALES COMPARISON APPROACH $ _____

INDICATED VALUE BY INCOME APPROACH (If Applicable)   Estimated Market Rent $ _____ /Mo. x Gross Rent Multiplier _____ = $ _____

This appraisal is made ☐ "as is" ☐ subject to the repairs, alterations, inspections or conditions listed below ☐ subject to completion per plans & specifications.

Conditions of Appraisal: _____

Final Reconciliation: _____

The purpose of this appraisal is to estimate the market value of the real property that is the subject of this report, based on the above conditions and the certification, contingent and limiting conditions, and market value definition that are stated in the attached Freddie Mac Form 439/FNMA form 1004B (Revised _____).

I (WE) ESTIMATE THE MARKET VALUE, AS DEFINED, OF THE REAL PROPERTY THAT IS THE SUBJECT OF THIS REPORT, AS OF _____ (WHICH IS THE DATE OF INSPECTION AND THE EFFECTIVE DATE OF THIS REPORT) TO BE $ _____

APPRAISER:	SUPERVISORY APPRAISER (ONLY IF REQUIRED):	
Signature	Signature	☐ Did ☐ Did Not
Name	Name	Inspect Property
Date Report Signed	Date Report Signed	
State Certification # _____ State	State Certification # _____ State	
Or State License # _____ State	Or State License # _____ State	

Freddie Mac Form 70 6/93   PAGE 2 OF 2   Fannie Mae Form 1004 6-93

Figure 9.2b

DEFINITION OF MARKET VALUE: The most probable price which a property should bring in a competitive and open market under all conditions requisite to a fair sale, the buyer and seller, each acting prudently, knowledgeably and assuming the price is not affected by undue stimulus. Implicit in this definition is the consummation of a sale as of a specified date and the passing of title from seller to buyer under conditions whereby: (1) buyer and seller are typically motivated; (2) both parties are well informed or advised, and each acting in what he considers his own best interest; (3) a reasonable time is allowed for exposure in the open market; (4) payment is made in terms of cash in U. S. dollars or in terms of financial arrangements comparable thereto; and (5) the price represents the normal consideration for the property sold unaffected by special or creative financing or sales concessions* granted by anyone associated with the sale.

*Adjustments to the comparables must be made for special or creative financing or sales concessions. No adjustments are necessary for those costs which are normally paid by sellers as a result of tradition or law in a market area; these costs are readily identifiable since the seller pays these costs in virtually all sales transactions. Special or creative financing adjustments can be made to the comparable property by comparisons to financing terms offered by a third party institutional lender that is not already involved in the property or transaction. Any adjustment should not be calculated on a mechanical dollar for dollar cost of the financing or concession but the dollar amount of any adjustment should approximate the market's reaction to the financing or concessions based on the appraiser's judgment.

CERTIFICATION AND STATEMENT OF LIMITING CONDITIONS

CERTIFICATION: The Appraiser certifies and agrees that:

1. The Appraiser has no present or contemplated future interest in the property appraised; and neither the employment to make the appraisal, nor the compensation for it, is contingent upon the appraised value of the property.

2. The Appraiser has no personal interest in or bias with respect to the subject matter of the appraisal report or the participants to the sale. The 'Estimate of Market Value' in the appraisal report is not based in whole or in part upon the race, color, or national origin of the prospective owners or occupants of the property appraised, or upon the race, color or national origin of the present owners or occupants of the properties in the vicinity of the property appraised.

3. The Appraiser has personally inspected the property, both inside and out, and has made an exterior inspection of all comparable sales listed in the report. To the best of the Appraiser's knowledge and belief, all statements and information in this report are true and correct, and the Appraiser has not knowingly withheld any significant information.

4. All contingent and limiting conditions are contained herein (imposed by the terms of the assignment or by the undersigned affecting the analyses, opinions, and conclusions contained in the report).

5. This appraisal report has been made in conformity with and is subject to the requirements of the Code of Professional Ethics and Standards of Professional Conduct of the appraisal organizations with which the Appraiser is affiliated.

6. All conclusions and opinions concerning the real estate that are set forth in the appraisal report were prepared by the Appraiser whose signature appears on the appraisal report, unless indicated as 'Review Appraiser'. No change of any item in the appraisal report shall be made by anyone other than the Appraiser, and the Appraiser shall have no responsibility for any such unauthorized change.

CONTINGENT AND LIMITING CONDITIONS: The certification of the Appraiser appearing in the appraisal report is subject to the following conditions and to such other specific and limiting conditions as are set forth by the Appraiser in the report.

1. The Appraiser assumes no responsibility for matters of a legal nature affecting the property appraised or the title thereto, nor does the Appraiser render any opinion as to the title, which is assumed to be good and marketable. The property is appraised as though under responsible ownership.

2. Any sketch in the report may show approximate dimensions and is included to assist the reader in visualizing the property. The Appraiser has made no survey of the property.

3. The Appraiser is not required to give testimony or appear in court because of having made the appraisal with reference to the property in question, unless arrangements have been previously made therefor.

4. Any distribution of the valuation in the report between land and improvements applies only under the existing program of utilization The separate valuations for land and building must not be used in conjunctions with any other appraisal and are invalid if so used.

5. The Appraiser assumes that there are no hidden or unapparent conditions of the property, subsoil, or structures, which would render it more or less valuable. The Appraiser assumes no responsibility for such conditions, or for engineering which might be required to discover such factors.

6. Information, estimates, and opinions furnished to the Appraiser, and contained in the report, were obtained from sources considered reliable and believed to be true and correct. However, no responsibility for accuracy of such items furnished the Appraiser can be assumed by the Appraiser.

7. Disclosure of the contents of the appraisal report is governed by the Bylaws and Regulations of the professional appraisal organizations with which the Appraiser is affiliated.

8. Neither all, nor any part of the content of the report, or copy thereof (including conclusions as to the property value, the identity of the Appraiser, professional designations, reference to any professional appraisal organizations, or the firm with which the Appraiser is connected), shall be used for any purposes by anyone but the client specified in the report, the borrower if appraisal fee paid by same, the mortgagee or its successors and assigns, mortgage insurers, consultants, professional appraisal organizations, any state or federally approved financial institution, any department, agency, or instrumentality of the United States or any state or the District of Columbia, without the previous written consent of the Appraiser; nor shall it be conveyed by anyone to the public through advertising, public relations, news, sales, or other media, without the written consent and approval of the Appraiser.

9. On all appraisals, subject to satisfactory completion, repairs, or alterations, the appraisal report and value conclusion are contingent upon completion of the improvements in a workmanlike manner.

Date: _____ Appraiser(s) _____

Freddie Mac
Form 439 JUL 86-1

MCS, Richardson, Texas 75082 (214) 699-7783

Fannie Mae
Form 1004B JUL 86-1

Figure 9.2c

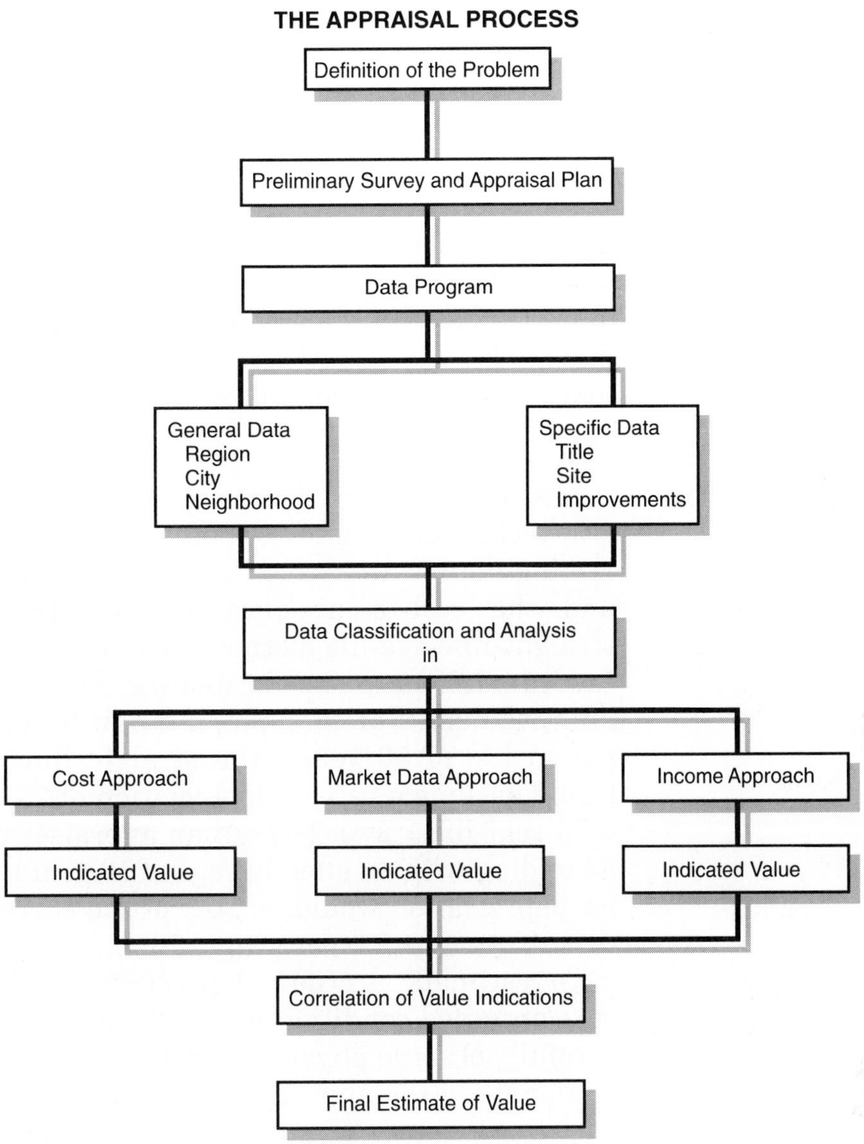

THE APPRAISAL PROCESS

Figure 9.3

3. *Estimate and then subtract accrued depreciation to arrive at present value of the improvement.* Current replacement cost new, less depreciation = present value of the improvements.

4. *Add value of land to present value of the improvements.* Land value + present value of improvements = estimate of value.

To estimate the value of the land, appraisers usually compare recent vacant lot sales, adjusting their estimates for the differences in location, topography, size, shape, and so on.

Estimate Replacement Cost

To estimate the current replacement cost of buildings, appraisers first measure the square footage (exterior length × width). The square footage of the house is measured separately from the garage, patios, and porches. Then based upon the construction quality of the building they are appraising, appraisers obtain estimates from local contractors regarding construction costs per square foot. In addition to local contractors, square foot costs and other construction information can be obtained by subscribing to cost-estimating publications. Once accurate costs per square foot are obtained, the appraiser multiplies this figure times the square footage of the building. Figures for fencing, cement work, and landscaping are then added to arrive at the current replacement cost of the improvement.

Estimate Depreciation

To estimate accrued depreciation, appraisers can use several techniques. The two most common methods of determining depreciation are the straight-line/age-life method and the cost-to-cure/observed condition method. The straight-line/age-life method assumes that depreciation occurs annually at an even rate over the estimated life of the improvement. For example, if a new building has an estimated life of 50 years, the straight-line/age-life method would assume a rate of depreciation of 2% per year (100% ÷ 50 year life = 2%). Thus, if an appraiser were appraising a building with an effective age of 10 years, the subtraction for depreciation would be 20% of the current replacement cost (10 years × 2% per year = 20%).

To estimate accrued depreciation using the cost-to-cure/observed condition method requires the appraiser to carefully observe physical, functional, and economic depreciation; then the appraiser estimates what it would cost to cure this depreciation. If some of the depreciation is incurable, the appraiser estimates the permanent loss in value. The sum of the cost to cure, plus the permanent loss in value, equals the estimated depreciation. Once the accrued depreciation has been estimated, this figure is subtracted from the current replacement cost to arrive at the present value of the improvements.

The final step in the cost approach is the easiest. The estimated value of the land is added to the estimated present value of the improvements to arrive at the estimated value of the total real property.

ADVANTAGES AND DISADVANTAGES OF THE COST APPROACH

The cost approach is appropriate for appraising newly constructed buildings, and unique, special-purpose properties and public buildings such as schools and libraries. The cost approach usually sets the highest limits on value, with the thought being that the most a person will pay for real property is what it would cost to replace the property.

On the negative side, the cost approach does not always measure the individual amenities of the property, such as location, or outside influences like neighborhood surroundings. Also it is difficult to accurately convert depreciation into dollar figures. Thus, on older properties the likelihood of errors in estimating depreciation increases with the age of the building. Also, in a declining real estate market, what it cost to build a property may be much higher than what buyers are currently willing to pay. Figure 9.4 is an example of an appraisal using the cost approach.

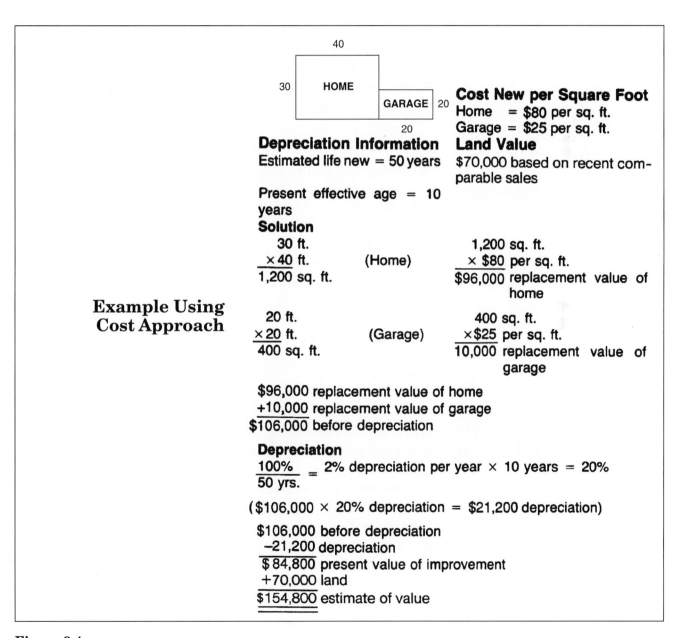

Example Using Cost Approach

40

30   HOME

GARAGE   20

20

Cost New per Square Foot
Home   = $80 per sq. ft.
Garage = $25 per sq. ft.

Depreciation Information
Estimated life new = 50 years

Land Value
$70,000 based on recent comparable sales

Present effective age = 10 years

Solution

30 ft.	
× 40 ft.	(Home)
1,200 sq. ft.	

1,200 sq. ft.
× $80 per sq. ft.
$96,000 replacement value of home

20 ft.	
× 20 ft.	(Garage)
400 sq. ft.	

400 sq. ft.
× $25 per sq. ft.
10,000 replacement value of garage

$96,000 replacement value of home
+10,000 replacement value of garage
$106,000 before depreciation

Depreciation

$$\frac{100\%}{50 \text{ yrs.}} = 2\% \text{ depreciation per year} \times 10 \text{ years} = 20\%$$

($106,000 × 20% depreciation = $21,200 depreciation)

$106,000 before depreciation
−21,200 depreciation
$ 84,800 present value of improvement
+70,000 land
$154,800 estimate of value

Figure 9.4

INCOME APPROACH

The *income approach* to value is based on the premise that a property is worth the present value of the future income to be produced by the property. In other words, what an investor should be willing to pay today for a property is directly related to what the investor expects to receive from the property in the future. Financial analysts have developed a technique called *capitalization* which mathematically computes the present value of the future income produced by real estate.

The determination of the value by the income approach can be viewed as a series of steps:

1. Estimate gross annual income.
2. Estimate vacancies and uncollectible rents and subtract this from gross annual income to arrive at the effective gross income, also called the gross operating income.
3. Estimate annual expenses and subtract these from the effective gross income to arrive at the net operating income.
4. Select the proper capitalization rate.
5. Divide the capitalization rate into the net operating income to arrive at an estimate of value.

These steps can be summarized as follows:

	Gross annual income
Less	− Vacancy factor and uncollectible rents
Equals	Effective gross income
Less	− Annual expenses
Equals	Net operating income

$$\frac{\text{Net operating income}}{\text{Capitalization rate}} = \text{Estimate of property's value}$$

EXPLANATION OF THE INCOME APPROACH

Gross annual income is the maximum amount of income a property can expect to make if fully occupied 100% of the time and assuming rents are at the going market rate. Appraisers recognize that 100% occupancy all the time is unrealistic. Vacancies and turnovers will occur. Also, some tenants will skip out on their rent. Therefore, appraisers subtract an estimate for vacancies and uncollectibles to arrive at the effective gross income.

After computing the effective gross income the appraiser totals the annual operating expenses. Operating expenses are the costs of running and maintaining the property. Examples include:

Property taxes	Supplies
Insurance premiums	Utilities
Repairs	Accounting and legal advice
Maintenance	Advertising
Management fees	Reserves for replacement

Real estate loan payments and income tax depreciation deductions are *not* considered operating expenses because they are not used to run the building. Therefore, they are not deducted to arrive at net income.

Once annual operating expenses are calculated, they are subtracted from the effective gross income to arrive at the net operating income. *Net operating income* is the income the property produces after deducting operating expenses, but before real estate loan payments.

The next step in the income approach is to select the appropriate capitalization rate. A *capitalization rate* can be defined as the rate necessary to attract an average investor to invest in the property being appraised. The capitalization rate reflects a return on the funds invested, as well as a return (recapture) of the investment. The determination of the appropriate capitalization rate is the most difficult aspect of the income approach to value. The techniques for the selection of a capitalization rate are complex and beyond the scope of this book. For our purpose visualize the capitalization rate as being the rate that other like properties are returning to their owners.

The final step in the income approach is to divide the capitalization rate into net operating income to arrive at an estimate of value.

$$\frac{\text{Net operating income}}{\text{Capitalization rate}} = \text{Estimate of value}$$

The income approach to value is appropriate for income-producing properties such as apartment buildings, commercial office buildings, and retail stores. Figure 9.5 is an example of an appraisal using the income approach.

MARKET APPROACH (COMPARABLE SALES)

The market approach to value is based on the principle of substitution. The *principle of substitution* states that a buyer should not pay more for a home than the price it takes to acquire a comparable home. Therefore, the market approach is also known as the *comparison sales approach to value.*

<table>
<tr><td rowspan="20">Example Using Income Approach</td><td colspan="2">A 15-unit apartment with fair market rents of $700 per unit. The estimated factor for vacancies and uncollectibles is 5 percent. Annual operating expenses include:</td></tr>
</table>

Property taxes	$9,450	
Insurance	$1,000	
Management & accounting	$10,000	
Repairs and others	$12,000	

The capitalization rate selected by the appraiser is 10 percent.

Solution

Gross annual income	$126,000	($700 x 15 units x 12 months)
Less vacancies and uncollectibles	−6,300	($126,000 × 5%)
Effective gross income	$119,700	
Less annual expenses	−32,450	($9,450 + 1,000 + 10,000 + 12,000)
Net operating income	$87,250	

$$\frac{\text{Net operating income}}{\text{Capitalization rate}} \quad \frac{\$87,250}{10\%} = \$872,500 \quad \text{Estimate of value}$$

If the capitalization rate selected had been 9 percent, the value would be:

$$\frac{\$87,250}{9\%} = \$969,444 \quad \text{If the capitalization rate were 11 percent,}$$

the value would be $\dfrac{\$87,250}{11\%} = \$793,181.$

Observe this rule: *The higher the capitalization rate, the lower the value.* Therefore, you can see that the selection of the appropriate capitalization rate is very critical! *The selection of an inappropriate capitalization rate can greatly distort value.*

Figure 9.5

To apply the market approach, an appraiser gathers data on current sales of properties that are similar to the property being appraised. Ideally, the comparable properties should be in the same neighborhood and be similar in size, style, quality, and contain similar internal characteristics as the subject property.

Each comparable used must also be what is called a *market sale*. A market sale is a sale in which a property is sold using normal financing techniques, and the buyer and the seller were fully informed and knowledgeable about the real estate market. If either the buyer or the seller were under any duress or strain, such as divorce, death in the family, or financial reversals, the appraiser will discard the sale as not being a good comparable sale. For the market approach to be valid the sales used for comparison must reflect normal market conditions, not sales sold under abnormal circumstances.

Once the comparable properties are selected (three properties are usually the minimum; five are better), the appraiser then makes adjustments for the differences between the comparable properties and the subject property being appraised. In essence, what the appraiser does is take sales prices of the comparable properties and adjust these prices to reflect what the comparable properties would have sold for if they had the characteristics of the subject property. The results of this process will produce an indicated market value range for the property being appraised. Figure 9.6 is an example of an appraisal using the market approach.

VALUE RANGE FOR MARKET APPROACH EXAMPLE

If the comparables in the market approach example (Figure 9.6) were near the location of the subject home and had the same lot size and overall condition of the subject home, the comparables A, B, C would have sold for somewhere between $169,900 and $170,500; these figures reflect the indicated market value range.

VALUE CONCLUSIONS FOR MARKET APPROACH EXAMPLE

Subject home in Figure 9.6 should sell for somewhere between $169,900 and $170,500. Final estimate is $170,000, as Comparable B is most comparable in the opinion of the appraiser.

This is a highly simplified example of the market approach, but it does show the basic concept of how the market approach attempts to adjust known comparable sales to reflect what the comparables should have sold for if the comparables had the characteristics of the subject property. As consumers, people use an informal market approach when they shop for automobiles, furniture, clothes, and most other types of consumer purchases. When it comes to real estate, appraisers simply formalize the process by reducing the comparative facts to writing.

The market approach to value is not the main technique used when appraising income property, but it is an excellent approach to use when appraising homes, especially when the local home market is highly active with many comparable sales in the immediate neighborhood.

USE OF GROSS MULTIPLIERS

Appraisers have designed a method for quickly obtaining a rough estimate of value using what are called gross monthly rent multipliers (GMRM), also known as gross rent

Example Using Market Approach

Assume that the subject property is a medium quality, 25-year old, three-bedroom home, which has a two-car garage. The square footage of the home is 1,300 square feet. The appraiser locates three similar homes that have recently sold in the neighborhood at fair market prices. All have identical square footage and number of rooms.

Comparables

Data	Comparable A	Comparable B	Comparable C
Price paid	$173,900	$171,500	$166,000
Location	better than subject property	equal to subject property	equal to subject property
Lot size	equal to subject property	larger than subject property	smaller than subject property
Overall condition	better than subject property	equal to subject property	worse than subject property

Dollar Adjustment Factors per the Opinion of the Appraiser

Location difference	$1,000
Lot size difference	$1,500
Overall condition difference	$3,000

Adjustments

Data	Comparable A	Comparable B	Comparable C
Price paid	$173,900	$171,500	$166,000
Location	−1,000	0	0
Lot size	0	−1,500	+1,500
Overall condition	−3,000	0	+3,000
Price comparables would have sold for if they were like the subject home	$169,900	$170,000	$170,500

Figure 9.6

multipliers (GRM), if annual rents, instead of monthly rents, are used. A *gross multiplier* is a ratio between sales price and rental rates. The gross monthly rent multiplier is found by dividing the sales price of a home by its monthly rent.

EXAMPLE

$$\frac{\text{Sales Price}}{\text{Monthly rental rate}} \quad \frac{\$170,000}{\$1,000} = 170 \text{ Gross monthly rent multiplier}$$

The gross rent multiplier is found by dividing the sales price of a home by it annual rent.

$$\frac{\text{Sales price}}{\text{Annual rent}} \quad \frac{\$170,000}{\$12,000} = 14.17 \text{ Gross rent multiplier}$$
$$(\$1,000/\text{mo.} \times 12)$$

An appraiser does this for many sales until a trend develops. When asked to conduct an appraisal on a home, the appraiser will do a complete market approach (comparable sales) to arrive at an estimate of value. To recheck the results of the market approach, the appraiser may also do a cost approach and an income approach. For a home, a full-blown income approach is not needed, so the gross rent multiplier approach often is used instead.

The appraiser will locate comparable homes, determine their gross multipliers, then select the most appropriate multiplier. Next, the appraiser will determine the fair market rent of the subject home. Then the gross multiplier is multiplied by the fair market rent to arrive at an estimate of value.

EXAMPLE. After carefully selecting comparable sales, the appraiser determines that the gross monthly rent multiplier should be 170. The fair market rent of the home is $1,100. Therefore, gross monthly rent multiplier × monthly rent = estimate of value.

170 × $1,100 = $187,000 Estimate of value

RECONCILIATION AND FINAL ESTIMATE OF VALUE

The process of bringing together the three indications of value derived through the market, cost, and income approaches is the final step in the appraisal process. This process is called *correlation or reconciliation.* When reconciling, the appraiser gives full consideration to each approach; then, based on judgment and experience, the appraiser arrives at one final value or price.

Correlation or reconciliation is not the averaging of the three approaches! Averaging gives equal weight to each approach, and this is wrong. For any given property, one of the approaches is better and should be given more weight.

The final value estimate is not given in odd dollars and cents. The final estimate of value usually is rounded to the nearest $100, $500, or $1,000, depending upon the value of the property.

CHAPTER SUMMARY

Appraisers are required to be licensed or certified for all transactions involving federal insurance or regulation. An appraisal license or certificate is distinct and separate from a real estate license.

An appraisal is defined as an estimate or opinion of value. Although there are many types of value, the value sought most often is the market value.

For a property to have value, four elements are necessary: utility, scarcity, demand, and transferability. Once value has been established, social, economic, political, and physical forces cause value to change. Appraisal theory rests on certain principles such as highest and best use, change, supply and demand, substitution, and conformity, plus several others.

Depreciation is defined as a loss in value from any cause. Depreciation of real estate is caused by physical deterioration, functional obsolescence, and economic obsolescence. Depreciation can be classified as curable or incurable or as accrued or accrual for depreciation.

The appraisal process can be viewed as a series of steps leading to a final estimate of value. The appraisal techniques include the cost approach, income approach, and market approach. In certain instances the gross multiplier technique is also used to estimate value.

The selection of a single final estimate of value is called correlation or reconciliation. Final value conclusions are submitted in a written report, which may be a letter form report, a short-form report, or a narrative report.

IMPORTANT TERMS AND CONCEPTS

Appraisal

Appreciation

Correlation (reconciliation)

Cost approach

Depreciation

Economic and social obsolescence

Elements of value

Functional obsolescence

Gross multipliers

Income approach

Market approach

Market value

Physical deterioration

Principles of substitution

Value in use (utility value)

PRACTICAL APPLICATION

1. A special use property consists of the following: the land value is $300,000; the main structure is 200 feet × 40 feet, a storage building is 35 feet × 15 feet. A cement slab and other improvements have a present value of $27,000. The main structure has an effective age of 20 years with an estimated life new of 50 years. The replacement cost of the main structure is $65 per square foot. The storage building has an effective age of 15 years with an estimated life new of 30 years. The replacement cost of the storage building is $20 per square foot. Using the cost approach, what is the estimated value of the property? (Round answer to nearest $1,000.)

2. An 11,000-square-foot commercial property rents for $1 per square foot per month on a triple net lease to a highly rated tenant with 10 years to go on the lease. The only cost to the landlord is 5% of gross rents for miscellaneous expenses not covered by the net lease. A comparable property sold for $1,500,000 and had a net operating income of $135,000. Based only on this information, what is the estimated value of the commercial property? (Round answer to nearest $1,000.)

3. You are doing a listing presentation for Ms. Seller's home, which does not have a swimming pool. You have found three comparable homes that have sold recently in the subdivision. Comparable A sold for $257,000 and is in better condition and has a larger lot, plus a pool. Comparable B sold for $240,000, is in similar condition

to Ms. Seller's home, but it has a smaller lot and no pool. Comparable C sold for $225,000 and is in worse condition than Ms. Seller's home and has a smaller lot and no pool. The adjustments are as follows: for pool $1,000, condition $3,000, and $10,000 for lot size. Based only on this information, what do you think should be the listing price of Ms. Seller's home? (Round answer to nearest $1,000.)

REVIEWING YOUR UNDERSTANDING

1. An appraisal is defined as:
   a. market price
   b. an estimate of value
   c. loan value
   d. actual selling price

2. For most home buyers, the value they would like to know is:
   a. market value
   b. tax value
   c. insurance value
   d. resale value

3. The best use of land is that use which produces the greatest net return to the land. This is the:
   a. principle of change
   b. principle of substitution
   c. principle of conformity
   d. principle of highest and best use

4. Loss in value in a home because of a poor floor plan is called:
   a. physical determination
   b. functional obsolescence
   c. economic obsolescence
   d. book depreciation

5. The most comprehensive type of appraisal report is the:
   a. restricted (letter)
   b. summary (short form)
   c. self-contained (narrative)
   d. negotiated (based on estimated value)

6. For existing residential homes, the best appraisal approach is usually the:
   a. market approach
   b. income approach
   c. cost approach
   d. capitalization approach

7. Given: land is valued at $35,000; cost new per square foot: home $80, garage $25; Estimated life: new 50 years, present effective age, 10 years. What is the estimated value of the property? (See Figure 9.7.)
   a. $110,400
   b. $163,000
   c. $173,000
   d. $145,400

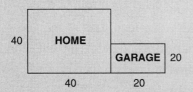

Figure 9.7

8. Find the value, by use of the income approach (round to nearest $100). Given: four-unit apartment rents for $500 per unit per month; vacancy factor 5%; annual expenses $8,000; capitalization rate 10½%.
   a. $141,000
   b. $164,900
   c. $250,000
   d. $173,500

9. Gross monthly multiplier is 125 and fair market rent of condo is $575 per month. The estimate of value is:
   a. $71,875
   b. $70,000
   c. $57,500
   d. $125,000

10. According to the California Office of Real Estate Appraisers, the most comprehensive appraisal skill level is:
    a. licensed appraiser
    b. certified-residential
    c. certified-general
    d. broker

11. When evaluating a 20-year-old home, the appraiser assigns it an age of only 10 years because of the extremely good care taken by the owner. This is an example of:
    a. effective age
    b. chronological age
    c. actual age
    d. physical age

12. The rule is: The higher the capitalization rate, the
    a. higher the value
    b. lower the value
    c. lower the risk
    d. higher the net income

13. Which of the following is false?
    a. All things equal, the higher the demand the higher the price.
    b. An example of physical deterioration is a worn-out roof.
    c. Depreciation for income tax purposes is different from depreciation for appraisal purposes.
    d. Price, value, and cost are the same concept.

14. A change in zoning is what type of force that influences values?
    a. functional
    b. physical
    c. political
    d. observed

15. The principle that states that the value of one home tends to be influenced by the price of acquiring equally desirable homes is called the principle of:
    a. progression
    b. supply and demand
    c. substitution
    d. conformity

16. Which of the following best describes the cost approach to value?
    a. land value + replacement cost = value
    b. land value + replacement cost – depreciation = value
    c. land value + net income ÷ capitalization rate = value
    d. land value + adjusted value of comparables = value

17. Similar homes rent for $900 per month and sell for $162,000. The home you would like to buy could rent for $925. What is its estimate of value?
    a. $162,000
    b. $164,500
    c. $166,500
    d. $168,000

18. When considering the purchase of a home with fix-up potential, it is important to remember that the most difficult depreciation to cure (correct) is:
    a. physical
    b. functional
    c. economic
    d. deferred

19. For property to have value, there must be four elements. All of the following are elements of value, except:
    a. transferability
    b. scarcity
    c. utility
    d. price

20. One of the last steps in the appraisal process is known as correlation, or:
    a. averaging the three values
    b. reconciliation
    c. establishing the median value
    d. discounting the values to a single value

Chapter 10

The Role of Escrow and Title Insurance Companies

Chapter Preview   Closing a real estate transaction is a highly technical process. Escrow and title insurance companies provide valuable services that help consumers and real estate agents to smoothly and efficiently close a real estate transaction. At the conclusion of the chapter, you will be able to:

1. Define escrow and list the legal requirements for a valid escrow

2. Describe the basic services provided by title insurance companies

3. Explain the difference between a CLTA standard and an ALTA extended coverage policy of title insurance

4. Explain various closing costs and indicate who normally pays for each closing cost

10.1 ESCROW

Definition of Escrow   In a real estate sale, an escrow is a process whereby a neutral third party acts as the closing agent for the buyer and the seller. (See Figure 10.1.) The escrow officer assumes the responsibility of handling all the paperwork and

Figure 10.1

disbursement of funds to close out a real estate transaction. The Civil Code defines an escrow as:

> A grant may be deposited by the grantor with a third person, to be delivered on the performance of a condition, and, on delivery by the depository, it will take effect. While in the possession of the third person, and subject to condition, it is called an escrow.

Escrows can be used for a variety of business transactions, such as sale or exchange of real estate, sale or encumbrance of personal property, sale or pledging of securities, sale of the assets of a business (bulk sale), sale of a promissory note secured by a deed of trust, and the transfer of liquor licenses. By far the most common reason for the use of an escrow is to handle the sale and transfer of real estate. The clerical aspects of transferring title to real estate are detailed and complicated; therefore, buyers, sellers, lenders, and real estate agents prefer to use trained escrow officers.

Legal Requirements for a Valid Escrow

There are two essential requirements for a valid escrow:

1. There must be a binding contract between the seller (grantor) and the buyer (grantee).
2. There must be the conditional delivery of transfer instruments and monies to a neutral third party.

The binding contract can be in any legal form, such as a deposit receipt, agreement of sale, exchange agreement, or mutual instructions from the buyer and the seller. The escrow instructions signed by the buyer and seller supplement the terms of the original purchase agreement, and the two contracts are interpreted together. If there is a conflict between the purchase contract and the escrow instructions, the usual rule is that the most recent contract prevails. In most cases, this would be the signed escrow instructions.

Confidentiality of Escrows

Escrow instructions are confidential. Only the principals and their agents in the transaction are entitled to see the escrow instructions, and then, only insofar as the instructions pertain to mutual items in the transaction. For example, both the buyer and the seller are entitled to see each other's escrow instructions regarding the sales price, down payment, and other terms of the sale. But how much the seller is netting from the sale is no business of the buyer. Likewise, the buyer's financing arrangement with an institutional lender is no business of the seller who is cashing out of the transaction.

If the escrow holder receives conflicting instructions from the principals, the escrow officer simply refuses to proceed until the parties settle their differences. An escrow officer cannot give legal advice and may bring an action in court forcing the principals in the escrow to litigate their differences. This legal action is called an *interpleader action.*

Status of the Escrow Holder

An escrow is a limited agency. The only obligations to be fulfilled by the escrow holder are those set forth in the instructions connected with the transaction. Before a real estate sale is recorded, the escrow officer is the dual agent for both the buyer and the seller. After the deed is recorded, the escrow officer becomes the individual agent for each party.

This distinction is important, especially if an unethical escrow officer should steal money from the escrow company. If the escrow officer embezzles the money before the seller is entitled to it, the buyer suffers the loss. But if the money is embezzled after the seller has become entitled to it, the loss falls on the seller, because it is now considered to be the seller's money.

Regulation of Escrow Holders

Title insurance companies, banks, trust companies, or attorneys can handle escrows without obtaining an escrow license. However, independent escrow companies must be incorporated and can handle escrows only after obtaining a special license from the California Corporations Commissioner. Independent escrow companies are common in Southern California, whereas title insurance companies and financial institutions handle most of the escrows in Northern California.

Who Decides Which Escrow Company to Use?

The selection of an escrow company is negotiated between the buyer and seller. The real estate agent cannot dictate which escrow company to use. If a real estate agent has a financial interest in an escrow company, the law requires the agent to disclose this interest to the buyer and the seller before a final selection is made. Real estate brokers can legally handle escrows without obtaining a special escrow license if the broker is an agent for the buyer or the seller in the transaction.

Once an escrow company is selected, who pays the fee? The payment of the escrow fee is an item that is negotiable between buyer and seller. The decision as to who pays this fee will vary throughout the state. In some geographic areas the seller usually pays; in other areas the buyer usually pays; in some areas the fee is split between the buyer and the seller.

Services Provided by Escrow Holders

For a fee, the escrow holder carefully collects, prepares, and safeguards the instructions, documents, and monies required to close the transaction. Upon receipt of written instructions from all parties (that is, buyer, seller, lender, real estate agent), the escrow instructions are compared to determine if the parties are in mutual agreement. An escrow officer can do no more or no less than the instructions received.

When the parties are in agreement and all instruments and monies have been deposited, the escrow officer then sees that title is transferred. The following are some of the services performed by an escrow company:

1. Prepares buyer's and seller's escrow instructions; prepares deed and other needed documents, such as promissory notes and deeds of trust as instructed from all parties
2. Requests the demand for payoff for the seller's loan from the lending institution; or in the case of an assumption, requests a beneficiary statement from the lending institution
3. Collects the structural pest control report and the notice of work completed, if any

4. Collects the required fire insurance policy
5. Balances the accounting details, including adjustments and prorations of the taxes, interest, insurance, and assessments and rents, if any
6. Collects the balance of monies required to close the transaction
7. Verifies that the appropriate documents are recorded. After transfer has occurred, the escrow file is audited. The escrow officer then disburses the monies, issues itemized closing statements to all parties, and orders the title insurance policy

SPECIAL INTEREST TOPIC

North versus South

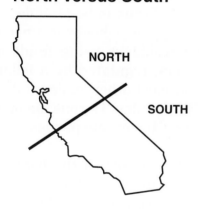

Escrow practices differ between Southern and Northern California. In Southern California, independent escrow companies are common, and they handle a considerable number of the real estate transactions. Title insurance companies provide the title services, but escrow companies do the actual closing of the sale. Because of the severe recession in the 1990s, many Southern California independent escrow companies have gone out of business, or merged with other escrow companies, or were purchased by title companies. Some lending institutions also provide escrow services in Southern California. In Northern California, most escrows are handled by title insurance companies that have extensive escrow departments with many branch offices.

One other point of difference has to do with the timing of the signing of escrow instructions. In Southern California, it is common to have the buyer and seller sign escrow instructions shortly after they sign their purchase agreement. This may be 30 or 60 days before the actual close of escrow. In many Northern California counties, escrow instructions are usually not signed until a day or two before the actual close of escrow.

Termination of Escrows

Escrows are usually terminated by completion of the sale, and in the case of a refinance, upon completion of the loan process. If the transaction is not completed, the escrow may then be canceled by mutual agreement of all parties. The escrow company is entitled to receive partial payment of escrow fees for services rendered to date.

All the conditions required by escrow instructions must be performed within the time limit set forth in the escrow agreement. The escrow officer has no authority to enforce or accept the performance after the time limit provided in the instructions. When the time limit provided in the escrow has expired and neither party to the escrow has performed in accordance with the terms, upon receiving mutual written releases, the parties are entitled to the return of their respective papers and documents from the escrow officer.

Escrows and RESPA

The Real Estate Settlement Procedures Act (RESPA) is a federal law that requires certain forms to be provided regarding closing costs. The law applies whenever a person purchases an owner-occupied residence using funds obtained from institutional lenders, regulated by a federal agency. Virtually all banks and most other lenders fall directly or indirectly under RESPA's rules. The one major exception would be real estate loans by private parties—they are usually exempt from RESPA.

RESPA rules require a lender to furnish the borrower with a special information booklet and a good faith estimate of closing costs when the prospective borrower files an application for a real estate loan. RESPA rules prohibit any kickbacks or unearned fees from being listed as closing costs. The law expressly states that only valid, earned, closing costs shall be charged the buyer or seller. Any violators can be punished by up to one year in jail and/or a $10,000 fine.

Most of the burden for implementing RESPA falls upon the real estate lender. However, escrow agents are also involved. RESPA requires the use of a Uniform Settlement Statement (HUD-1) which must itemize all closing charges. Upon request, the escrow agent must let the borrower-buyer inspect the Uniform Settlement Statement one day before the close of escrow. In addition, the escrow officer must see that all parties receive a copy of the Uniform Settlement Statement after the close of escrow.

An escrow holder is a neutral third party who, for a fee, will handle the paperwork involved in transferring title and/or in placing a new loan on real property. Escrow companies are licensed by the state of California. However, banks, attorneys, and title insurance companies can act as escrow holders without obtaining a special license. A real estate broker can act as an escrow holder only if the broker is an agent for either the buyer or seller.

ESCROWS—SUMMARIZED

Technical Reasons for an Escrow

1. To provide a custodian for funds and documents who can make concurrent delivery
2. To provide a clearinghouse for payments
3. To provide an agency for computing prorations

Essentials of a Valid Escrow

1. Must have a binding contract between buyer and seller
2. Must have conditional delivery of transfer instruments to a third party

Termination of an Escrow

1. By full performance and closing
2. Mutual cancellation by the parties
3. Revocation by a party

10.2 TITLE INSURANCE COMPANIES

Title insurance companies are incorporated businesses that provide these basic services:

1. Search and gather public records relating to the legal title of real property
2. Examine and interpret the title records that have been gathered
3. Insure an owner or lender against financial loss resulting from certain unreported defects in the title

Title Search

A title search can be conducted in one of two ways. The first is the "courthouse search." Under this method, a title person goes to the county courthouse and searches through the public records, seeking information pertaining to a particular property under examination. The title searcher then reproduces the information and presents the items to a title examiner for interpretation.

The second method is for a title company to maintain its own "title plant." A title plant is really a condensed courthouse where records affecting real property are copied, usually microfilmed or computerized, and filed for future reference. When a title search is ordered, the title person has only to select the needed information from the title plant. This reduces the need for frequent trips to the county courthouse, thereby saving valuable time for the title company and the customer.

Title Examination

The actual examination and interpretation of the title is done by a highly skilled title examiner (not an attorney) whose task is to review each document and create what is known as a *chain of title*. A chain of title is an unbroken history of all the title transfers, beginning with the document originally transferring title from the government to private ownership and ending with the document vesting title in the current owner.

In addition to identifying the correct owner, the title examiner determines what and how various encumbrances, such as taxes, deeds of trust, easements, and so on, affect the ownership. When the examination is complete the data is compiled into a *preliminary title report* which lists the owner(s) name, the legal description of the property, the status of property taxes and special assessments, and the various encumbrances against the property. This preliminary title report does not insure, but is the basis upon which a title company is willing to insure the owner's title.

Title Insurance

In the early days of California, title insurance did not exist. Land holdings were large and population sparse. Property frequently was transferred simply by the delivery of a symbol in the presence of a witness.

As population and migration increased, land holdings were divided and sold to incoming strangers. Boundaries became confused and it was difficult to identify ownerships. To combat this confusion, when California became a state in 1850, the legislature enacted recording statutes. These recording statutes created depositories, namely the county recorder's office, to collect and file title documents for public use. Soon the recorder's offices became too complex for many lay people to use. Specialists called *abstractors* began searching and compiling courthouse records. For a fee, these abstractors would publish their findings on a specific parcel of land.

To protect the public, the need arose for a system to guard against the errors, omissions, and incorrect judgments that abstractors might make. This need for additional assurance led to the concept of title insurance.

Today, a title insurance policy insures the ownership of land and the priority of a lien (deed of trust, contract of sale, and so on) subject to the encumbrances revealed in the title examination. The owner and/or lender is insured that a thorough search has been made of all public records affecting a particular property.

Types of Title Insurance Policies

Title insurance policies are divided into two basic groups, the *standard policy* and the *extended coverage policy*. The standard policy is the most widely used and can be divided into three subtypes:

1. *Standard owner's policy,* which insures the owner for the amount of the purchase price
2. *Standard lender's policy,* which insures the lender for the amount of the loan
3. *Standard joint protection policy,* which co-insures the owner and lender under one policy

The standard policy is frequently referred to as a *CLTA policy*. CLTA stands for California Land Title Association, a state trade association for title insurance companies.

Included in the standard coverage policy is the assurance that title is free and clear of all encumbrances of public record, other than the items revealed in the title examination and listed as exceptions in the title policy. Under the standard policy, the title company does not make a physical inspection of the property and therefore excludes from coverage unrecorded items that could affect the title. For example, unrecorded easements are excluded, as well as the rights of parties in possession other than the owner, such as tenants or squatters. Also excluded from standard policy coverage are violations of environmental laws, zoning and other government ordinances affecting the use of the property, nondeclared assessments, and some items regarding mining and water claims.

Extended Coverage Policy

The extended coverage policy was originally established for real estate lenders. This policy requires the title company to make a physical inspection of the property and insures against certain unrecorded title risks excluded under the standard policy. In some cases the extended coverage policy is requested and issued to homeowners, but not other types of property owners. The extended coverage policy is commonly referred to as an *ALTA policy*. ALTA stands for American Land Title Association, a national trade association for title insurance companies.

How Much Does Title Insurance Cost?

Title insurance premiums, like most other types of insurance premiums, are calculated based upon the dollar amount of insurance coverage. Owner's title policies are issued for the purchase price of the property, whereas lender's title policies are issued for the loan amount. Therefore, owners of more expensive property pay higher title fees than owners of less expensive property. Title fees are established by title companies themselves, not any government agency. Competition keeps rates between title companies comparable.

Unlike other forms of insurance—such as automobile, fire, or life insurance, which require annual premiums—a title insurance fee is paid only once. The title policy stays in force as long as the owner retains title to the property. Once title is transferred, the title policy coverage ceases, and the new owner must obtain his or her own title insurance policy.

TITLE INSURANCE PROCESS

Search → Examination → Chain of title → Preliminary report → Escrow → Title policy

A title insurance policy insures that a thorough examination has been made of all public records affecting the property in question, and that the owner has acquired ownership free from title defects of public record, subject only to the encumbrances revealed in the title examination and the exceptions recited in the title insurance policy. It means that the owner has a marketable title that can be transferred to others.

Standard Coverage Policy (CLTA)

1. Risks normally insured against:
   (a) Most matters disclosed by public records
   (b) Certain off-record risks, such as forgery or incompetence of parties
2. Risks not normally insured against:
   (a) Matters not disclosed by public records
   (b) Environmental laws, zoning, and other government ordinances regarding the use of the property
   (c) Certain mining and water claims
   (d) Defects known to the insured before the property was purchased and not revealed to the title company before the sale

Extended Coverage Policy (ALTA)

1. Risks covered:
   (a) All those listed under the standard coverage policy, plus
   (b) Unperfected mechanic's liens
   (c) Unrecorded physical easements
   (d) Facts a correct survey would show
   (e) Certain water claims
   (f) Rights of parties in possession, including tenants and owners under unrecorded instruments
2. Risks not normally covered:
   (a) Environmental laws, zoning, and other government ordinances affecting the use of the property
   (b) Defects known to the insured before the property was insured but not revealed to title company by the insured

For an additional charge, an insured can purchase special endorsements to cover items normally excluded under the CLTA or ALTA policies.

TITLE INSURANCE SUMMARIZED

TITLE POLICY

Who Pays for the Title Insurance?

The payment of the owner's policy fee is a negotiable item between the buyer and the seller. However, in different geographical areas the method of payment varies. In some areas it is customary to split the title fee between the buyer and the seller. In some areas the seller normally pays the title fee, and in others the buyer pays. The lender's policy title fee is almost always paid by the borrower-buyer.

Who Decides Which Title Insurance Company to Use?

This is another negotiable item between the buyer and seller. The usual custom is for the party paying the title fee to select the title company. Real estate regulations prohibit a real estate agent from dictating which title insurance company to use. If the real estate agent should happen to have a financial interest in the title company selected, the agent must disclose this fact to both the buyer and seller.

Evolution of Title Protection

FIRST CAME

Abstract of Title

A summary of title prepared by an early-day specialist, with no guarantees of accuracy

THEN

Certificate of Title

A certificate stating the name of the owner and a list of encumbrances. No guarantee of accuracy

THEN

Guarantee of Title

A title search in which an abstract company guaranteed the accuracy of the search

AND TODAY

Title insurance

Creation of an insurance company that issues a title policy and insures the accuracy of results. If insured suffers an insured loss, a claim is filed similar in nature to any other type of insurance. Title insurance led to the use of the grant deed and elimination of the warranty deed in California. (See Chapter 2 for details regarding deeds.)

Typical Escrow and Title Insurance Fees

Sales Price	Escrow Fee	Title Insurance Fee	Combined
$ 50,000	$ 600	$ 475	$ 1,075
100,000	600	615	1,215
150,000	750	765	1,515
200,000	900	915	1,815
250,000	1,050	1,055	2,105
300,000	1,200	1,195	2,395
350,000	1,350	1,320	2,670
400,000	1,500	1,445	2,945
450,000	1,650	1,570	3,220
500,000	1,800	1,695	3,495

For illustrative purposes only. Fees vary from company to company.

10.3 CLOSING COSTS

Closing costs refer to the expenses paid by the buyer and the seller upon the sale of property. Some people attempt to estimate closing costs by using simple rules of thumb, such as "3% of the sales price" or some other rough figure. However, rules of thumb are not accurate. The only sure way to determine actual closing costs is to list and price each individual item.

It must be stressed that the payment of the closing costs is a negotiable topic between the buyer and seller. There is no law requiring that certain closing costs are the responsibility of the buyer or the seller. The only exception deals with some government-backed loans where regulations prohibit the buyer from paying certain closing costs. However, by custom, certain closing costs are typically paid by the buyer, and other costs are usually paid by the seller.

Buyer's Closing Costs

Buyer's (borrower) closing costs can be divided into two categories: (1) nonrecurring closing costs, and (2) recurring closing costs.

Nonrecurring closing costs are one-time charges paid upon the close of escrow. Recurring closing costs are prepaid items that the buyer pays in advance to help offset expenses that will continue as long as the buyer owns the property.

Nonrecurring Closing Costs Usually Paid by the Buyer

1. *Loan origination fee.* A fee charged by a lender to cover the expenses of processing a loan. The fee is usually quoted as a percentage of the loan amount. For example,

a $1\frac{1}{2}\%$ loan fee for a $100,000 loan would be $1\frac{1}{2}\% \times$ $100,000 = $1,500 loan fee.

2. *Appraisal fee.* A fee charged by an appraiser for giving an estimate of property value. The fee for a simple appraisal will vary throughout the state, with $350 or more being a typical charge for a single-family residence. Appraisal fees for income properties such as apartments or office buildings are considerably higher.

3. *Credit report fee.* Before a lender grants a loan, the borrower's credit is checked at a credit agency. The credit report usually costs from $40 to $60.

4. *Structural pest control inspection fee.* A fee charged by a licensed inspector who checks for termites, fungus, dry rot, pests, and other items that might cause structural damage. For a home in an urban area the fee is usually from $125 and up.

5. *Tax service fee.* A fee paid to a tax service company that, for the life of the loan, each year reviews the tax collector's records. If a borrower fails to pay the property taxes, the tax service company reports this to the lender, who can then take steps to protect the loan against a tax foreclosure sale. This fee usually runs from $50 to $80.

6. *Recording fees.* This covers the cost of recording the deed, deed of trust, and other buyer-related documents. Most counties charge $7 to record a single-page document.

7. *Notary fees.* Signatures on documents to be recorded must be notarized. Notary publics typically charge $10 or more per signature.

8. *Assumption fee.* A fee paid to a lender if the buyer "assumes" the loan—that is, agrees to take over and continue to pay the seller's existing loan.

9. *Title and escrow fees.* Buyer's responsibility in buyer-pays areas—areas where it is customary for the buyer to pay the title and escrow fees.

Recurring Closing Costs Usually Paid by the Buyer

1. *Hazard insurance.* A one-year premium for insurance against fire, storm, and other risks. The minimum coverage is the amount of the real estate loan, but buyers are advised to purchase greater amounts if they make a large down payment toward the purchase price. Many owners purchase comprehensive homeowner's packages.

2. *Tax proration.* In California the property tax year runs from July 1 through June 30 of the following year. If the seller has prepaid the taxes, the buyer reimburses the

seller for the prepaid portion. Prorations are discussed in detail in Chapter 6.

3. *Tax and insurance reserves.* This is also known as an impound account or trust account. If a buyer's (borrower's) monthly loan payment is to include taxes and insurance, as well as principal and interest, the lender sets up a reserve account. Depending upon the time of the year (the date taxes and insurance are due relative to the date escrow closes), a lender will want the buyer to prepay one to six months of taxes and insurance premiums into this reserve account. Once an adequate reserve account is established, tax and insurance bills are forwarded to the lender for payment. At the end of the year, adjustments are made to assure that adequate amounts are in the trust fund for the next year.

4. *Interest due before the first loan payment.* Interest on real estate loans is typically paid in arrears. For example: Escrow closes September 15, with the first loan payment due November 1. The payment due November 1 covers the interest due for the month of October. How is the interest from September 15 to September 30 collected? It is collected in advance at close of escrow and is called prepaid interest. If escrow closed on the first of a month, there would be no prepaid interest if the first payment was due the first of the following month.

Seller's Closing Costs

The closing costs paid by a seller are one-time, nonrecurring expenses. After the close of escrow, the seller is divested of ownership and therefore has no recurring expenses attached to ownership such as property taxes and hazard insurance. Again it must be emphasized that the payment of a particular closing expense is negotiable between the buyer and seller. The list below is merely a guideline to closing costs usually paid by the seller as the result of custom and/or agreement.

Closing Costs Usually Paid by the Seller

1. *Transfer tax.* A tax charged when title is transferred. The county has a documentary transfer tax that is computed at $1.10 per $1,000 (or 55 cents per $500 or fraction thereof) of the sales price. For example, if a $190,000 home is sold for cash, the state documentary transfer tax would be $190,000 sales price ÷ 1,000 = 190 × $1.10 = $209 tax.

    For a more detailed explanation of the state documentary transfer tax, see Chapter 6. In addition to the county documentary transfer tax, some cities in California have enacted a municipal transfer tax that must be collected at the close of escrow.

2. *Prepayment penalty.* A charge by a lender when a borrower pays off a loan before the required due date. Many times when a property is sold, the buyer obtains financing to cover the sales price. In the process the seller's existing mortgage is paid off to make way for the buyer's new mortgage. If the seller's mortgage has a prepayment clause, the seller pays this penalty as a closing cost. Most loans do not have prepayment penalties. But if they do, the actual prepayment penalties vary by lender. A typical prepayment penalty might be six months' interest on the outstanding loan balance at the time of payoff, after subtracting 20% of the original loan amount. (See Chapter 7 for details.)

3. *Structural pest control work.* Customarily the buyer pays for the structural pest control inspection fee, and the seller pays for corrective work. However, in some areas the seller pays for both the inspection and the corrective work.

4. *Real estate brokerage commission.* The commission is normally quoted as a percentage of the sales price. A 6% commission with a sales price of $190,000 would be an $11,400 closing cost for the seller.

5. *Discount points.* On some government-backed loans the seller may pay discount points to increase a lender's yield on a loan. One point is equal to 1% of the buyer's loan amount.

6. *Recording and notary fees.* Fees for recording seller-oriented documents, such as a deed of reconveyance to clear off an old loan.

7. *Title and escrow fees.* Seller's responsibility in seller-pays areas—areas where it is customary for the seller to pay the title and escrow fees.

8. *Natural hazard disclosure fees.* To provide seller-required disclosures for earthquake, flood, fire, and other hazards.

Summary of Closing Costs

BUYER USUALLY PAYS

1. Loan origination fee
2. Appraisal fee
3. Credit report
4. Structural pest control inspection fee
5. Tax service fee
6. Recording fees

7. Notary fees
8. Assumption fee
9. Title and escrow fees in buyer-pays areas
10. Hazard insurance
11. Interest on loan before first payment

SELLER USUALLY PAYS

1. Transfer tax
2. Prepayment penalty
3. Structural pest control work fee
4. Real estate brokerage commission
5. Discount points on government-backed loans
6. Recording and notary fees
7. Title and escrow fees in seller-pays areas
8. Natural hazard disclosure fees

THE FOLLOWING ITEMS ARE USUALLY PRORATED BETWEEN THE BUYER AND SELLER

1. Property taxes
2. Interest if loan is assumed by buyer
3. Hazard insurance if existing policy is assumed by buyer
4. Rents if the property is tenant-occupied income property

CHAPTER SUMMARY

Escrow is the use of a neutral third party to act as the closing agent in a real estate transaction. To be valid, an escrow requires a binding contract and a conditional delivery of transfer instruments. Escrow companies must comply with the Real Estate Settlement Procedures Act (RESPA).

Title insurance companies, institutional lenders, attorneys, and independently licensed companies can handle escrows. A real estate broker can handle an escrow if he or she is an agent for either the buyer or seller in the transaction.

Title insurance companies search and gather public title records, examine and interpret the records, and then issue policies of title insurance. The two major types of title insurance policies are the CLTA standard and the ALTA extended coverage policies. Certain items are not included in title insurance coverage, and therefore consumers should be aware that these excluded items are their responsibility.

Closing costs can be classified as recurring and nonrecurring. Recurring closing costs are prepaid items that the buyer pays in advance to help offset expenses that will continue as long as the buyer owns the property. Nonrecurring closing costs are one-time charges paid upon the close of escrow.

The payment of escrow fees, title insurance, and closing costs is an item of negotiation between the buyer and the seller. However, by custom, certain closing costs are typically paid by the buyer, whereas other costs are usually paid by the seller. This custom varies throughout the state of California. Escrow and closing practices differ between Northern and Southern California.

IMPORTANT TERMS AND CONCEPTS

Abstractor

ALTA policy

Beneficiary statement/demand

Chain of title

CLTA policy

Escrow

Extended coverage policy

HUD-1 closing statement

Nonrecurring closing costs

Preliminary report

Recurring closing costs

RESPA

Standard policy

PRACTICAL APPLICATION

1. Seller and buyer are in escrow for the sale of a home. In the area it is customary for the seller to pay for the CLTA title policy. The deposit receipt states that the seller will pay for the title policy, but the escrow instructions signed by all parties state that all title and escrow fees will be split 50/50. Just prior to close of escrow, the buyer submits amended instructions for the escrow officer to charge the entire CLTA policy to the seller. The seller refuses to proceed with the escrow. As the buyer's real estate agent, what might you do to solve this problem?

2. Acme Title Company has a policy of giving real estate licensees who refer business to Acme Title a dinner for two, plus tickets to a professional sporting event. Without your suggestion, both the buyer and seller asked that Acme Title Company be the title insurer. As the real estate agent in the transaction, what are the legal and ethical issues?

3. A $213,575 existing ARM loan at 7% will be assumed by the buyer. The seller has made the October 1 payment and escrow will close on October 19 (use 18 days as buyer is responsible for the day escrow closes). Using a 360-day year, what are the escrow debit and credit charges to the buyer and seller for the interest proration?

1. For an escrow to be binding, there must be a:
   a. conditional delivery of transfer instruments
   b. contract between the parties
   c. neutral third party
   d. all of the above

2. Which of the following must have an escrow license?
   a. title insurance companies
   b. independent escrow companies
   c. real estate brokers if they handle escrows in which they are also the agent
   d. all of the above

3. A history of all title transfers of a particular parcel of land is called a:
   a. preliminary report
   b. chain of title
   c. abstract of title
   d. guarantee of title

4. A CLTA title policy is also known as:
   a. an extended coverage policy
   b. an ALTA coverage policy
   c. a standard coverage
   d an all-inclusive policy

5. Which of the following is a nonrecurring closing cost?
   a. title insurance fee
   b. real property tax proration
   c. interest on new real estate loan
   d. hazard insurance premium

6. A title insurance policy especially designed for lenders, which requires the title company to make a physical inspection of the property, is called:
   a. a CLTA standard policy
   b. a joint protection policy
   c. an all-inclusive policy
   d. an ALTA extended coverage policy

7. Annual real property taxes of $720 are paid for the current fiscal year. Escrow closes April 1, and the taxes are to be prorated. Therefore the:
   a. seller will be charged (debited) $180
   b. seller will be credited $180
   c. buyer will be credited $180
   d. buyer will be debited $540

8. The sales price is $150,000, with buyer obtaining a new VA guaranteed loan. The seller agrees to pay off the existing $100,000 FHA-insured loan. The seller also agrees to pay the county documentary transfer tax, which is:

   a. $55

   b. $110

   c. $145

   d. $165

9. Although the payment of closing costs is negotiable between the buyer and seller, the buyer usually pays for the:

   a loan origination fee

   b. broker's commission

   c. prepayment penalty

   d. transfer tax

10. Sales price for a rural home is $80,000; buyer pays all cash; seller pays off old loan of $45,000. Seller also pays 5% broker commission, documentary transfer tax, $300 prepayment penalty, plus $500 in other closing costs. How much will the seller net from escrow?

   a. $35,000

   b. $30,112

   c. $49,888

   d. $45,000

11. All of the following are covered by title insurance policies, except:

   a. forged deeds

   b. liens of record

   c. environmental violations

   d. incompetent owners of record

12. If the parties in an escrow are in conflict and cannot agree as to what to do, the escrow officer can bring a court action called:

   a. an abstractor

   b. an interpleader

   c. a judgment

   d. a writ

13. The use of the HUD-1 closing statement is required by:

   a. Regulation Z

   b. Truth-in-lending

   c. ECOA

   d. RESPA

14. The title records in the office of the title company are called a title:

   a. survey

   b. examination

   c. plant

   d. chain

15. Which of the following is a recurring closing cost?

   a. tax service

   b. property taxes

   c. credit report

   d. recording fee

16. Which of the following is a nonrecurring closing cost?

   a. notary fee

   b. homeowner association dues

   c. interest on existing loans

   d. fire insurance

17. Sales price is $300,000; buyer obtains a new 80% loan and pays 1% loan fee, $25 tax service fee, $350 property tax proration, $100 structural pest control inspection charge, $525 hazard insurance, and one-half of the $900 escrow fee. Based on this information, how much total cash will the buyer need to close escrow?
    a. $1,450
    b. $3,750
    c. $63,850
    d. $64,450

18. The most extensive title assurance is:
    a. certificate of title
    b. abstract of title
    c. guarantee of title
    d. insurance of title

19. Escrow officers cannot:
    a. give legal advice
    b. draft deeds for the parties in escrow
    c. prepare documents for recording
    d. do any of the above

20. Property taxes for the year are $1,080, paid to July 1 of the year. Escrow closes May 1; therefore, the escrow officer will prorate the prepaid property taxes as follows:
    a. $180 credit to seller
    b. $180 credit to buyer
    c. $900 debit to seller
    d. $900 debit to buyer

Chapter 11

Landlord and Tenant Relations

Chapter Preview   The relationship between landlords and tenants can be calm and enjoyable, or it can be turbulent, with frustration and confusion on both sides. The California legislature is constantly passing laws related to landlords or tenants. Many problems between landlords and tenants are caused by a lack of understanding of the legal rights and duties of each party. At the conclusion of the chapter, you will be able to:

1. Define a lease and then list four types of leasehold estates

2. Outline the requirements needed for a valid lease or rental agreement

3. Explain the difference between a sublease and an assignment of a lease

4. Discuss the duties and responsibilities landlords and tenants owe to each other

5. Describe how tenants can be lawfully evicted

6. Explain the services provided by professional property managers

11.1 LEASES   A lease is a contract between an owner, called a *lessor,* or *landlord,* and a *lessee,* or *tenant.* A tenant is given the right to possess and use the landlord's property in exchange for *rent*. California law requires that all leases for more than one year must be in writing to be valid.

A lease or rental agreement for one year or less need not be in writing to be valid. However, a prudent person should reduce all rental and lease agreements to writing. In this chapter the terms lease and rental agreement are used interchangeably.

Types of Leasehold Estates

In Chapter 2, a distinction was made between a *freehold estate* and a *less-than-freehold estate*. It was stated that a freehold estate is an interest in real property as an owner, whereas a less-than-freehold estate is an interest in real property as a tenant. Less-than-freehold estates are also known as *leasehold estates* or *chattel real*. There are four types or classifications of leasehold estates, as illustrated in Figure 11.1 and described in the following list.

1. *Estate for years (tenancy for a fixed term)*. A leasehold that continues for a fixed time span. The term estate for years is misleading because the fixed time span can be for a single day, week, month, year, or years. Therefore, a signed lease for five years, and a signed lease for one month, may both be estates for years. To eliminate this confusion, estates for years are beginning to be called a *tenancy for a fixed term*.
2. *Estate from period to period (periodic tenancy)*. A leasehold that continues from period to period (day, week, month, year) with no specified termination date. Each party agrees to renew or terminate at the end of each period. A month-to-month rental agreement is an example of an estate from period to period.

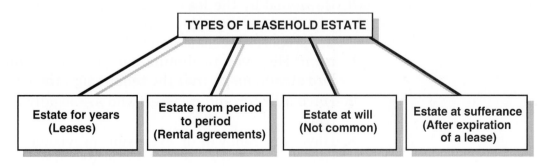

Figure 11.1

3. *Estate at will.* A leasehold that can be terminated without notice at any time by the lessor or the lessee. An estate at will has no definite termination date listed in the lease. The California legislature has passed laws stating that both the lessor and the lessee must give advance notice prior to the termination of an estate at will.

4. *Estate at sufferance.* A leasehold where a lessee retains possession of the land after the expiration of a lease. For example, a lessee has a five-year lease which expired today. The lessor and the lessee have not decided upon renewal terms. Under these circumstances the lessee's estate for years is converted to an estate at sufferance until a decision is made about the future rights of the lessee. The landlord can enter into another lease agreement or ask the lessee to leave.

Requirements for a Valid Lease

For a lease to be valid, it must:

1. Be in writing, if the term is for more than one year. Any alterations must also be in writing.

2. Contain the names of the lessor and lessee.

3. Contain a sufficient description of the property. In some cases a street address is sufficient for a simple residential lease. In other cases, it may be wise to include a complete legal description in addition to the common street address.

4. Show the amount of rent and the manner of payment. An example might be a rent of $30,000, payable $500 per month for five years.

5. State the duration or time period the lease is to run, or in the case of a periodic tenancy, the periods involved. According to law, urban property cannot be leased for more than 99 years and rural agricultural land for more than 51 years.

6. Be signed by the lessor. Technically, a lessee need not sign the lease to make it valid. The lessee's possession of the property is considered to be acceptance of the agreement. However, to eliminate misunderstanding, a landlord should insist that the tenant sign the lease.

7. Have a lessor and a lessee who are legally able to contract.

8. Have any renewal or extension provisions in boldface type. A renewal or extension provision is a clause that automatically renews or extends the lease if the lessee remains in possession after expiration of the lease.

See Figure 11.2 for a sample residential rental agreement form.

Other Provisions

Although not legally required, a lease should also state who is responsible for utilities and maintenance. If there are special rules, regarding noise, guests, parking, pets, and so on, they should be noted in the rental agreement. The intended use of the property should be specified as well as the maximum number of tenant occupants per rental unit as allowed by law. A lease should also note the right, if any, the tenant may have to remove fixtures attached by the tenant.

Security Deposits

On a residential rental, a security deposit cannot exceed more than two months' rent on unfurnished dwellings or three months' rent on furnished units. The security deposit must be refunded within 21 days after the tenant vacates the property.

However, if properly worded, the security deposit can be used to offset back rent, damages caused by the tenant, or to clean the premises left dirty by the tenant. If an offset is used, the landlord must provide the tenant with an itemized statement showing all charges within 21 days after the tenant vacates. *No security deposit can be labeled as nonrefundable.* The landlord is still allowed to collect the first month's rent in addition to the security deposit already noted.

Assignment versus Sublease of the Lease

An *assignment* of a lease transfers the entire leasehold interest to another party, including the prime liability and responsibility to make payments to the lessor (landlord). Figure 11.3 illustrates an assignment of a lease.

Under an assignment the original Lessee A is removed from the transaction and all rights and duties pass to Assignee B. Assignee B is now primarily liable for the lease.

A *sublease* transfers only a part of the term of the lessee to a sublessee. The original lessee is still liable to the lessor (landlord) for the terms and conditions of the lease. Figure 11.4 illustrates a sublease.

Sublessee B pays Lessee A, who pays the lessor. In essence, there are two contracts—the original lease between lessor and Lessee A, and another contract between Lessee A and Sublessee B. Each contract stands alone. If Sublessee B does not pay Lessee A, Lessee A

CALIFORNIA
ASSOCIATION
OF REALTORS®

RESIDENTIAL LEASE OR
MONTH-TO-MONTH RENTAL AGREEMENT

_____ ("Landlord") and

_____ , ("Tenant") agree as follows:

1. PROPERTY:
   A. Landlord rents to Tenant and Tenant rents from Landlord, the real property and improvements described as: _____
   _____ ("Premises").
   B. The following personal property is included: _____
2. TERM: The term begins on (date) _____ ("Commencement Date"), **(Check A or B):**
   ☐ **A. Month-to-month:** and continues as a month-to-month tenancy. Either party may terminate the tenancy by giving written notice to the other at least 30 days prior to the intended termination date, subject to any applicable local laws. Such notice may be given on any date.
   ☐ **B. Lease:** and shall terminate on (date) _____ at _____ AM/PM.
   Any holding over after the term of this Agreement expires, with Landlord's consent, shall create a month-to-month tenancy which either party may terminate as specified in paragraph 2A. Rent shall be at a rate equal to the rent for the immediately preceding month, unless otherwise notified by Landlord, payable in advance. All other terms and conditions of this Agreement shall remain in full force and effect.
3. RENT:
   A. Tenant agrees to pay rent at the rate of $ _____ per month for the term of the Agreement.
   B. Rent is payable in advance on the **1st (or** ☐ _____**) day** of each calendar month, and is delinquent on the next day.
   C. If Commencement Date falls on any day other than the first day of the month, rent shall be prorated based on a 30-day period. If Tenant has paid one full month's rent in advance of Commencement Date, rent for the second calendar month shall be prorated based on a 30-day period.
   D. PAYMENT: The rent shall be paid to (name) _____ , at (address) _____
   _____ , or at any other location specified by Landlord in writing to Tenant.
4. SECURITY DEPOSIT:
   A. Tenant agrees to pay $ _____ as a security deposit. Security deposit will be ☐ given to the Owner of the Premises; or ☐ held in Owner's Broker's trust account.
   B. All or any portion of the security deposit may be used, as reasonably necessary, to: (1) cure Tenant's default in payment of rent, Late Charges, NSF fees, or other sums due; (2) repair damage, excluding ordinary wear and tear, caused by Tenant or by a guest or licensee of Tenant; (3) clean Premises, if necessary, upon termination of tenancy; and (4) replace or return personal property or appurtenances. **SECURITY DEPOSIT SHALL NOT BE USED BY TENANT IN LIEU OF PAYMENT OF LAST MONTH'S RENT.** If all or any portion of the security deposit is used during tenancy, Tenant agrees to reinstate the total security deposit within five days after written notice is delivered to Tenant. Within three weeks after Tenant vacates the Premises, Landlord shall (1) furnish Tenant an itemized statement indicating the amount of any security deposit received and the basis for its disposition, and (2) return any remaining portion of security deposit to Tenant.
   C. No interest will be paid on security deposit, unless required by local ordinance.
   D. If security deposit is held by Owner, Tenant agrees not to hold Broker responsible for its return. If security deposit is held in Owner's Broker's trust account, **and** Broker's authority is terminated before expiration of this Agreement, **and** security deposits are released to someone other than Tenant, **then** Broker shall notify Tenant, in writing, where and to whom security deposit has been released. Once Tenant has been provided such notice, Tenant agrees not to hold Broker responsible for security deposit.
5. MOVE-IN COSTS RECEIVED/DUE:

Category	Total Due	Payment Received	Balance Due	Date Due
Rent from _____ to _____ (date)				
*Security Deposit				
Other _____				
Other _____				
Total				

   *The maximum amount that Landlord may receive as security deposit, however designated, cannot exceed two month's rent for an unfurnished premises, and three month's rent for a furnished premises.
6. PARKING: (Check A or B)
   ☐ **A.** Parking is permitted as follows: _____
      The right to parking ☐ is, ☐ is not, included in the rent charged pursuant to paragraph 3. If not included in the rent, the parking rental fee shall be an additional $ _____ per month. Parking space(s) are to be used for parking operable motor vehicles, except for trailers, boats, campers, buses or trucks (other than pick-up trucks). Tenant shall park in assigned space(s) only. Parking space(s) are to be kept clean. Vehicles leaking oil, gas or other motor vehicle fluids shall not be parked on the Premises. Mechanical work or storage of inoperable vehicles is not allowed in parking space(s) or elsewhere on the Premises.
   OR ☐ **B.** Parking is not permitted on the Premises.
7. STORAGE: (Check A or B)
   ☐ **A.** Storage is permitted as follows: _____
      The right to storage space ☐ is, ☐ is not, included in the rent charged pursuant to paragraph 3. If not included in rent, storage space shall be an additional $ _____ per month. Tenant shall store only personal property Tenant owns, and shall not store property that is claimed by another or in which another has any right, title, or interest. Tenant shall not store any improperly packaged food or perishable goods, flammable materials, explosives, or other inherently dangerous material.
   OR ☐ **B.** Storage is not permitted on the Premises.
8. LATE CHARGE/NSF CHECKS: Tenant acknowledges that either late payment of rent or issuance of a non-sufficient funds ("NSF") check may cause Landlord to incur costs and expenses, the exact amount of which are extremely difficult and impractical to determine. These costs may include, but are not limited to, processing, enforcement and accounting expenses, and late charges imposed on Landlord. If any installment of rent due from Tenant is not received by Landlord within **5 (or** ☐ _____**) calendar days** after date due, or if a check is returned NSF, Tenant shall pay to Landlord, respectively, an additional sum of $ _____ as Late Charge and $25.00 as a NSF fee, either or both of which shall be deemed additional rent. Landlord and Tenant agree that these charges represent a fair and reasonable estimate of the costs Landlord may incur by reason of Tenant's late or NSF payment. Any Late Charge or NSF fee due shall be paid with the current installment of rent. Landlord's acceptance of any Late Charge or NSF fee shall not constitute a waiver as to any default of Tenant. Landlord's right to collect a Late Charge or NSF fee shall not be deemed an extension of the date rent is due under paragraph 3, or prevent Landlord from exercising any other rights and remedies under this Agreement, and as provided by law.

Tenant and Landlord acknowledge receipt of copy of this page, which constitutes Page 1 of _____ Pages.
Tenant's Initials (_____) (_____)   Landlord's Initials (_____) (_____)

REBS | Published and Distributed by:
REAL ESTATE BUSINESS SERVICES, INC.
a subsidiary of the CALIFORNIA ASSOCIATION OF REALTORS®
525 South Virgil Avenue, Los Angeles, California 90020
PRINT DATE
R OCT 97

┌─ OFFICE USE ONLY ─┐
│ Reviewed by Broker │
│ or Designee _____ │
│ Date _____ │
└──────────────────┘

EQUAL HOUSING OPPORTUNITY

LANDLORD'S COPY
RESIDENTIAL LEASE OR MONTH-TO-MONTH RENTAL AGREEMENT (LR-14 PAGE 1 OF 3) REVISED 10/97

Figure 11.2a (Reprinted with permission, _California Association of Realtors®._ Endorsement not implied.)

Premises: _____ Date _____

9. **CONDITION OF PREMISES:** Tenant has examined Premises, all furniture, furnishings, appliances and landscaping, if any, and fixtures, including smoke detector(s).
   (Check one:)
   ☐ **A.** Tenant acknowledges that these items are clean and in operative condition, with the following exceptions _____

   OR ☐ **B.** Tenant's acknowledgement of the condition of these items is contained in an attached statement of condition, (such as C.A.R.'s MIMO-11).
   OR ☐ **C.** Tenant will provide Landlord a list of items which are damaged or not in operable condition within 3 (or ☐ _____) days after Commencement Date, not as a contingency of this Agreement but rather as an acknowledgement of the condition of the Premises.
   OR ☐ **D.** Other: _____

10. **NEIGHBORHOOD CONDITIONS:** Tenant is advised to satisfy him or herself as to neighborhood or area conditions, including schools, proximity and adequacy of law enforcement, crime statistics, registered felons or offenders, fire protection, other governmental services, proximity to commercial, industrial or agricultural activities, existing and proposed transportation, construction and development which may affect noise, view, or traffic, airport noise, noise or odor from any source, wild and domestic animals, other nuisances, hazards, or circumstances, facilities and condition of common areas, conditions and influences of significance to certain cultures and/or religions, and personal needs, requirements and preferences of Tenant.

11. **UTILITIES:** Tenant agrees to pay for all utilities and services, and the following charges: _____
    except _____, which shall be paid for by Landlord. If any utilities are not separately metered, Tenant shall pay Tenant's proportional share, as reasonably determined by Landlord.

12. **OCCUPANTS:** The Premises are for the sole use as a personal residence by the following named persons **only:** _____

13. **PETS:** No animal or pet shall be kept on or about the Premises without Landlord's prior written consent, except _____

14. **RULES/REGULATIONS:** Tenant agrees to comply with all rules and regulations of Landlord which are at any time posted on the Premises or delivered to Tenant. Tenant shall not, and shall ensure that guests and licensees of Tenant shall not, disturb, annoy, endanger, or interfere with other tenants of the building or neighbors, or use the Premises for any unlawful purposes, including, but not limited to, using, manufacturing, selling, storing, or transporting illicit drugs or other contraband, or violate any law or ordinance, or commit a waste or nuisance on or about the Premises.

15. **CONDOMINIUM/PLANNED UNIT DEVELOPMENT:** ☐ (If checked) The Premises is a unit in a condominium, planned unit, or other development governed by an owner's association. The name of the owner's association is _____.
    Tenant agrees to comply with all covenants, conditions and restrictions, by-laws, rules and regulations and decisions of owner's association. Landlord shall provide Tenant copies of rules and regulations, if any. Tenant shall reimburse Landlord for any fines or charges imposed by owner's association or other authorities, due to any violation by Tenant, or the guests or licensees of Tenant.

16. **MAINTENANCE:**
    A. Tenant shall properly use, operate, and safeguard Premises, including if applicable, any landscaping, furniture, furnishings, and appliances, and all mechanical, electrical, gas and plumbing fixtures, and keep them clean and sanitary. Tenant shall immediately notify Landlord, in writing, of any problem, malfunction or damage. Tenant shall pay for all repairs or replacements caused by Tenant, or guests or invitees of Tenant, excluding ordinary wear and tear. Tenant shall pay for all damage to Premises as a result of failure to report a problem in a timely manner. Tenant shall pay for repair of drain blockages or stoppages, unless caused by defective plumbing parts or tree roots invading sewer lines.
    B. ☐ Landlord, ☐ Tenant, shall water the garden, landscaping, trees and shrubs, except _____
    C. ☐ Landlord, ☐ Tenant, shall maintain the garden, landscaping, trees, and shrubs, except _____

17. **ALTERATIONS:** Tenant shall not make any alterations in or about the Premises, without Landlord's prior written consent, including: painting, wallpapering, adding or changing locks, installing antenna or satellite dish, placing signs, displays or exhibits, or using screws, fastening devices, large nails or adhesive materials.

18. **KEYS/LOCKS:**
    A. Tenant acknowledges receipt of (or Tenant will receive ☐ prior to the Commencement Date, or ☐ _____):
    ☐ _____ key(s) to Premises,   ☐ _____ remote control device(s) for garage door/gate opener(s).
    ☐ _____ key(s) to mailbox,   ☐ _____
    ☐ _____ key(s) to common area(s), ☐ _____
    B. Tenant acknowledges that locks to the Premises ☐ have, ☐ have not, been re-keyed.
    C. If Tenant re-keys existing locks or opening devices, Tenant shall immediately deliver copies of all keys to Landlord. Tenant shall pay all costs and charges related to loss of any keys or opening devices. Tenant may not remove locks, even if installed by Tenant.

19. **ENTRY:** Tenant shall make Premises available to Landlord or representative for the purpose of entering to make necessary or agreed repairs, decorations, alterations, or improvements, or to supply necessary or agreed services, or to show Premises to prospective or actual purchasers, tenants, mortgagees, lenders, appraisers, or contractors. Landlord and Tenant agree that twenty-four hours notice (oral or written) shall be reasonable and sufficient notice. In an emergency, Landlord or representative may enter Premises at any time without prior notice.

20. **SIGNS:** Tenant authorizes Landlord to place For Sale/Lease signs on the Premises.

21. **ASSIGNMENT/SUBLETTING:** Tenant shall not sublet all or any part of Premises, or assign or transfer this Agreement or any interest in it, without prior written consent of Landlord. Unless such consent is obtained, any assignment, transfer or subletting of Premises or this Agreement or tenancy, by voluntary act of Tenant, operation of law, or otherwise, shall be null and void, and, at the option of Landlord, terminate this Agreement. Any proposed assignee, transferee or sublessee shall submit to Landlord an application and credit information for Landlord's approval, and, if approved, sign a separate written agreement with Landlord and Tenant. Landlord's consent to any one assignment, transfer, or sublease, shall not be construed as consent to any subsequent assignment, transfer or sublease, and does not release Tenant of Tenant's obligation under this Agreement.

22. ☐ **LEAD PAINT (CHECK IF APPLICABLE):** Premises was constructed prior to 1978. In accordance with federal law, Landlord gives, and Tenant acknowledges receipt of, the disclosures on the attached form (such as C.A.R. Form FLD-14) and a federally approved lead pamphlet.

23. **POSSESSION:** If Landlord is unable to deliver possession of Premises on Commencement Date, such Date shall be extended to date on which possession is made available to Tenant. If Landlord is unable to deliver possession within 5 (or ☐ _____) **calendar days** after agreed Commencement Date, Tenant may terminate this Agreement by giving written notice to Landlord, and shall be refunded all rent and security deposit paid.

24. **TENANT'S OBLIGATIONS UPON VACATING PREMISES:** Upon termination of Agreement, Tenant shall: (a) give Landlord all copies of all keys or opening devices to Premises, including any common areas; (b) vacate Premises and surrender it to Landlord empty of all persons; (c) vacate any/all parking and/or storage space; (d) deliver Premises to Landlord in the same condition as referenced in paragraph 9; (e) clean Premises, including professional cleaning of carpet and drapes; (f) give written notice to Landlord of Tenant's forwarding address, and (h) _____.

    All improvements installed by Tenant, with or without Landlord's consent, become the property of Landlord upon termination.

25. **BREACH OF CONTRACT/EARLY TERMINATION:** In addition to any obligations established by paragraph 24, in event of termination by Tenant prior to completion of the original term of Agreement, Tenant shall also be responsible for lost rent, rental commissions, advertising expenses, and painting costs necessary to ready Premises for re-rental.

26. **TEMPORARY RELOCATION:** Tenant agrees, upon demand of Landlord, to temporarily vacate Premises for a reasonable period, to allow for fumigation, or other methods, to control wood destroying pests or organisms, or other repairs to Premises. Tenant agrees to comply with all instructions and requirements necessary to prepare Premises to accommodate pest control, fumigation or other work, including bagging or storage of food and medicine, and removal of perishables and valuables. Tenant shall only be entitled to a credit of rent equal to the per diem rent for the period of time Tenant is required to vacate Premises.

27. **DAMAGE TO PREMISES:** If, by no fault of Tenant, Premises are totally or partially damaged or destroyed by fire, earthquake, accident or other casualty, which render Premises uninhabitable, either Landlord or Tenant may terminate Agreement by giving the other written notice. Rent shall be abated as of date of damage. The abated amount shall be the current monthly rent prorated on a 30-day basis. If Agreement is not terminated, Landlord shall promptly repair the damage, and rent shall be reduced based on the extent to which the damage interferes with Tenant's reasonable use of Premises. If damage occurs as a result of an act of Tenant or Tenant's guests, only Landlord shall have the right of termination, and no reduction in rent shall be made.

Tenant and Lanlord acknowledge receipt of copy of this page, which constitutes Page 2 of _____ Pages.
Tenant's Initials (_____) (_____) Landlord's Initials (_____) (_____)

OFFICE USE ONLY
Reviewed by Broker
or Designee _____
Date _____

PRINT DATE
R OCT 97

LANDLORD'S COPY

RESIDENTIAL LEASE OR MONTH-TO-MONTH RENTAL AGREEMENT (LR-14 PAGE 2 OF 3) REVISED 10/97

Exhibit 11.2b

273

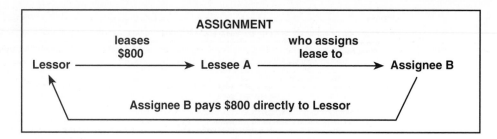

Figure 11.3

must still pay the lessor. In Figure 11.4, Lessee A is said to hold a "sandwich lease." In other words, Lessee A is wedged between the lessor and the sublessee. A lessor may insert a clause in the lease prohibiting any assignment or sublease without the prior written approval of the lessor.

Lease With Option to Buy

Under a lease with option to buy (purchase), property is rented for a period of time, at the end of which the lessee is given the right to purchase per a set of agreed terms. The lessee (tenant/optionee) is not required to buy, but may if he or she wishes. If the lessee does exercise the option, the lessor/optionor must sell.

A lease with option to buy should not be confused with a concept known as the first right of refusal. Under a first right of refusal, the lessor (landlord) is not required to sell. However, if the lessor does wish to sell, the lessee (tenant) will be given the first chance to buy.

Major Types of Leases

1. *Gross lease.* Tenant pays flat rental amount, and the landlord is responsible for taxes, maintenance, and insurance.

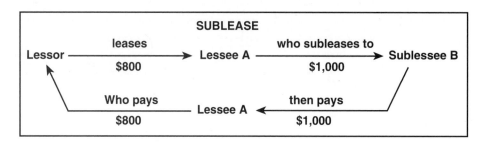

Figure 11.4

2. *Triple net lease.* Tenant pays rent, and tenant also pays the landlord's property taxes, maintenance, and hazard insurance. This type of lease is used when leasing commercial property on a long-term basis. Rather than being called a triple net lease, this is sometimes merely referred to as a "net" lease.

3. *Percentage lease.* Rent is based on a percentage of the tenant's gross sales—sometimes uses a combination flat rent, plus a certain percentage of the tenant's gross sales. Usually the higher the tenant's gross sales, the smaller the percentage. The lower the tenant's sales volume, the higher the percentage.

Important Concepts

1. *Extension of a lease.* The continuation of an old lease would be an extension. For example, an existing lease is about to expire so the lessor and lessee agree to extend the lease for one year using the same terms and conditions.

2. *Renewal of a lease.* This occurs when the existing lessor and lessee renegotiate a new lease upon the expiration of the existing lease. The terms and conditions are frequently different than the terms of the old lease.

3. *Escalator clause.* This clause allows the landlord to increase the rent during the term of the lease if costs increase. Frequently tied to the consumer price index or producer price index.

11.2 DUTIES AND RESPONSIBILITIES OF LANDLORDS AND TENANTS

In exchange for rent, a landlord surrenders use and possession of the property to a tenant. Under this arrangement a landlord owes the tenant certain duties and responsibilities, which include:

Landlord's Duties and Rights

1. If the property is residential, there is an *implied right of habitability*. The landlord, in essence, guarantees that the dwelling meets minimum housing and health codes.

2. Landlords have the right to periodically inspect the property, but they must give *advance notice*. Most lease agreements state that the landlord must give 24 or 48 hours' notice. In cases of emergency, to protect the property, a landlord is allowed to enter the premises without

giving advance notice. In short, a landlord or property manager, with proper notice, can be a supervisor, but not a "snoopervisor" of the property.

3. With residential property, a landlord is usually held liable for injuries resulting from unsafe conditions in common areas such as stairwells, hallways, and the surrounding grounds. If the defects or dangers are caused by tenant negligence, then the liability for injuries may shift from the landlord to the tenant. On nonresidential structures, the liability for keeping the premises safe is frequently shifted from landlord to tenant via the use of triple net lease terms.

4. A landlord is not allowed to interfere with the tenant's use and quiet enjoyment of the property. If the tenant is abiding by the terms of the rental agreement, frequent and uncalled for intrusions by a pesky landlord can be grounds for the tenant to cancel the rental agreement and possibly seek damages in court.

5. According to state and federal laws, a landlord cannot refuse to rent to a tenant based on (a) race, color, national origin, (b) religion or creed, (c) sex or marital status, and (d) physical handicap, unless it can be proven that the building poses a danger to the handicapped person. Also, landlords cannot refuse to rent to families with children. Certain senior citizen housing projects are allowed to exclude children.

6. Under current law (as of January 1999), a landlord can terminate a month-to-month rental agreement by serving the tenant with a 30-day notice. The landlord does not need to give the tenant a reason, nor does the tenant need to be in violation of the terms of the rental agreement. However, if the tenant can prove that the landlord's actions are unfair, based upon the anti-discriminatory laws noted previously, the tenant can sue the landlord. Also, it must be stressed that if a tenant has a signed lease for a specified duration (estate for years) a landlord cannot force the tenant (lessee) to leave unless the tenant violates the terms of the lease agreement.

LANDLORD   TENANT

Tenant's Duties and Rights

A tenant owes a landlord certain duties and responsibilities. In turn, a tenant has certain rights. Tenant duties and rights are summarized as follows:

1. Tenants are expected to pay the rent when due and not damage the property beyond normal wear and tear.
2. Tenants who have month-to-month rental agreements are required to give at least a 30-day notice before vacating the property. A landlord can sue for 30 days' rent if a tenant fails to give the landlord a 30-day notice before vacating.

3. Tenants can be held liable for injuries to guests or customers resulting from unsafe conditions caused by the tenant's negligence. Tenants should purchase their own renter's insurance policy to protect their valuables in case of fire, storm damage, and theft. Most renter's insurance policies also provide personal liability protection for the tenant.

4. Tenants have a duty not to interfere with the rights of other tenants.

5. A tenant has the right to use and enjoy the property. If the tenant is unreasonably bothered by the landlord or another person, the tenant has the right to abandon the property and pay no further rent. This process is called *constructive eviction.*

6. In California, all residential rentals must meet minimum housing and health codes. The responsibility for meeting the codes rests with the landlord. If the property falls below standards because of damage or negligence caused by the tenant, the landlord can bring legal action against the tenant. On the other hand, if, through no fault of the tenant, the dwelling falls below housing codes, the tenant can demand that the landlord make the needed repairs. If the landlord refuses, the tenant can abandon the property and not be liable for future rent. The tenant may elect to use a rental offset procedure outlined in the California Civil Code.

Rental Offset If a residential landlord refuses to make needed repairs, Section 1942 of the Civil Code allows a tenant to spend up to one month's rent to make the repairs. The paid repair bill can then be used to offset the next month's rent. The basic rules are:

1. The tenant must give the landlord written notice and adequate time to make the repairs.

2. If the landlord refuses, the tenant may spend up to one month's rent on the repairs, then deduct the cost of repairs from the following month's rent.

3. A tenant can use a rental offset *only twice in any 12-month period* and only for needed repairs, not decorative changes. In most cases, a tenant cannot charge for his or her own labor, only repair parts. However, if a tradesperson makes the repairs, both parts and labor can be

used for the offset. If a tenant spends more than one month's rent, the excess cannot be applied against subsequent rental payments.

Current law prohibits a landlord from taking retaliatory action, such as serving an eviction notice or raising the rents, for a period of 180 days after the tenant's use of the rental offset.

Rental Payments to Neutral Escrow

In some instances, needed repairs may exceed one month's rent and tenants may be reluctant to use the limited offset provisions noted earlier. Under these circumstances, *it might be possible* for the tenants to make their rental payments to a neutral escrow, with instructions to deliver the rents to the landlord after the property has been brought up to minimum housing standards. *Caution: This is a recent concept and should never be exercised without the advice of an attorney.*

11.3 EVICTIONS AND OTHER WAYS TO TERMINATE RENTAL AGREEMENTS

Eviction occurs when a tenant is dispossessed by operation of law. It must be stressed that the eviction process is a legal procedure in court. Landlords cannot resort to "self-help" actions such as changing the locks, shutting off utility services, seizing the tenant's property in lieu of rent, or threatening the tenants with bodily harm. If a landlord commits an illegal act, such as the ones noted earlier, the tenant can sue the landlord.

Unlawful Detainer Action

The process of removing a tenant from possession involves a series of steps.

1. Landlord serves the tenant with a three-day or 30-day notice, depending upon the circumstances.
2. If the tenant fails to abide by the notice, the landlord files an unlawful detainer action in court.
3. If the landlord wins, the court awards the landlord a judgment. The landlord then asks for a writ of possession authorizing the sheriff to evict the tenant.
4. The sheriff sends tenant an eviction notice; if tenant fails to leave, the sheriff then physically removes the tenant.

Three-Day versus 30-Day Notice

A tenant is served a three-day notice when the tenant has defaulted on rent or has violated other terms of the rental agreement. A 30-day notice is served when the tenant has not violated the rental agreement, but the landlord wants the tenant to leave. If the tenant has a fixed-term lease (estate for years), a landlord cannot serve a notice unless the terms of the lease have been violated by the lessee. The exception is, serving notice to the lessee that the lease will not be renewed upon expiration. (See the sample three-day serving notice in Figure 11.5.)

Serving Notice

The procedure for serving notice can be summarized as follows:

1. The notice must be personally delivered to the tenant(s).

OR

2. If the tenant(s) is absent, a copy should be left with someone of suitable age; then a copy must be mailed to the tenant(s) at place of residence.

OR

3. If no one is home, a copy may be affixed in a conspicuous place on the property; then a copy must be mailed to the tenant(s).

Slipping the notice under the door or putting it in the mailbox is not sufficient delivery. Also, it is a good idea to have the notice served by someone other than the landlord. If the sheriff, marshall, or constable serves the notice, it will have the maximum impression on the tenant(s).

Superior Court*

Landlords bring unlawful detainer actions in superior court. In superior court these actions have a priority on the court's calendar, and an early hearing is usually granted. An attorney generally is needed for a superior court action, and this helps assure the landlord that legal procedures will be correctly followed. This is important if a landlord or tenant appeals to a higher court. Unlawful detainer actions can no longer be heard in small claims court.

Sheriff Evicts the Tenant

After a writ of possession has been granted the landlord, the sheriff sends the tenant an eviction notice. After approximately five days, if the tenant has not left, the sheriff physically removes the tenant, but not the tenant's possessions. The tenant's possessions are impounded according to the lien laws.

* A recent law combined municipal and superior courts in most counties.

To _____

_____

_____

NOTICE TO PAY RENT
OR SURRENDER POSSESSION

NOTICE IS HEREBY GIVEN that, pursuant to the agreement by which you hold possession of the above-described premises there is now due and unpaid rent for said premises in the total sum of $_____, being the rent that became due on_____ for the period from_____, at a monthly rental of $_____.

WITHIN THREE DAYS after service of this notice on you, you are required to pay said rent in full, or to deliver up possession of said premises to the undersigned, or legal proceedings will be commenced against you to recover possession of said premises, to declare said agreement forfeited, and to recover TREBLE RENTS AND DAMAGES for the unlawful detention of said premises.

Dated:_____

Signed:_____

Figure 11.5

Delays and Appeals

With an increasing awareness of tenant's rights, many tenant action groups have effectively designed delay and appeal processes that can extend an unlawful detainer action for many months. This dramatically increases the landlord's costs, both in attorney time and lost rents. From the landlord's point of view, the best protection is to make sure that a lawful, careful screening takes place before a tenant moves in. Once an unethical tenant moves in, it can become very expensive to have the tenant removed.

Termination of Lease

Few leases or rental agreements are ever terminated because of eviction. Most leases are terminated for the following reasons:

1. *Expiration of time.* The time period for the lease is up, and new terms are not negotiated.
2. *Mutual consent.* The lessor and lessee agree to terminate the lease with no additional liability on either side.

In addition, leases can be terminated because of destruction of the premises; government action, such as condemnation; or a breach of terms and conditions by the lessor or lessee.

Mobile Home Park Tenants

A mobile home park is usually a development where lots are rented to mobile home owners. The tenants own their mobile homes, but they are tenants of the land. In California, there are special laws for mobile home park tenants that differ from the typical landlord/tenant laws. A mobile home tenant in a park *cannot be evicted unless:*

1. The tenant fails to comply with local and state laws
2. The tenant annoys other tenants
3. The tenant fails to abide with reasonable park rules
4. The tenant fails to pay the rent and other agreed charges
5. The tenant has his or her rights condemned by government
6. The use of the park changes

The mobile home tenant who is in violation must be given at least a 60-day notice, rather than the three-day or 30-day notice rules for regular tenants.

If the mobile home cannot be moved without a permit, the law requires that a tenant must have a reasonable notice to vacate. The tenant cannot be required to move merely to make space available for a person to purchase a mobile home from the park owner. In addition, there are many other special rules that apply to tenants in mobile home parks.

11.4 PROPERTY MANAGEMENT

As an investment, real estate offers a hedge against inflation, income tax advantages, and, in some cases, provides an annual cash income. However, real estate needs managerial attention, and this frequently discourages investors who do not wish to be bothered by tenants. An alternative might be to employ a professional property manager.

Field of Property Management

Property management is a specialty within the real estate business. Property managers represent owners by screening tenants, negotiating rental agreements, hiring personnel to maintain the building and grounds, and hiring on-site residential managers. California rules state that an apartment building or complex with 16 or more rental units must have an on-site residential manager. In addition, property managers are responsible for rent collection and the keeping of accounting records for income tax purposes.

Property managers range from real estate brokers who handle a few properties for their clients to large corporate firms that manage hundreds of units, including commercial properties such as office buildings and shopping centers.

An off-site property manager must be a licensed real estate broker, but on-site residential managers do not need a real estate license. Key employees of the property management company must be bonded. The Institute of Real Estate Management, affiliated with the National Association of Realtors, issues the nationally recognized designation, Certified Property Manager (CPM). The CPM designation is achieved after meeting rigorous educational and experience requirements.

Compensation

Property management firms are usually paid a percentage of the rents collected. The percentage is negotiable and varies from firm to firm. For a large structure with many rental units, the fee may be as low as 1% or 2% of gross rents collected. On small units such as rental homes and duplexes, the fee may be 10% or more. The fee for renting resort properties may be 20% or even 25% of rents collected. Some property managers may charge a flat rate rather than a percentage of rents collected.

Property management fees do not include the cost of maintenance, but only the management of the property. If maintenance or repairs are needed, the manager sees that the work is done, but the bill is paid by the property owner, or deducted from the rent proceeds.

When a property manager is hired, the manager and the owner sign a management contract. This contract designates the property manager as the owner's agent and lists all the duties and responsibilities of the parties. To be enforceable, the management contract must meet the legal requirements of California contract law.

CHAPTER SUMMARY

A lease is a contract between an owner called the lessor and a tenant called the lessee. A lessee is given possession in exchange for rent. Leases for more than one year must be in writing to be valid.

Types of leasehold estates are estate for years, estate from period to period, estate at will, and estate at sufferance. Leases on urban property cannot exceed 99 years, whereas leases for agricultural land cannot exceed 51 years.

Security deposits on residential properties cannot exceed two months' rent on unfurnished dwellings and three months' rent on furnished dwellings.

An assignment of a lease transfers the entire leasehold interest to another person, whereas a sublease transfers only a part of the leasehold interest to a sublessee.

Rental payments can be paid on a gross, net, or percentage basis. An escalator clause allows the landlord to raise the rent during the term of the lease.

A landlord's duties and rights may include an implied condition of habitability, advance notice prior to inspection, 30-day advance notice when ordering the tenant to vacate, and an obligation not to discriminate when renting property.

A tenant's duties and rights include paying the rent when due, not damaging the property, and giving the landlord 30 days' notice when vacating. Under certain conditions, a tenant can use a rent offset for repairs if the property falls below minimum housing standards.

Eviction occurs when a tenant is dispossessed by process of law. The tenant must be served with either a three-day or a 30-day notice depending upon the circumstances.

The action of suing for eviction is called unlawful detainer action. If a writ of possession is granted, the sheriff evicts the tenant. Delays and appeals by a tenant can extend the eviction process by several months.

In addition to eviction, leases can be terminated by expiration of time, mutual consent, destruction of the premises, government action, or breach of terms and conditions.

Property management is a specialty within the real estate business. Property managers represent owners by finding tenants, caring for the property, and maintaining proper accounting records. Property managers are usually paid a fee based on the rents collected.

IMPORTANT TERMS AND CONCEPTS

Assignment of lease

Certified property manager (CPM)

Estate at sufferance

Estate for years

Estate from period to period

Eviction notices

Gross lease

Lease with option to buy

Less-than-freehold estate

Lessee

Lessor

Net lease

Percentage lease

Refundable security deposit

Rental offset

Sandwich lease

Sublease

Unlawful detainer action

PRACTICAL APPLICATION

1. An apartment is rented for $800 per month with a $1,000 security deposit. While moving out, the tenant informs the landlord that the water heater leaks. After inspecting the water heater, the landlord believes that the leak was caused when the tenant banged the water heater while moving out. The cost of the repair is $100. How would you handle the security deposit issue if you were the landlord?

2. A tenant has a one-year lease that terminates December 1, 2000. The terms of the lease state that no pets are allowed. On October 1, 2000 a neighbor calls the landlord to complain that the tenant's dog barks too often and too long. The landlord tells the tenant that the dog must go, but the tenant refuses to remove the dog. List the next legal steps the landlord must do to get rid of the dog.

3. As an owner of a 5-unit apartment complex you are thinking about hiring a professional property manager. The property manager quotes a fee of 8% of collected rents. Each apartment rents for $750 per month with a vacancy factor of 5%. You are in a combined federal and state tax bracket of 31%. What is the annual after-tax cost of the property manager?

REVIEWING YOUR UNDERSTANDING

1. Ms. Brown leases her summer cabin to Mr. Greene for the months of June, July, and August of a designated year. Mr. Greene has an estate:
   a. for years
   b. from period to period
   c. at sufferance
   d. of monthly rental

2. Urban property cannot be leased for more than:
   a. 99 years
   b. 51 years
   c. 15 years
   d. no time limit

3. An assignment of a lease differs from a sublease in that an assignment:
   a. transfers liability to the new occupant
   b. involves two lease contracts: (1) lessor to lessee, and (2) lessee to sublessee
   c. requires that the original lessee still be primarily liable to the lessor
   d. none of the above

4. Under which lease does the tenant pay rent, property taxes, maintenance, and hazard insurance?
   a. gross lease
   b. triple net lease
   c. flat lease
   d. escalator lease

5. A residential tenant may expect the landlord to make necessary repairs to keep the dwelling habitable. If the landlord does not, the tenant may make repairs and offset the rent up to:
   a. $700 maximum
   b. one month's rent
   c. reasonable cost
   d. $1,000 maximum

6. It is illegal to screen and eliminate potential tenants based on:
   a. marital status, sex
   b. race, color, creed
   c. religion, physical handicap
   d. all of the above

7. If a tenant has violated the terms of the rental agreement or lease, before the tenant can be evicted the tenant must be served a:
   a. 1-day notice
   b. 3-day notice
   c. 30-day notice
   d. 60-day notice

8. If an unfurnished apartment rents for $600 per month, the maximum security deposit the landlord may ask for is:
   a. $100
   b. $500
   c. $600
   d. $1,200

9. The legal process by which a tenant is evicted is called:
   a. an eviction action
   b. an ejectment action
   c. a possessory action
   d. an unlawful detainer action

10. The professional designation CPM stands for:
    a. Certificate of Public Management
    b. Certified Practical Manager
    c. Certificate of Practical Management
    d. Certified Property Manager

11. At the end of the lease, the lessee may purchase the property under agreed terms and the lessor must sell. This is an example of:
    a. lease with option to buy
    b. first right of refusal
    c. sublease
    d. assignment of lease

12. The law that states certain leases must be in writing to be enforceable is the:
    a. Statute of Escribe
    b. Statute of Limitations
    c. Statute of Conveyance
    d. Statute of Frauds

13. A landlord wishes to ask the month-to-month tenant to leave because the landlord wishes to occupy the rental home. The landlord will need to serve the tenant with a:
    a. 30-day notice
    b. 3-day notice
    c. eviction order
    d. writ of possession

14. A landlord who is uniform in application can refuse to rent based on all of the following, except:
    a. poor credit
    b. inadequate income
    c. the existence of children
    d. too many pets

15. Assuming the tenant takes possession, in order to be valid a rental agreement for six months must contain:
    a. signatures of the lessor and lessee
    b. written terms
    c. the amount and payment terms of the rent
    d. none of the above

16. The interest a tenant has in real estate is known as a:
    a. freehold estate
    b. less than freehold estate
    c. tenant right estate
    d. fee simple absolute estate

17. Regarding security deposits:
    a. the maximum for a unfurnished apartment is three months' rent
    b. no security deposit can be labeled nonrefundable
    c. the deposit must be less than the first month's rent
    d. all unused deposits must be refunded in seven days

18. Month-to-month tenants in a mobile home park can be requested to leave only for specified reasons and must be served with a:
    a. 90-day notice
    b. 60-day notice
    c. 30-day notice
    d. 3-day notice

19. Most unlawful detainer actions are heard in:
    a. superior court
    b. small claims court
    c. appellate court
    d. Supreme Court

20. In an apartment complex, an on-site resident manager is required if there are:
    a. 4 or more units
    b. 8 or more units
    c. 12 or more units
    d. 16 or more units

Chapter 12

Land-Use Planning, Subdivisions, and Other Public Controls

Chapter Preview   This chapter highlights the principles of government land-use planning, and stresses zoning and subdivision regulations. Condominiums, planned unit developments, and the selling of undivided interests are also discussed. The chapter concludes with an explanation of fair housing laws. At the conclusion of the chapter, you will be able to:

1. Describe the main goals of a community general plan

2. Explain the difference between government use of police power and eminent domain and give two examples of each

3. List the major characteristics of the Subdivision Map Act and the Subdivided Lands Act

4. Describe a common interest development and discuss the differences between a condominium and a planned unit development

5. List the major fair housing laws that prohibit discrimination in the selling or renting of real estate

12.1 GOVERNMENT LAND-USE PLANNING

Government land-use controls are controversial. Some people feel that land is a commodity to be bought and sold like any other product. They consider any type of land-use control an infringement on free enterprise. At the other extreme are those who believe land is a resource that belongs to all the people, the use of which should be completely controlled by government. Somewhere in the middle is the view that land is both a commodity and a resource that should be privately owned, but used constructively to benefit society.

Private Deed Restrictions

Most attention regarding land-use control has focused on government regulations. However, it should be noted that for many years covenants, conditions, and restrictions (CC&Rs) in deeds have been used by private individuals to regulate real estate usage.

California owners are allowed to limit the use of land by contract as long as the restrictions are not a violation of the law. Thus, land-use controls are not new, but in the last 50 years the bulk of the controls have shifted from private imposition to government imposition. Private deed restrictions were discussed in more detail in Chapter 3.

Public Land-Use Controls

Industrialization and urban crowding have created a need for public controls to maintain order and promote social harmony. One way to maintain order is to control the use of land. The two main powers that allow government to control land use are police power and the power of eminent domain.

Police power refers to the constitutional right of government to regulate private activity to promote the general health, welfare, and safety of society. Police power has often been used in the United States to direct land use. Major real estate examples of police power include zoning ordinances, building and health codes, set-back requirements, environmental regulations, and rent controls. Of the many police power enactments, zoning, subdivision, and environmental regulations emerge as the most influential methods for controlling land use.

Police power allows government to regulate private land use without the payment of compensation. The power of eminent domain is different in that it allows the government to acquire title to private land for public use in exchange for the payment of just compensation. Eminent domain is used for a variety of government land-use projects, such as highways, public housing, and urban renewal.

All levels of government may exercise the power of eminent domain regardless of how unwilling the property owner may be. The main issue in most eminent domain cases is the amount of compensation. The courts have ruled that the property's fair market value is the proper basis for determining compensation. In addition, most federal and some state agencies must also pay for moving and other miscellaneous expenses incurred by those being displaced.

Planning   The dictionary defines "planning" as "thinking out acts and purposes beforehand." When applied to cities and counties, planning can be defined as anticipating and achieving community goals in light of social, economic, and physical needs. Planning requires that a community analyze its assets and liabilities, establish its goals, and then attempt to achieve these goals using land-use control as a primary tool.

California law requires that every incorporated city and county must have a planning commission. A *planning commission* is composed of citizens appointed by the members of the city council or board of supervisors. Planning commissioners advise the elected officials on land-use matters. The planning commission only makes recommendations— the final decision on planning rests with the city council or board of supervisors, depending upon who has jurisdiction.

In addition to planning commissions, many cities and counties have planning departments. *Planning departments* are agencies within city and county government, staffed with professionally trained planners. Planning department employees provide technical services for the planning commissions, elected officials, and citizens.

State law requires every city and county to develop a *general plan,* which outlines the goals and objectives for the community. The general plan then lists the steps needed to achieve these goals.

General Plan   The establishment of a community general plan requires three major steps: (1) resource analysis, (2) formulation of community goals, and (3) implementation of the plan.

RESOURCE ANALYSIS   The first step is to recognize the individual character of the community. What are its strong points? What are its weaknesses? To accomplish this, several substudies will be required, including an economic base study, a population trend study, a survey of existing land use, a city facilities study, and an analysis of the community's financial resources. Once a resource inventory has been taken, the next step is to formulate community goals in light of its resources.

FORMULATION OF COMMUNITY GOALS   The formulation of community goals is the most difficult phase of urban planning because of the conflict between various special interest groups, each trying to secure and establish its own definition of the community goal. In spite of this problem, citizen input should be encouraged. A community plan must be based on the desires of community residents as a whole, not on the desires of staff planners alone.

Once the goals are established, a comprehensive plan to achieve these objectives must be formulated. The plan is frequently referred to as the general plan or the master plan, and it should encompass all social, economic, and physical aspects of the projected growth. The plan should be long-range but provide for short-range flexibility as the need for modification arises. Under no circumstances must the master plan be viewed as an inflexible, permanent fixture that will never require modification. A community's attitude and resources can change, and the general plan must be modified to comply with these changes.

IMPLEMENTATION OF THE PLAN

The final step in urban planning is to implement the general plan. The implementation phase requires local government to use police power, eminent domain, taxation, and control over government spending to enact the plan. As previously indicated, the three most powerful tools for implementing a community plan are zoning, subdivision, and environmental regulations.

Zoning

Zoning refers to the division of land into designated land-use districts. In its simplest form, zoning districts are divided into residential use, commercial use, industrial use, and rural use. Each use in turn can have several subclasses. For example, residential can be broken down into single-family, multifamily, and mobile home zones. Commercial zones are usually divided into retail, office, and wholesale space. Industrial zones are divided into light industry and heavy industry, and rural zones into agricultural, resource, or recreational uses.

Zoning as a land-control tool was not common in the United States until the 1920s; prior to this time there was some doubt about the constitutionality of zoning, although early zoning laws can be traced to colonial times. However, in 1926 the U.S. Supreme Court held that zoning was a reasonable exercise of government police power. Since this decision, every state has passed legislation allowing individual cities and counties to enact zoning ordinances.

Early zoning ordinances were aimed at safety and nuisance control. The idea was to use zoning to protect individual property values by prohibiting offensive use of surrounding land. The use of zoning has gradually been expanded, and now it is used to "promote the general welfare" of the entire community.

INCLUSIONARY ZONING

Inclusionary zoning is an ordinance that requires a builder of new residential housing to set aside a designated number of units for low- and moderate-income people. If the developer refuses to provide the designated units, the building permit is denied.

In some cases, instead of providing inclusionary units, the builder is required to pay into a fund that the government then uses to provide low- and moderate-income housing. To encourage participation in the program, the builder is allowed to construct more units per acre than normal.

The economic reality is that the prices of the regular units are frequently increased to offset the builder's losses on the inclusionary units. This shifts the burden of providing affordable housing from the government to the private market.

CONTROVERSY: LOCAL VERSUS STATE AND FEDERAL PLANNING

Historically, planning has been a local matter. Each community developed its own plans within the confines of its own territorial limits. In the process, each community attempted to optimize its own social and economic well-being, frequently at the expense of surrounding areas. For example, the planning of a smelly industrial plant on the border of one city has a spillover effect on the neighboring community located downwind.

The growth of multicity metropolitan areas has led the state to mandate planning on a regional basis. Water and sewage systems, rapid transit, highway traffic patterns, airports, and pollution controls are some examples of regional planning. However, from a political point of view, there is a wide-scale resistance to the creation of another layer of government. Moreover, local government officials are reluctant to surrender some of their power to regional or state commissioners.

Opposition to federal and state controls also comes from individuals who feel that the power of land regulation should be limited to local government. They fear that planning on a state and federal level will be insensitive to local needs. Who is correct? Like most land-use controls, the correct answer depends on one's value judgment. However, the current trend is toward more regional, state, and federal control over land use.

Examples of federal laws include the *National Environmental Policy Act,* which requires an environmental impact report on all projects using federal funding, and the *Clean Air Act,* which requires businesses (including real estate developers) to meet air quality standards. The federal government has declared that development cannot take place in "wetlands" for fear of damaging wildlife habitat. The definition of what constitutes "wetlands" has created numerous lawsuits.

Examples of state laws include: *The Coastline Conservation Act,* creating controls on the 1,000-mile California coast; the *California Environmental Quality Act,* which requires an environmental impact report on major real estate projects; and the *Subdivision Map Act* and *Subdivided Lands Act,* which controls the creation of subdivisions in the state.

Source: From *Essentials of Real Estate Economics,* 4th ed., by D. J. McKenzie and R. M. Betts (Englewood Cliffs, N.J. Regents/ Prentice Hall, 1996, p. 486).

SUMMARY OF PLANNING TERMS

Planning commission. An appointed body of citizens charged with the responsibility of advising the elected board of supervisors or city council members in matters of land use

Planning department. City or county staff employees who lend professional and technical assistance to elected officials and citizens

Zone. An area defined on a map by a boundary line within which the land-use regulations are the same

Rezoning. The process of changing land-use regulations on property from one zone to another

Variance. A deviation from the zoning regulations for a particular parcel

Condition. A requirement imposed by government in connection with the approval of a permit or a division of property

Development plans. Plans showing the details of the proposed development. Normally includes plot plan, architectural renderings, and statistical information relative to acreage, building area, units, and parking. In most cases an environmental impact study will be required.

Standard subdivision. A division of property into five or more parcels

Lot split. A division of property into two, three, or four parcels

Architectural review. Certain zoning areas where a special citizens' group approves or rejects the proposal based on its architectural compatibility with the surrounding area

Appeal. The right to request review of a negative planning commission decision. The appellate process goes from the planning commission, to the board of supervisors or city council, to the courts.

12.2 SUBDIVISIONS

Another important use of police power is *subdivision regulation.* Poorly conceived subdivisions, with inadequate streets and facilities, can become a burden to taxpayers in later years when expensive redevelopment is needed to correct earlier oversights. Proponents of subdivision controls believe that the origin of slums and urban blight can be traced to inadequate regulations. Opponents disagree, noting that today's slums are the result of government ordinances that prevent land from rising to its economic highest and best use.

Today, subdivision regulations are used in all areas of California. Real estate developers are frequently required to provide water, sewer, paved streets, sidewalks, street lights, and school and park sites as a condition of being allowed to subdivide. The idea is to plan for the future at the inception and to require the purchaser of the subdivided lot, not the community as a whole, to pay the expense of added community facilities. Like all public controls, subdivision regulations are controversial because they require the surrender of some individual rights in an attempt to promote the general welfare.

Subdivision Laws

There are two basic laws under which subdivisions are controlled in California—the Subdivision Map Act and the Subdivided Lands Act. The *Subdivision Map Act* covers the division of land into two or more lots for the purpose of sale, lease, or financing, whether now or in the future. The Subdivision Map Act is administered by local officials and is concerned with the physical aspects of the subdivision, such as design, streets, sewers, and so on. The Subdivision Map Act outlines the procedure for filing subdivision maps to legally create a subdivision. (See Figure 12.1.)

The *Subdivided Lands Act* defines a subdivision as the division of land into five or more lots for the purpose of sale, lease, or financing, whether now or in the future. The Subdivided Lands Act is administered by the California real estate commissioner and is primarily concerned with the marketing aspects of the subdivision. The basic objective of the Subdivided Lands Act is to protect the purchasers of

SUBDIVISION

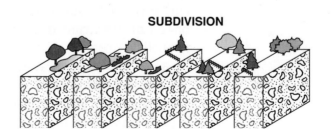

BASIC OUTLINE OF SUBDIVISION
MAP PREPARATION AND APPROVAL

PRELIMINARY PLANNING

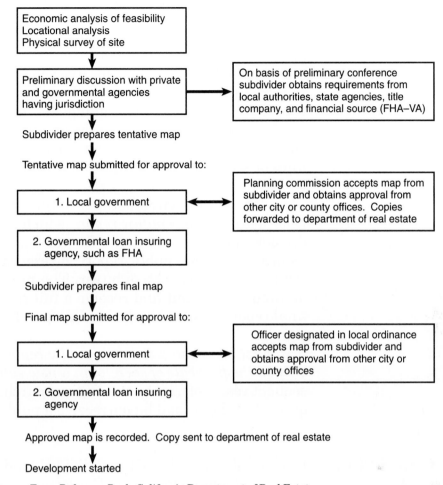

Economic analysis of feasibility
Locational analysis
Physical survey of site

Preliminary discussion with private and governmental agencies having jurisdiction

On basis of preliminary conference subdivider obtains requirements from local authorities, state agencies, title company, and financial source (FHA–VA)

Subdivider prepares tentative map

Tentative map submitted for approval to:

1. Local government

Planning commission accepts map from subdivider and obtains approval from other city or county offices. Copies forwarded to department of real estate

2. Governmental loan insuring agency, such as FHA

Subdivider prepares final map

Final map submitted for approval to:

1. Local government

Officer designated in local ordinance accepts map from subdivider and obtains approval from other city or county offices

2. Governmental loan insuring agency

Approved map is recorded. Copy sent to department of real estate

Development started

Source: From *Reference Book*, California Department of Real Estate.

Figure 12.1

property in new subdivisions from fraud and misrepresentation when buying new subdivided land.

No new subdivision of five or more parcels located in California can be offered for sale until the real estate commissioner issues a public report. The final public report is not issued until the commissioner is satisfied that the developer has met all statutory requirements, with particular emphasis on the establishment of financial arrangements to assure completion of any promised facilities. *The issuance of a public report does not mean that in the eyes of the commissioner the subdivision is a good investment.* It merely means that the subdivider has conformed to all laws and regulations.

Before each lot in a new subdivision can be sold, the subdivider must deliver a copy of the commissioner's final public report to the prospective buyer. The prospective buyer must then sign a statement acknowledging that he or she has received and read the public report, and this signed copy must be kept on file by the subdivider for three years. Only after these steps have taken place can the subdivider sell each lot.

The public report is good for five years; however, the law requires the commissioner to issue an amended public report when a material change occurs regarding the subdivision. Examples of material changes could include changes in contract forms, physical changes such as lot lines or street lines, or a sale of five or more lots to a single buyer.

Under certain circumstances, the commissioner can issue a *preliminary public report,* which will allow the subdivider to take reservations for purchase pending the issuance of the final public report. A reservation is not binding upon the prospective buyer. The prospective buyer is allowed to back out and receive a full refund up until the final report is issued and a binding purchase agreement is signed.

It must be stressed that the public report process applies only on the first sale of each lot in a new subdivision. A subsequent resale of a lot by the original purchaser does not require that the second buyer receive a public report.

Out-of-State and Foreign Land

Effective January 1, 1996, subdivided land located in other states and offered for sale in California does not need to obtain a formal public report from the California Department of Real Estate. Instead, out-of-state subdividers must include specific disclaimers in all advertising and sales agreements. Foreign properties offered for sale in California have very few restrictions; it is basically a buyer-beware situation. All California buyers should seek legal advice before purchasing an out-of-state or out-of-country property.

Red Tape

The actual processing of a subdivision is frequently a costly and time-consuming process. The data needed to complete the required forms are highly technical and beyond the skills of average property owners. The services of title officers, surveyors or engineers, contractors, and attorneys often are required. The average subdivision will take many months to process—major development can take years. Delays are costly and, in the end, these costs are borne by the consumer.

Subdivision Laws Summarized

Subdivided Lands Act	Subdivision Map Act
Five or more lots or parcels	Two or more lots or parcels
No contiguity requirement	Land must be contiguous units
160 acres and larger parcels designated as such by government survey are exempt	No exemption for 160 acres and larger
Administered by California real estate commissioner	Administered by local officials
Requires a final public report	No public report required

Currently a debate is raging: increased regulations are designed to protect the consumer and the environment, but on the other hand, consumers must pay for these regulations via higher prices. Are the protections worth the price? This is a value-judgment question that each person must answer.

Land Project Right to Rescind Sale

A land project is defined as a speculative subdivision of 50 or more lots located in a sparsely populated area of the state. These types of subdivisions are frequently sold only after intensive promotion in urban areas, long distances away from the development.

A purchaser of a lot in the land project is allowed a limited time *after the sale* to "cool off" and rescind, or cancel, the purchase contract and receive a full refund with no further obligations. As of January 1999, the right to rescind extends for 14 days after the signing of the purchase agreement. But in the future, regulations might extend this period. (Also see the section on time-sharing ownership regarding the right to rescind sale.)

Interstate Land Sales Full-Disclosure Act

A federal law known as the *Interstate Land Sales Full-Disclosure Act* regulates land sales between two or more states. If a developer of 50 or more lots located in one state wishes to market the lots in another state(s), the developer must conform to this law.

Basically the law requires the developer to obtain a public report issued by the Department of Housing and Urban Development (HUD) and to deliver a copy of the public report to each prospective buyer. This law is an attempt to reduce the number of fraudulent land sales that take place by mail or through out-of-state advertising.

12.3 COMMON INTEREST DEVELOPMENTS (CID)

An increase in population has caused an increase in urban land prices. As land becomes more scarce and prices begin to rise, there is a tendency to intensify development to obtain more living units per acre. Common Interest Developments in the form of condominiums, planned unit developments (PUDs), stock cooperatives, and community apartments are examples of intensified owner-occupied developments that differ from the traditional single-family-home type of subdivision. All these developments are considered subdivisions and are regulated by state law.

Condominiums

A *condominium* is a type of real estate ownership, not a type of structure. In a condominium, a person owns his or her own apartment-type living unit. In a legal sense, a condominium owner acquires a fee title interest in the airspace of the particular unit and an undivided interest (with other condominium owners) in the land plus all other common areas, such as hallways, elevators, carports, and recreational facilities. A condominium is sometimes called a "vertical" subdivision.

Each condominium owner has his or her own individual deed, real estate loan, and separate property tax assessment. A condominium interest is bought and sold like any other parcel of real estate.

All condominiums have owner associations that elect a governing board. The governing board is responsible for the management of the complex, and sees to it that the building and common areas are maintained. The owners' association also sets the dues for each owner's share of the maintenance.

Condominium developments are expected to continue to gain an increasing share of the housing market. In some areas, there has been a tendency to convert existing renter-occupied apartments into owner-occupied condominiums. This has caused controversy because condo conversion reduces the supply of rental units, thereby making it more difficult for renters to find affordable housing. On the other hand, a condo conversion increases the supply of owner-occupied housing, thereby making it easier for owners to find affordable housing. Therefore, it is expected that the condo-conversion controversy will rage on for years.

Planned Unit Development (PUD)

A planned unit development (PUD) is often confused with a condominium. They are not the same! In a PUD a person owns his or her own living unit and lot, plus an undivided interest in the common areas. A condominium owner owns his or her own living unit, but not his or her own lot. A PUD is often referred to as a "townhouse development," but this is incorrect, as a townhouse is a type of architecture and not a type of ownership. In a PUD there is no one living in the airspace above or below the owner, as is found in a condominium. PUDs are frequently located in the suburbs, whereas condominiums are usually located in urban areas. They are both found in resort areas such as Lake Tahoe and Hawaii.

PUDs are similar in operation to condominiums. An owners' association levies dues for upkeep and maintenance of the common areas. In addition, each property owner has covenants, conditions, and restrictions in his or her deed that dictate the do's and don'ts of ownership.

Stock Cooperatives and Community Apartments

A *stock cooperative* is a corporation formed for the purpose of holding title to a building. Each shareholder of the entire corporation is given the right to occupy a living unit, but the entire building is owned by the corporation. A sale of a share in the corporation also passes the right of occupancy to a living unit within the stock cooperative.

A *community apartment* is created when a group of people jointly purchase an undivided interest in an entire apartment complex. Then each person is given the right to occupy a particular apartment unit. The undivided share can be sold, and the new purchaser acquires the right to live in the particular apartment.

Under a stock cooperative and a community apartment, each person *does not* receive an individual deed, real estate loan, or property tax assessment. All the shareholders and undivided interest owners must agree to pool their funds each month to make the mortgage payment, pay the property taxes, and pay for the upkeep and maintenance.

Stock cooperatives and community apartments are not as popular as condominiums and PUDs. Most people prefer their own individual deed, real estate loan, and property tax assessment which are present in condominiums and PUDs but not in stock cooperatives or community apartments.

Disclosure Requirements

When a unit in an existing common interest development is offered for sale, the seller must provide, *as a minimum,* to a prospective buyer prior to the close of escrow:

1. A copy of the existing conditions, covenants, and restrictions, articles of incorporation, owners' association by-laws, governing documents, and a current financial statement on the owners' association

2. A written statement of any known pending special assessments, claims, or litigation against the seller or the owners' association

3. A current statement showing whether the seller has any unpaid assessments or dues owed to the owners' association

Recreational Developments Selling Undivided Interests

Recreational land developments can be found throughout California. The developer usually begins with a large parcel of land, subdivides the land, and then sells parcels to individual owners. In some cases the parcels are fully developed, and in other cases just vacant lots are sold.

An alternative to subdividing recreational land into individual parcels is to keep the original large parcel intact and sell undivided interests or shares in the whole. An example might be a developer who has 1,000 acres of land and is considering subdividing the land into 1,000 one-acre lots to be sold to 1,000 recreational users. An alternative might be to sell a $1/1000$ undivided interest to 1,000 recreational users. By selling 1,000 undivided interests, each owner has the right to use all 1,000 acres instead of just one acre, as would be the case if a traditional subdivision were created.

As of January 1999, a buyer of an undivided interest has 72 hours to rescind the sale and receive a full refund. The marketing of undivided interest is controlled by the state subdivision laws and private deed restrictions similar to condominiums and PUDs.

Time-Sharing Ownership

Another interesting concept is that of time-sharing ownership. Under time sharing, a person buys an interest in a building—for example, a condominium in a resort area—where the right of occupancy is limited to a specified calendar time period. An example might be 12 people who pool their funds and each person purchases a $1/12$ interest in a Lake Tahoe condominium. Each person's $1/12$ interest gives that person the right to occupy the condominium for a month. The month or the time period is designated in the deed or by a separate instrument. This is a way to own your vacation home for the exact time period you desire, for an expense that covers just the pro rata time of occupancy.

There are other derivations of time-sharing ownership, such as purchasing the right of occupancy for a designated time period each year. But the purchaser does not acquire an interest in the land. Many time-share resorts have exchange privileges with other resorts, allowing a time-share owner to move from location to location.

The time-sharing owners need covenants, conditions, and restrictions in deeds, as well as an owners' association to govern the use and maintenance of the unit. The buyer of a time share has 72 hours to rescind the purchase contract for any reason and receive a full refund.

12.4 HOUSING AND CONSTRUCTION LAWS

State Laws and Regulations

State housing laws. State housing laws, or codes, establish minimum housing standards for the entire state. State housing codes are enforced by local, not state, building inspectors. The state housing law is a uniform code that must be adopted by all cities and counties in California.

Local building codes. Until 1970, local codes were allowed to deviate from the state housing laws. However, with the passage of the state uniform housing codes, local variances are permitted only if a study finds sufficient reason to deviate from the state uniform code.

Contractor's license law. State law requires every person who engages in the business of a contractor to be licensed. A property owner doing his or her own work, for his or her own use, must build according to codes, but is exempt from the contractor license law. On the other hand, if an owner wishes to build with the intention to offer the finished real estate project for sale, a licensed contractor must do the work.

Environmental impact regulations. A housing or real estate development will usually require an environmental review before a building permit is issued. The builder will need to prepare either a Negative Impact Report (NIR) if a minor project with no or limited environmental concern, or a costly, fully documented Environmental Impact Report (EIR) if a major project. The purpose of both reports is to address what impact the real estate construction will have on the social, economic, physical, and biological environment. Then the report must state what steps the builder will take to reduce the impact on the environment, including not building the project in the first place.

12.5 FAIR HOUSING

EQUAL HOUSING OPPORTUNITY

State Laws and Regulations

Over the years, several federal and state laws have been passed making it against public policy to discriminate in real estate based on race, color, religion, sex, marital status, national origin, ancestry, family status, or mental or physical handicap. The courts will not tolerate discrimination, and violators can expect to be fined and/or jailed.

Unruh Civil Rights Act. This state law makes it unlawful for persons engaged in business in California, including real estate agents, to discriminate when providing business products and services. Examples of unlawful conduct include "steering" and "block busting." *Steering* is the unlawful directing of a prospective buyer or tenant to certain neighborhoods or the refusal to tell about the availability of housing in another neighborhood. *Block busting* is attempting to create panic selling by telling existing property owners that minority groups have targeted their neighborhoods for purchase. Steering and block busting are illegal; the penalties include loss of a real estate license, and severe criminal and civil charges, plus fines.

California Fair Housing Act (Rumford Act). This state law forbids discrimination in the sale, rental, lease, or financing of practically all types of housing. The staff of the Department of Fair Employment and Housing investigates complaints from people who believe they have been discriminated against in housing. If the staff feels a violation has occurred, a hearing is held with the Commission of Fair Employment and Housing. If the Commission rules that discrimination has occurred, they have the power to order the sale or rental of the property. In addition, the Commission has the power to levy fines. A person who has suffered discrimination has a right to by-pass the Commission process and bring a direct law suit in court. The state of California believes that fair housing is so important that it requires all real estate agents to take a three-hour fair housing course as a condition for keeping a real estate license.

Housing Financial Discrimination Act, also known as the Holden Act. This state law prohibits financial institutions from engaging in discriminatory loan practices. This law attempts to prohibit "redlining." Redlining is a loan practice under which a lender refuses to grant a housing loan in certain geographic areas based on neighborhood trends, regardless of the worthiness of the borrower or of the individual home.

Commissioner's rules and regulations. The California real estate commissioner has issued numerous regulations regarding housing discrimination. These regulations detail the types of discriminatory conduct that, if practiced by a real estate licensee, will be the basis for disciplinary action that can result in a suspension, fine, or even a prosecution by the local district attorney.

Federal Laws

Civil Rights Act of 1968 and 1988 Amendments. This comprehensive law states that, within constitutional limits, fair housing should prevail throughout the United States. This act left it up to the courts to determine the constitutionality of this law.

Jones v. Mayer *Case*. In this landmark case, the U.S. Supreme Court interpreted and applied an act of Congress, passed in 1866 right after the Civil War. The constitutionality rested on the Thirteenth Amendment, which prohibits slavery. Using the Act of 1866 and the Thirteenth Amendment, the U.S. Supreme Court upheld the provisions of the Civil Rights Act of 1968.

In short, what the *Jones v. Mayer* case means is that the Unruh and Rumford acts apply in California, and what discriminations they might not cover are now prohibited by federal law.

1988 Amendments to the Civil Rights Act of 1968. The 1988 Amendments broaden the definition of handicap to include anyone with a disability that impairs "major life activities." Thus, property owners cannot discriminate because of AIDS, cancer, and alcoholism. People with mental disorders, including past drug users, are also protected. Per the 1988 Amendments, current drug abusers, transvestites, or anyone who can be proved to be a current threat to the health, safety, or property of others, is not considered a protected class. To be safe, any refusal to sell or rent for any reason other than inadequate income or credit, should first be reviewed by the property owner's attorney. The 1988 Amendments also made it a federal violation to discriminate against families with children, unless the development is an approved senior citizen project.

Many Other Laws   In addition to the laws listed earlier, there are numerous other laws and regulations that directly or indirectly attempt to prohibit discrimination in housing. The point being stressed is that all real estate owners, agents, managers, and lenders must give the public an equal opportunity to acquire real estate.

CHAPTER SUMMARY   Two powers that allow government to control land use are police power and the power of eminent domain. Major police power tools include zoning, building and health codes, and subdivision regulations.

Cities and counties in California must have a planning commission. In addition, most cities and counties also have planning departments. The planning commission and elected officials must adopt a general plan that outlines the goals and objectives for the community. The three most powerful tools for implementing the general plan are zoning, subdivision regulations, and environmental regulations.

The two major subdivision laws are the Subdivision Map Act and the Subdivided Lands Act. The Subdivision Map Act is administered by local officials and is mostly concerned with the physical aspects of the subdivision. The Subdivided Lands Act is administered by the California real estate commissioner and is primarily concerned with the marketing aspects of the subdivision. The key element of the Subdivided Lands Act is the required public report, which must be delivered to each prospective buyer of a lot in a new California subdivision.

Common interest developments such as condominiums, planned unit developments (PUDs), stock cooperatives, and community apartments are examples of intensified owner-occupied developments that differ from the traditional single-family-dwelling type of subdivision.

Over the years laws have been passed making it against public policy to discriminate in the sale, lease, or renting of housing. The Unruh Civil Rights Act and the California Fair Housing Act (Rumford Act) are two California antidiscrimination laws. The Civil Rights Act of 1968 and the 1988 Amendments is a federal law that prohibits discrimination in housing.

IMPORTANT TERMS AND CONCEPTS

California Fair Housing (Rumford) Act

Civil Rights Act of 1968 and 1988

Commission on Fair Employment and Housing

Common interest developments

Condominium

Eminent domain

Environmental impact report

General plan

Planned unit development (PUD)

Planning commission

Police power

Public report

Selling undivided interests

Subdivided Lands Act

Subdivision Map Act

Unruh Civil Rights Act

Zoning

PRACTICAL APPLICATION

1. You are the real estate agent for an owner of vacant land currently zoned residential. You and the owner believe that growth trends have changed and that the highest and best use of the land would be for commercial development. You apply to the planning commission for a rezone to commercial use. The planning commission turns down your proposal. The owner wishes to appeal the planning commission decision. What is the appeal process?

2. Explain how a condominium differs from a PUD and a stock cooperative. Why are they all called common-interest developments?

3. You just listed a $300,000 home for sale. Twenty days later the seller calls to tell you that the neighbors are concerned that the home might be sold to a minority person and that the seller does not want the home shown to potential minority buyers. How should you respond?

1. Which of the following is an example of government use of police power?
   a. rent controls
   b. building codes
   c. zoning ordinances
   d. all of the above

2. The Subdivision Map Act is administered by:
   a. California real estate commissioner
   b. local officials
   c. California Department of Urban Planning
   d. Department of Housing and Urban Development (HUD)

3. Before a developer can sell a lot in a new California subdivision, the prospective buyer must receive a copy of the:
   a. preliminary title report
   b. builder's warranties
   c. public report
   d. zoning ordinances

4. A developer from Nevada wishes to sell 300 Las Vegas lots to California residents and open sales offices in Los Angeles and San Francisco. The developer need not conform to the:
   a. Subdivision Map Act
   b. CA Department of Real Estate sales agreement disclosures requirements
   c. CA Department of Real Estate advertising disclosures requirements
   d. Interstate Land Sales Full-Disclosure Act

5. The right of the consumer, within a specified time, to rescind a land purchase contract and receive a full refund applies to new:
   a. urban subdivisions of 50 lots or more
   b. suburban subdivisions of 50 lots or more
   c. farmland of 50 acres or more
   d. land projects of 50 lots or more

6. A development where a person individually owns his or her living unit, but has an undivided interest with the other owners in the land and common areas, is a:
   a. planned unit development
   b. townhouse
   c. condominium
   d. stock cooperative

7. The selling of a 1/2500 share in a Northern California recreational ranch is an example of:
   a. an undivided interest
   b. a condominium
   c. a PUD
   d. a time-sharing ownership

8. A person cannot refuse to sell a home based on the buyer's
   a. physical handicap
   b. marital status
   c. sex
   d. cannot refuse based on all of the above

9. The law that prevents agents from discriminating when providing real estate services is:
   a. Fair Housing Act
   b. Rumford Act
   c. Unruh Civil Rights Act
   d. Housing Financial Discrimination Act

10. The law that makes it illegal for real estate lenders to redline a neighborhood is:
    a. California Fair Housing Act
    b. Rumford Act
    c. Unruh Civil Rights Act
    d. Housing Financial Discrimination Act

11. Which of the following is the best example of a common interest development?
    a. condominium
    b. single-family home
    c. tenant-occupied apartment building
    d. mobile home park

12. Recorded CC&Rs and an owners' association are mandatory for:
    a. a condominium
    b. single-family home
    c. tenant-occupied apartment building
    d. mobile home park

13. A deviation from the established zone requirements is called:
    a. a lot split
    b. a negative impact report
    c. a rezoning
    d. a variance

14. If private deed restrictions allow some use that is prohibited by zoning, the rule is that:
    a. zoning prevails
    b. private deed restrictions prevail
    c. rezoning is allowed
    d. spot zoning will be required

15. A simple lot split is governed by the:
    a. Subdivided Lands Act
    b. Subdivision Lot Division Act
    c. Subdivision Map Act
    d. Subdivision Land Project Act

16. The Civil Rights Act of 1968 and 1988 Amendments does not protect against discrimination in housing if a person is:
    a. a current controlled-substance abuser
    b. an alcoholic
    c. an AIDS victim
    d. confined to a wheelchair

17. The illegal act of directing potential buyers and tenants to certain neighborhoods is called:
    a. block busting
    b. directing
    c. locating
    d. steering

18. If the real estate commissioner issues a Preliminary Public Report for a subdivision, a developer is allowed to:
    a. sell the lots
    b. reserve the lots
    c. finance the lots
    d. escrow the lots

19. The power of eminent domain requires government agencies to:
    a. regulate but not buy the private property
    b. pay just compensation for the private property
    c. include the private property in the general plan
    d. take public property

20. Prior to issuing a building permit involving a minor project with little if any environmental damage, the local government may require an:
    a. environmental impact report
    b. public subdivision report
    c. property tax report
    d. negative impact report

Chapter 13

Introduction
to Taxation

Chapter Preview   Government levies taxes to generate revenue to help pay for government expenditures. This chapter presents the principles of real property and income taxation, two forms of taxation that have a direct impact on real estate ownership. At the conclusion of the chapter, you will be able to:

1. Describe the real property assessment procedure as required by Proposition 13

2. List the rules regarding the date and manner of payment of real property taxes; describe the tax sale procedure in the event of nonpayment of property taxes

3. Explain homeowner's, veteran's, and senior citizen's property tax exemptions

4. List the income tax advantages of real estate ownership, including the changes resulting from recent revisions in the law

13.1 REAL PROPERTY TAXES   In California, property taxes used to be levied by cities and counties on an ad valorem basis. *Ad valorem* is a Latin phrase that means "according to value." Under the concept of ad valorem, owners of higher valued property pay more in property taxes than owners of lower valued property.

With the passage of Proposition 13, property taxes in California are now levied using a system based upon date of acquisition, which is not a pure ad valorem system.

Assessment Procedure

On June 6, 1978, the voters of California passed Proposition 13, the Jarvis-Gann initiative. Proposition 13 limits real property taxes to 1% of the full cash value of the real property, plus an amount for local assessments and bonds.

No Change in Ownership Since March 1, 1975

Under the terms of Proposition 13, if there has been no change in ownership since March 1, 1975, the 1975 value shall be the initial full cash value. To this figure the assessor is allowed to add an inflation factor of 2% per year, *compounded* to arrive at full cash value for the present tax year. For example, assume that a person has owned his or her home since March 1, 1975. The 1975 value was $60,000. The 1976 full cash value would be $60,000 plus 2%, or $61,200; 1977 would be $61,200 plus 2% or $62,424, and so on until the present tax year is reached. In this example, for the year 2000 the value for tax purposes will be $98,436. Therefore, the maximum real property tax for the 2000–2001 tax year will be 1% of $98,436, or only $984.36, plus any amount needed to pay for voter-approved bonds, less any exemptions such as the California homeowner's exemption. Again, this applies only if there is no change in ownership since March 1, 1975.

It must be stressed that in this example the value for tax purposes bears no relationship to the actual current market value of the property. A home worth $60,000 in 1975 may be worth $250,000 or more currently. But the property would only be taxed at a value of $98,436! A bargain for the property owner. Whereas, as noted later, a property next door purchased today for the market value of $250,000 would be taxed at 1% and would require payment of a property tax of $2,500!

Change in Ownership Since March 1, 1975

When there is a change in ownership, such as a sale, gift, or inheritance, *the new owner's full cash value for tax purposes shall be the sales price or value of the property as of the date of transfer.* To this figure the assessor is allowed to add the inflation factor of 2% per year to arrive at full cash value. A supplemental tax bill is then mailed to the new owner.

Using the previous example, if a property worth $60,000 in 1975 is sold in 2000 for $250,000, the new owner's full cash value for 2000 will be $250,000 + 2%, or $255,000.

Therefore, the maximum real property tax for the 2000–2001 tax year will be 1% of $255,000, or $2,550, plus any amount needed to pay for voter-approved bonds, less any exemptions, such as the California homeowner's exemption.

As you can see, whenever there is a change in ownership, the full cash value for tax purposes is adjusted to the current market value of the property. In many cases this can result in a dramatic increase in real property taxes from what the former owner was paying.

Is This Discrimination?

Opponents of Proposition 13 have long contended that this law discriminates against recent buyers. Opponents point out that similar properties side by side could have dramatically different property tax bills depending upon when each owner purchased the property. Is this a form of discrimination based on unequal taxation? In a U.S. Supreme Court case, it was held that Proposition 13 is constitutional and not a form of illegal discrimination.

Other Adjustments

On new construction since March 1, 1975, full cash value for tax purposes is the real estate value at the *time of completion* plus the inflation factor of 2% per year to the present tax year. If you add improvements to your existing home, such as a swimming pool or a new bathroom, does this affect your tax bill? Yes! Does it mean that the entire home is brought up to current market value for tax purposes? No! What happens is that your home keeps its present full cash value as shown on the tax records before your new improvements. Then the new improvements are valued separately as of the date of completion. Each of these figures is adjusted by the 2% yearly figure, and the sum of these two figures equals full cash value for tax purposes.

Transfers between spouses, such as changing title from joint tenancy to community property or a deed of property from one spouse to the other spouse, are not considered transfers for property tax purposes. This means the county assessor *will not* reappraise the property and increase the property tax.

It should be noted that during the real estate crash of the early to mid-1990s when property values dropped, the tax assessor did not automatically increase tax values by the 2% factor allowed under Proposition 13. In some cases property tax values were lowered and property taxes owed declined.

Special Treatment for Senior Citizens

Another law, Proposition 60, allows homeowners 55 years of age and over to transfer their base year property tax value to another home of equal or less value in the *same county* and keep the low assessment they had on their former home. Example: Couple purchased a home in 1985 for $100,000 and for property tax purposes the assessed value is now $121,900 but the home is worth $200,000. If the couple sells for $200,000 and buys a home in the same county for $190,000 they can take their $121,900 assessment to the new home, rather than be assessed for the $190,000 purchase price. This results in the following property tax savings: $121,900 × 1% = $1,219 property tax, versus $190,000 × 1% = $1,900 property tax.

Proposition 90 allows the same concept to be applied if a home is purchased in *another county,* but only if that county's Board of Supervisors chooses to apply Proposition 90. Proposition 90 is scheduled to sunset January 1999 unless extended by the legislature.

Real Property Tax Dates

Real property taxes cover a fiscal year that begins July 1 and runs through June 30 of the following year. For example, the fiscal tax year for 2000–2001 would begin July 1, 2000, and end June 30, 2001.

The real property tax becomes a lien on January 1 preceding the fiscal tax year. Using our previous example, on January 1, 2000, a lien is placed on all taxable real estate for the 2000–2001 tax year, which begins July 1, 2000. (See Figure 13.1.)

The real property tax can be paid in two equal installments. The first installment is due November 1 and is delinquent if not paid by 5:00 P.M. December 10. If December 10 falls on a weekend or holiday, the tax is due by 5:00 P.M. the next business day. The second installment is due on February 1 and is delinquent if not paid by 5:00 P.M. April 10. Again, if April 10 falls on a weekend or holiday, the tax is due by 5:00 P.M. on the next business day.

REAL PROPERTY TAX YEAR

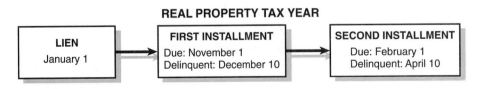

LIEN January 1	FIRST INSTALLMENT Due: November 1 Delinquent: December 10	SECOND INSTALLMENT Due: February 1 Delinquent: April 10

Figure 13.1

If a taxpayer wishes, both installments can be paid when the first installment is due. A 10% penalty is added to each installment that is not paid on time. If both installments become delinquent, a small additional charge is added to the 10% penalty.

As a memory tool, some people use the acronym NDFA, which stands for "No Darn Fooling Around" with property taxes!

Tax Sale

If an owner fails to pay real property taxes when due, on June 30 the tax collector publishes a notice of "intent to sell" the property to the State of California because of unpaid taxes. This sale is not a real sale, but rather what is known as a *book sale*. The property owner still owns the real estate, but the owner's name is entered into a delinquent account book, and this begins a five-year redemption period.

During this five-year period an owner can redeem the property by paying back taxes, interests, and other penalties and costs. Delinquent taxes can be paid in five annual installments as long as the current taxes are paid on time. For example, assume that a taxpayer owes three years worth of back property taxes. If the owner pays the current year's taxes, the tax collector will allow the owner to make partial payments on the back taxes, rather than demand full payment of all back taxes.

If after five years the property taxes are still unpaid, the delinquent property is deeded to the state, and the former owner loses title. But as long as the state holds title, the former owner still has the right of redemption.

However, the state also has the right to sell tax-deeded property to other public agencies or to private parties. Once the state sells the property, the former owner loses the right of redemption.

Public Auction

The sale of tax-deeded property is conducted by the county tax collector who must first obtain the permission of the local board of supervisors and the state controller.

The actual sale is a public auction that begins with a minimum bid that varies with each parcel being sold. All tax sales are for cash, as the state or county will not finance the sale. The successful bidder receives a *tax deed*. Under current title insurance practices, the holder of tax-deeded property can acquire title insurance after a period of one year.

Real Property Tax Exemptions

Because of special laws, certain owners of real estate are partially or totally exempt from the payment of property taxes. For example, government-owned real estate such as public buildings, parks, and school sites is exempt from property taxation. Some churches and other religious properties are not charged property taxes. In addition, there are special exemptions for homeowners, veterans, and senior citizens.

CALIFORNIA HOMEOWNER'S EXEMPTION

Under current law (January 1999), an owner-occupied residential dwelling is entitled to a $7,000 deduction from full appraisal value. For example, if an owner-occupied home is assigned a $180,000 full cash value by the assessor, a $7,000 homeowner's exemption is subtracted from this figure to obtain a $173,000 taxable value.

$180,000	Full cash value
− 7,000	Less homeowner's exemption
$173,000	Taxable value

Then according to Proposition 13, the actual tax will be $1,730 ($173,000 × 1%), plus any amount needed to pay for voter-approved bonds. In short, the California Homeowner's Exemption is worth $70 ($7,000 × 1%).

To claim the homeowner's exemption, a person must have been the owner and in residence on or before January 1, and must file for the exemption by February 15 with the assessor's office. Once filed, the exemption remains in effect until title is transferred or the exemption is terminated by actions of the owner. If a homeowner should miss the February 15 deadline, he or she can still file by December 1, but will receive only 80% ($5,600) of the $7,000 exemption.

VETERAN'S EXEMPTION

A California resident who has served in the military during time of war is entitled to a $4,000 exemption on the full value of the property. However, a person may not have both a homeowner's exemption and a veteran's exemption on the same property. Therefore, a veteran who owns only one home is wise to take the homeowner's exemption of $7,000, instead of the veteran's exemption of only $4,000. But if a veteran owns other real estate in addition to a personal residence, the veteran's exemption may be applied against the other property. But current rules prohibit a veteran whose net worth exceeds a designated sum from using the veteran's exemption. The designated net worth is subject to change, so a veteran should contact a veteran's official or tax consultant before applying for the veteran's exemption.

Upon the death of an eligible veteran, the exemption rights are extended to the unmarried surviving spouse or to a pensioned father or mother. *Special rules exist for disabled veterans* because of injuries incurred in military service. In some cases, the disabled veteran may not be required to pay any property tax. The California Department of Veterans Affairs should be contacted regarding the special rules for disabled California veterans.

EXEMPTIONS FOR SENIOR CITIZENS

In recent years several laws have been enacted to help senior citizens, many of whom live on fixed incomes. Under some laws a senior citizen may be defined as a person 55 years of age or older, whereas under other laws the age limit is moved up to 62 years or older.

In California there are special laws that may allow a partial or total refund of property taxes for certain senior citizens. In addition, the California legislature has passed laws allowing certain senior citizens to defer the payment of property taxes due on their home. The way it works is that the state pays the property taxes due the county and city. Then the state places a lien against the senior citizen's home, which accrues interest. The postponed taxes and interest run for an indefinite period. The state can recover on the lien only when the senior citizen dies, sells, or no longer occupies the home.

The rules that determine the eligibility of senior citizens for special tax treatment are constantly changing; therefore, senior citizens should contact the local tax assessor or senior citizen's action council for the latest information.

OTHER EXEMPTIONS

Property tax exemptions of one sort or another also exist for a variety of other owners of real estate. Timber, growing crops, young orchard trees, grapevines less than three years old, churches, nonprofit organizations, all qualify in some way for property tax exemptions. In addition, property tax incentives are used to keep agricultural land from being converted to urban use.

Special Assessments

Special assessments are different from real property taxes. Real property taxes help pay for the general operation of local government, whereas special assessments are levied to pay for a specific improvement such as streets and sewers. Special assessment liens usually are on a parity with property tax liens and often are collected at the same time.

A frequently used special assessment law is the Street Improvement Act of 1911. This law is used by cities and counties for street improvements. What usually occurs is that local government or a specially formed district hires a contractor to install or improve streets. Each owner along the street is liable for a pro rata share of the cost. The owner can pay in full within 30 days after completion, or the local government can sell bonds to raise the revenue to pay the contractor. If the project goes to bond, the property owners can pay their prorated share in installments over a period of time. Failure to pay a special assessment can result in a loss in the property owner's title, similar in nature to a tax sale.

Another program is the Mello-Roos Community Facilities Act of 1982. This law is used as a way to finance public services in newly developed areas. Examples of services include waste treatment plants, parks, schools, fire stations, and so on. Under this program, the owners in the assessment district pay for the facilities in their neighborhood, rather than have these facilities paid for by owners in other neighborhoods. This Mello-Roos Act can result in extra-high taxes, above the normal property tax, and should be made known to any new buyer before a purchase takes place.

Taxing Personal Property

As a general rule, only tangible personal property used in business is subject to taxes. Intangible property, such as shares of stock, loans due, as well as household furnishings and personal effects, are not taxed.

Personal property taxes are divided into secured and unsecured categories, depending upon whether the owner of the personal property also owns the real estate where the personal property is located. There are many rules that apply to personal property, but they are beyond the scope of this book. Local tax assessors have prepared numerous pamphlets to explain the personal property tax procedures. All businesspersons are encouraged to obtain these pamphlets.

13.2 INCOME TAXES

Income taxes are levied by both the federal government and the state of California. The income tax is a progressive tax. The federal and state rates increase as the income levels being taxed increase.

The buying and selling of real estate have significant income tax consequences. In some cases, the income tax aspects are more important than the price of the property. Income tax aspects of a real estate transaction should be considered *before* the sale, not after. Once a sale takes place, it is too late to go back and restructure the sale to take advantage of any tax laws that were overlooked.

Income tax laws are complicated and constantly changing. Before entering into a complicated real estate transaction, a person should seek the advice of an income tax specialist, such as an attorney or accountant.

Major Income Tax Advantages for Homeowners

Income tax laws favor homeowners over renters by granting various income tax incentives for becoming a homeowner.

1. Interest paid on real estate loans is deductible against personal income to reduce tax liability, subject to the interest limitation noted on page 319, item #1.

2. Property taxes paid are also deductible against personal income.

3. The old 24-month trade-up and 55-year-old rules have been abolished. The new law states that there will be no tax on gain up to $250,000 for singles and $500,000 for married people who file joint returns. No age limits, no restrictions even if you previously used the 55-year-old exemption. Unmarried co-owners will get up to a $250,000 exclusion for each person if each meets the ownership and occupancy rules.

   To qualify, the home must have been your principal residence for at least 2 years during the 5 years prior to the sale. Only one spouse must be the owner during this time. *But* both spouses must have lived there for the 2-year period to get the maximum exemption of $500,000 with a joint filing.

   If you have lived less than 2 years in the present home, but sold a previous home and deferred gain under the old 24-month trade-up rule into the present home, the years spent in the previous home can be counted to meet the 2-year holding period rule.

4. The full exclusion can be used only once every 2 years. If the home is sold for a gain before the 2-year holding period is achieved, the gain will be fully taxable unless the sale is due to a job change or major illness. Then a pro rata formula will be used to separate tax exempt from taxable gain.

   Example:
   Owned and lived in a home only 18 months and then due to a job change it was sold for a gain. The formula will probably be as follows:

   $$\frac{18 \text{ months}}{24 \text{ months}} = 75\%$$

   for single $250,000 × 75% = $187,500 maximum exclusion
   for marrieds $500,000 × 75% = $375,000 maximum exclusion
   (The law does not state if days or months formula will be used)

REAL ESTATE ASPECTS OF THE TAX REFORM ACT 1986, TAX REVENUE ACT 1987, TAXPAYER RELIEF ACT OF 1997, AND OTHER RECENT REVISIONS

Summary of Rules for Homeowners

1. Mortgage interest deductions are allowed for acquisition debt (purchase money loan) up to a maximum loan of $1 million on all combined mortgages on a first and second residence. If you borrow more than $1 million, the interest paid on the excess over $1 million is not deductible. No interest deduction is allowed for three or more personal-use homes. This affects all home buyers who acquired their home after October 13, 1987.

2. For the refinance of an existing home, the remaining loan balance on acquisitions loan(s) plus $100,000 will be the maximum refinance loan allowed if the homeowner wishes to deduct all the interest as a qualified home loan.

3. The $250,000 for singles and $500,000 for joint-filing married couples exemption noted on page 318 are still valid.

4. Installment sale treatment is still allowed for homeowners.

Summary of Rules for Income Property Owners

1. Depreciation (cost recovery) on buildings and improvements is 27½ years for residential rental and with longer periods for nonresidential rental, and the straight-line method must be used.

2. Rental property mortgage interest is fully deductible against rental income with no dollar loan limits such as the $1 million cap placed on homeowners. However, any tax loss created by interest and depreciation deductions will fall under the passive tax loss rules listed herein.

3. Real estate rentals are considered "passive" investments and produce either passive income or passive loss, depending upon the property's cash flow. The general rule is that a passive real estate loss can only be used to offset other passive income, NOT active or portfolio income such as salaries, commissions, profits, interest, and dividends. Prior to tax law changes, real estate losses could be used to offset active or portfolio income.

4. Special $25,000 exception to the passive loss rules if a person meets the following test:

   a. Be an individual owner of 10% or more interest in rental real estate

   b. Be actively involved in the management (can use property managers but you must make the key decisions)

   c. Have a modified adjusted gross income of $100,000 or less

   If the owner of rental real estate meets this test, he or she can use up to $25,000 in passive losses from real estate to offset active or portfolio income, such as salaries and interest, after first offsetting passive income.

5. If the rental property owner's modified adjusted gross income exceeds $100,000, then the $25,000 amount is reduced $1 for every $2 above the $100,000. Any unused passive losses from rental real estate can be carried forward to reduce future passive income and gain upon sale of the property. The passive loss rules do not eliminate the investor's right to use real estate losses. However, the law's changes will, in some cases, delay the right to use the loss until a later date, such as the date of resale.

6. The right for a real estate investor to do a 1031 tax-deferred exchange remains the same; recent tax law changes have not eliminated this technique.

7. Installment sales treatment for real estate investors is still allowed. Installment sale treatment for real estate dealers has been abolished.

There are many other tax law changes, but these are the items that have a major impact on real estate. The preceding is listed for information purposes and should not be considered tax advice. For tax advice a person should seek competent tax advisors.

1. Homeowners with gains of more than $250,000 for singles and $500,000 for married people. They will be taxed at capital gain rates for the excess over these dollar amounts . . . no deferral techniques available.

2. Loss on the sale of a personal home will not be tax deductible.

Major Income Advantages for Investment Property Owners

1. Interest on real estate loans and property taxes paid is deductible against the rental income earned by the property.

2. Repairs, maintenance, management, insurance, and other operating expenses are also deductible. Note: Repairs, maintenance, and other operating expenses are not deductible for homeowners on their own residences, only on investment real estate.

3. Depreciation deduction allowances can be used to shelter income. The depreciation deduction consists of a yearly allowance for wear, tear, and obsolescence, which will permit the property owner to recover the original cost over the useful life of the property. Land is not depreciable, only the improvements such as buildings, fences, and so on. Depreciation cannot be taken on owner-occupied residential homes; it can be taken only on income real estate. Depreciation deductions reduce the taxable income, thereby giving the property owner more after-tax cash flow. However, tax law changes place restrictions on how real estate losses can be used to shelter income other than rents.

4. Under certain circumstances, an investment property owner can enter into a tax-deferred exchange. If properly structured, an investor can exchange one like property for another without paying immediate income taxes on the former property. The tax liability is not eliminated, but rather postponed until the investor disposes of the new property in a taxable transaction—usually a sale. Some people incorrectly call this a "tax-free" exchange, but technically it is only a tax-deferred exchange. To structure an Internal Revenue Code, Section 1031, tax-deferred exchange, an investor must not receive "boot." Boot is defined as unlike property received in an exchange. The receipt of boot creates a tax liability on the boot. Examples of boot include cash, notes, personal property and so on. There are many technical rules regarding a tax-deferred exchange, and no one should proceed without the advice of tax counsel.

5. An installment sale is another way to reduce tax liability upon the sale of real estate. This method of selling allows the seller to carry back paper and spread the gain

from the sale over a period of years. Rather than paying the entire tax in the year of sale, the seller pays income taxes only on that portion of the gain received in the form of payments in any one year. Once again, it must be stressed that advice of tax counsel should be sought to make sure the sale qualifies for installment reporting.

State Income Tax

In some ways, California income tax law is patterned after the federal laws. However, there are some notable differences that should be discussed with a tax expert. For example, the tax brackets for individuals and corporations are different for state income tax as opposed to the federal income taxes. There are special rules regarding new residents and their need to file a California income tax statement. All of these state tax laws, plus many others, are administered by the California franchise tax board.

For most real estate transactions, the impact of federal income taxes is more important than the impact of state income taxes. But careful tax planning should attempt to minimize both federal and state income taxes.

Special Withholding Rules for Foreign and Out-of-State Sellers

Under the Foreign Investment in Real Property Tax Act (FIRPTA), the federal government requires that 10% of the sales price of property owned by a foreigner must be withheld for a possible income tax liability. California Revenue and Taxation Code Sections 18805 and 26131 require a $3\frac{1}{3}\%$ withholding for state income taxes if the seller is a *foreigner or a resident of another state*. Both of these laws put the burden for compliance on the *buyer not the seller*. Both of these laws have exceptions and exemptions that can be complicated and tricky. If a person is purchasing California property from a foreigner or a U.S. citizen who lives in another state, the buyer might wish to check with a tax expert to make sure the income tax laws are being correctly applied before the sale takes place.

13.3 OTHER TAXES

Documentary Transfer Tax

Upon the transfer of real estate, a documentary transfer tax of $0.55 per $500 of consideration or fraction thereof ($1.10 per $1,000) is levied. If the property being transferred is in an unincorporated area, all the tax goes to the county where the property is located. If the property is located in an incorporated city, the city and county divide the tax proceeds.

The tax is levied on the full price of the property if there is an all-cash sale or if the buyer obtains a new loan that cashes the seller out. If the buyer assumes the seller's existing loan, the transfer tax is levied only on the equity being transferred. (See Chapter 6 for detailed examples of the documentary transfer tax.)

Estate and Inheritance Tax

In some cases, the federal government taxes the estates of deceased persons. The state of California has eliminated inheritance taxes. There are several ways to reduce or, in some cases, avoid the payment of estate taxes. The methods are technical and complicated and frequently require the use of inter vivos (living) or testamentary trusts. At all times the services of an attorney should be used. For futher information, see Internal Revenue Publication 559.

Gift Taxes

The federal government, but not the state of California, has tax laws that apply to gifts of real and personal property. A gift is a voluntary transfer of property from the owner called the donor to the receiver called the donee.

The federal law allows a tax-free gift (as of January 1999) of $10,000 of value per donee per year. This $10,000 is scheduled to slowly increase after the year 2000. The use of gift tax exclusions during the life of the donor can often be used to save estate taxes upon death. Gift tax laws are complicated, and professional tax advice should be sought when planning an estate to minimize taxes by use of gifts.

Miscellaneous Taxes

Sales and use taxes occasionally arise in certain broker transactions—for example, the sale of a business opportunity or a mobile home. In circumstances where sales tax is involved, it is the responsibility of the real estate agent to see that escrow instructions are correctly drafted to account for the tax liability.

Unemployment insurance fees, workman's compensation fees, and Social Security taxes may need to be collected when a real estate salesperson is hired by a broker and acts as an employee instead of as an independent contractor.

CHAPTER SUMMARY

Property taxes in California are levied on a modified ad valorem basis and usually change when a property is transferred to a new owner. Two classifications of property taxes are: (1) real property taxes, and (2) personal property taxes. With passage of the Jarvis-Gann Initiative (Proposition 13) the maximum real property tax allowed is 1% of full cash value, plus 2% annual inflationary factor, plus an additional sum to pay for voter-approved bonds that affect the property.

If there has been no change in ownership since March 1, 1975, the tax year 1975–1976 is the base year for computing full cash value. A change in ownership after March 1, 1975, will cause the full cash value for tax purposes to be increased to the sales price or value as of the date of transfer. There are special rules for the handling of remodeling and additions that will cause the taxable value to rise.

Real property taxes are paid over a fiscal year beginning July 1 and ending June 30. The first installment is due November 1 and delinquent if not paid by December 10. The second installment is due February 1 and delinquent if not paid by April 10. Real property taxes become a lien January 1 preceding the fiscal tax year. If the required taxes are not paid, the owner's title will eventually revert to the state of California for delinquent taxes.

Real property tax exemptions include $7,000 on appraised value for homeowners, $4,000 for qualified veterans, and special exemptions for senior citizens. There are several other property tax exemptions for certain classes of property such as timber, growing crops, and so on.

Income taxes are levied by both federal and state government. Income taxes are progressive—that is, the tax rate increases as the income level increases. The buying and selling of real estate has significant income tax consequences. Sometimes the income tax aspects are more important than price. Income tax laws are complicated and constantly changing. Before entering into a real estate transaction, a person should seek the advice of a qualified tax expert.

Other taxes that could have an impact on real estate are estate taxes, gift taxes, transfer taxes, and use and sales taxes.

IMPORTANT TERMS AND CONCEPTS

Ad valorem

California homeowner's exemption

Depreciation deduction

Estate taxes

Fiscal property tax year

Installment sale

Proposition 13

Senior citizen exemption

Special assessments

Tax-deferred exchange

Tax sale

1. Counting local bonds, the typical property tax in your community runs .012 of the sales price and homeowner's insurance runs .005 of the sales price. As a real estate agent you are showing potential buyers a $225,000 home that will require an 80% loan at 8% amortized for 30 years. Based on this information, what will be the initial monthly housing payment of PITI (principal, interest, $\frac{1}{12}$ taxes, and $\frac{1}{12}$ insurance)? Hint: You will need to use a financial calculator or the amortization table in Chapter 6.

2. Married homeowners, who have owned and lived in their main home for eight years, sell their $750,000 home and have a $300,000 gain. They file joint returns and their federal capital gain tax bracket is 20%. Based on this information, how much will they owe in federal taxes due to the sale of their home?

3. A homeowner refinances and takes out a 125% equity loan. How much of the interest on this loan is deductible for federal income taxes?

REVIEWING YOUR UNDERSTANDING

1. Under Proposition 13, the maximum real property tax cannot exceed what percent of full cash value, after adjustments for inflation, voter-approved bonds, and exemptions?
   a. 1%
   b. 2%
   c. 5%
   d. 10%

2. Real property taxes become a lien on:
   a. February 1
   b. January 1
   c. December 1
   d. November 1

3. Real property is deeded to the state if property taxes are delinquent for:
   a. one year
   b. three years
   c. five years
   d. seven years

4. If full cash value of a condo is $90,000, what will be the taxable value after subtraction for a homeowner's exemption?
   a. $80,000
   b. $90,000
   c. $86,000
   d. $83,000

5. The second installment of real property taxes is due:
   a. November 1
   b. December 10
   c. February 1
   d. April 10

6. Which of the following is incorrect?
   a. To obtain the full homeowner's exemption, a person must file by February 15.
   b. The California veteran's exemption is $4,000.
   c. Property taxes are collected by the assessor.
   d. Special assessments are liens on real property.

7. A single homeowner can exclude the taxable gains from the sale of a home up to:
   a. $100,000
   b. $150,000
   c. $250,000
   d. $500,000

8. A married couple who files joint returns can exclude gain on their home up to:
   a. $100,000
   b. $150,000
   c. $250,000
   d. $500,000

9. Income real estate is entitled to use:
   a. tax-deferred exchanges
   b. installment sale provisions
   c. depreciation deductions on improvements
   d. all of the above

10. The passive loss rules apply to:
    a. principal residence
    b. vacant land
    c. rental real estate
    d. personal automobiles

11. In a Section 1031 tax-deferred exchange, the receipt of unlike property is called:
    a. basis
    b. boot
    c. basics
    d. bases

12. Examples of laws that create special assessments above and beyond basic property taxes are the Street Improvement Act of 1911 and:
    a. Proposition 13
    b. Proposition 60
    c. The Assessment Act of 1974
    d. The Mello-Roos Community Facilities Act of 1982

13. Sales price $250,000 and the buyer is to assume an existing loan of $190,000; the documentary transfer tax is:
    a. $275
    b. $209
    c. $110
    d. $66

14. The homeowner's property tax exemption is worth how much in actual tax savings?
    a. $7,000
    b. $700
    c. $70
    d. $7

15. When a seller carries paper to spread out the taxable gain over a series of years, this is called:
    a. installment reporting
    b. a 1031 exchange
    c. a capital gain
    d. tax elimination

16. Which of the following cannot legally take a depreciation tax deduction on their property?
    a. apartment building owner
    b. retail store owner
    c. farm building owner
    d. homeowner, for that portion of the home not used as a business

17. Under certain guidelines, which proposition allows homeowners 55 years or older to transfer their property tax basis to another home in the same county?
    a. Proposition 13
    b. Proposition 60
    c. Proposition 90
    d. Proposition 1034

18. For a homeowner, which of the following expenses are deductible for income tax purposes?
    a. condo association dues
    b. fire insurance
    c. property taxes
    d. two of the above

19. The government person who maintains the property tax rolls is the
    a. assessor
    b. collector
    c. council person
    d. none of the above

20. A "book sale" refers to a sale:
    a. where income taxes are deferred
    b. for accounting purposes for delinquent property taxes
    c. where tax delinquent property is deeded to a buyer
    d. to remove paid liens

Chapter 14

Single-Family Homes and Mobile Homes

Chapter Preview This chapter explores the characteristics of a house, including construction details, roof styles, and architectural designs. Mobile homes, condominiums, and vacation or second homes are also presented. At the conclusion of the chapter, you will be able to:

1. Identify major construction terms associated with home building

2. Differentiate among various architectural styles

3. List the advantages and disadvantages of buying versus renting a home

4. Discuss the advantages and disadvantages of owning a mobile home, condominium, or vacation home

14.1 HOME CONSTRUCTION STYLES There are many varieties of home construction styles, but the three most common types are one-story, split level, and two-story homes.

Obviously the *one-story* home is the most simple to build and the easiest to maintain, but it occupies more land per square foot of living space than the others.

The *split-level* home is popular in California because of the better utilization of land of varying topography as well as the pleasing cosmetic effect. However, it is usually more expensive to build.

The *two-story* home has a lower cost per square foot because a single foundation and roof supports two floors of living area. But the principal disadvantage is the stairs to climb to reach the second floor. Also, the difficulty of reaching exterior portions for repair and maintenance presents some problems.

Roof Styles
There are numerous roof styles, but the major ones are as follows:

The *gable* roof is a pitched roof with two sloping sides that meet at the top.

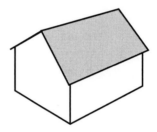

A *gambrel* roof has a steeper lower slope with a flatter upper slope above—usually found on barns. This is also called a Dutch barn roof.

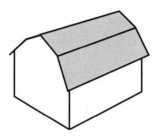

A *hip* roof is a pitched roof with sloping sides and ends—all sides slope to the eaves.

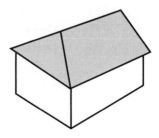

A *mansard* roof is a French-style roof with a sloping lower part on all sides and a flat top.

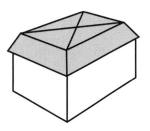

Architectural Styles

It would be an impossible task to become familiar with all architectural designs. However, descriptions of the most common are:

A *colonial* style is usually referred to as early American. Generally it is two stories, with a gable roof, and shutters on the windows.

COLONIAL

The *California Cape Cod* style has a high-pitched roof, large chimney, wood siding and shutters, and is usually two stories high.

CALIFORNIA CAPE COD

Monterey (Spanish) style is a large two-story building, white stucco, red tile roof, with the second-story balcony having decorative iron railings.

Modern or contemporary style is one story, ultramodern, with plenty of glass and open walls.

MODERN OR CONTEMPORARY

California bungalow or ranch style is a one-story structure, with a low-pitched roof and sliding-glass windows and a ground-hugging (sprawling) floor plan.

CALIFORNIA BUNGALOW/RANCH

California Mediterranean is a two-story stucco home combining many flavors of Spain, France, and Italy. This style has been very popular since the late 1980s in Southern California subdivisions.

CALIFORNIA MEDITERRANEAN

Source: California Department of Real Estate and Loraine Norton, *The California Real Estate Consultant,* Upper Saddle River, N.J.: Prentice Hall, 1996.

CONSTRUCTION DETAILS

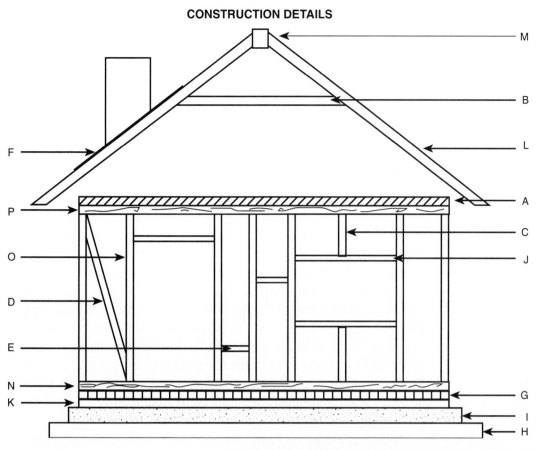

A CEILING JOIST. Horizontal beams supporting ceiling
B COLLAR BEAM. A beam that connects opposite rafters above the floor
C CRIPPLES. Short vertical piece 2 × 4 above or below an opening
D DIAGONAL BRACE. A brace across corner of structure to prevent swaying
E FIRE STOP. Short board or wall between studs to prevent fire spreading
F FLASHING. Metal sheet usually around chimney to prevent water seepage
G FLOOR JOIST. Horizontal beams supporting floor
H FOOTING. Base or bottom of a foundation wall
I FOUNDATION. The supporting portion of structure resting on footing
J LINTEL. A horizontal board over a door or window also called header
K MUDSILL. Perimeter board anchored directly to foundation
L RAFTERS. Boards designed to support roof loads
M RIDGE BOARD. Highest board in the house supporting upper ends
N SOLE PLATE. Usually 2 × 4 on which wall and studs rest
O STUDS. Vertical boards 2 × 4 supporting the walls every 16″ (on center)
P TOP PLATE. A horizontal board fastened to upper end of studs

Other Construction Terms
    Board Foot = used to measure lumber, contains 144 cubic inches
    R–VALUE = ranking of insulation materials
    EER = Energy Efficiency Rating

Figure 14.1

14.2 MOBILE HOMES

Because building codes, zoning laws, and other practices, as well as inflation, make it difficult to build low-cost conventional houses, many families have turned to mobile homes as a solution.

A mobile home is defined by the California health and safety code as "a vehicle designed and equipped to contain not more than two dwelling units, to be used without permanent foundation."

Mobile homes in the past were confused with trailers. The major difference is that trailers usually provide temporary housing only, whereas a mobile home is a permanent living unit. The word "mobile" may be confusing; actually, studies show that once in place, mobile homes are seldom moved. They are usually located in mobile home parks, although in many rural areas they can be found on individual lots.

The Mobile Home Parks Act defines a mobile home park as "any area or tract of land where one or more mobile home lots are rented or leased." The rental operation of a mobile home park is within the jurisdiction of the State Department of Housing and Community Development. If a mobile home park has five or more lots for sale or lease, it is considered a subdivision and consequently subject to subdivision laws.

Under certain circumstances, mobile homes purchased after July 1, 1980, can be taxed as real property if they are attached to a permanent foundation.

Types of Mobile Homes

The four basic types of mobile homes are illustrated here.

Single, 8-foot, and 10-foot-wide units.

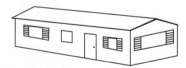

Single, 12-foot-wide units.

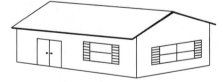

Multiple wide, double wide, or triple wide units.

Quads—four units together.

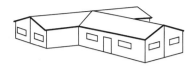

Legal Requirements Related to Mobile Homes

In order to list or sell a mobile home, a real estate licensee must comply with special aspects of the real estate law.

1. *New mobile homes cannot be sold by real estate licensees,* but only through mobile home dealers licensed by the Department of Housing and Community Development.
2. *A real estate licensee can sell used mobile homes* provided the mobile homes have already been registered with the state and are on a lot or in a mobile home park.
3. The mobile home must be capable of being transported over a road. The hitch must be attached to the unit or stored underneath, and the axles must still be attached to the frame.
4. The licensee is responsible for the proper completion and delivery of the title to the buyer.
5. Notification of transfer of ownership must be made within 10 days of the date of the sale.
6. All fees must be paid to the state within 10 days of the sale date.
7. No concealment of a material fact or any other fraudulent act may be committed.
8. Mobile homeowners pay an In Lieu Tax similar to regular property taxes paid by homeowners.
9. If the mobile home was manufactured after June 15, 1976, it must have a Department of Housing and Urban Development (HUD) tag, guaranteeing its proper construction.

Violations of Business and Professions Code

Under this code, real estate licensees may have their licenses suspended or revoked if they are found guilty of any of the following:

1. Failure to provide for delivery of proper certificate of ownership of the mobile home
2. Have knowingly participated in the purchase or sale of a stolen mobile home
3. Submitted a check, draft, or money order to the state for payment of mobile home fees and the draft is dishonored upon presentation to the bank

Financing Mobile Homes

Because mobile homes are considered to be personal property, the method of encumbering the ownership is through a security agreement instead of a deed of trust.

Mobile homes can be financed through FHA, VA, and Cal-Vet loans. In addition, conventional loans are available from banks and other real estate lenders. Most mobile home loans are amortized over a 15- to 20-year period. Interest rates on mobile home loans are usually higher than on conventional home loans.

Termination of Tenancy in a Mobile Home Park

The Civil Code provides for the termination of tenancy by the landlord of a mobile-home-park tenant, when any of these occur:

1. Failure of the tenant to comply with local ordinances and state laws and regulations related to mobile homes
2. Conduct of the tenant upon park premises that constitutes a substantial annoyance to other tenants
3. Failure of the tenant to comply with reasonable rules and regulations of the mobile home park
4. The nonpayment of rent, utility charges, or incidental service charges
5. Failure to maintain the mobile home in a reasonable state of repair acceptable to park management.

In recent years there has been considerable legislation, as well as many disputes and lawsuits, regarding rents and other occupancy issues at mobile home parks. The complete rights and duties of landlords and tenants in a mobile home park is too extensive to cover in this textbook. Interested parties should research The Mobilehome Residency Law, Civil Code 798, and The Mobilehome Parks Act, Sections 18200, et. seq., of the Health and Safety Code.

Advantages of Mobile Home Ownership

1. The price of traditional homes has risen so rapidly that many families, young adults, and senior citizens are purchasing mobile homes because of their lower prices as compared to conventional homes.
2. Mobile home parks are relatively quiet places to live.
3. There is a definite feeling of security, because there is usually only one entrance or exit and most residents know who lives in the mobile home park.
4. Mobile homes are transportable.

5. The quality and amenities of mobile homes have improved over the years.

6. Better financing terms are now available for mobile home purchasers.

7. There is minimal yard maintenance or none at all.

Disadvantages of Mobile Home Ownership

1. Mobile homes can depreciate rapidly.

2. Mobile homes usually have a lower resale value than conventional houses.

3. The terms of loans offered by lenders are usually not as favorable as conventional homes.

4. When your mobile home is located in a mobile home park, you may be required to buy extras, such as steps with handrails or skirting to conceal wheels.

5. Many cities and counties have severe restrictions regarding the placement of mobile homes; therefore, sites are often difficult to obtain.

Converting a Mobile Home to Real Property

For a mobile home to become real property, the following four conditions must be met:

1. The mobile homeowner must obtain a building permit.

2. The mobile home must be placed on a permanent foundation.

3. The mobile homeowner must obtain a certificate of occupancy.

4. A document stating that the mobile home is attached to a permanent foundation must be recorded.

Once this takes place, a mobile home is considered real property, and all the laws of real estate apply.

14.3 CONDOMINIUMS

A *condominium* is a system of individual fee ownership of a unit in a multifamily structure, combined with joint ownership of common areas of the structure and the land.

Advantages of Condominium Ownership

1. You can sell your own unit as you would a regular home.

2. Insurance companies offer special packages for condominium owners.

3. It combines the benefits of owning a house with the advantages of apartment living.

4. You receive the same tax benefits as a homeowner.

5. You build an equity with each payment as you do in a regular home.

6. There is little or no yard work to perform.

7. Common areas that are part of your ownership can include game rooms, swimming pools, tennis courts, and putting greens.

8. The law offers some protection to the owner, in that he or she cannot be made to leave because of certain infractions of by-laws and regulations of the governing owners' association.

Disadvantages of Condominium Ownership

1. You are responsible for all building maintenance problems in your unit.

2. You may be required to pay your share of the association fees to cover maintenance costs in common areas, even if you disagree with the expenditure.

3. Sometimes the developer controls parking and recreation areas, for which he or she may charge extra fees.

4. You will find yourself living rather compactly in close proximity to neighbors. Noises emanating from swimming pool and game areas may prove distracting.

Basic Items to Check When Buying a Condominium

1. If the building is new, check on the reputation of the builder. If an existing building, check with agents, neighbors, owners' associations, and government agencies to see if there have been complaints regarding the quality of construction.

2. Read all legal documents carefully including any conditions, covenants, and restrictions, as well as governing documents of the owners' association (consult an attorney if necessary).

3. Make sure you know the amount and coverage of any homeowner association fees. What are they now? When were they raised last? Are there any pending lawsuits against the homeowners' association?

4. Ask yourself these specific questions:

   a. Is exterior and/or interior maintenance included in the established fees?

   b. Are there any restrictions on the sale or lease of individual units? How many units are tenant-occupied, as opposed to owner-occupied?

   c. Are there any warranties on equipment? If so, for how long?

   d. Does the developer have reserve funds in case of an emergency?

e. Are you required to pay maintenance costs for unsold units?

f. Is there enough insurance to protect against fire, liability, theft, and other risks?

5. What experience has the real estate agent had regarding the sale and financing of condominiums?

14.4 VACATION HOMES

Many people own a second or vacation home. Second homes typically include (1) a cabin in the mountains, (2) a cottage by the lake, (3) a house near the beach, or (4) a chalet near a ski slope.

Where You Buy Is Important

You should ask yourself these questions before you make your final decision regarding ownership of a second home:

1. Can I tolerate close neighbors, or do I want complete privacy?

2. Do I want a place close to everyday conveniences or one that is "out of sight and sound"?

3. Depending upon the area chosen, can I afford it? If not, can I interest someone in a joint venture?

4. What is the resale potential? Will the home be difficult to resell if I need to get my money out?

A Second Home as an Investment

There are five major factors that determine investment potential. They are risk, liquidity, management, tax aspects, and appreciation potential.

Risk is the chance you take that you may lose all or part of your initial investment. The risk involved in a second home as an investment will depend upon the market conditions at the time of purchase and resale. Second-home investments are usually considered a greater risk than a principal residence, and this is reflected in the higher interest rates lenders charge for a second-home loan compared to the interest rate on a loan to buy a principal residence.

Liquidity refers to the ability to quickly convert your investment to cash. Real estate is not as liquid as other investments, such as stocks or bonds. However, if the second home is priced right, it can usually be sold in a reasonable length of time. Before you buy a second home, check out the resale history of the area.

Management refers to the cost and time involved in overseeing the investment. Real estate requires a considerable amount of management. On nearby real estate investments you may choose to manage the property yourself. But if the second home is a considerable distance away, you will need to pay for local management to oversee, maintain, and check up on the property.

Tax aspects refers to the income tax laws and their impact on the investment. Owners of second homes are allowed to deduct the interest on loans and payment of property taxes. If the second home is rented out for a portion of time, a complex set of income tax rules applies. A vacation or second home is no longer the tax haven that it once was—see your tax advisor before you buy. Today most vacation homes are purchased to enjoy; they are not purchased as tax shelters.

Appreciation refers to an increase in value when demand exceeds supply. California real estate, as a whole over a length of time, has tended to increase significantly in value. But at any given time, prices can decline because of a current decline in demand. The second or vacation home market is usually more volatile than the regular home market.

14.5 SHOULD YOU RENT OR BUY?

Keep in mind that the advantages in renting will closely parallel the disadvantages of buying, and the disadvantages in renting will closely relate to the advantages of buying.

Advantages of Renting and Disadvantages of Buying

1. Only a comparatively small outlay of money is required to rent, usually the first and last months' rents and a security deposit. When you purchase, you are usually required to pay a sizable down payment of 5% to 20% of the purchase price as well as closing costs.

2. There is less risk in renting because your initial outlay is limited. You don't stand to lose much even if you decide to move earlier than you had planned. In purchasing, whenever you invest money there is a greater risk that you might lose some or all of it if property values decline.

3. In the short run, when you rent your costs are fixed. You know pretty well how much your rent will be each month, so you can usually budget accordingly. In buying, the mortgage payment may or may not remain stable depending upon whether the loan has a fixed or adjustable rate; property taxes and maintenance costs will increase over time.

4. In renting, if the neighborhood should decline, you can move without suffering a personal loss because of a de-

cline in real estate values. Renting gives greater mobility than owning.

5. When you rent, you can take the money that otherwise would be used to buy a home and deposit it in a savings account or buy stocks and bonds giving you greater liquidity. When you purchase real estate, your money is usually tied up and sometimes difficult to pull out to meet a financial emergency.

6. When you rent, you don't have the same responsibility for maintenance as you do when you own your own property. You can take a vacation trip without worrying about the maintenance and upkeep of the property. If you are the owner, the responsibility for maintenance is yours.

Advantages of Buying and Disadvantages of Renting

1. If you buy a home it could be an investment for the future. Well-located properties usually increase in value over the long run. During recessions there may be a short-term drop in prices, but over the long term the average California home has experienced appreciation. When you rent, you have only rent receipts to show for your expenditure at the end of each month.

2. As a homeowner, you are allowed to deduct your property taxes and interest payments from personal income before you are required to pay federal or state income taxes.

3. Pride of ownership and security make people feel comfortable and permanent in their own homes. Many homeowners cement that security by becoming involved in community affairs, working around the yard, and making minor repairs. On the other hand, it is difficult to establish permanence in a rented home. At the whim of the landlord you may be asked to leave or to pay higher rent in order to stay.

4. A home is usually larger than an apartment unit, allowing plenty of room for activities. Few apartment units provide the same freedom of movement as a home. In addition, you can build on to your home if you need more space.

5. There are fewer restrictions placed on homeowners. They can have pets if they wish. They can even play the stereo after 10:00 P.M. if they wish!

6. Homeowners are frequently viewed as more secure credit risks than renters.

These items are just a few of the advantages and disadvantages of owning versus renting.

CHAPTER SUMMARY

This chapter discussed the characteristics of one-story, two-story, and split-level homes. Various architectural designs, roof styles, and construction details were illustrated. The principles of mobile home, condominium, and vacation home ownership were discussed. The chapter ended with an explanation of the pros and cons of buying versus renting real estate.

IMPORTANT TERMS AND CONCEPTS

Condominiums
Double-wide mobile homes
Gable roof
Hip roof
Mansard roof

Mobile home
Single story
Single-wide mobile homes
Split-level home
Two-story home

PRACTICAL APPLICATION

1. Starting with the ground, using the construction illustration in the book, move from the ground to the sole plate of a standard home giving the construction name for each item in the correct sequence.

2. List the four conditions required in California to convert a mobile home to real property.

3. As a real estate agent you are attempting to convince a renter that buying a home makes more economic sense than renting. List five advantages of owning a home.

REVIEWING YOUR UNDERSTANDING

1. The ownership of a mobile home is transferred by means of a:
   a. deed
   b. certificate of ownership
   c. bill of sale
   d. sales agreement

2. All fees relating to licensing or transferring of title to mobile homes must be paid to the:
   a. Department of Housing and Community Development
   b. Department of Motor Vehicles
   c. Department of Real Estate
   d. Division of Mobile Homes

3. All other things being equal, the least cost per square foot should be found in a:
   a. one-story home
   b. split-level home
   c. ranch-style home
   d. two-story home

4. When you rent as opposed to owning, you have the ability to move faster to another location. This is called:
   a. liquidity
   b. convenience
   c. mobility
   d. permanence

5. Of the numerous roof styles, which of the following fits this description: "A pitched roof with sloping two sides that meet at the top"?
   a. gambrel
   b. hip
   c. mansard
   d. gable

6. What style of house fits this description: "A large two-story building with red tile roof and decorative iron railings"?
   a. modern or contemporary
   b. California bungalow
   c. Monterey (Spanish.
   d. colonial

7. A real estate licensee can sell used mobile homes if the mobile home:
   a. is registered with the state
   b. has at least 800 square feet
   c. qualifies for conventional financing
   d. is preapproved by the Department of Real Estate

8. The proper payment for the transfer fee for the sale of a mobile home must be made within:
   a. 5 days
   b. 10 days
   c. 15 days
   d. 20 days

9. For a mobile home to be considered real estate it must be:
    a. in a mobile home park
    b. on a permanent foundation
    c. approved by the FHA
    d. preapproved by the Department of Real Estate

10. Once a mobile home is converted to real property, title to the mobile home is transferred using a:
    a. deed
    b. bill of sale
    c. pink slip
    d. certificate of ownership

11. In terms of complication, the most difficult tenant to evict is one located in:
    a. an apartment building
    b. a mobile home park
    c. a duplex
    d. a home

12. The highest point in a standard frame house is:
    a. collar beam
    b. rafters
    c. ridge board
    d. header

13. In the construction of a home, the board above a window is called a:
    a. brace
    b. sole plate
    c. header
    d. stud

14. A piece of lumber 1 inch thick and 12 inches by 12 inches in size contains:
    a. 1 board foot
    b. 2 board feet
    c. 3 board feet
    d. 4 board feet

15. The foundation of a standard built home sits upon the:
    a. mudsill
    b. collar beam
    c. footing
    d. stud

16. The ultimate responsibility for the management of an entire condominium building after all the individual units have been sold rests with the:
    a. original developer
    b. lender
    c. owners' association
    d. government

17. Regarding second homes:
    a. They always make for good investments.
    b. They provide extraordinary tax write-offs.
    c. They are easier to finance than a first home.
    d. They are usually purchased to enjoy, not as investments.

18. An advantage of owning instead of renting includes:
    a. mobility
    b. control
    c. liquidity
    d. less risk

19. For income tax purposes, a second homeowner who does not rent out the property is allowed to:
    a. sell and within 24 months trade up into another second home and defer the gain on the sale
    b. deduct property taxes and loan interest
    c. deduct the cost of repairs and maintenance
    d. sell and use the 55-year-old, once-in-a-lifetime exemption

20. The advantage of owning over renting a home includes:
    a. more liquidity
    b. more mobility
    c. less initial investment
    d. income tax deductions

Chapter 15
A Career in Real Estate

Chapter Preview   A career in real estate can be an exciting opportunity for certain people. The various types of job opportunities within the real estate industry may offer a greater potential for movement and advancement than many other areas of employment. The real estate business is a people-oriented industry. Real estate professionals help or assist customers and clients to achieve their financial and investment goals. Thus, a career in real estate can lead to a wide range of employment activities from the entry level of sales agent to the sophisticated role of the real estate counselor. However, there are pitfalls to consider! Not everyone can succeed in real estate. It is definitely not to be viewed as a get-rich-quick industry. Success takes dedication and hard work. At the conclusion of the chapter, you will be able to:

1. Describe the major career fields in the real estate industry

2. List the requirements to become a licensed real estate salesperson or broker

3. Review the personal items to consider before becoming a real estate agent

At the end of this chapter you will find Appendix A and Appendix B. Appendix A describes the rules for real estate licensees who sell Business Opportunities. Appendix B is a reprint from the Department of Real Estate, describing the procedure and content of the state real estate examination.

Following the appendices, you will find a complete 150-question practice real estate examination similar in format to the state examination.

15.1 STRUCTURE OF THE REAL ESTATE INDUSTRY

Although this chapter focuses on the rules for obtaining a real estate license, anyone interested in a career in real estate should recognize the diversity of the industry. In addition to acting as an agent for the buying and selling of properties, a career in real estate could include many other activities. Real estate-oriented people are needed in the areas of construction, financing, escrow, appraising, management, land development, and other related specialties. Each of these areas offers opportunities for well-trained people. Some of these specialties require a real estate license, whereas others may require a different license, or no license at all.

Real Estate Agents

The potential as a real estate sales agent is unlimited. A variety of opportunities exists as a result of the growth in America's population and the continued expansion of our nation's economy. As a consequence, real estate agents are needed to assist people who wish to buy, sell, or develop real estate.

A real estate salesperson's license qualifies one to work for a real estate broker as a selling agent. Although a new licensee may be considered an expert in the eyes of the public and the law, most new agents soon realize that additional training and education are necessary in order to live up to the public's expectations.

As a salesperson becomes more experienced, he or she may wish to become a real estate broker. Brokers are allowed to own and operate their own business. A real estate salesperson cannot solely own and operate a real estate firm; he or she must be affiliated with a broker.

Sometimes a real estate brokerage company will handle all kinds of properties, or it may specialize in just residential, commercial, industrial, farm, or vacant land sales. Some real estate brokers may wish to become consultants and work on a fee-per-hour basis rather than be paid a sales commission.

Although the field of real estate is complex, there are boundless opportunities for personal satisfaction as well as the potential for above-average income. A person who plans on entering the field of real estate must remember that experience, education, integrity, and resourcefulness are the characteristics that the public expects to see in real estate agents.

However, success will not be easy. Real estate is a competitive business, and the failure and turnover rates for new licensees are very high. Later in this chapter the reasons for failure are discussed in detail.

Real Estate Trade Associations

People who choose real estate as a career quickly become aware of real estate trade associations. The largest is the National Association of REALTORS® (NAR) which is identified by the symbol ®. The National Association of REALTORS® owns the nationally recognized designation REALTOR®. Only members of the National Association of Realtors can use the term REALTOR®. In California, the unauthorized use of the term REALTOR® constitutes a violation of Department of Real Estate regulations.

The National Association of REALTORS® is broken down into state associations, each of which provides services to their state members. The California Association of REALTORS® (CAR) is the state-affiliated group that provides services for California members. The major objectives of the California Association of REALTORS® (CAR), as set forth in its constitution, are:

1. To unite its members
2. To promote high standards
3. To safeguard the land-buying public
4. To foster legislation for the benefit and protection of real estate
5. To cooperate in the economic growth and development of the state

The California Association of REALTORS® is in turn divided into numerous local groups called Association of REALTORS® or Boards of REALTORS®. Local associations are usually broken down by cities or counties.

The main thrust of REALTOR® trade groups is to provide information and education for their members, and to pursue political agendas that are favorable to the ownership of real estate. This is achieved using publications, seminars, state–national–international conventions, videos, cassettes, and various training sessions. Another advantage of association membership is the substantial savings on insurance and other health benefits through group rates.

Another national real estate organization is the National Association of Real Estate Brokers. This trade association was formed in 1947 and consists of predominantly African-American real estate brokers whose members are called "REALTISTS®." The organization has several state chapters and local boards throughout the United States.

A REALTIST® must be a member of a local board as well as a member of the national organization. Both nationally and locally, REALTISTS® are working for better housing for the communities they serve. In many cases, individuals are both REALTORS® and REALTISTS® by virtue of voluntary dual membership.

Professional Designations and Code of Ethics

If an agent wishes to specialize in a particular aspect of real estate, trade associations provide advanced training leading to certified designations. Once earned, the professional designations enjoy a national recognition and usually lead to higher income for the designee.

Virtually all trade associations have a code of ethics for their members. If trade association members violate the code of ethics, it is grounds for dismissal from the group and the loss of the benefits of membership.

Other Real Estate Employment

In addition to sales jobs, real estate trained salaried positions may be available as a loan officer, appraiser, escrow officer, or title officer. These salaried jobs are with financial institutions, appraisal companies, escrow companies, title companies, and some government agencies. Real estate developers and contractors frequently hire salaried personnel who need a real estate background.

Additional opportunities for real estate students can exist in local, state, and federal governments. These may include a variety of occupational levels such as right-of-way agents, appraisers, leasing negotiators, planners, and HUD housing program staff.

15.2 LICENSE REQUIREMENTS AND COMPETITION

Real Estate Salespersons

The current requirements (1999) to become a real estate salesperson are:

1. Must be at least 18 years of age and a legal U.S. resident.
2. Must not have a past criminal record. Conviction of a crime that is either a felony or involves moral turpitude may result in the denial of a license.

3. Must take a college-level course in real estate principles before sitting for the salesperson examination. This course can be taken at an accredited college or at a private vocational school approved by the Department of Real Estate.

4. Must be able to pass the state examination consisting of 150 multiple-choice questions to be answered within a three-and-one-quarter-hour time period. A passing score is 105 or more correct answers representing 70% and up.

   The salesperson's examination is given as needed at designated locations in California, usually San Francisco, Los Angeles, San Diego, Sacramento, and Fresno. The examination is difficult, and a failure rate of 50% or more is common.

5. After passing the examination, you must submit the required license fee on an approved application form along with a set of classifiable fingerprints.

6. A conditional sales license is granted for 18 months, during which time two broker-level courses must be completed. Then the remaining term of a four-year license is issued. If the two additional broker-level courses are completed before taking the sales examination, upon passage of the examination and the proper filing of an application, a four-year license is issued. There is no need for the 18-month conditional license.

Real Estate Brokers

Current requirements to become a real estate broker are:

1. Must be at least 18 years of age and a legal U.S. resident.
2. Must not have a past criminal record. Conviction of a crime that is either a felony or involves moral turpitude may result in the denial of a license.
3. Must complete at least eight approved real estate courses. The following five must be taken:
   a. Real Estate Practice
   b. Legal Aspects of Real Estate
   c. Real Estate Finance
   d. Real Estate Appraisal
   e. Real Estate Economics or Accounting
   f. Then any three of the following courses for a grand total of eight courses: real estate principles, business law, property management, real estate office, administration, escrow, mortgage loan brokering or another approved advanced real estate course. The courses

must be taken through an accredited college or at a private vocational school approved by the real estate commissioner.

4. Must complete the experience requirements which consist of two years' full-time experience as a real estate salesperson, or its equivalent. "Equivalent" is experience in an allied field such as title, escrow, or finance. Equivalence can in some cases include education in lieu of experience, such as an accredited college degree.

5. Must pass the state examination consisting of 200 multiple-choice questions to be answered within five hours with a score of 150 or more correct answers, representing a score of 75% or better. The test for the broker's license is more difficult than the salesperson's examination, and the failure rate is frequently high, averaging approximately 50%.

6. Must complete the license application and pay the proper fee.

7. The broker's examination is given monthly or more often depending upon demand at the locations mentioned earlier for the sales examination.

Real estate licensees are allowed to sell business opportunities as well as real estate. See Appendix A of this chapter for details regarding business opportunities.

State Examination

For a detailed explanation of the state real estate examination and official Department of Real Estate instructions, see Appendix B of this chapter. Also a complete 150-question examination, including answers, in a format similar to the sales examination, is presented for your review following Appendix B.

Continuing Education Requirements

All licensees must show proof of completing a minimum of 45 clock hours of real estate commissioner-approved continuing education before a real estate license will be renewed. The rule is not 45 hours per year, but rather 45 hours within the four-year licensing period. The first 45-hour renewal must include four separate 3-hour courses covering the topics of ethics, agency, fair housing, and trust fund handling. These four mandatory classes must total 12 hours. On a licensee's second four-year renewal a six-hour mandatory survey course on current updates on ethics, agency, fair housing, and trust fund handling is required.

The remaining classes to total 45 hours can be on various topics of a licensee's choosing as long as the classes are pre-approved for continuing education by the California Department of Real Estate. A passing score on a test is required on all correspondent continuing education classes. No testing is required on live and video continuing education seminars.

If a real estate salesperson obtains a broker's license before the time to renew the salesperson license, the new broker will not need to meet the continuing education requirement until the renewal date of the broker's license.

Department of Real Estate–approved continuing education courses are offered throughout the state by private enterprises, as well as by real estate trade associations and California colleges.

The California Department of Real Estate— A Summary

The Department of Real Estate is a public agency that has responsibility over certain real estate activities in California. Here are some key points:

1. The California Real Estate Commissioner is appointed by the Governor and serves as the chief executive of the Department of Real Estate.

2. The Commissioner administers the Real Estate Law and issues regulations that have the force of law and become a part of the California Administrative Code.

3. The Commissioner and the Department screen applicants for licenses and investigate complaints against licensees. After a proper hearing, if a licensee has violated a law or regulation, the Commissioner can restrict, suspend, or revoke a real estate license.

   Restricted License: allows licensee to continue to work, but under limited conditions

   Suspended License: a temporary loss of license

   Revoked License: a loss of license

4. A real estate license is required when a person performs a real estate act for another for compensation. The compensation may be in the form of a commission, fee, salary, or anything of value. The following exceptions do not need a real estate license:

   a. Principal handling his or her own affairs

   b. Attorney in fact acting under a power of attorney

c. Appraiser (needs special license not issued by the Department of Real Estate, but rather issued by the Office of Real Estate Appraisers)

d. Attorney at law (Lawyer) while performing duties as an attorney. If the attorney charges a fee as a broker, then a real estate license is required.

e. Trustee selling under a deed of trust

f. Residential on-site property manager. A full-service, off-site property manager must have a real estate license.

5. As of January 1999, the fine for an unlicensed person who receives an illegal commission is $10,000 for an individual and $50,000 for a corporation. The fine for paying a commission to an unlicensed person is $100.

6. Fictitious Business Name. A licensed broker, corporation, or partnership may operate under a fictitious name (DBA, Doing Business As) if the name is approved by the Commissioner.

7. A corporate real estate license requires an officer to be licensed as a broker. A partnership real estate license requires one partner to be licensed as a broker. A real estate salesperson and a broker can form a real estate brokerage partnership.

8. Prepaid Rental Listing License. A special license that allows licensee to collect a fee for supplying a prospective tenant with a list of available rentals. This does not allow licensee to negotiate rental contracts or perform any other real estate activity. Real estate brokers can collect a prepaid fee without a special license if done at their regular place of business.

9. Real Estate Advisory Commission. Consists of the Commissioner and 10 other members appointed by the Commissioner. Six members are real estate brokers, four are public members. The purpose of the Real Estate Advisory Commission is to advise the Commissioner on real estate matters important to the industry and the public.

Real Estate Licensees in California

Statistics provided by the Department of Real Estate indicate that the total number of real estate licensees fluctuates with the real estate market. When the market is good the number of real estate licensees increases. When the real estate market drops so does the number of licensees, but this drop lags the drop in the market. As of January 1999, there were approximately 300,000 real estate licensees in California. Approximately 30% were brokers and 70% salespersons.

The greatest number of licensees is involved with the buying and selling of homes as opposed to other real estate activities. One can enter the real estate market as a salesperson with only a small amount of initial capital, and the opportunity does exist to earn a good income. Compensation, on the other hand, is largely based on earnings from commissions. As a consequence, anyone contemplating a real estate sales career should be aware that they are in direct competition with a large number of licensees whose numbers tend to expand with the real estate market.

How About a Part-Time Real Estate Job?

Many potential licensees hope to work part-time until their sales volume will support full-time employment. However, many brokers will not hire part-time salespeople. The reason relates to the time and financial cost to train part-time salespersons and the requirement for fully employed staff to follow or cover the part-timer's assignment and client contacts. Unless covered in a suitable manner, part-time salespeople can create management and personnel problems for brokers and their staffs. This does not mean that part-time real estate salespeople are unwanted, but rather that part-timers usually are not as successful as fully committed salespeople.

Working Hours and Fringe Benefits

The person who decides to enter real estate on a full-time basis will initially face the prospect of long hours, including evenings and weekends. Evenings and weekends are the only hours some prospective buyers and sellers have free to discuss real estate needs.

In addition, many times the fringe benefits that come with other jobs may not exist. For example, paid vacations, insurance benefits, or retirement funds are not common in the real estate business. If a real estate salesperson wants these items, he or she usually must pay for them out of his or her own earnings. If fringe benefits are of overriding concern, each prospective salesperson should explore these areas of question prior to joining a particular firm.

Realistic Picture

Real estate sales and related activities can offer unlimited opportunities for motivated individuals. Perseverance and hard work, coupled with good training and additional educational course work, can help a person become financially independent and provide a valuable service for the public.

Real estate is not a get-rich-quick business—it takes work and a willingness to be helpful and understanding.

15.3 PERSONAL PREPARATION TO ENTER THE REAL ESTATE INDUSTRY

Some people enter real estate sales with unrealistic expectations for earnings that do not materialize, and this results in a negative employment experience. If possible, a prospective licensee should meet with a real estate instructor or career counselor and an experienced real estate broker and discuss what it takes to succeed in the local real estate market. Some community colleges offer an internship program, where students work in a local real estate office while taking real estate courses.

Personal Checklist

1. If at all possible an interest inventory test, such as the Strong Inventory Test, should be taken. These tests indicate a person's interests and what vocations are suited to these interests. These tests are available at most local community colleges. Call the college's registrar, student service office, or assessment center for information.

2. If the local college has a career center, check with a counselor to verify which real estate courses are required. A call to a Department of Real Estate-approved private vocational school can provide the same information. Many are listed in the telephone book. Be sure to discuss the cost for textbooks, registration fees, matriculation requirements, class hours, as well as the total scope of real estate course offerings.

3. Once the arrangements for a course of study have been established, it is a good idea to check the local real estate employment market. The executive officers of local real estate associations and boards can give indications of the sales activities in the local area. These indicators might include a list of the number of real estate salespeople, listings and sales activities, and average dollar volume of business. The real estate sections of many local newspapers are now publishing these statistics.

4. Select an area where you might like to work and survey the real estate offices within this territory. Go in several offices and take a look around. Although a brief look does not indicate the success of a real estate company, it does give some important first impressions.

5. Check local newspaper real estate advertisements to determine which real estate offices are working which neighborhoods.

6. Narrow the real estate office choices to perhaps one to five offices, and then attempt to identify the personnel

within these offices. If possible, make an appointment with an employed salesperson to discuss the activities within each office. This can provide valuable facts concerning management, number of employees, rapport, and so on. Many times the decision to attempt to join a firm is made at this time.

7. Once the selection process is narrowed, an appointment should be made for an interview with either the owner-broker or the personnel manager. Prior to doing so, however, an application form should be requested (for many small offices, application forms are not used). The form should be completed in advance of the appointment and accompanied by a personal resume.

To assure a more informative interview, list specific questions you may wish to ask. The list should include questions regarding the existing number of salespeople, support personnel, training programs, commission splits, advertising and listing policies, employee–independent contractor arrangements, commission ratios once certain sales quotas have been reached, personal costs for office expenses (telephone), and fringe benefits if any.

This suggested list of questions does not intend to imply that the applicant is to interview management! However, not asking enough questions can lead to regret later. A well-conducted interview usually brings out important information for both the salesperson and the real estate company.

Questions to Ask Yourself Before You Enter the Real Estate Business

1. Why am I leaving my current employment? Are my reasons valid and logical, or are they emotional?
2. How many sales per month will I need to generate enough commission dollars to earn to equal my present salary? (This projection should include money set aside for income taxes and insurance.)
3. What arrangements will be made for annual vacations and holidays?
4. What about the fringe benefits—health, life, dental packages? How will these be paid for?
5. Will I have to work on weekends and during evening hours? If so, will this be continuous? If not, for how long? How will this affect my lifestyle? My family?
6. Do I have the stamina and energy it takes to be in sales?
7. Are my personality traits such that I will be continually charged and challenged? Can I take the peaks and valleys of real estate sales?

8. Am I financially prepared to begin a career in real estate sales? Do I have the money to carry myself and my family for a period of time before sales start to materialize. In addition, the prospective salesperson should recognize that there are continuing out-of-pocket expenses such as:

   a. Local board, state, and national professional fees

   b. The cost to drive and maintain a suitable automobile for use in escorting clients to and from properties. (This would include repair costs, additional gasoline mileage, and comprehensive insurance coverage.)

   c. Incidental daily costs that arise in connection with food services for clients, such as, coffee, luncheons, or dinners

   d. Monthly office costs—telephone, listing materials, keys for properties

   e. Personal appearance, which requires a businesslike wardrobe, personal grooming, or the uniform wardrobe required by certain franchise offices

9. How will my family or my other relationships cope with the change? Are they supporting my decision?

This list of questions is not intended to be presented as a negative overview of real estate sales, but rather as a serious review of what must be considered for a successful and professional entrance into the real estate field.

Ending Note

The real estate business provides an opportunity for a personally challenging and a financially rewarding career, but it is not "easy for the taking." With dedication and hard work, you can become a successful real estate salesperson, earn a substantial income, and open up opportunities for personal investments.

CHAPTER SUMMARY

Real estate offers many avenues for employment. In addition to sales, opportunities exist in the fields of real estate appraisal, finance, escrow, title insurance, construction, and development. Real estate trade associations, such as the National Association of Realtors®, the National Association of Real Estate Brokers, and the California Association of Realtors®, provide valuable services to their members and the public.

Real estate licensees are regulated by the California Department of Real Estate (DRE). The DRE is headed by the real estate commissioner, who is appointed by the governor.

The 10-member Real Estate Advisory Commission advises the commissioner on matters of importance to the industry and the public.

The basic requirements to become a real estate salesperson are being 18 years of age or older, be a legal U.S. resident, completing an approved course in real estate principles, passing the 150-question state examination with a score of 70% or better, completing an application, and paying all fees. A temporary 18-month license is issued pending completion of two college-level real estate broker courses. Once the two additional courses are completed, the license is extended for the remaining portion of a four-year term. A real estate salesperson must work for a broker.

The basic requirements to become a real estate broker are being 18 years of age or older, be a legal U.S. resident, completing eight approved real estate courses, having two years' experience as a real estate salesperson or its equivalent, passing a 200-question state examination with a score of 75% or better, completing an application, and paying all fees. A real estate broker's license is good for four years. A real estate broker is allowed to operate his or her own real estate office and hire real estate salespeople.

To renew a real estate sales or broker's license, a person must complete 45 hours of DRE-approved continuing education classes. Within the first 45-hour renewal period, a licensee must take four separate three-hour courses in ethics, agency, fair housing, and trust fund handling.

Prior to entering the real estate business a person should conduct a serious self-appraisal. The real estate business offers many opportunities for self-motivated people, but it is not a get-rich-quick business.

IMPORTANT TERMS AND CONCEPTS

California Association of Realtors® (CAR)

Department of Real Estate (DRE)

National Association of Real Estate Brokers (NAREB)

National Association of Realtors® (NAR)

Real estate broker license requirements

Real estate commissioner

Real estate salesperson license requirements

REALTIST®

REALTOR®

PRACTICAL APPLICATION

1. As a new California real estate salesperson licensee, what are the educational requirements during the first four years of your license?

2. After being a California real estate salesperson for five years, you acquire your California real estate broker license. What are the continuing education requirements during the first four years of your broker license?

3. What is meant by the term "bulk sale"? (See the appendix to this chapter.)

REVIEWING YOUR UNDERSTANDING

1. The term "REALTOR®" can only be used by a member of the:
   a. National Association of Real Estate Brokers
   b. National Association of Realtors
   c. National Association of Real Estate Councils
   d. All of the above

2. "REALTISTS®" are members of the:
   a. National Association of Real Estate Brokers
   b. National Association of Realtors
   c. National Association of Real Estate Councils
   d. all of the above

3. Real estate appraisers are licensed by the:
   a. Department of Property Valuation
   b. Office of Real Estate Appraisers
   c. Department of Real Estate
   d. Office of Valuations and Standards

4. A real estate salesperson is usually employed on a commission basis and receives payment directly from the:
   a. buyer
   b. seller
   c. broker
   d. lender

5. Which of the following best describes the real estate business?
   a. easy money business
   b. competitive business
   c. noncompetitive business
   d. generous employer-paid benefits

6. In addition to real property, a real estate licensee is allowed to act as an agent for the sale of:
   a. automobiles
   b. new, unregistered mobile homes
   c. travel trailers
   d. business opportunities

7. Before being allowed to sit for the state real estate sales examination, an applicant must:
   a. take 45 hours of approved continuing education
   b. be 21 years old
   c. take two broker-level courses
   d. take a course in real estate principles

8. Once a person passes the state real estate sales examination, files an application and pays the fees, a temporary license may be issued for 18 months pending completion of:
   a. 45 hours of approved continuing education
   b. eight approved college-level broker courses
   c. four approved college-level broker courses
   d. two approved college-level broker courses

9. To sit for the real estate broker's examination, an applicant must first do all the following, *except:*
   a. take 45 hours of approved continuing education
   b. take eight approved college-level broker courses
   c. have two years' real estate sales experience or its equivalent
   d. pay the required examination fee

10. Once a real estate license has been issued, renewal of the license every four years requires:
    a. 45 hours of approved continuing education
    b. a re-examination
    c. two approved college-level broker courses
    d. two years of full-time real estate experience or its equivalent

11. The California Real Estate Commissioner is:
    a. elected by the voters
    b. appointed by the California Association of Realtors®
    c. appointed by the governor
    d. elected by the California legislature

12. After a proper hearing, if a licensee has violated a law or regulation, the real estate commissioner can restrict, suspend, or revoke a real estate license. If a licensee is allowed to continue to work under limited outlined conditions, the real estate license is called a:
   a. restricted license
   b. suspended license
   c. revoked license
   d. temporary license

13. The fine for an unlicensed person who receives an illegal commission is:
   a. $100
   b. $1,000
   c. $10,000
   d. $100,000

14. In a typical real estate sale, which of the following does not need a real estate license to handle their portion of the transaction?
   a. listing salesperson
   b. selling agent
   c. original broker
   d. buyer's attorney

15. The Real Estate Advisory Commission consists of the commissioner and how many other members?
   a. 5
   b. 10
   c. 15
   d. 20

Questions 16–20 refer to business opportunities as outlined in Appendix A of this chapter.

16. A business opportunity is defined as the sale of all of the following, *except:*
   a. operating business
   b. inventory
   c. goodwill
   d. real estate

17. The financial statement that shows the position of a business on a given day is called a:
   a. profit and loss statement
   b. balance sheet
   c. net worth sheet
   d. cash flow statement

18. The financial statement that shows the operations of a business over a period of time, usually one year, is called a:
   a. profit and loss statement
   b. balance sheet
   c. net worth sheet
   d. cash flow statement

19. Under bulk sales rules, the buyer must give public notice at least:
    a. 5 days before transfer takes place
    b. 7 days before transfer takes place
    c. 10 days before transfer takes place
    d. 12 days before transfer takes place

20. The payment for the expectation of continued patronage is called:
    a. blue sky
    b. intangible goods
    c. goodwill
    d. site value

Appendix A
Business Opportunities

A real estate license allows an agent to sell business opportunities. A business opportunity is defined as the sale or lease of a business, including stock, trade fixtures, trade name, and goodwill. This involves the sale of personal property, and all the rules of personal property apply.

The essential elements of the sale of a business opportunity include:

1. A bill of sale is the written instrument that passes title to personal property.
2. The financial statements needed when a business is sold are:
   a. Balance Sheet—Shows the financial position of the business as of a given date

   Assets. Things of value owned by the business

   Liabilities. Unpaid debts and expenses of the business

   Net Worth. Owners' equity, the difference between the assets and liabilities
   b. Profit and Loss Statement—Shows the profit and loss of the business during a specific time period.

Gross Income   (Revenue from sales)
–Expenses   (Cost of goods and expenses)
Net Income   (Profit)

3. Bulk Sales Rules apply when a business is sold that involves inventory. A bulk transfer is defined as the transfer of a major portion of inventory other than a sale to customers. Transferee (buyer) must give public notice 12 business days before transfer takes place. The notice requires recording a Notice of Intent to Sell Bulk and publishing it in a newspaper of general circulation. The purpose of this is to let creditors of the seller file a claim if trade credit is still owed on the inventory.

    If the buyer and seller do not comply with the bulk sale law, the sale is valid between them, but is void against the creditors who can then attach the inventory.

4. Other terms and definitions are:

    a. Goodwill. Expectation of continued public patronage
    b. Turnover. Number of times the inventory is sold per year
    c. Sales and Use Tax. A tax on the sale of personal property
    d. Alcoholic Beverage Control Act (ABC). Rules involving the sale of a liquor license. One of these rules states that the person must be of good moral character. If a new license is issued by the state, the initial fees are relatively modest. But once issued, because the number of liquor licenses is limited by population, a free market develops and the price for a liquor license can skyrocket.

Appendix B*

The Real Estate License Examinations

The Commissioner is required by law to ascertain by written examination the competency qualifications of applicants for a real estate license (Section 10153 of the Business and Professions Code). Examination requirements cannot be waived (Sections 10153 and 10158 of the Business and Professions Code and Commissioner's Regulation 2761). An application to take the examination may be obtained by calling or writing any of the Department of Real Estate district offices. A pamphlet entitled "Instructions to License Applicants" that gives detailed instructions on license application and qualification procedures is furnished with each application.

This section is devoted to the license examination process itself, giving some idea of the extent and scope of the examinations for real estate broker and salesperson licenses.

EXAMINATION PURPOSE

Real estate license examinations are designed to test the candidate's practical knowledge of real estate, appraisal techniques, and the handling of real estate transactions in the best interest of the principals. It must be emphasized that a few personal experiences with real estate transactions will not usually give the exam candidate knowledge of sufficient scope and depth to enable the candidate to pass the examination.

Every effort is made to construct the examinations in such a way as to give the candidate for a license an opportunity to demonstrate his or her knowledge of the fundamentals of real estate and the ability to handle transactions properly without endangering the interests of the public.

*Reprinted from the *Reference Book*, published by the California Department of Real Estate.

Business and Professions Code Section 10153 requires that the Commissioner structure an examination as follows:

Section 10153. In addition to the proof of honesty and truthfulness required of any applicant for a real estate license, the Commissioner shall ascertain by written examination that the applicant, and in case of a corporation applicant for a real estate broker's license, that each officer, or agent thereof through whom it proposes to act as a real estate licensee, has all of the following:

(a) An appropriate knowledge of the English language, including reading, writing and spelling and arithmetical computations common to real estate and business opportunity practices.

(b) An understanding of the principles of real estate and business opportunity conveyancing, the general purposes and general legal effect of agency contracts, deposit receipts, deeds, mortgages, deeds of trust, chattel mortgages, bills of sale, land contracts of sale, leases, and of the principles of business and land economics and appraisals.

(c) A general and fair understanding of the obligations between principal and agent, the principles of real estate and business opportunity practice and the canons of business ethics pertaining thereto, and the provisions of Part I (commencing with Section 10000) and, of Chapter 1 (commencing with Section 11000) of Part 2, and the regulations of the Real Estate Commissioner as contained in Title 10 of the California Code of Regulations.

Exam Preparation

Unless the applicant for a real estate broker or salesperson license has had experience with the various instruments used in real estate transactions, has good general knowledge of real estate fundamentals, and of the obligations of an agent as well as familiarity with the laws and regulations governing an agent's activities, it is suggested that serious study be undertaken prior to taking the examination. Even those persons well grounded in these areas will find a review extremely valuable. It is well to remember that a substantial number of those who take the real estate license examination fail to pass it.

Real estate practice in the last two decades has become much more professional in its outlook. As transactions become more and more complex, the licensee is expected to have a broader knowledge of the field of real estate. This knowledge must be acquired through a combination of academic channels and experience. Therefore, it is important that the person striving for real estate licensure be adequately prepared before appearing for the examination. The Reference Book and the Real Estate Law book published by the Department touch on most of those subjects covered in the examinations.

In addition, there are a number of excellent textbooks on California real estate law, practice, finance, economics and appraising available at public libraries and bookstores. Resident courses of study in the previously mentioned subjects and others are offered by universities, state universities, community colleges, the University of California Extension and private vocational schools.

For those who prefer independent study (correspondence instruction), the University of California (Berkeley) and some private vocational schools offer basic real estate courses for home study.

EXAMINATION CONSTRUCTION

The Department of Real Estate's testing program primarily follows guidelines and techniques set by the State Personnel Board and other test authorities. The format and outline of all real estate license examinations as we know them today were originally created through a research grant to the University of California in 1956. Since that time several research studies have been conducted to update the test specifications. The most recent study was conducted in 1986 by the Educational Testing Service. The study researched the tasks performed by brokers and salespersons and the knowledge areas necessary to competently perform these tasks. They found differences in the level and amount of knowledge required of salespersons and brokers in performing their work. These differences account for the variation in weighting in the test outlines presented herein. Because knowledge requirements for entry-level salespersons and brokers have changed, new salesperson and broker licensing examinations are constantly being developed to conform with the findings and recommendations of the most recent validation study.

Examination weighting as of January 1996. The weighting may be subject to change in the future.

The subject matter covered in the examinations is based on laws and procedures applicable within the state of California. As new broker and salesperson licensing examinations are developed, each of the content areas is weighted as indicated on the test outlines presented later. The subject matter outlines are presented to assist applicants for licensure in preparing for the licensing examination.

REAL ESTATE SALESPERSON LICENSING EXAMINATION TEST OUTLINE AND CONTENT WEIGHTINGS

General Topics   **Overall Weightings**

REAL PROPERTY AND LAWS RELATING
TO OWNERSHIP 11%
    Ownership of property
    Encumbrances
    Public power over property
TAX IMPLICATIONS OF REAL ESTATE OWNERSHIP 8%
    Knowledge of current tax laws affecting real estate ownership
VALUATION/APPRAISAL OF REAL PROPERTY 15%
    Methods of appraising and valuing property
    Factors that may influence value estimate
FINANCING REAL ESTATE 17%
    Sources of financing
    Common clauses in mortgage instruments
    Types of loans
    Terms and conditions
TRANSFER OF PROPERTY 10%
    Titles
    Escrow reports
REAL ESTATE PRACTICE 22%
    Listing of real property
    Sales contracts
    Marketing
BROKERAGE: RESPONSIBILITIES AND FUNCTIONS
OF SALESPERSONS 17%
    State real estate laws and regulations
    Laws relating to fair practices
    Knowledge of trends and developments
    Knowledge of forms and calculations

REAL ESTATE BROKER LICENSING EXAMINATION TEST OUTLINE AND CONTENT WEIGHTINGS

REAL PROPERTY AND LAWS RELATING TO OWNERSHIP 9%
    Ownership of property
    Encumbrances
    Public power over property
TAX IMPLICATIONS OF REAL ESTATE OWNERSHIP 8%
    Knowledge of current tax laws affecting real estate ownership

VALUATION/APPRAISAL OF REAL PROPERTY 15%
    Methods of appraising and valuing property
    Factors that may influence value estimate
FINANCING REAL ESTATE 16%
    Sources of financing
    Common clauses in mortgage instruments
    Types of loans
    Terms and conditions
TRANSFER OF PROPERTY................................... 9%
    Title
    Escrow reports
REAL ESTATE PRACTICE.................................. 21%
    Listing of real property
    Sales contracts
    Marketing
BROKER'S RESPONSIBILITY FOR OFFICE MANAGEMENT 22%
    State real estate laws and regulations
    Laws relating to fair practices
    Knowledge of trends and developments
    Knowledge of forms and calculations

Question Writing

The license examination is similar to an achievement test, in that it is a mastery test of a specific knowledge. Given that the examination is not competitive, its nature becomes qualifying and no set quota or rank of applicants is required. The examination process is not designed to predict future success in the business of real estate. It is meant to select the better qualified or competent over the less competent or less knowledgeable applicants.

To construct a good measuring device, it is essential that the component parts be consistent with relevancy to the subject matter and the knowledge being evaluated. Accordingly, each question or item is a test in itself and must meet the technical characteristics demanded of the test as a whole.

EXAMINATION RULES AND GRADING

The time allowed to complete an examination is subject to change as examination content and construction may dictate. Currently, applicants for a broker license are allowed a maximum of five hours to complete the test—$2\frac{1}{2}$ hours in the morning and $2\frac{1}{2}$ hours in the afternoon. A candidate for a real estate salesperson license is allowed $3\frac{1}{4}$ hours to complete the test. To pass an examination, a broker candidate must answer at least 75% of the questions correctly out of a total of 200 and the candidate for a salesperson license must correctly answer 70% of the questions out of 150. Tests are objective, consisting of multiple-choice items, and they are impersonally graded by mechanical means.

Experience shows that an applicant for either a broker or a salesperson license who has earnestly applied himself or herself in preparing for the test has no difficulty finishing within the prescribed time limits. Naturally, the examination for broker license is more comprehensive in nature than the test for a real estate salesperson license.

Applicants are urged to arrive at the designated place for the examination promptly, and preferably 15 minutes prior to the scheduled time for the start of the test. Anxiety about being late and missing part of the time allotted to complete the test is detrimental to the candidate's chances of passing the examination. Also late examinees are required to waive the normal allotted time.

The usual rules for examinations apply—conversation is not permitted, the use of notes or references to texts is strictly forbidden, dishonest practice of any kind will result in a nonpassing grade, and may be grounds for denying future examinations (Business and Professions Code Section 10153.1 and Regulation

2763). Pursuant to legislation that became effective January 1, 1984, the Department and other testing agencies are affected by the provisions of law relating to test security. This legislation added Sections 496 and 497 to the Business and Professions Code. These sections provide that the Department may deny, suspend, revoke or restrict the license of an applicant or licensee who subverts or attempts to subvert a licensing examination. Conduct that constitutes subversion includes but is not limited to the following:

1. Removing exam material from a test site

2. Reproducing exam material without authorization

3. Using paid test takers for the purpose of reconstructing an examination

4. Using improperly obtained test questions to prepare persons for examination

5. Selling, distributing, or buying exam material

6. Cheating during an exam

7. Possessing unauthorized equipment or information during an examination

8. Impersonating an examinee or having an impersonator take an examination

Examination Sessions

In administering examinations, the same procedure is followed in both morning and afternoon sessions. The applicant receives prepared instructions, scratch paper, an examination booklet, answer sheet, and a special pencil. Answers must be recorded on the answer sheet and care must be exercised in marking the space provided for the examinee's selection of what examinee considers to be the correct alternative. Following is an example:

EXAMINATION BOOKLET	ANSWER SHEET

22. When examinees and licensees refer to the Reference Book, as published by the Department of Real Estate, they should use:
(a) the first edition
(b) any edition available
(c) the 1960 edition
(d) the latest edition published
	A B C D
	22 O O O O
	    A B C D
	23 O O O O
	    A B C D
	24 O O O O
	    A B C D
	25 O O O O

It is most important that the number on the answer sheet coincide with the number of the question in the examination booklet because misplaced answers become wrong answers. If more than one answer is marked on a question, no credit is given for that question. An answer may be changed by erasing and marking another.

No question is meant to be a trick or catch question. Interpret the words according to their commonly accepted meanings. Look over the entire test before beginning to work and apportion your time to the best advantage. It is wise to read all questions completely and attempt to answer every question.

Check carefully to be sure you have not skipped any pages and that you have matched the numbers on the answer sheet to the numbers in the examination booklet, as there may be more numbers on the answer sheet than there are questions in the examination booklet.

Nothing but the examination booklet, the answer sheet, a special pencil, and slide rule or silent, battery-operated, pocket-size, electronic calculator without a print-out capability or an alphabetic keyboard, are allowed on your desk, other than the single page scratch paper for arithmetical calculations with which you will be supplied and which you MUST turn in with your answer sheet and examination booklet on completing the test.

New test items must be prepared periodically and new examinations constructed to reflect the changing conditions in the field of real estate. This is also necessary to maintain the validity and reliability of the license testing process in California, where such a large number of real estate license exams are given during the course of each year.

One of the most difficult tasks in the preparation of an effective exam is the preparation of test items phrased in such a manner that they truly probe the applicant's knowledge without making him or her wonder about their meaning. The questions must not be too difficult, too easy, unimportant, or inappropriate for any reason.

Multiple Choice Exam

All test items in the real estate exams are multiple choice. Each multiple choice item is constructed to provide several answers that seem to be correct. Although the examinee may feel that more than one answer has some element of correctness, the examinee must be able to eliminate the incorrect responses and choose the best answer.

Question Analyses

The following analyses of multiple choice questions should be helpful to the examinee preparing for a license exam.

1. Under no circumstances may a broker:
   - (a) receive a commission from both buyer and seller
   - (b) appoint a subagent
   - (c) misrepresent material facts
   - (d) sell the principal's property to a relative
   - (a) is incorrect. A broker may receive a commission from both parties provided both buyer and seller have knowledge of the arrangement.
   - (b) is incorrect. A broker may get prior consent from the principal to appoint other brokers as subagents to cooperate in selling the property.
   - (c) is correct. A material misrepresentation of fact is fraud. Acts of fraud are violations of law.
   - (d) is incorrect. The broker may sell to any purchaser provided the principal has full knowledge.

2. A valid bill of sale must contain:
   - (a) a date
   - (b) an acknowledgment
   - (c) the seller's signature
   - (d) a verification
   - (a) is incorrect. Although a date is advisable it is not required.
   - (b) is incorrect. The law does not require an acknowledgment.
   - (c) is correct. A bill of sale is an instrument that has been executed (signed) and delivered to convey title to personal property.
   - (d) is incorrect. Verification means to confirm the correctness of an instrument by an affidavit or oath. Verification may be desirable but not required.

Be alert for questions that call for a response such as: "All of the following statements are correct, except"; or "Which of the following are not liens?" In the following sample question, for example, three of the responses would be correct. The answer called for, however, is the incorrect statement.

3. A valid deed must contain all of the following, except:
   - (a) the signature of the grantor
   - (b) a granting clause
   - (c) an adequate description of the property
   - (d) an acknowledgment of the grantor's signature

A deed is a written instrument used to convey title to real property.

    (a) is a correct statement. The grantor is the person who passes title to another and without grantor's signature title will not pass.

    (b) is a correct statement. The granting clause is necessary to evidence the intent of the grantor.

    (c) is a correct statement. The property being transferred must be described so the grantor knows exactly what property is being conveyed to the grantee.

    (d) is the incorrect statement. An acknowledgment is only necessary to enable the deed to be recorded but is not required to make the deed valid.

Sample Multiple Choice Items

The following multiple choice items are examples of the types of questions that may appear in the examination. No answers are provided because it is felt the student may more effectively use these examples to test retention of material studied by answering them and checking answers against appropriate sources.

1. Real estate taxes become a lien on the property:
   (a) on July 1st of the applicable tax year
   (b) the first Monday of November of the fiscal tax year
   (c) if not paid by December 10 of the tax year
   (d) on January 1st of each year

2. Tax delinquent real property not redeemed by the owner during the 5-year statutory redemption period is deeded to:
   (a) the city
   (b) the county
   (c) the state
   (d) the school district

3. Crowell bought the contents of a store for $9,300. Crowell sold the goods for $33\frac{1}{3}\%$ more than they cost, but lost 15% of the selling price in bad debts. His profit on the venture was:
   (a) $18\frac{1}{3}\%$
   (b) $1,240
   (c) $1,860
   (d) $3,100

4. In a typical percentage lease, rent is calculated as a percentage of:
   (a) assets of the lessee's business
   (b) net sales of the lessee's business
   (c) gross sales of the lessee's business
   (d) net taxable income of the lessee's business

5. The position of trust assumed by the broker as an agent for a principal is described most accurately as:
   (a) a gratuitous relationship
   (b) a trustor relationship
   (c) a fiduciary relationship
   (d) an employment relationship

6. The Federal Housing Administration's role in financing the purchase of real property is to:
   (a) act as the lender of funds
   (b) insure loans made by approved lenders
   (c) purchase specific trust deeds
   (d) do all of the above

7. The instrument used to remove the lien of a trust deed from record is called a:
   (a) satisfaction
   (b) release
   (c) deed of reconveyance
   (d) certificate of redemption

8. Which item would be used by an appraiser in arriving at a net income for capitalization purposes?
   (a) cost of loans against the property
   (b) allowance for rent loss and vacancies
   (c) federal income tax
   (d) reserve for appreciation of buildings

9. The type of mortgage loan that permits borrowing additional funds at a later date is called:
   (a) an equitable mortgage
   (b) a junior mortgage
   (c) an open-end mortgage
   (d) an extendible mortgage

10. Private restrictions on the use of land may be created by:
    (a) private land use controls
    (b) written agreement
    (c) general plan restrictions in subdivisions
    (d) all of the above

11. Which approach to value would be given most consideration in an appraisal of a shopping center?
    (a) market data
    (b) cost
    (c) summation
    (d) income

12. A quitclaim deed conveys only the present right, title, and interest of the:
    (a) grantor
    (b) servient tenement
    (c) grantee
    (d) property

13. Broker Carter negotiated a lease for 3,000 square feet of warehouse storage space at a monthly rental of $2.00 per sq. ft. Carter's commission is 8% of the first year's gross rent. Carter will receive:
    (a) $4,720
    (b) $5,360
    (c) $5,760
    (d) none of the above

14. You are a California real estate broker. A prospect is referred to you by an out-of-state broker and a sale is consummated by you. You want to split your commission with the cooperating broker. Under the California Real Estate Law:
    (a) you may pay a commission to a broker of another state
    (b) you cannot divide a commission with a broker of another state
    (c) you can pay a commission to a broker of another state only if he is also licensed in California
    (d) none of the above

15. A loan to be completely repaid, principal and interest, by a series of regular equal installment payments is a:
    (a) straight loan
    (b) balloon payment loan
    (c) fully amortized loan
    (d) variable rate mortgage loan

16. The age of a house can be determined most accurately by inspecting which of the following:
    (a) physical condition of the house
    (b) architectural style of the house
    (c) tax assessor's records
    (d) recorded subdivision map

17. In a legal sales contract, the seller is often referred to as the:
    (a) trustor
    (b) divisor
    (c) donor
    (d) vendor

18. The instrument used to secure a loan on personal property is called a:
    (a) bill of sale
    (b) trust deed
    (c) security agreement
    (d) bill of exchange

19. Community property is property owned by:
    (a) churches
    (b) husband and wife
    (c) the municipality
    (d) the community

20. An apartment complex cost $450,000. It brings in a net income of $3,000 per month. The owner is making what percentage of return on the investment?
    (a) 7%
    (b) 8%
    (c) 11%
    (d) none of the above

21. A person holding title to real property in severalty would most likely have:
    (a) a life estate
    (b) an estate for years
    (c) ownership in common with others
    (d) sole ownership

22. Under the Federal Truth-in-Lending Law, two of the most critical facts that must be disclosed to buyers or borrowers are:
    (a) duration of the contract and discount rate
    (b) finance charge and annual percentage rate
    (c) carrying charge and advertising expense
    (d) installment payments and cancellation rights

23. Appraisals of single-family dwellings are usually based on:
    (a) capitalization of rental value
    (b) asking prices of comparable houses
    (c) sales prices of comparable properties
    (d) the assessed valuations

24. A contract based on an illegal consideration is:
    (a) valid
    (b) void
    (c) legal
    (d) enforceable

25. The California "standard form" policy of title insurance on real property insures against loss occasioned by:
    (a) a forgery in the chain of recorded title
    (b) liens or encumbrances not disclosed by official records
    (c) rights of parties in possession of the property
    (d) actions of governmental agencies regulating the use or occupancy of the property

26. A house sold for $113,900, which was 11% more than the cost of the house. The cost of the house was most nearly:
    (a) $99,960
    (b) $100,400
    (c) $101,370
    (d) $102,610

27. A secured real property loan usually consists of:
    (a) financing statement and trust deed
    (b) the debt (note) and the lien (deed of trust)
    (c) FHA or PMI insurance
    (d) security agreement and financing statement

28. During escrow, if an unresolved dispute should arise between the seller and buyer preventing the close of escrow, the escrow holder may legally:
    (a) arbitrate the dispute as a neutral party
    (b) rescind the escrow and return all documents and monies to the respective parties
    (c) file an interpleader action in court
    (d) do any of the above

29. Copies of all listings, deposit receipts, cancelled checks, and trust records must be retained by a licensed real estate broker for:
    (a) one year
    (b) two years
    (c) three years
    (d) five years

30. Parallel wooden members used to support floor and ceiling loads are called:
    (a) rafters
    (b) joists
    (c) headers
    (d) studs

31. When a loan is fully amortized by equal monthly payments of principal and interest, the amount applied to principal:
    (a) and interest remains constant
    (b) decreases while the interest payment increases
    (c) increases while the interest payment decreases
    (d) increases by a constant amount

32. Joint ownership of real property by two or more persons each of whom has an undivided interest (not necessarily equal) without right of survivorship is a:
    (a) tenancy in partnership
    (b) tenancy by the entireties
    (c) tenancy in common
    (d) leasehold tenancy

33. A "loss in value from any cause" is a common definition of:
    (a) economic obsolescence
    (b) depreciation
    (c) principle of contribution
    (d) adverse leverage

34. Which of the following is a lien?
    (a) an easement
    (b) a zoning restriction
    (c) an attachment
    (d) all of the above are liens

35. An owner sold a lot with a front footage of 120 feet and a depth of 300 feet for $3.50 a square foot. What was the selling price?
    (a) $12,600
    (b) $16,200
    (c) $54,500
    (d) $126,000

36. If an appraiser finds that the fair rent for a vacant parcel is $700 per month and the interest rate is 11%, what is the approximate indicated land value?
    (a) $54,545
    (b) $69,280
    (c) $76,360
    (d) $105,000

37. Economic obsolescence could result from each of the following, except:
    (a) new zoning laws
    (b) a city's leading industry moving out
    (c) misplacement of improvements
    (d) an outdated kitchen

38. Which of the following is an appraiser's primary concern in the analysis of residential property?
    (a) marketability and acceptability
    (b) square foot area
    (c) functional utility
    (d) fixed and operating expenses

39. A subordination clause in a trust deed may:
    (a) permit the obligation to be paid off ahead of schedule
    (b) prohibit the trustor from making an additional loan against the property before the trust deed is paid off
    (c) allow for periodic renegotiation and adjustment in the terms of the obligation
    (d) give priority to liens subsequently recorded against the property

40. In order to evaluate a vacant commercial site, an appraiser decides to use the land residual technique. Here is the information the appraiser gathered:
    Cost new of a proper building—$250,000;
    Estimated net income before recapture $32,800 per year; interest rate—8.5%;
    Estimated remaining economic life of building—40 years
    What is the approximate estimated value of the land using this technique?
    (a) $31,000
    (b) $47,000
    (c) $48,182
    (d) $62,353

41. In the diagram shown, how many square feet are contained in the living area of the dwelling only?
    (a) 2,236
    (b) 2,272
    (c) 2,476
    (d) Cannot be computed from information given.

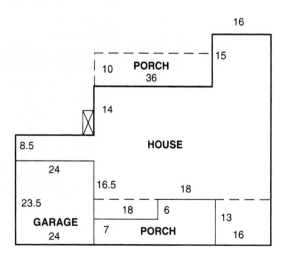

42. A contractor obtained a construction loan, and the loan funds are to be released in a series of progress payments. Most lenders disburse the last payment when the:
(a) building is completed
(b) notice of completion is filed
(c) buyer approves the construction
(d) period to file a lien has expired

43. To estimate the value of a parcel of real property an appraiser concentrated only on the cost to the buyer of acquiring a comparable, substitute parcel. This estimate approach is most similar to which of the following appraisal methods?
(a) cost
(b) income
(c) market
(d) none of the above

44. Brown purchased a $1,400 note secured by a second mortgage for investment purposes. The seller allowed a 15% discount. The note provided for monthly payments of $122 including interest at 9% per annum over a one-year term. Brown received all payments on the above terms. The yield on Brown's investment expressed as a percentage is:
(a) 23%
(b) 31%
(c) 34%
(d) 40%

45. The covenant of quiet enjoyment most directly relates to:
(a) nuisances maintained on adjoining property
(b) possession of real property
(c) title to real property
(d) all of the above

46. An interest in real property may be acquired either by prescription or by adverse possession. The interest resulting from prescription is:
(a) the right to use another's land
(b) a possessory title
(c) an equitable interest
(d) a private grant

47. Generally the taking of private land by governmental bodies for public use is governed by due process of law, and is accomplished through:
(a) exercise of the police power
(b) eminent domain
(c) reverter
(d) escheat

48. Governmental land use planning and zoning are important examples of:
(a) exercise of eminent domain
(b) use of police power
(c) deed restrictions
(d) encumbrances

49. Capitalization is a process whereby an appraiser:
(a) converts income into capital value
(b) determines depreciation reserves
(c) establishes cost of capital investment
(d) finds gross income or equity capital

50. In arriving at an effective gross income figure, an appraiser of rental property makes a deduction for:
(a) real property taxes
(b) repairs
(c) vacancy
(d) depreciation

AUTHORS' NOTE

As mentioned under the section entitled "Sample Multiple Choice Items," the Department of Real Estate Reference Book does not give the answers to the 50 questions presented in the DRE book. The authors believe the correct answers are as follows:

1. (D) 2. (C) 3. (B) 4. (C) 5. (C) 6. (B) 7. (C) 8. (B) 9. (C) 10. (D) 11. (D) 12. (A) 13. (C) 14. (A) 15. (C) 16. (C) 17. (D) 18. (C) 19. (B) 20. (B) 21. (D) 22. (B) 23. (C) 24. (B) 25. (A) 26. (D) 27. (B) 28. (C) 29. (C) 30. (D) 31. (C) 32. (C) 33. (B) 34. (C) 35. (D) 36. (C) 37. (D) 38. (A) 39. (D) 40. (D) 41. (C) 42. (D) 43. (C) 44. (D) 45. (B) 46. (A) 47. (B) 48. (B) 49. (A) 50. (C)

A complete 150-question practice examination, with answers, can be found in your textbook beginning on the next page.

Practice Examination

There is an old education adage that says the best way to learn is to "read, recite, and review." To help with your review, we present a 150-question practice examination. Real estate principles cover such a vast amount of material that every single topic cannot be tested. But the questions that follow are a representative sample of the types of questions that frequently appear in examinations.

TEST-TAKING TIPS

1. Take three passes through the examination. The first time through answer only the questions you know for sure, skipping everything else. This will give you a sense of success and allow you to get a feel for the examination. The second time through answer those questions you think you know, skipping those that are completely unfamiliar to you. The third time through, guess. **Remember to go back and answer all the questions**.

2. Reading pitfalls: Make sure you read all the answer choices. Sometimes an answer may appear correct, but another reading reveals the actual correct answer. Watch out for questions that say "**except for**," "**which is not**," and so on. The wording is confusing and you may select the wrong answer if you are not careful.

3. Here are some guessing suggestions:
   (a) Take the longest answer.
   (b) Do not take "all of the above" unless you can identify two answers as being right.
   (c) Two answers will be close and two answers are obviously wrong. Eliminate the obviously wrong two and select the most logical of the remaining two.

4. Math phobia: If math is not your strong point, leave the math until last. If you have done well on the rest of the examination, missing every math question will not usually cause you to fail. If you cannot do a math question, just take a wild guess.

5. Take the entire exam in one sitting in quiet surroundings. Upon completion, check your answers and look up the textbook discussion regarding the questions you missed.

DO NOT WRITE ON THE EXAMINATION. RUN SEVERAL PHOTO COPIES OF THE ANSWER SHEET ON THE NEXT PAGES. THIS TYPE OF ANSWER SHEET IS CURRENTLY (JANUARY 1996) USED BY THE DEPARTMENT OF REAL ESTATE FOR THE STATE EXAMINATION. THIS PROCEDURE WILL ALLOW YOU TO RETAKE THE EXAMINATION SEVERAL TIMES FOR PRACTICE.

DEPT. OF REAL ESTATE - ANSWER SHEET

RE FORM-420 (12/81) **PRINT CLEARLY**

SIDE 1

1. WRITE YOUR IDENTIFICATION NUMBER IN THE SPACES PROVIDED BELOW.

2. BELOW EACH DIGIT OF YOUR IDENTIFICATION NUMBER BLACKEN THE CIRCLE THAT CORRESPONDS TO THE DIGIT IN THAT COLUMN.

IDENTIFICATION NUMBER

1. EXAMINEE NAME (LAST, FIRST, & MIDDLE)

2. EXAMINEE SIGNATURE ▶

3. TITLE ☐ BROKER ☐ SALESPERSON

4. SESSION ☐ AM ☐ PM

5. EXAMINATION DATE

6. BIRTHDATE

7. EXAMINATION LOCATION ☐ LA ☐ SAC ☐ SF ☐ SD ☐ SA ☐ FR ☐ _____

8. EXAMINATION CODE NUMBER

9. BOOK NUMBER

PROPER MARK ● IMPROPER MARKS ⊙ ◐ ⊘ ⊗

IMPORTANT: ERASE CLEANLY ANY ANSWER YOU WISH TO CHANGE. SEE IMPORTANT MARKING INSTRUCTIONS ON SIDE 2.

ENTER FIRST 3 LETTERS OF LAST NAME
(A B C D E F G H I J K L M N O P Q R S T U V W X Y Z)

	A	B	C	D		A	B	C	D		A	B	C	D		A	B	C	D		A	B	C	D
1	○	○	○	○	21	○	○	○	○	41	○	○	○	○	61	○	○	○	○	81	○	○	○	○
2	○	○	○	○	22	○	○	○	○	42	○	○	○	○	62	○	○	○	○	82	○	○	○	○
3	○	○	○	○	23	○	○	○	○	43	○	○	○	○	63	○	○	○	○	83	○	○	○	○
4	○	○	○	○	24	○	○	○	○	44	○	○	○	○	64	○	○	○	○	84	○	○	○	○
5	○	○	○	○	25	○	○	○	○	45	○	○	○	○	65	○	○	○	○	85	○	○	○	○
6	○	○	○	○	26	○	○	○	○	46	○	○	○	○	66	○	○	○	○	86	○	○	○	○
7	○	○	○	○	27	○	○	○	○	47	○	○	○	○	67	○	○	○	○	87	○	○	○	○
8	○	○	○	○	28	○	○	○	○	48	○	○	○	○	68	○	○	○	○	88	○	○	○	○
9	○	○	○	○	29	○	○	○	○	49	○	○	○	○	69	○	○	○	○	89	○	○	○	○
10	○	○	○	○	30	○	○	○	○	50	○	○	○	○	70	○	○	○	○	90	○	○	○	○
11	○	○	○	○	31	○	○	○	○	51	○	○	○	○	71	○	○	○	○	91	○	○	○	○
12	○	○	○	○	32	○	○	○	○	52	○	○	○	○	72	○	○	○	○	92	○	○	○	○
13	○	○	○	○	33	○	○	○	○	53	○	○	○	○	73	○	○	○	○	93	○	○	○	○
14	○	○	○	○	34	○	○	○	○	54	○	○	○	○	74	○	○	○	○	94	○	○	○	○
15	○	○	○	○	35	○	○	○	○	55	○	○	○	○	75	○	○	○	○	95	○	○	○	○
16	○	○	○	○	36	○	○	○	○	56	○	○	○	○	76	○	○	○	○	96	○	○	○	○
17	○	○	○	○	37	○	○	○	○	57	○	○	○	○	77	○	○	○	○	97	○	○	○	○
18	○	○	○	○	38	○	○	○	○	58	○	○	○	○	78	○	○	○	○	98	○	○	○	○
19	○	○	○	○	39	○	○	○	○	59	○	○	○	○	79	○	○	○	○	99	○	○	○	○
20	○	○	○	○	40	○	○	○	○	60	○	○	○	○	80	○	○	○	○	100	○	○	○	○

DEPT. OF REAL ESTATE—ANSWER SHEET

IMPORTANT DIRECTIONS FOR MARKING ANSWERS

PRACTICE

	A	B	C	D
1	○	○	○	○
2	○	○	○	○
3	○	○	○	○
4	○	○	○	○
5	○	○	○	○

- Use only the black lead pencil provided.
- Do NOT use ink or ballpoint pens.
- Make heavy black marks that fill the circle completely.
- Erase cleanly any answer you wish to change.
- Make no stray marks on the answer sheet.
- NOTE: IMPROPER MARKS MAY SIGNIFICANTLY DELAY THE RELEASE OF YOUR RESULTS.

EXAMPLES

RIGHT
1 ● ○ ○ ○

WRONG
2 ○ ◐ ○ ○

WRONG
3 ○ ○ ⊗ ○

WRONG
4 ○ ○ ○ ◉

WRONG
5 ○ ○ ○ ◔

DO NOT WRITE IN THIS SPACE

#	A B C D	#	A B C D	#	A B C D	#	A B C D	#	A B C D
101	○ ○ ○ ○	121	○ ○ ○ ○	141	○ ○ ○ ○	161	○ ○ ○ ○	181	○ ○ ○ ○
102	○ ○ ○ ○	122	○ ○ ○ ○	142	○ ○ ○ ○	162	○ ○ ○ ○	182	○ ○ ○ ○
103	○ ○ ○ ○	123	○ ○ ○ ○	143	○ ○ ○ ○	163	○ ○ ○ ○	183	○ ○ ○ ○
104	○ ○ ○ ○	124	○ ○ ○ ○	144	○ ○ ○ ○	164	○ ○ ○ ○	184	○ ○ ○ ○
105	○ ○ ○ ○	125	○ ○ ○ ○	145	○ ○ ○ ○	165	○ ○ ○ ○	185	○ ○ ○ ○
106	○ ○ ○ ○	126	○ ○ ○ ○	146	○ ○ ○ ○	166	○ ○ ○ ○	186	○ ○ ○ ○
107	○ ○ ○ ○	127	○ ○ ○ ○	147	○ ○ ○ ○	167	○ ○ ○ ○	187	○ ○ ○ ○
108	○ ○ ○ ○	128	○ ○ ○ ○	148	○ ○ ○ ○	168	○ ○ ○ ○	188	○ ○ ○ ○
109	○ ○ ○ ○	129	○ ○ ○ ○	149	○ ○ ○ ○	169	○ ○ ○ ○	189	○ ○ ○ ○
110	○ ○ ○ ○	130	○ ○ ○ ○	150	○ ○ ○ ○	170	○ ○ ○ ○	190	○ ○ ○ ○
111	○ ○ ○ ○	131	○ ○ ○ ○	151	○ ○ ○ ○	171	○ ○ ○ ○	191	○ ○ ○ ○
112	○ ○ ○ ○	132	○ ○ ○ ○	152	○ ○ ○ ○	172	○ ○ ○ ○	192	○ ○ ○ ○
113	○ ○ ○ ○	133	○ ○ ○ ○	153	○ ○ ○ ○	173	○ ○ ○ ○	193	○ ○ ○ ○
114	○ ○ ○ ○	134	○ ○ ○ ○	154	○ ○ ○ ○	174	○ ○ ○ ○	194	○ ○ ○ ○
115	○ ○ ○ ○	135	○ ○ ○ ○	155	○ ○ ○ ○	175	○ ○ ○ ○	195	○ ○ ○ ○
116	○ ○ ○ ○	136	○ ○ ○ ○	156	○ ○ ○ ○	176	○ ○ ○ ○	196	○ ○ ○ ○
117	○ ○ ○ ○	137	○ ○ ○ ○	157	○ ○ ○ ○	177	○ ○ ○ ○	197	○ ○ ○ ○
118	○ ○ ○ ○	138	○ ○ ○ ○	158	○ ○ ○ ○	178	○ ○ ○ ○	198	○ ○ ○ ○
119	○ ○ ○ ○	139	○ ○ ○ ○	159	○ ○ ○ ○	179	○ ○ ○ ○	199	○ ○ ○ ○
120	○ ○ ○ ○	140	○ ○ ○ ○	160	○ ○ ○ ○	180	○ ○ ○ ○	200	○ ○ ○ ○

DO NOT WRITE IN THIS SPACE

NCS Trans-Optic 08-15193:321

DEPT. OF REAL ESTATE - ANSWER SHEET

SIDE 1

1. WRITE YOUR IDENTIFICATION NUMBER IN THE SPACES PROVIDED BELOW.

2. BELOW EACH DIGIT OF YOUR IDENTIFICATION NUMBER BLACKEN THE CIRCLE THAT CORRESPONDS TO THE DIGIT IN THAT COLUMN.

IDENTIFICATION NUMBER

RE FORM-420 (12/81)   PRINT CLEARLY

1. EXAMINEE NAME (LAST, FIRST, & MIDDLE)

2. EXAMINEE SIGNATURE
   ▶

3. TITLE
   ☐ BROKER   ☐ SALESPERSON

4. SESSION
   ☐ AM   ☐ PM

5. EXAMINATION DATE

6. BIRTHDATE

7. EXAMINATION LOCATION
   ☐ LA   ☐ SAC   ☐ SF   ☐ SD   ☐ SA   ☐ FR   ☐ _____

8. EXAMINATION CODE NUMBER

9. BOOK NUMBER

PROPER MARK ●   IMPROPER MARKS ⊙ ◐ ⊘ ⊗

IMPORTANT: ERASE CLEANLY ANY ANSWER YOU WISH TO CHANGE.
SEE IMPORTANT MARKING INSTRUCTIONS ON SIDE 2.

ENTER FIRST 3 LETTERS OF LAST NAME

(Answer grid, questions 1–100, each with options A B C D)

DEPT. OF REAL ESTATE—ANSWER SHEET

IMPORTANT DIRECTIONS FOR MARKING ANSWERS

PRACTICE

	A	B	C	D
1	○	○	○	○
2	○	○	○	○
3	○	○	○	○
4	○	○	○	○
5	○	○	○	○

- Use only the black lead pencil provided.
- Do NOT use ink or ballpoint pens.
- Make heavy black marks that fill the circle completely.
- Erase cleanly any answer you wish to change.
- Make no stray marks on the answer sheet.
- NOTE: IMPROPER MARKS MAY SIGNIFICANTLY DELAY THE RELEASE OF YOUR RESULTS.

EXAMPLES

RIGHT
1 ● ○ ○ ○
WRONG
2 ○ ⊘ ○ ○
WRONG
3 ○ ○ ⊗ ○
WRONG
4 ○ ○ ○ ◎
WRONG
5 ○ ○ ○ ◉

DO NOT

WRITE

IN THIS

SPACE

	A B C D		A B C D		A B C D		A B C D		A B C D
101	○○○○	121	○○○○	141	○○○○	161	○○○○	181	○○○○
102	○○○○	122	○○○○	142	○○○○	162	○○○○	182	○○○○
103	○○○○	123	○○○○	143	○○○○	163	○○○○	183	○○○○
104	○○○○	124	○○○○	144	○○○○	164	○○○○	184	○○○○
105	○○○○	125	○○○○	145	○○○○	165	○○○○	185	○○○○
106	○○○○	126	○○○○	146	○○○○	166	○○○○	186	○○○○
107	○○○○	127	○○○○	147	○○○○	167	○○○○	187	○○○○
108	○○○○	128	○○○○	148	○○○○	168	○○○○	188	○○○○
109	○○○○	129	○○○○	149	○○○○	169	○○○○	189	○○○○
110	○○○○	130	○○○○	150	○○○○	170	○○○○	190	○○○○
111	○○○○	131	○○○○	151	○○○○	171	○○○○	191	○○○○
112	○○○○	132	○○○○	152	○○○○	172	○○○○	192	○○○○
113	○○○○	133	○○○○	153	○○○○	173	○○○○	193	○○○○
114	○○○○	134	○○○○	154	○○○○	174	○○○○	194	○○○○
115	○○○○	135	○○○○	155	○○○○	175	○○○○	195	○○○○
116	○○○○	136	○○○○	156	○○○○	176	○○○○	196	○○○○
117	○○○○	137	○○○○	157	○○○○	177	○○○○	197	○○○○
118	○○○○	138	○○○○	158	○○○○	178	○○○○	198	○○○○
119	○○○○	139	○○○○	159	○○○○	179	○○○○	199	○○○○
120	○○○○	140	○○○○	160	○○○○	180	○○○○	200	○○○○

DO

NOT

WRITE

IN

THIS

SPACE

PRACTICE EXAMINATION

1. A "loss in value from any cause" is a definition of:
   (a) economic obsolescence
   (b) depreciation
   (c) leverage
   (d) goodwill

2. A couple recently married and each had children from a previous marriage. They wish to take title to property so that they each could pass their share to their own children by will. The best form of title would be:
   (a) joint tenancy
   (b) severalty
   (c) community property
   (d) tenancy in whole

3. A valid deed passes title when it is:
   (a) signed
   (b) recorded
   (c) delivered
   (d) acknowledged

4. When a governmental body takes private real estate for public use, the process is called:
   (a) eminent domain
   (b) police power
   (c) zoning
   (d) adverse possession

5. The main purpose of the Truth-in-Lending Act is to:
   (a) prevent usury
   (b) require disclosure of credit terms
   (c) reduce the cost of credit
   (d) regulate annual percentage rates

6. The difference between judgment liens and mechanic's liens is:
   (a) mechanic's liens are general liens
   (b) mechanic's liens can take priority before they are recorded
   (c) mechanic's liens are voluntary liens
   (d) judgment liens are involuntary liens

7. Private restrictions (CC&Rs) cannot be conveyed by:
   (a) deed
   (b) written agreement
   (c) easement
   (d) general plan restrictions in a subdivision

8. On September 1, 2000, Garcia agreed to purchase Chan's home. Both parties agreed that possession would take place October 30, 2000, and that property taxes would be prorated as of date of possession. On December 1, 2000, Chan paid the property taxes for the year 2000–2001. According to the escrow closing statement, which of the following is true?
   (a) Garcia paid Chan for 8 months' taxes
   (b) Garcia paid Chan for 4 months' taxes
   (c) Chan paid Garcia for 8 months' taxes
   (d) Chan paid Garcia for 4 months' taxes

9. A quitclaim deed conveys only the present rights of the:

(a) grantor

(b) servient tenant

(c) grantee

(d) trustee

10. To have a valid recorded homestead, certain elements are essential. Which of the following is not essential?

(a) a description of the property

(b) a statement of residence

(c) to be a married person

(d) to be recorded

11. A licensed loan broker arranged for a loan and has the borrower sign the required statement. The broker then discovers that there is a lien that the borrower did not disclose. If the loan cannot be arranged due to the lien, the borrower would be liable for:

(a) cost and expenses incurred to date

(b) no cost and expenses

(c) all cost and expenses and half the commission

(d) none of the above

12. A person purchased a property for $200,000, which was equal to $4.75 per square foot. The rectangular lot was 300 feet deep. The cost per front foot was:

(a) $1,425

(b) $950

(c) $827

(d) $793

13. Which of the following is not essential to form an agency?

(a) a fiduciary relationship

(b) agreement of the parties

(c) consideration

(d) competent parties

14. An owner sells a property for cash and receives $67,100 from escrow. The only expenses were a 6% commission and $517 in other expenses. The property sold for:

(a) $71,643

(b) $71,933

(c) $72,591

(d) $73,137

15. A real estate agent must disclose all material facts to a seller principal. Which of the following is considered a material fact?

(a) the buyer's racial background

(b) the agent's knowledge of a pending better offer

(c) the lender's requirement that a buyer pay a loan fee

(d) that the buyer has a medical problem

16. In appraising improved property, the least important factor is:

(a) sales price

(b) highest and best use

(c) prices of comparables

(d) assessed value

17. Community apartments and condominium projects fall within the subdivision laws of the California Real Estate Law when they contain:

(a) one or more units

(b) two or more units

(c) three or more units

(d) five or more units

18. Studs are attached to rest upon the:

(a) mud sill

(b) subfloor

(c) header

(d) sole plate

19. A person borrowed 80% of the value of a condo. The loan interest rate was 9%. The first-year interest was $5,050. The value of the condo was:

(a) $63,313

(b) $65,459

(c) $70,139

(d) none of the above

20. Adams, Brown, and Chow are owners of commercial land as joint tenants. Adams dies and is survived by Brown and Chow. Which is correct?

(a) Brown and Chow receive title by succession.

(b) The joint tenancy is terminated.

(c) Adams's interest terminates.

(d) Brown and Chow are now tenants in common.

21. To completely fence the NW quarter of the SE quarter of Section 3 would take how much fencing?

(a) 2 miles

(b) 1 mile

(c) ½ mile

(d) ¼ mile

22. When both the landlord and tenant mutually agree to cancel a lease, their action is called:

(a) a termination

(b) a rescission

(c) a release

(d) an abandonment

23. An amortized loan has equal monthly installments consisting of:

(a) interest alone

(b) principal alone

(c) principal and interest

(d) principal, interest, taxes, and insurance

24. Which of the following is an operating expense to be subtracted from gross income when appraising a property using the income approach?

(a) interest payments

(b) principal payments

(c) property taxes

(d) all of the above

25. The word "emblements" refers to:

(a) attachments to a contract

(b) growing crops

(c) machinery

(d) fixtures on a building

26. A salesperson working for a broker had been wrongfully selling information to a loan company. When the broker, who had been using reasonable supervision, discovered this, the salesperson was fired. Based upon the information given:

(a) the broker is probably not liable if he or she had no knowledge of the wrongdoing

(b) both the salesperson and the broker are liable

(c) there is no liability

(d) the salesperson is licensed to sell loan information in his name only

27. Which of the following is worded incorrectly?

(a) Federal National Mortgage Association (Fannie Mae)

(b) Government National Mortgage Association (Ginnie Mae)

(c) Federal Housing Association (FHA)

(d) Department of Veterans Affairs (DVA)

28. Williams entered into a 9-month oral lease on July 1 to start on September 1 at a rate of $1,000 per month. On August 15, Williams backs out of the lease. The lease is:

(a) unenforceable

(b) enforceable

(c) void

(d) restricted by the Statute of Frauds

29. Title insurance does not protect a buyer against:

(a) forgery in the chain of title

(b) lack of capacity of the grantor

(c) recorded easements

(d) zoning restrictions

30. If state housing codes conflict with local codes, usually:

(a) state codes prevail

(b) local codes prevail

(c) the stricter of the two prevail

(d) the more lenient of the two prevail

31. A broker received deposits from principals and incorrectly placed the funds in a safe for several days before putting the funds in the broker's trust fund account at the bank. The broker is guilty of:

    (a) conversion

    (b) commingling

    (c) misrepresentation

    (d) fraud

32. A husband dies intestate. His separate property is distributed to his wife and two children as follows:

    (a) all to the wife

    (b) half to the wife and half to the children

    (c) all to the children

    (d) one third to the wife, the rest to the children

33. Under the Subdivided Lands Act, the Real Estate Commissioner is primarily concerned with:

    (a) physical design and layout

    (b) health facilities

    (c) financing and marketing arrangements

    (d) none of the above

34. Jones leases a home from Santos under a 3-month written lease. Upon expiration of the lease, Jones retains possession. Santos has not decided upon the next step. Jones has an estate at:

    (a) will

    (b) sufferance

    (c) years

    (d) tenancy

35. An investor has an apartment building with no vacancies in which each unit rents for $600. The investor raises the rent 15% and suffers a 15% vacancy factor. Rental income:

    (a) increases

    (b) decreases

    (c) remains the same

    (d) the question cannot be answered with the information given

36. A valid homestead is filed by a head of a household. The residence is later sold to a buyer giving a grant deed. The sale is:

    (a) invalid unless an abandonment of homestead is recorded

    (b) valid

    (c) unenforceable if the grantee wishes to back out

    (d) void because of lack of implied warranties

37. The maximum amount of personal funds a broker may have in a trust fund account to cover charges and not be guilty of commingling is:

    (a) $50

    (b) $200

    (c) $500

    (d) $1,000

38. Property is being sold where the buyer is going to take over the seller's existing loan. To avoid legal conflict before closing, the real estate agent should check to be sure the loan does not include:

(a) a release clause

(b) a prepayment penalty

(c) an alienation clause

(d) a subordination clause

39. The stated policy of the Real Estate Commissioner is to create an equal opportunity industry. This means agents should:

(a) maintain an attitude free from bias

(b) realize that race, creed, and color are not material facts

(c) do unto others as you would have them do unto you

(d) all of the above

40. A subdivider sold five lots to one buyer and optioned five other lots to another buyer. The subdivider must:

(a) notify the Department of Real Estate of a material change

(b) close the option sales within three business days

(c) record the sales within five business days

(d) not sell five lots to a single purchaser

41. Under the Federal Truth-in-Lending Law (Regulation Z), certain borrowers have———days to rescind the loan:

(a) 30

(b) 10

(c) 5

(d) 3

42. A seller employed a broker under an open listing. The seller indicated to the broker that the roof leaked. While showing the home to a buyer, the broker stated that the roof was in good condition. After the sale the buyer discovered that the roof leaked. The buyer would logically sue:

(a) only the broker

(b) both the seller and broker for specific performance

(c) both the seller and broker for damages

(d) only the seller

43. Under Division 6 of the Uniform Commercial Code (Bulk Sale), a public notice must be given 12 days before transfer by the:

(a) seller

(b) buyer

(c) creditors

(d) all of the above

44. The value of the subject property as set by the price of comparable properties is based on the principle of:

(a) change

(b) regression

(c) substitution

(d) highest and best use

45. A California real estate broker sold a ranch in Montana to a California resident. A Montana broker assisted in the sale. To show appreciation, the California broker gave part of the commission to the Montana broker. This action was:

    (a) unlawful, because the California broker was not licensed in Montana

    (b) unlawful, because the Montana broker was not licensed in California

    (c) lawful

    (d) none of the above

46. Income tax benefits for homeowners include deductions for:

    (a) interest on home loans

    (b) depreciation on buildings

    (c) expenses and repairs

    (d) all of the above

47. All Realtors in California are bound by which Code of Ethics?

    (a) National Mortgage Brokers Association

    (b) National Association of Real Estate Brokers

    (c) National Association of Realtors

    (d) all of the above

48. In issuing a policy of title insurance, the title company is least likely to make an on-site inspection if the policy is:

    (a) a CLTA standard owners policy

    (b) an ALTA extended policy

    (c) a construction loan policy

    (d) a lender's policy

49. A real estate broker must retain copies of all listings and deposit receipts for how many years?

    (a) 1

    (b) 3

    (c) 4

    (d) 5

50. The first half of real property taxes are due and payable on November 1. They become delinquent after December 10, at which time a penalty is added to the amount. The penalty is:

    (a) 10%

    (b) 8%

    (c) 6%

    (d) 3%

51. A Notice of Nonresponsibility is usually posted and recorded by an owner when a:

    (a) bulk sale takes place

    (b) tenant makes repairs

    (c) transfer of title takes place

    (d) mechanic's lien is filed

52. Covenants and conditions are frequently placed in deeds. If a covenant or condition is breached, the enforcement is:

(a) more severe for a condition

(b) more severe for a covenant

(c) equal for both a condition and a covenant

(d) under current law neither can be enforced

53. Which of the following is not a fiduciary relationship?

(a) broker to seller

(b) trustor to beneficiary

(c) attorney to client

(d) attorney-in-fact to principal

54. An appraiser determines that the market rent for a parcel of land is $700 per month and that interest (capitalization) rates should be 11%. The approximate value is:

(a) $54,545

(b) $69,280

(c) $76,360

(d) $105,000

55. A parcel of land is planned to be divided into nine parcels, with the intention of selling three parcels per year for each of the next three years. The owner:

(a) must satisfy the Subdivision Map Act

(b) must report to the Real Estate Commissioner, but need not conform to the Subdivision Map Act

(c) must comply with the Subdivision Map Act and the Subdivided Lands Act

(d) need not comply with any special law, as fewer than five lots are being sold in any one year

56. Which of the following is a less-than-freehold estate?

(a) fee simple defeasible

(b) fee simple absolute

(c) leasehold estate

(d) life estate

57. A lease that lies between the primary lease and the sublessee is a:

(a) sandwich lease

(b) percentage lease

(c) ground lease

(d) wedge lease

58. An easement acquired by prescription can be lost by nonuse for a period of:

(a) 5 years

(b) 3 years

(c) 2 years

(d) 1 year

59. A corporation built a large tract of homes and hired a handyman to take care of the maintenance. He was given extra compensation for showing the homes on weekends to prospective buyers.
   (a) The corporation is not in violation of real estate regulations.
   (b) The handyman could be fined for showing homes without a license.
   (c) As an employee, the handyman does not need a license to show homes.
   (d) All corporate employees and officers selling the homes must be licensed.

60. After a Trustee's Sale, any money remaining after paying lienholders and costs is remitted to the:
   (a) trustor
   (b) trustee
   (c) beneficiary
   (d) mortgagor

61. The person who acquires title to real property under the terms of a will is known as the:
   (a) devisee
   (b) administrator
   (c) testator
   (d) executrix

62. A "commercial acre" is:
   (a) 43,560 sq. ft.
   (b) a normal acre, less deductions for streets and setbacks
   (c) an acre zoned for commercial use
   (d) 42,513 sq. ft.

63. Legal seizure of property to be held for payment of money, pending the outcome of a lawsuit, is called:
   (a) a writ of execution
   (b) an attachment
   (c) an abstract of judgment
   (d) a lis pendens

64. Shay gives a quitclaim deed to Wilson for a parcel of real estate. Wilson does not record the deed. Which of the following is true?
   (a) Deed is invalid as between Shay and Wilson.
   (b) Deed is invalid as between Shay and Wilson but valid to subsequent recorded interest.
   (c) Deed is valid as between Shay and Wilson but invalid as to subsequent recorded interest without notice.
   (d) Deed is valid as between Shay and Wilson and valid as to subsequent recorded interest without notice.

65. When public records are used to establish a chain of title, a written summary of the results is known as:
   (a) a guarantee of title
   (b) an abstract of title
   (c) an opinion of title
   (d) an affidavit of title

66. After a mortgage is executed and recorded, title:
    (a) remains with the mortgagor
    (b) transfers to the mortgagee
    (c) is given to the trustee
    (d) remains with the trustor

67. A real estate contract by a married couple under the age of 18 is:
    (a) void
    (b) voidable
    (c) unenforceable
    (d) valid

68. An exclusive agency listing differs from an exclusive right-to-sell listing in that:
    (a) only the exclusive right-to-sell listing must have a definite termination date
    (b) the broker is entitled to a commission if the owner sells the property under the exclusive agency listing
    (c) only the exclusive right-to-sell listing must be in writing to be enforceable
    (d) under the exclusive right-to-sell listing, the broker is entitled to a commission no matter who sells the property during the term of the listing

69. A buyer in a land project can rescind the purchase for any reason and obtain a refund within:
    (a) 3 days
    (b) 5 days
    (c) 10 days
    (d) 14 days

70. Which of the following represents the four essentials of value?
    (a) scarcity, cost, demand, utility
    (b) utility, transferability, cost, demand
    (c) transferability, utility, demand, scarcity
    (d) demand, cost, utility, price

71. All of the following are contracts, except:
    (a) escrow instructions
    (b) a listing agreement
    (c) a deed
    (d) a deposit receipt

72. The cost approach to value has limited use when appraising:
    (a) a new building
    (b) tract homes
    (c) museum buildings
    (d) special-purpose properties

73. When an agent violates antidiscrimination regulations, the Real Estate Commissioner can:
    (a) sue for damages
    (b) file a criminal action
    (c) revoke a license
    (d) all of the above

74. Zowski holds a life estate measured by his own life. He leased the property to Anderson for five years, but died two months later. The lease is:

    (a) still valid

    (b) no longer valid

    (c) invalid from the inception

    (d) binding on the heirs of Zowski

75. An owner sold a lot for $70,400, realizing a 20% profit over what was originally paid for the lot. The profit is:

    (a) $11,733

    (b) $14,080

    (c) $13,714

    (d) $12,509

76. Which of the following is not essential to a general contract?

    (a) that it be in writing

    (b) mutual consent

    (c) capable parties

    (d) lawful object

77. An example of a lender who frequently uses loan correspondents and funds large commercial loans is a:

    (a) savings bank

    (b) commercial bank

    (c) credit union

    (d) life insurance company

78. RESPA (Real Estate Settlement Procedures Act) requires that certain lenders and/or closers must deliver a Uniform Settlement Statement to the borrower and seller within:

    (a) 10 days after the loan commitment

    (b) 3 days prior to closing

    (c) 5 days after closing

    (d) on or before the date of closing

79. A deeds a title to B with the condition that B never sell alcoholic beverages on the property. B has a:

    (a) less-than-freehold estate

    (b) fee simple absolute

    (c) fee simple defeasible

    (d) periodic tenancy

80. An abstract of judgment can be recorded:

    (a) in any county

    (b) only in the county where the judgment is to be placed

    (c) only in the county where the debtor has real property

    (d) only in the county where the creditor resides

81. The amount of real estate sales commission is:

    (a) regulated by the Real Estate Commissioner

    (b) subject to negotiation

    (c) fixed by trade groups

    (d) governed by state law

82. A roof that is pitched with two sloping sides is called a:
    (a) hip
    (b) gable
    (c) mansard
    (d) gambrel

83. A contract that is executory:
    (a) has not been performed
    (b) has been signed
    (c) is completed
    (d) has been notarized

84. How much money would have to be invested at a 7% return to give an investor $200 per month?
    (a) $34,286
    (b) $48,000
    (c) $43,705
    (d) $39,325

85. A person who feels he or she has been discriminated against in seeking housing can file a complaint with:
    (a) the Federal Trade Commission
    (b) the Rumford Commission
    (c) the Unruh Commission
    (d) the Fair Employment and Housing Commission

86. If a borrower fails to make a loan payment, which financing instrument would be to the borrower's advantage?
    (a) deed of trust
    (b) mortgage
    (c) contract of sale
    (d) lease

87. After a loan has been granted, rapid unanticipated inflation would most benefit a:
    (a) borrower with an ARM loan
    (b) fixed-interest rate beneficiary
    (c) trustor with fixed interest rate
    (d) trustee

88. The most difficult depreciation to correct is:
    (a) physical
    (b) economic
    (c) functional
    (d) accrued

89. Properties A and B each have a value of $200,000. Property A was appraised using a capitalization rate of 9%, whereas Property B was appraised using a capitalization rate of 10%.
    (a) Property B has more income than Property A.
    (b) Property B has less income than Property A.
    (c) Property A and Property B have the same income.
    (d) none of the above

90. Which of the following is not appurtenant or incidental to the land?

    (a) stock in mutual water company

    (b) an easement

    (c) reasonable airspace

    (d) a picked crop

91. Recording of an instrument gives:

    (a) actual notice

    (b) constructive notice

    (c) preliminary notice

    (d) recorded notice

92. A rate of interest that exceeds the legal rate is the:

    (a) nominal rate

    (b) going rate

    (c) stated rate

    (d) none of the above

93. The Federal National Mortgage Association (Fannie Mae) was primarily created to:

    (a) insure low-income housing loans

    (b) increase the amount of money available to finance housing

    (c) insure bank depositors for up to $100,000 per account

    (d) lengthen the term for real estate loans

94. Broker Sanchez and Broker Roberts both have an open listing on a home. Broker Sanchez showed the home to a buyer who decided not to make an offer. A month later, Broker Roberts showed the same home to the same buyer who then decided to buy. The seller owes a commission to:

    (a) Broker Sanchez only

    (b) Broker Sanchez and Broker Roberts

    (c) Broker Roberts only

    (d) Broker Sanchez, who will need to split it with Broker Roberts

95. Both the buyer and the seller initial the liquidated damages clause in a deposit receipt. Later the buyer backs out. The seller is entitled to:

    (a) actual damages

    (b) no damages

    (c) punitive damages

    (d) liquidated damages

96. A person borrowed $2,500 on a straight note. In eight months, $150 in interest was paid. The interest rate is:

    (a) 8.4%

    (b) 9%

    (c) 10.1%

    (d) 10.6%

97. If a dispute arises during escrow and the buyer and seller cannot agree, the escrow holder may legally:

(a) file an interpleader action

(b) return all funds to the respective parties

(c) cancel the escrow

(d) do all of the above

98. The SW quarter of the NW quarter of the SE quarter of the SE quarter of the NW quarter of a section contains:

(a) 1¼ acres

(b) 2½ acres

(c) 5 acres

(d) none of the above

99. A couple on a deed that reads "husband and wife" without indicating how the title is to be held will be presumed to:

(a) be joint tenants

(b) hold community property

(c) be tenants in common

(d) hold severalty ownership

100. An owner hired a broker to act as property manager and collect rent from tenants. Rents are due on the first of the month. On June 1, the broker collected rents from all but one of the tenants. The next day the owner died. On June 2, the broker asked the remaining tenant for the rent. The tenant refused to give the rent money to the broker. The tenant:

(a) must give the rent to the broker

(b) should not give the rent to anyone but the heirs or the court

(c) is in default by not giving the rent to the broker

(d) need not pay the rent

101. Which of the following employment situations is primarily concerned with results, not direction, of work?

(a) employer-employee

(b) jobber

(c) independent contractor

(d) agent

102. If there is no notice of completion, a subcontractor must file a mechanic's lien in:

(a) 10 days

(b) 30 days

(c) 60 days

(d) 90 days

103. Which of the following is not issued by the Department of Real Estate?

(a) real estate broker license

(b) prepaid rental listing license

(c) real estate sales license

(d) escrow license

104. The fine for an unlicensed person who receives a real estate commission is:
    (a) $10,000
    (b) $1,000
    (c) $100
    (d) none of the above

105. Probate hearings are handled in:
    (a) Superior Court
    (b) Municipal Court
    (c) Small Claims Court
    (d) Inheritance Court

106. An out-of-state developer wishes to sell lots to Californians. All of the following apply, except:
    (a) sales agreements must carry a disclaimer approved by the California Real Estate Commissioner
    (b) advertising must carry a disclaimer approved by the California Real Estate Commissioner
    (c) the Subdivision Map Act will be enforced
    (d) all of the above apply

107. The $500,000 exemption on the profits from the sale of a qualified principal residence apply for homeowners who are:
    (a) 50 years or older
    (b) married and file joint tax returns
    (c) native Californians only
    (d) earning income of $125,000 or less

108. Equity in real property is the:
    (a) cash-flow value
    (b) total of all mortgages
    (c) difference between mortgage balance and value
    (d) appraised value

109. The maximum time urban real estate can be leased is:
    (a) 99 years
    (b) 51 years
    (c) 30 years
    (d) 15 years

110. Which of the following is not required to acquire title to unimproved land by adverse possession?
    (a) minimum of five years
    (b) open and notorious use
    (c) color of title or claim of right
    (d) that the acquiring party live on the property

111. Certain unities are required to maintain a joint tenancy relationship. They are:
    (a) grantee, unity, possession, claim
    (b) time, title, interest, unity
    (c) interest, time, title, possession
    (d) ownership, time, title, interest

112. The Health and Safety Code specifies minimum standards for water and sewer facilities in a new subdivision. Approval and control for local water and sewer rest with the:
    (a) Health Officer
    (b) Real Estate Commissioner
    (c) Building Inspector
    (d) Planning Commissioner

113. Most real estate syndicates in California use which form of ownership?
    (a) corporation
    (b) limited partnership
    (c) real estate investment trust
    (d) joint venture

114. The words "procuring cause" would have the most important meaning under which circumstance?
    (a) a lawsuit by the buyer
    (b) a dispute between brokers over a commission
    (c) a disagreement between buyer and seller
    (d) a dispute over loan proceeds

115. Which of the following would violate the advertising provisions of the Truth-in-Lending Law? Ads that state:
    (a) no money down
    (b) $100,000 all-cash sale
    (c) $200,000 price, easy terms
    (d) qualification for FHA financing

116. In the event that a seller backs out of a valid purchase contract, all of the following are true, except:
    (a) the buyer could sue for damages
    (b) the buyer could sue for specific performance
    (c) the broker could sue for damages
    (d) the broker could sue for specific performance

117. A federal law regarding the sale of subdivided lots is the:
    (a) Subdivision Map Act
    (b) Interstate Land Sales Full Disclosure Act
    (c) Land Project Act
    (d) Subdivided Lands Act

118. The instrument used to transfer title to personal property is the:
    (a) deed
    (b) bill of lading
    (c) lease
    (d) bill of sale

119. An example of functional obsolescence is a:
    (a) one-car garage
    (b) cracked foundation
    (c) truck route in front of a home
    (d) detrimental change in zoning

120. When the Real Estate Commissioner receives a valid complaint against a licensee, the Commissioner institutes action against the licensee under the:

(a) Business and Professions Code

(b) Administrative Procedures Code

(c) Real Estate Code

(d) Rules and Regulations Code

121. When a business opportunity is sold, frequently a price is paid for continued patronage. This continued patronage is called:

(a) goodwill

(b) blue sky

(c) turnover

(d) future sales

122. A cloud on the title could be created by:

(a) a recorded homestead

(b) a deed of trust paid, but never reconveyed

(c) an easement for utility poles

(d) recorded covenants and conditions

123. A written agency between a real estate broker and a principal would not be:

(a) executed

(b) implied

(c) expressed

(d) a contract

124. The lowest interest rates and costs would probably be found with:

(a) CAL-Vet loans

(b) FHA loans

(c) conventional loans

(d) VA loans

125. When a real estate broker acts exclusively for the buyer or seller, but not for both, it is called a:

(a) dual agency

(b) exclusive agency

(c) divided agency

(d) single agency

126. The most important factor in estimating the value of residential homes is:

(a) square footage

(b) demand by ready, willing, and able buyers

(c) floor plan

(d) rent

127. Which of the following is correct regarding net listings?

(a) They are not allowed in California.

(b) The broker has the exclusive right to sell the property.

(c) The broker is required to disclose the full commission prior to close of sale.

(d) The seller's net cannot exceed the difference between the sales price and the appraised value.

128. Once an abstract of judgment is recorded it remains in force for:
   (a) 1 year
   (b) 3 years
   (c) 5 years
   (d) 10 years

129. The "secondary mortgage market" refers to:
   (a) the resale of existing loans
   (b) the granting of second loans
   (c) mortgage brokers who arrange loans
   (d) none of the above

130. Real estate loans that are pegged to some index and in which the interest rate may change during the term of the loan are called:
   (a) conventional loans
   (b) FHA loans
   (c) ARM loans
   (d) seller carry loans

131. The unauthorized use of the term "Realtor®" is:
   (a) a criminal offense
   (b) a violation of California Real Estate Law
   (c) not a problem if the person is a licensed broker
   (d) not punishable in California

132. If a tenant is late on the rent, an owner should serve:
   (a) a 30-day notice
   (b) a 3-day notice
   (c) an unlawful detainer warrant
   (d) an eviction notice

133. Once a real estate broker's license has been revoked or suspended, his or her sales associates can:
   (a) be paid commissions earned prior to the suspension
   (b) collect rents as property managers
   (c) continue to work on existing listings
   (d) take new listings with a post date on the contract

134. A woman died and left an estate. Thirty-seven percent went to her husband, 18% went to each of the two sons and one daughter. The rest went to a college foundation. The college foundation received $37,000. The daughter's share was:
   (a) $74,000
   (b) $84,000
   (c) $96,000
   (d) $124,000

135. Adams sells Blackacre to Baker. Baker places the deed to Blackacre in his safety deposit box without recording same. Baker lets Adams retain possession of Blackacre. Some time later, Adams sells Blackacre to Collins. Collins records her deed and takes possession of Blackacre from Adams. When Baker gains knowledge of the transfer from Adams to Collins, he could do which of the following?
   (a) Record his prior deed and charge Collins rent.
   (b) Take possession away from Collins and let Collins collect the money she paid to Adams.
   (c) Sue Collins.
   (d) Do nothing regarding Collins if she had no prior knowledge of the transfer to Baker.

136. Personal property attached to a building in such a way that it becomes part of the building is known as:

(a) an appurtenance

(b) a fixture

(c) an attachment

(d) a dedication

137. The situation by which property reverts to the state for lack of heirs is called:

(a) escheat

(b) eminent domain

(c) condemnation

(d) intestate succession

138. When work is done per the Street Improvement Act of 1911, property owners are allowed to pay their pro rata share within how many days before it goes to bond?

(a) 30

(b) 60

(c) 90

(d) 180

139. The real property tax year runs:

(a) January 1 to December 31

(b) March 1 to February 28

(c) July 1 to June 30

(d) December 10 to December 9

140. Ingress and egress apply to:

(a) fee simple

(b) lease

(c) encumbrance

(d) less than freehold

141. In qualifying a buyer for a loan, the least important is:

(a) regular income

(b) spouse's income

(c) monthly debts

(d) overtime pay

142. Rates for title insurance are established by:

(a) title insurance companies

(b) the Department of Real Estate

(c) the Department of Insurance

(d) the Corporation Commissioner

143. A duly licensed real estate salesperson may lawfully receive a commission from the:

(a) seller

(b) escrow holder

(c) broker

(d) all of the above

144. A real estate broker would not be disciplined by the Real Estate Commissioner for:
    (a) making a secret profit
    (b) making a false promise
    (c) making a misrepresentation
    (d) acting as a dual agent with full knowledge and approval of all parties

145. "Time is of the essence" would most likely be found in which contract?
    (a) a deposit receipt
    (b) a listing agreement
    (c) an option
    (d) a lease

146. The important case of the U.S. Supreme Court that prohibits discrimination in housing is:
    (a) *Wellenkamp v. Wilson*
    (b) *Jones v. Mayer*
    (c) *Unruh v. Smith*
    (d) *Rumford v. Brown*

147. The maximum commission allowed on a $5,000 second trust deed loan due in seven years is:
    (a) $250
    (b) $500
    (c) $750
    (d) $1,000

148. The maximum amount allowed from the Real Estate Recovery Fund for all parties in a single judgment case against a broker is:
    (a) $10,000
    (b) $25,000
    (c) $50,000
    (d) $100,000

149. A corporation is prohibited from holding title as:
    (a) joint tenants
    (b) tenancy in partnership
    (c) tenants in common
    (d) severalty

150. In a 1031 real estate exchange, taxable unlike property is called:
    (a) like for like
    (b) basis
    (c) foreign property
    (d) boot

Answers to Practice Examination

As you grade your practice examination, keep track of each question missed. A passing score is 105 questions correct (70%).

After you compute your score, go back and reread each question missed, then look up the explanation in the textbook. Wait a day or two, review the glossary in the textbook, and then take the examination again.

1. (b) Chapter 9

2. (c) Chapter 2

3. (c) Chapter 2

4. (a) Chapter 12

5. (b) Chapter 7

6. (b) Chapter 3

7. (c) Chapter 3

8. (a) Chapter 6

9. (a) Chapter 2

10. (c) Chapter 3

11. (c) Chapter 7

12. (a) $200,000/$4.75 = 42,105.26 sq. ft./300 = ft. 140.35 front ft., then $200,000/140.35 = $1,425

13. (a) Chapter 5 (fiduciary is result of agency, not needed to form an agency)

14. (b) $67,100 + 517 = (94% of total) $67,617/0.94 = $71,933

15. (b) Chapter 5

16. (d) Chapter 9

17. (b) Chapter 12 (Subdivision Map Act 2 or more units)

18. (d) Chapter 14

19. (c) $5,050/0.09 = 56,111/0.80 = $70,139 value

20. (c) Chapter 2

21. (b) Chapter 2

22. (a) Chapter 11

23. (c) Chapter 7

24. (c) Chapter 9

25. (b) Chapter 1

26. (b) Chapter 4

27. (c) Chapter 8

28. (b) Chapter 11

29. (d) Chapter 10

30. (c) Chapter 12

31. (b) Chapter 4

32. (d) Chapter 2

33. (c) Chapter 12

34. (b) Chapter 11

35. (b) Chapter 9 (15% rent increase will not cover 15% vacancy)

36. (b) Chapter 3

37. (b) Chapter 4

38. (c) Chapter 7

39. (d) Chapter 12

40. (a) Chapter 12

41. (d) Chapter 7

42. (c) Chapter 4 (by inference, not stated)

43. (b) Chapter 15

44. (c) Chapter 9

45. (c) Chapter 4

46. (a) Chapter 13

47. (c) Chapter 15

48. (a) Chapter 10

49. (b) Chapter 5

50. (a) Chapter 13

51. (b) Chapter 3

52. (a) Chapter 3

53. (b) Chapter 7

54. (c) $700 × 12 mo. = $8,400/0.11 = $76,364

55. (c) Chapter 12

56. (c) Chapter 11

57. (a) Chapter 11

58. (a) Chapter 3

59. (b) Chapter 15

60. (a) Chapter 7

61. (a) Chapter 2

62. (b) Chapter 2

63. (b) Chapter 3

64. (c) Chapter 2

65. (b) Chapter 11

66. (a) Chapter 7

67. (d) Chapter 5

68. (d) Chapter 5

69. (d) Chapter 12

70. (c) Chapter 9

71. (c) Chapter 5

72. (b) Chapter 9

73. (c) Chapter 15

74. (b) Chapter 3

75. (a) $70,400/1.20 = $58,667, then $70,400 less $58,667 = $11,733

76. (a) Chapter 5 (only contracts under Statute of Frauds need be in writing, not a general contract)

77. (d) Chapter 8

78. (d) Chapter 10

79. (c) Chapter 2

80. (a) Chapter 3

81. (b) Chapter 5

82. (b) Chapter 14

83. (a) Chapter 5

84. (a) $200 mo. × 12 mo. = $2,400/0.07 = $34,286

85. (d) Chapter 12

86. (b) Chapter 7

87. (c) Chapter 7

88. (b) Chapter 9

89. (a) Chapter 6

90. (d) Chapter 1

91. (b) Chapter 2

92. (d) Chapter 7 (usury)

93. (b) Chapter 8

94. (c) Chapter 5

95. (d) Chapter 5

96. (b) $150/8 = $18.75 mo. × 12 mo. = $225 int. yr./$2,500 loan = 9%

97. (a) Chapter 10

98. (d) Chapter 2

99. (b) Chapter 2

100. (b) Chapter 4

101. (c) Chapter 4

102. (d) Chapter 3

103. (d) Chapter 15

104. (a) Chapter 15
105. (a) Chapter 2
106. (c) Chapter 12
107. (b) Chapter 13
108. (c) Glossary
109. (a) Chapter 11
110. (d) Chapter 2
111. (c) Chapter 2
112. (a) Chapter 12 (not stated in text, but by inference)
113. (b) Chapter 2
114. (b) Glossary
115. (a) Chapter 7
116. (d) Chapter 5
117. (b) Chapter 12
118. (d) Chapter 15
119. (a) Chapter 9
120. (b) Chapter 15
121. (a) Chapter 15
122. (b) Chapter 7
123. (b) Chapter 5
124. (a) Chapter 8
125. (d) Chapter 4
126. (b) Chapter 9
127. (c) Chapter 5
128. (d) Chapter 3

129. (a) Chapter 8
130. (c) Chapter 7
131. (b) Chapter 15
132. (b) Chapter 11
133. (a) Chapter 15 (not stated in text, but true)
134. (a) $18\% \times 3 = 54\%$ children's share, then $54\% + 37\% = 91\%$ husband and children combined, then $100\% - 91\% = 9\%$ college share, then daughter has twice as much as college, $\$37,000 \times 2 = \$74,000$
135. (d) Chapter 2
136. (b) Chapter 1
137. (a) Chapter 2
138. (a) Chapter 13
139. (c) Chapter 13
140. (c) Chapter 3
141. (d) Chapter 8 (not stated in text, but true)
142. (a) Chapter 10
143. (c) Chapter 4
144. (d) Chapter 4
145. (a) Chapter 5
146. (b) Chapter 12
147. (c) Chapter 7
148. (d) Chapter 4
149. (a) Chapter 2
150. (d) Chapter 13

Answers to Practical Application Questions

Chapter 1

1. Requiring an application fee and a set of approved plans infringes on the Right to Use and the Right to Enjoy by placing a cost on the homeowner. On the other hand, requiring that the new addition meet housing codes ensures that the existing and subsequent owner(s) will have a safer home. As mentioned in the textbook, the Bundle of Rights are not absolute or unlimited; they are subject to the actions of government, which in turn is accountable to the people via the election process.

2. In absence of an agreement to the contrary, all items of personal property can usually be removed by the seller. If the facts of the case show that the prefab storage shed merely rested on the ground, it is probably personal property. If it was bolted down on a cement slab or attached to a foundation, it probably is real property and should stay with the land. If the issue is too close to call, the courts tend to favor the buyer. This entire issue could have been avoided if the parties had mentioned the outcome of the shed in the purchase contract.

3. Trade fixtures are added by tenants as items needed to run a business, while regular fixtures are added by tenants for personal use. The presumption is that business tenants are automatically allowed to remove trade fixtures when they leave. Personal fixtures carry no automatic removal presumption. Whether regular fixtures can or cannot be removed will depend upon individual circumstances. In both cases, any legal removal carries with it the responsibility to repair all damages the removal may cause. Once again any conflict can be avoided by discussing the issue in the rental contract.

Chapter 2–Part I

1. 165 acres, which looks like the shaded area below.

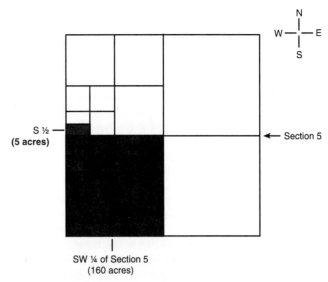

S ½
(5 acres)

← Section 5

SW ¼ of Section 5
(160 acres)

160 acres + 5 acres = 165 acres

2. The basic rule is that the first additional bid over the initial accepted bid must be 10% of the first $10,000 and 5% of any excess.

Therefore:
$$\begin{array}{ll} & \$200{,}000 \text{ initial bid} \\ - & 10{,}000 \times 10\% = \$1{,}000 \\ & \$190{,}000 \times 5\% \ = \$9{,}500 \\ \hline & \$10{,}500 \end{array}$$

$200,000 initial bid + $10,500 = $210,500 required for the first additional bid over the initial bid. Any bids after this may be in any amounts at the pleasure of the probate judge.

3. Williams is probably right because a grant deed carries after-acquired title, which means after the grantor deeds the property, if he or she should later acquire an additional interest in the property, that interest automatically passes to the grantee.

Chapter 2–Part II

1. Upon Washington's death, the lease with Santos is cancelled since a life tenant cannot lease beyond the life of the designated person in a life estate. Possession will go to the heirs of Adams.

2. Nuygen and Battino are tenants in common as they do not have the unities of time, title, or interest. The percentage of interest in the properties is as follows: Nuygen now has his original 50% + Harris' 25% for a total of 75% interest in the 20 acres. Battino has a 25% interest in the 20 acres. When Harris sold one half to Battino, Harris was still a joint tenant with Nuygen on the remaining one half and the right of survivorship applies. This illustrates how confusing things can get when joint tenants sell off portions of their interest in real estate.

3. The community property issues for the court to look at are as follows: The family home is obviously community property, but the five-unit apartment is going to be a legal issue. When Sara's parents left her the apartments, the inheritance was her separate property. The placing of the rental money in a separate account in her name alone showed intent to keep it separate property. But when Sara used the rental income to pay for the children's college tuition, that

may be perceived as using the funds for a community property responsibility and a form of commingling. Sara's attorney will try to prove the money was a mere gift and not a pledging of the rental proceeds for a community purpose. Bill's attorney may take the opposite argument. It could create a nasty situation. The moral to the story is if you are married and wish to maintain separate property, it is best to operate under the guidance of a competent attorney.

Chapter 3

1. An easement by prescription is an attempt to obtain the right to travel over the land of another, while adverse possession is an attempt to take title to the land of another. Both require hostile, open, and notorious use for at least 5 years under a claim of right or color of title. But adverse possession also requires the payment of the property taxes for at least 5 years, while easement by prescription does not.

2. a. Preliminary Notice should be served within 20 days from the first furnishing of labor or materials on your home site.
b. A Notice of Completion should be filed by you within 10 days after the completion of the home.
c. After filing your Notice of Completion, the general contractor has 60 days to file a lien, while the subcontractors have 30 days.
d. If your Notice of Completion is filed incorrectly and hence is invalid, all workers have 90 days to file a lien.
e. If a mechanic's lien is filed, it will automatically terminate if court action is not instituted within 90 days.

3. $250,000 home value
   - 125,000 to holder of first loan
   - 35,000 to holder of home equity second loan
   - 75,000 to owner of home per head of household exemption
   $ 15,000 remainder to be applied toward the judgment creditor's $25,000 debt.

Chapter 4

1. Vista Realty is probably a dual agent for both Alvarez and Patel because both salespeople work for the same real estate office. Or maybe Patel is completely unrepresented. If Salesperson Ames and Salesperson Jones worked for different real estate companies it then would be possible to have Vista Realty represent just the seller and the other real estate company represent just the buyer.

2. Both Acme Properties and Lake Realty are probably guilty of misrepresentation. The incorrect square footage and wrong lot size was probably an honest mistake, and not outright fraud, but a misrepresentation is a misrepresentation. Lake Realty will have a difficult time declaring that they are innocent because they relied on the information supplied by Acme Properties. The salesperson from Acme Properties should have said: "Here are the measurements provided by Lake Realty, the listing agent. I have not verified the numbers and you should not make any decisions until you have an appraiser or other qualified person check their accuracy."

3. The heirs are right. The seller's death prior to accepting the offer automatically canceled the listing contract with Excellent Realty. Excellent Realty's contention that a commission was earned prior to the seller's death due to the $160,000 offer is incorrect. $160,000 is less than the listed price of $175,000 and it would take the seller's formal acceptance of the $160,000 offer to waive the required $175,000 listing price.

Chapter 5

1. Sally has a bilateral (promise for a promise, e.g., rent for occupancy), expressed (written), executed (signed and moved in), valid real estate contract (lease). Although she is only 17, by virtue of her military service she is an emancipated minor and legally able to contract.

2. The legal issues to consider: Sunrise Realty was given the exclusive authorization and right to sell listing for 180 days. Vargas cancelled the listing in 90 days without a legal release from Sunrise Realty. The sale took place through Ambrosini Properties during the 180 day time period that Vargas had given to Sunrise Realty. In a similar situation, a California court ruled that a seller could not unilaterally cancel the listing, that the permission of the listing agent was required, and that the seller must pay a second full commission to the original listing company.

3. A Real Estate Transfer Disclosure Statement is required on all 1–4 residential units, even rental units, even if the property is being sold "as is," even if the buyer does not care about the condition of the house. The parties cannot agree to "waive" the Real Estate Transfer Disclosure Statement on residential 1–4 unit sales. The seller is legally liable to disclose all known defects and the agent is responsible to conduct a physical inspection and disclose the results of said inspection. Agents are not normally liable for hidden defects not disclosed by sellers, nor revealed to the agent or buyer. However, the agent should submit in writing a suggestion to the buyer to seek out and use professional contractors and inspectors to determine the extent of the physical damage, prior to purchasing the property "as is." Frequently, the purchase contract, signed by the buyer, seller, and real estate agent, has this provision preprinted. But to be extra safe, an additional separate notice to this effect would not hurt.

Chapter 6

1. $244.75 divided by $1.10 = $222.50 × $1,000 = $222,500 originally paid by the seller. Then $300,000 less $222,500 = $77,500 profit divided by $222,500 paid = 34.8% approximate profit.

2. The N $\frac{1}{2}$ and the NW $\frac{1}{4}$ of the SW $\frac{1}{4}$ of Section 9 = 360 acres × $5,000 per acre = $1,800,000 sale price × 10% commission = $180,000 total commission × 50% = Broker B's share of $90,000 × 60% = $54,000, your share as the salesperson.

3. 2,000 square feet × $80 per square foot = $160,000 and 500 square feet × $30 per square foot = $15,000. Thus, $160,000 home + $15,000 garage + $60,000 land and other improvements = $235,000 total cost × 1.20 = $282,000 resale price to make a 20% profit. Proof: $282,000 resale price divided by 1.20 = $235,000 cost.

Chapter 7

1. $200,000 interest-only loan × 6% = $12,000 divided by 12 months = $1,000 current monthly payment. Second year equals: $200,000 × 8% = $16,000 divided by 12 months = $1,333.33 monthly payment. Third year equals: $200,000 × 10% = $20,000 divided by 12 months = $1,666.67 monthly payment. Fourth year 11% cap rate is reached; therefore: $200,000 × 11% = $22,000 divided by 12 months = $1,833.33 monthly payment.

2. The homeowner has until five days prior to the date of the foreclosure sale to make up back payments and all foreclosure costs to save the home. Using the figures given, that would be $2,000 back payments + $1,000 foreclosure costs, or a total of $3,000. If the homeowner waits until the five days prior or the date of sale, the lender can then demand the entire loan balance of $175,000 + $2,000 back payments + $1,000 in foreclosure costs. Some owners who find themselves

in this predicament, using the services of an attorney, file bankruptcy in an attempt to buy some time against the foreclosure.

3. $15,000 junior lien for 10 years has a maximum commission rate of 15%, plus a maximum of 5% of the loan amount for additional costs and expenses, not to exceed $700. Therefore: $15,000 × 15% = $2,250 commission; $15,000 × 5% = $750 other costs, with a maximum allowed of only $700. Thus: $15,000 less $2,250 commission, less $700 additional costs and expenses = $12,050 net to the homeowner. But the homeowner will be required to repay $15,000 plus interest on the $15,000, driving the effective rate of interest considerably higher than the interest rate stated on the note.

Chapter 8–Part I

1. $3,000 gross monthly income × 28% = $840 qualified maximum housing payments not counting debts. $3,000 × 36% = $1,080 less $300 long-term monthly debts = $780 qualified counting monthly debts. Therefore, $780—the lesser of the two—applies. This illustrates how too much in long-term debt reduces a person's ability to qualify for a larger loan, which in turn reduces the ability to qualify for a more expensive home.

2. People can either spend or save (invest) their after-tax income and profits. If people decide to spend excessively this will reduce the supply of savings available for loans. This in turn may drive up interest rates and make it more difficult for people to qualify for real estate loans and that will slow down the real estate market. On the other hand, if people choose to raise their level of savings, all things being equal, this should increase the supply of funds available for loans and interest rates should remain affordable. Affordable interest rates tend to stimulate the real estate market. Of course, if taken to extremes, if everybody only saved and did not spend, the economy would crash and nobody would borrow to buy anything at any interest rate!

3. $180,000 loan balance × .0025 = $450 annual PMI cost divided by 12 months = $37.50 reduction in the monthly loan payment if the PMI coverage is cancelled.

Chapter 8–Part II

1. Minimum cash required is 3%, therefore $150,000 price × 3% = $4,500 cash required to close escrow if the seller pays all other closing costs.

2. Due to no down payment on this VA-guaranteed loan, the sales price and the loan amount are the same. Therefore:
$150,000 loan × 2.5% (1% loan fee + 1.5% funding fee) = $3,750 + $500 other closing costs = $4,250 cash required to close escrow.

3. $150,000 Cal-Vet price × 2% down payment = $3,000 + $700 other costs = $3,700 cash required to close escrow.

Chapter 9

1. 200 × 40 foot main structure = 8,000 square feet × $65 per square foot = $520,000 replacement cost new; 20-year effective life × 2% (100% divided by 50 years) = 40% depreciation factor; $520,000 × 40% = $208,000 depreciation. Therefore:
$520,000 replacement cost new
−208,000 depreciation
$312,000 present value of main structure

35×15 foot storage building = 525 square feet $\times$ \$20 per square foot = \$10,500 replacement cost new; 15-year effective life $\times$ 3.33% (100% divided by 30 years) = 50% depreciation factor; \$10,500 $\times$ 50% = \$5,250 depreciation. Therefore:

$10,500 replacement cost new
$\underline{-\ 5,250}$ depreciation
$ 5,250 present value of the storage building

$312,000 present value of main structure
+   5,250 present value of storage building
+   27,000 present value of cement slab and other improvements
$\underline{+300,000}$ land value
$644,250 or \$644,000 estimated value of the special use property

2. 11,000 square feet $\times$ \$1 $\times$ 12 months = \$132,000 gross rents;

$132,000 gross rents
$\underline{-\quad 6,600}$ expenses (\$132,000 $\times$ 5%)
$125,400 net operating income

$$\frac{\$135,000 \text{ net income of comparable property}}{\$1,500,000 \text{ comparable property}} = 9\% \text{ comparable cap rate}$$

$$\frac{\$125,400 \text{ net operating income}}{.09 \text{ capitalization rate}} = \$1,393,333 \text{ or } \$1,393,000 \text{ estimated value}$$

3.

	Comparable A	Comparable B	Comparable C
Price paid	$257,000	$240,000	$ 225,000
Pool	− 1,000	0	+ 0
Condition	− 3,000	0	+ 3,000
Lot size	− 10,000	+ 10,000	+ 10,000
	$243,000	$250,000	$ 238,000

$250,000 is the best listing price estimate, based on Comparable B having the least number of adjustments.

Chapter 10

1. The issue here is to save the transaction. The buyer's agent could note that the buyer did sign escrow instructions to split the title fee 50/50, even though the original deposit receipt said the seller would pay. The latest contract usually applies, unless the buyer made an honest mistake and misread the instructions. Perhaps the agent could mention that if the transaction falls through, the buyer might lose his or her deposit. Also, the issue of a court action interpleader might be pursued by the escrow holder. The bottom line is that if the transaction falls apart, the buyer will not get the home, the seller won't get the full sale proceeds, and the agent will not get a full commission. If the issue is a total stumbling block, ultimately the agent might agree to pay the buyer's 50% portion just to close the transaction. This may not be "fair," but that might be what it takes to solve the problem.

2. There are many issues here: California has an anti-rebate law that prohibits title companies from paying real estate licensees for the placement of title insurance. The fine can be up to \$10,000 and/or one year in jail for both the title representative and the real estate agent. Federal RESPA rules prohibit kickbacks and unearned fees paid to real estate agents. Real estate commissioner regulations prohibit "secret profit" by real estate agents. The issue: do unsolicited dinner and sporting event tickets come under the anti-rebate, RESPA, and secret profit rules? It would take an attorney to check out each law! It is probably best to pass on the whole thing and tell the title company NO THANKS!

3. $213,575 × 7% = $14,950.25 divided by 360 days = $41.53 per day × 18 days = $747.51 proration, which will be a debit for the seller and a credit for the buyer because interest is paid in arrears on real estate loans.

Chapter 11

1. The landlord could proceed as follows: Within 21 days refund the security deposit, less damages beyond normal wear and tear. If the $100 damage to the water heater is beyond normal, then the landlord should withhold the $100 from the security deposit. The problem is proving that the leak was caused by damage, not normal wear and tear. From a purely practical point of view, many landlords will not hold the $100 from the security deposit for fear the tenant will make an issue, causing legal hassles, which could end up costing much more than $100.

2. The landlord should serve a 3-day (not a 30-day) notice to remove the dog or quit possession. If tenant complies, then the issue is settled. If the tenant does not remove the dog or move out, the next step for the landlord is to proceed with a formal unlawful detainer action. From pure cost point of view, sometimes it is cheaper to pay the tenant to move, rather than bear the cost of an unlawful detainer action.

3. 5 units × $750 per month × 12 months = $45,000 gross scheduled income per year, then:

$45,000	
− 2,250	vacancy factor ($45,000 × 5%)
$42,750	collected rents
× .08	property management rate
$ 3,420	property management fee paid
× .31	combined tax bracket
$ 1,060.20	tax savings when management fee is deducted

Therefore:	$3,420.00	property management fee paid
	−1,060.20	tax savings
	$2,359.80	after-tax cost of property management

Chapter 12

1. The appeal process is as follows: The planning commission decision can be appealed to the city council or the board of supervisors depending upon who has jurisdiction. If the city council or board of supervisors decision is not to your liking, a person can appeal to the courts. Then the decision of the highest court is final.

2. An owner of a condominium owns exclusively his or her air space within the condo unit, then has an undivided interest with the other owners in the building and land. A PUD owner owns his or her individual unit, inside and out, and owns the land immediately under the PUD. He or she has an equal undivided interest with the other PUD owners in the common areas. Under a stock cooperative, a corporation owns the property and each shareholder in the corporation is given the right to occupy a living unit. They all are called common interest developments because they all feature some joint form of ownership in common with other co-owners.

3. The agent should respond by stating any form of discrimination is illegal and carries a stiff fine and/or jail term for agents and owners. Also, good business ethics and a sense of fair play mean that all financially qualified people should have an equal right to own a home. Finally, if the owner insists upon discriminating, you should immediately cancel the listing.

Chapter 13

1. $225,000 \times 80\% = \$180,000$ loan at 8% for 30 years = $1,320.78 monthly payment using a financial calculator or $7.34 \times 180 = \$1,321.20$ approximate monthly payment using the amortization table in Chapter 6. $225,000 price $\times$ .017 (.012 property taxes plus .005 insurance) = $3,825 divided by 12 months = $318.75 per month for property taxes and insurance. Therefore: $1,320.78 + $318.75 = $1,639.53 by financial calculator or $1,321.20 + $318.75 = $1,639.95 using the amortization table in Chapter 6.

2. No federal capital gains tax is owed as the first $500,000 of gain is excluded for married homeowners who file joint returns and live in their main home for more than 2 years.

3. The federal tax code allows homeowners to deduct interest on the home equity loan up to the market value of the home. The interest paid on 25% of a 125% loan that exceeds the market value of the home will not be deductible if said funds are used to pay personal debts or expenditures. Homeowners should check with their tax person before entering into an equity loan to determine the current IRS rulings.

Chapter 14

1. Using the illustration in the book, starting with the ground and then building up, a standard home will have the footings, then the foundation, then the mudsill, then the floor joist, and finally the sole plate.

2. The four conditions are: (1) must obtain a building permit, (2) must be placed on a permanent foundation, (3) must obtain a certificate of occupancy, and (4) must record a document stating that the mobile home is attached to a permanent foundation.

3. Advantages of owning your home include: appreciation potential, tax advantages, privacy and control, pride of ownership, and better access to credit.

Chapter 15

1. As a new California real estate salesperson licensee, the educational requirements during the first four years of your license are: If not previously completed, during the first 18 months of your license you must complete two college or private vocational school (approved by DRE) college-level real estate courses consisting of real estate practice, or finance, or appraisal, or legal aspects, or economics, or accounting, or business law, or property management, or escrows, or office administration, or mortgage loan brokering, or other advanced real estate course approved by the DRE. Then you must complete within the first four years, four 3-hour DRE-approved courses in ethics, agency, fair housing, and trust fund handling.

2. As a California real estate broker licensee, the continuing educational requirements during the first four years of your license are: you must complete 45 hours of DRE-approved continuing education, including one 6-hour survey course updating ethics, agency, fair housing, and trust fund handling.

3. A bulk sale occurs when a business is sold that has inventory. If the bulk sale rules are not followed, a buyer of a business may find that they will pay twice for the same inventory: once to the seller who did not own the inventory outright and again to the creditor who has a claim on the inventory. All purchasers of businesses should seek the advice and guidance of an attorney to be sure that all bulk sale rules are followed.

Answers to Reviewing Your Understanding Questions

Chapter 1
1. (c), 2. (b), 3. (d), 4. (c), 5. (a), 6. (d), 7. (b), 8. (d), 9. (d), 10. (d), 11. (c), 12. (a), 13. (b), 14. (d), 15. (b), 16. (c), 17. (b), 18. (a), 19. (d), 20. (a)

Chapter 2—Part I
1. (d), 2. (d), 3. (b), 4. (d), 5. (d), 6. (a), 7. (b), 8. (c), 9. (c), 10. (a), 11. (a), 12. (c), 13. (a), 14. (d), 15. (c), 16. (b), 17. (b), 18. (c), 19. (a), 20. (d)

Chapter 2—Part II
1. (a), 2. (d), 3. (c), 4. (c), 5. (b), 6. (c), 7. (c), 8. (c), 9. (b), 10. (b), 11. (b), 12. (a), 13. (b), 14. (d), 15. (c), 16. (c), 17. (c), 18. (a), 19. (d), 20. (b)

Chapter 3
1. (c), 2. (b), 3. (d), 4. (b), 5. (a), 6. (c), 7. (d), 8. (b), 9. (a), 10. (b), 11. (c), 12. (a), 13. (c), 14. (d), 15. (b), 16. (a), 17. (b), 18. (c), 19. (d), 20. (d)

Chapter 4
1. (b), 2. (d), 3. (b), 4. (b), 5. (d), 6. (a), 7. (d), 8. (c), 9. (b), 10. (d), 11. (b), 12. (a), 13. (c), 14. (b), 15. (c), 16. (b), 17. (a), 18. (c), 19. (b), 20. (d), 21. (a), 22. (c), 23. (c), 24. (c), 25. (b)

Chapter 5
1. (d), 2. (d), 3. (c), 4. (b), 5. (d), 6. (a), 7. (b), 8. (d), 9. (c), 10. (c), 11. (a), 12. (c), 13. (c), 14. (a), 15. (d), 16. (d), 17. (a), 18. (b), 19. (c), 20. (c), 21. (c), 22. (d), 23. (a), 24. (d), 25. (b)

Chapter 6
1. (d), 2. (b), 3. (d), 4. (b), 5. (d), 6. (b), 7. (c), 8. (a), 9. (b), 10. (d), 11. (a), 12. (c), 13. (d), 14. (c), 15. (d), 16. (a), 17. (b), 18. (b), 19. (c), 20. (d)

Chapter 7
1. (d), 2. (c), 3. (a), 4. (b), 5. (d), 6. (d), 7. (a), 8. (b), 9. (a), 10. (a), 11. (d), 12. (c), 13. (c), 14. (b), 15. (a), 16. (c), 17. (b), 18. (d), 19. (b), 20. (c)

Chapter 8—Part I

1. (b), 2. (c), 3. (d), 4. (b), 5. (c), 6. (c), 7. (a), 8. (c), 9. (d), 10. (a)

Chapter 8—Part II

1. (c), 2. (a), 3. (b), 4. (d), 5. (b), 6. (c), 7. (b), 8. (b), 9. (d), 10. (a)

APPENDIX CASE STUDY

$1,245	Principal and interest
+ 175	Property taxes (2,100 ÷ 12)
+ 42	Property insurance (504 ÷ 12)
+ 38	Private mortgage insurance (PMI)
$1,500	Total monthly housing payment

$33,000 + 34,000 = $67,000 per year ÷ 12 months = $5,583 per month

$1,500 ÷ $5,583 = 26.9%

$1,500	Total monthly housing payment
+ 375	Car payment
+ 125	Furniture payment
$2,000	Total monthly credit obligations

$2,000 ÷ $5,583 = 35.8%

Yes, they qualify for the loan.

Chapter 9

1. (b), 2. (a), 3. (d), 4. (b), 5. (c), 6. (a), 7. (d), 8. (a), 9. (a), 10. (c), 11. (a), 12. (b), 13. (d), 14. (c), 15. (c), 16. (b), 17. (c), 18. (c), 19. (d), 20. (b)

Chapter 10

1. (d), 2. (b), 3. (b), 4. (c), 5. (a), 6. (d), 7. (b), 8. (d), 9. (a), 10. (b), 11. (c), 12. (b), 13. (d), 14. (c), 15. (b), 16. (a), 17. (c), 18. (d), 19. (a), 20. (a)

Chapter 11

1. (a), 2. (a), 3. (a), 4. (b), 5. (b), 6. (d), 7. (b), 8. (d), 9. (d), 10. (d), 11. (a), 12. (d), 13. (a), 14. (c), 15. (d), 16. (b), 17. (b), 18. (b), 19. (a), 20. (d)

Chapter 12

1. (d), 2. (b), 3. (c), 4. (a), 5. (d), 6. (c), 7. (a), 8. (d), 9. (c), 10. (d), 11. (a), 12. (a), 13. (d), 14. (a), 15. (c), 16. (a), 17. (d), 18. (b), 19. (b), 20. (d)

Chapter 13

1. (a), 2. (b), 3. (c), 4. (d), 5. (c), 6. (c), 7. (c), 8. (d), 9. (d), 10. (c), 11. (b), 12. (d), 13. (d), 14. (c), 15. (a), 16. (d), 17. (b), 18. (c), 19. (d), 20. (b)

Chapter 14

1. (b), 2. (a), 3. (d), 4. (c), 5. (d), 6. (c), 7. (a), 8. (b), 9. (b), 10. (a), 11. (b), 12. (c), 13. (c), 14. (a), 15. (c), 16. (c), 17. (d), 18. (b), 19. (b), 20. (d)

Chapter 15

1. (b), 2. (a), 3. (b), 4. (c), 5. (b), 6. (d), 7. (d), 8. (d), 9. (a), 10. (a), 11. (c), 12. (a), 13. (c), 14. (d), 15. (b), 16. (d), 17. (b), 18. (a), 19. (d), 20. (c)

Glossary

ALTA Owner's Policy	A residential owner's extended coverage policy that provides buyers or owners the same protection the ALTA policy gives to lenders. Also called an ALTA-R policy.
ALTA Title Policy	American Land Title Association approved title policy. A type of title insurance policy that expands the risks normally insured against under the standard type of policy to include unrecorded mechanic's liens; unrecorded physical easements; facts a physical survey would show; water and mineral rights; and rights of parties in possession, such as tenants and buyers under unrecorded instruments.
Abatement of Nuisance	Extinction or termination of a nuisance
Absolute Fee-Simple Title	Absolute or fee-simple title is one that is absolute and unqualified. It is the best title one can have.
Abstract of Judgment	A condensation of the essential provisions of a court judgment
Abstract of Title	A summary or digest of the conveyances, transfers, and any other facts relied on as evidence of title, together with any other elements of record that may impair the title
Abstraction	A method of valuing land. The indicated value of the improvement is deducted from the sales price.
Acceleration Clause	Clause in trust deed or mortgage giving lender right to call all sums owed to the lender to be immediately due and payable upon the happening of a certain event

414

Acceptance	When the seller or agent's principal agrees to the terms of the agreement of sale and approves the negotiation on the part of the agent and acknowledges receipt of the deposit in subscribing to the agreement of sale, that act is termed an acceptance
Access Right	The right of an owner to have ingress and egress to and from his/her property, also called right of way
Accretion	An addition to land from natural causes as, for example, from gradual action of the ocean or river waters
Accrued Depreciation	The difference between the cost of replacement new as of the date of the appraisal and the present appraised value
Accrued Items of Expense	Those incurred expenses that are not yet payable. The seller's accrued expenses are credited to the purchaser in a closing statement.
Acknowledgment	A formal declaration before a duly authorized officer by a person who has executed an instrument that such execution is his or her act and deed
Acoustical Tile	Blocks of fiber, mineral, or metal, with small holes or rough-textured surface to absorb sound; used as covering for interior walls and ceilings. Old tile may contain asbestos that can create a health problem.
Acquisition	The act or process by which a person procures property
Acre	A measure of land equaling 160 square rods, or 4,840 square yards, or 43,560 square feet, or a tract about 208.71 feet square
Ad Valorem	A Latin phrase meaning "according to value." Usually used in connection with real estate taxation.
Adjustments	A means by which characteristics of a residential property are regulated by dollar amount or percentage to conform to similar characteristics of another residential property
Administrator/trix	A person appointed by the probate court to administer the estate of a person deceased
Advance	Transfer of funds from a lender to a borrower in advance on a loan
Advance Commitment	The institutional investor's prior agreement to provide long-term financing upon completion of construction
Advance Fee	A fee paid in advance of any services rendered. The practice of obtaining a fee in advance for the advertising of property or businesses for sale. Said fees can be incorrectly obtained, thereby becoming a violation of real estate laws and regulations.
Adverse Possession	The open and notorious possession and occupancy under an evident claim or right, in denial or opposition to the title of another claimant
Affiant	A person who has made an affidavit

Affidavit	A statement or declaration reduced to writing sworn to or affirmed before some officer who has authority to administer an oath or affirmation
Affidavit of Title	A statement, in writing, made under oath by seller or grantor, acknowledged before a notary public, in which the affiant provides identification certifying that since the examination of title on the contract date there are no judgments, bankruptcies, or divorces, no unrecorded deeds, contracts, unpaid repairs or improvements or defects of title known and that the seller is in possession of the property
Affirm	To confirm, to aver, to ratify, to verify
Agency	The relationship between principal and agent that arises out of a contract, either expressed or implied, written or oral, wherein the agent is employed by the principal to do certain acts dealing with a third party
Agent	One who represents another from whom he or she has derived authority
Agreement of Sale	A written agreement or contract between seller and purchaser in which they reach a meeting of minds on the terms and conditions of the sale. Often called a deposit receipt.
Air Rights	The rights in real property to use the airspace above the surface of the land
Alienation	The transferring of property to another; the transfer of property and possession of lands, or other things, from one person to another
Alienation Clause	A clause that gives the lender the right to call a loan upon sale of real estate. Also called a due-on-sale clause.
Allodial Tenure	A real property ownership system where ownership may be complete except for those rights held by government. Allodial is in contrast to feudal tenure.
Alluvion	(Alluvium) Soil deposited by accretion; increase of earth on a shore or bank of a river
Amenities	Satisfaction of enjoyable living to be derived from a home; conditions of agreeable living or a beneficial influence arising from the location or improvements
American Institute of Real Estate Appraisers	A trade association of real estate appraisers.
AMO	Accredited Management Organization
Amortization	The liquidation of a financial obligation on an installment basis; also, recovery, over a period, of cost or value
Amortized Loan	A loan that is completely paid off, interest and principal, by a series of regular payments that are equal or nearly equal. Also called a level payments loan.
Annuity	A series of assured equal or nearly equal payments to be made over a period of time or it may be a lump-sum payment to be made in the fu-

ture. The series of installment payments due to the landlord under a lease is an annuity. So is the series of installment payments due to a lender. In real estate finance we are most concerned with the first definition.

Anticipation, Principle of   Affirms that value is created by anticipated benefits to be derived in the future

Appraisal   An estimate and opinion of value; a conclusion resulting from the analysis of facts

Appraiser   One qualified by education, training, experience, and tested by the state, who is hired to estimate the value of real and personal property based on experience, judgment, facts, and use of formal appraisal processes

Appropriation of   A legal term including the act or acts involved in the taking and reducing to personal possession of water occurring in a stream or other body of water, and of applying such water to beneficial uses or purposes

Appurtenance   Something annexed to another thing that may be transferred incident to it. That which belongs to another thing, as a barn, dwelling, garage, or orchard is incident to the land to which it is attached.

Architectural Style   Generally the appearance and character of a building's design and construction

ASA   American Society of Appraisers

Assessed Valuation   A valuation placed upon property by a public officer or board, as a basis for taxation

Assessed Value   Value placed on property as a basis for taxation

Assessment   The valuation of property for the purpose of levying a tax, or the amount of the tax levied

Assessor   The official who has the responsibility of determining assessed values for property taxes

Assignment   A transfer or making over to another of the whole of any property, real or personal, in possession or in action, or of any estate or right therein

Assignor   One who assigns or transfers property

Assigns; Assignees   Those to whom property shall have been transferred

Assumption Agreement   An undertaking or adoption of a debt or obligation primarily resting upon another person

Assumption Fee   A lender's charge for changing over and processing new records for a new owner who is assuming an existing loan

Assumption of Mortgage   The taking of title to property by a grantee, wherein he or she assumes liability for payment of an existing note secured by a mortgage or deed of trust against the property; becoming a co-guarantor for the payment of a mortgage or deed of trust note

Attachment	Seizure of property by court order, usually done to have it available in the event a judgment is obtained in a pending suit
Attest	To affirm to be true or genuine; an official act establishing authenticity
Attorney in Fact	One who is authorized to perform certain acts for another under a power of attorney; power of attorney may be limited to a specific act or acts, or be general
Avulsion	The sudden tearing away or removal of land by action of water flowing over or through it
Axial Growth	City growth that occurs along main transportation routes. Usually takes the form of star-shaped extensions outward from the center.
Backfill	The replacement of excavated earth into a hole or against a structure
Balloon Payment	Where the final installment payment on a note is more than twice as great as the preceding installment payments, and it pays the note in full; such final installment is termed a balloon payment
Bargain and Sale Deed	Any deed that recites a consideration and purports to convey the real estate; a bargain and sale deed with a covenant against the grantor's acts is one in which the grantor warrants that nothing has been done to harm or cloud the title
Baseboard	A board placed against the wall around a room next to the floor
Base and Meridian	Imaginary lines used by surveyors to find and describe the location of private or public lands
Base Molding	Molding used at top of baseboard
Base Shoe	Molding used at junction of baseboard and floor. Commonly called a carpet strip.
Batten	Narrow strips of wood or metal used to cover joints, interiorly or exteriorly; also used for decorative effect
Beam	A structural member transversely supporting a load
Bearing Wall or Partition	A wall or partition supporting any vertical load in addition to its own weight
Bench Marks	A location indicated on a durable marker by surveyors
Beneficiary	(1) One entitled to the benefit of a trust; (2) one who receives profit from an estate, the title of which is vested in a trustee; (3) the lender on the security of a note and deed of trust
Bequeath	To give or hand down by will; to leave by will

Bequest	That which is given by the terms of a will
Betterment	An improvement upon property that increases the property value and is considered a capital asset, as distinguished from repairs or replacements where the original character or cost is unchanged
Bill of Sale	A written instrument given to pass title of personal property from vendor to the vendee
Binder	An agreement to consider a down payment for the purchase of real estate as evidence of good faith on the part of the purchaser. Also, a notation of coverage on an insurance policy, issued by an agent, and given to the insured prior to issuing of the policy.
Blacktop	Asphalt paving used in streets and driveways
Blanket Mortgage	A single mortgage that covers more than one piece of real estate
Blighted Area	A declining area in which real property values are seriously affected by destructive economic forces, such as encroaching inharmonious property usages, infiltration of lower social and economic classes of inhabitants, and/or rapidly depreciating buildings
Board Foot	A unit of measurement of lumber that is one foot wide, one foot long, one inch thick; 144 cubic inches
Bona Fide	In good faith, without fraud
Boot	Unlike property received in an exchange that creates an income tax liability. Examples: Cash, notes, personal property
Bracing	Framing lumber nailed at an angle in order to provide rigidity
Breach	The breaking of a law, or failure of duty, either by omission or commission
Breezeway	A covered porch or passage, open on two sides, connecting house and garage or two parts of the house
Bridging	Small wood or metal pieces used to brace floor joists
Broker	A person employed by another, to carry on any of the activities listed in the license law definition of a broker, for a fee
B.T.U. (British thermal unit)	The quantity of heat required to raise the temperature of one pound of water one degree Fahrenheit
Building Code	A systematic regulation of construction of buildings within a municipality established by ordinance or law
Building Line	A line set by law a certain distance from a street line in front of which an owner cannot build on his or her lot (a setback line)
Building, Market Value of	The sum of money which the presence of that structure adds to or subtracts from the value of the land it occupies. Land valued on the basis of highest and best use.

Building Paper	A heavy waterproofed paper used as sheathing in wall or roof construction as a protection against air passage and moisture
Built-in	Cabinets or similar features built as part of the house
Bundle of Rights	Beneficial interests or rights
CBD	Central Business District
CC&Rs	Abbreviation for covenants, conditions, and restrictions
CPM	Certified property manager, a designation of the Institute of Real Estate Management
Capital Assets	Assets of a permanent nature used in the production of an income, such as land, buildings, machinery, and equipment. Under income tax law, they are usually distinguishable from "inventory," which comprises assets held for sale to customers in ordinary course of the taxpayers' trade or business.
Capital Gain	Income from the sale of an asset rather than from the general business activity. Capital gains are generally taxed at a lower rate than ordinary income.
Capitalization	In appraising, determining value of property by considering net income and percentage of reasonable return on the investment. Thus, the value of an income property is determined by dividing annual net income by the capitalization rate.
Capitalization Rate	The rate of interest which is considered a reasonable return on the investment, and used in the process of determining value based upon net income. It may also be described as the yield rate that is necessary to attract the money of the average investor to a particular kind of investment. This amortization factor can be determined in various ways—for example, by the straight-line depreciation method. (To explore this subject in greater depth, refer to current real estate appraisal texts.)
Casement Window	Frames of wood or metal that swing outward
Cash Flow	The net income generated by a property before depreciation and other noncash expenses
Caveat Emptor	Let the buyer beware. The buyer must examine the goods or property and buy at his or her own risk.
Center of Influence	One who, by nature of his or her relationships, is in a position to sway others
Certificate of Reasonable Value (CRV)	The Department of Veterans Affairs appraisal commitment of property value
Certificate of Taxes Due	A written statement or guarantee of the condition of the taxes on a certain property, made by the county treasurer of the county wherein the property is located. Any loss resulting to any person from an error in a

tax certificate shall be paid by the county which such treasurer represents.

Chain A unit of measurement used by surveyors. A chain consists of 100 links equal to 66 feet.

Chain of Title A history of conveyances and encumbrances affecting the title from the time the original patent was granted or as far back as records are available

Change, Principle of Holds that it is the future, not the past, that is of prime importance in estimating value

Characteristics Distinguishing features of a (residential) property

Chattel Mortgage A claim on personal property (instead of real property) used to secure or guarantee a promissory note. (See Security Agreement and Security Interest.)

Chattel Real An estate related to real estate, such as a lease on real property

Chattels Goods or every species of property, movable or immovable, that are not real property

Circuit Breaker An electrical device that automatically interrupts an electric circuit when an overload occurs; may be used instead of a fuse to protect each circuit and can be reset

Clapboard Boards, usually thicker at one edge, used for siding

Closing Statement An accounting of funds made to the buyer and seller separately. Required by law to be made at the completion of every real estate transaction.

Cloud on the Title Any conditions revealed by a title search that affect the title to property, usually relatively unimportant items, but which cannot be removed without a quitclaim deed or court action

Code of Ethics See Ethics

Collar Beam A beam that connects the pairs of opposite roof rafters above the attic floor

Collateral This is the property subject to the security interest. (See Security Interest.)

Collateral Security A separate obligation attached to a contract to guarantee its performance; the transfer of property or of other contracts, or valuables, to insure the performance of a principal agreement

Collusion An agreement between two or more persons to defraud another's rights by the forms of law or to obtain an object forbidden by law

Color of Title That which appears to be good title but which is not title in fact

Combed Plywood	A grooved building material used primarily for interior finish
Commercial Acre	A term applied to the remainder of an acre of newly subdivided land after the area devoted to streets, sidewalks and curbs, and so on, has been deducted from the acre
Commercial Paper	Bills of exchange used in commercial trade
Commission	An agent's compensation for performing agency duties; in real estate practice, a percentage of the selling price of property, percentage of rentals, and so forth
Commitment	A pledge or a promise or firm agreement
Common Interest Developments	Projects with individual ownership of buildings and common ownership of land. Examples: condominiums and planned unit developments.
Common Law	The body of law that grew from customs and practices developed and used in England "since the memory of man runneth not to the contrary"
Community	A part of a metropolitan area that has a number of neighborhoods that have a tendency toward common interests and problems
Community Property	Property accumulated through joint efforts of a married couple
Compaction	Whenever extra soil is added to a lot to fill in low places or to raise the level of the lot, the added soil is often too loose and soft to sustain the weight of the buildings. Therefore, it is necessary to compact the added soil so that it will carry the weight of buildings without the danger of their tilting, settling, or cracking.
Comparable Sales	Sales that have similar characteristics as the subject property and are used for analysis in the appraisal process
Competent	Legally qualified
Competition, Principle of	Holds that profits tend to breed competition and that excess profits tend to breed ruinous competition
Component	One of the features making up the whole property
Compound Interest	Interest paid on original principal and also on the accrued and unpaid interest that has accumulated
Conclusion	The final estimate of value, realized from facts, data, experience, and judgment
Condemnation	The act of taking private property for public use by a political subdivision; declaration that a structure is unfit for use
Condition	A qualification of an estate granted that can be imposed only in conveyances. They are classified as conditions precedent and conditions subsequent.
Condition Precedent	A condition that requires certain action or the happening of a specified event before the estate granted can take effect. An example would be

most installment real estate sales contracts which state that all payments shall be made at the time specified before the buyer may demand transfer of title.

Condition Subsequent When there is a condition subsequent in a deed, the title vests immediately in the grantee, but upon breach of the condition the grantor has the power to terminate the estate—for example, a condition in the deed prohibiting the grantee from using the premises as a liquor store

Conditional Commitment A commitment of a definite loan amount for some future unknown purchaser of satisfactory credit standing

Conditional Sales Contract A contract for the sale of property stating that delivery is to be made to the buyer, title to remain vested in the seller until the conditions of the contract have been fulfilled. (See Security Interest.)

Condominium A system of individual fee ownership of units in a multifamily structure, combined with joint ownership of common areas of the structure and the land. (Sometimes referred to as a vertical subdivision.)

Conduit Usually a metal pipe in which electrical wiring is installed

Confession of Judgment An entry of judgment upon the debtor's voluntary admission or confession

Confirmation of Sale A court approval of the sale of property by an executor, administrator, guardian, or conservator

Confiscation The seizing of property without compensation

Conformity, Principle of Holds that the maximum of value is realized when a reasonable degree of homogeneity of improvements is present

Conservation The process of utilizing resources in such a manner that minimizes their depletion

Consideration Anything of value given to induce entering into a contract; it may be money, personal services, or even love and affection

Constant The percentage that, when applied directly to the face value of a debt, develops the annual amount of money necessary to pay a specified net rate of interest on the reducing balance and to liquidate the debt in a specified time period. For example, a 6% loan with a 20-year amortization has a constant of approximately 8½%. Thus, a $10,000 loan amortized over 20 years requires an annual payment of approximately $850.00.

Construction Loans Loans made for the construction of homes or commercial buildings. Usually funds are disbursed to the contractor-builder during construction and after periodic inspections. Disbursements are based on an agreement between borrower and lender.

Constructive Eviction Breach of a covenant of warranty or quiet enjoyment, e.g., the inability of a lessee to obtain possession because of a paramount defect in title or a condition making occupancy hazardous

Constructive Notice	Notice given by the public records
Consumer Goods	These are goods used or bought for use primarily for personal, family, or household purposes
Contour	The surface configuration of land
Contract	An agreement, either written or oral, to do or not to do certain things
Contribution, Principle of	Holds that maximum real property values are achieved when the improvements on the site produce the highest (net) return, commensurate with the investment
Conventional Mortgage	A mortgage securing a loan made by investors without governmental underwriting—that is, not FHA-insured or VA-guaranteed
Conversion	Change from one character or use to another
Conveyance	This has two meanings. One meaning refers to the process of transferring title to property from one person to another. In this sense it is used as a verb. The other meaning refers to the document used to effect the transfer of title (usually some kind of deed). In this last sense, it is used as a noun.
Cooperative Ownership	A form of apartment ownership. Ownership of shares in a cooperative venture that entitles the owner to use, rent, or sell a specific apartment unit. The corporation usually reserves the right to approve certain actions such as a sale or improvement.
Corner Influence Table	A statistical table that may be used to estimate the added value of a corner lot
Corporation	A group or body of persons established and treated by law as an individual or unit with rights and liabilities or both, distinct and apart from those of the persons composing it. A corporation is a creature of law having certain powers and duties of a natural person. Being created by law it may continue for any length of time the law prescribes.
Corporeal Rights	Possessory rights in real property
Correction Lines	A system of compensating for inaccuracies in the government rectangular survey system due to the curvature of the earth. Every fourth township line, 24-mile intervals, is used as a correction line on which the intervals between the north and south range lines are remeasured and corrected to a full six miles.
Correlate the Findings	Interpret the data and value estimates to bring them together to a final conclusion of appraised value
Correlation	To bring the indicated values developed by the three appraisal approaches into mutual relationship with each other
Cost	A historical record of past expenditures or an amount that would be given in exchange for other things

Cost Approach	One of three methods in the appraisal process. An analysis in which a value estimate of a property is derived by estimating the replacement cost of the improvements, deducting therefrom the estimated accrued depreciation, then adding the market value of the land.
Counterflashing	Flashing used on chimneys at roofline to cover shingle flashing and to prevent moisture entry
Covenant	Agreements written into deeds and other instruments promising performance or nonperformance of certain acts or stipulating certain uses or nonuses of the property
Crawl Hole	Exterior or interior opening permitting access underneath building, as required by building codes
CRB	Certified residential broker
Cubage	The number or product resulting by multiplying the width of a thing by its height and by its depth and length
Curable Depreciation	Items of physical deterioration and functional obsolescence that are customarily repaired or replaced by a prudent property owner
Curtail Schedule	A listing of the amounts by which the principal sum of an obligation is to be reduced by partial payments and of the dates when each payment will become payable
Curtesy	The right that a husband has in a wife's estate at her death
Damages	The indemnity recoverable by a person who has sustained an injury, either in his person, property, or relative rights, through the act or default of another
Data Plant	An appraiser's file of information on real estate
Debenture	Bonds issued without security
Debtor	This is the party who "owns" the property that is subject to the security interest—previously known as the mortgagor or the pledgor
Deciduous Trees	Lose their leaves in the autumn and winter
Deck	Usually an open porch on the roof of a ground or lower floor, porch or wing
Decree of Foreclosure	Decree by a court in the completion of foreclosure of a mortgage, contract, or lien
Dedication	An appropriation of land by its owner for some public use accepted for such use by authorized public officials on behalf of the public
Deed	Written instrument that, when properly executed and delivered, conveys title

Deed Restriction	This is a limitation in the deed to a property that dictates certain uses that may or may not be made of the property
Default	Failure to fulfill a duty or promise or to discharge an obligation; omission or failure to perform any act
Defeasance Clause	The clause in a mortgage that gives the mortgagor the right to redeem his or her property upon the payment of obligations to the mortgagee
Defeasible Fee	Sometimes called a base fee or qualified fee; a fee-simple absolute interest in land that is capable of being defeated or terminated upon the happening of a specified event
Deferred Maintenance	Existing but unfulfilled requirements for repairs and rehabilitation
Deferred Payment Options	The privilege of deferring income payments to take advantage of the tax statutes
Deficiency Judgment	A judgment given when the security pledge for a loan does not satisfy the debt upon its default
Depreciation	Loss of value in real property brought about by age, physical deterioration, or functional or economic obsolescence. Broadly, a loss in value from any cause.
Depth Table	A statistical table that may be used to estimate the value of the added depth of a lot
Desist and Refrain Order	An order directing a person to desist and refrain from committing an act in violation of the real estate law
Deterioration	Impairment of condition. One of the causes of depreciation and reflecting the loss in value brought about by wear and tear, disintegration, use in service, and the action of the elements.
Devisee	One who receives a bequest made by will
Devisor	One who bequeaths by will
Directional Growth	The location or direction toward which the residential sections of a city are destined or determined to grow
Discount	An amount deducted in advance from the principal before the borrower is given the use of the principal. [See Point(s).]
Disintermediation	The relatively sudden withdrawal of substantial sums of money that savers have deposited with savings banks, commercial banks, and mutual savings banks. This term can also be considered to include life insurance policy purchasers' borrowing against the value of their policies. The essence of this phenomenon is that financial intermediaries lose within a short period of time, billions of dollars as owners of funds held by those institutional lenders exercise their prerogative of taking them out of the hands of these financial institutions.

Disposable Income	The after-tax income a household receives to spend on personal consumption
Dispossess	To deprive one of the use of real estate
Documentary Transfer Tax	A state-enabling act allows a county to adopt a documentary transfer tax to apply on all transfers of real property located in the county. Notice of payment is entered on the face of the deed or on a separate paper filed with the deed.
Donee	A person to whom a gift is made
Donor	A person who makes a gift
Dower	The right that a wife has in her husband's estate at his death
Dual Agency	Where a broker represents both the buyer and seller in a real estate transaction
Duress	Unlawful constraint exercised upon a person whereby the person is forced to do some act unwillingly
Earnest Money	Down payment made by a purchaser of real estate as evidence of good faith
Easement	Created by grant or agreement for a specific purpose, an easement is the right, privilege, or interest one party has in the land of another—for example, right of way
Eaves	The lower part of a roof projecting over the wall
Ecology	The relationship between organisms and their environment
Economic Life	The period over which a property will yield a return on the investment, over and above the economic or ground rent due to land
Economic Obsolescence	A loss in value caused by factors away from the subject property but adversely affecting the value of the subject property
Economic Rent	The reasonable rental expectancy if the property were available for renting at the time of its valuation
Effective Age of Improvement	The number of years of age that is indicated by the condition of the structure
Effective Date of Value	The specific day the conclusion of value applies
Effective Interest Rate	The percentage of interest that is actually being paid by the borrower for the use of the money
Eminent Domain	The right of the government to acquire property for necessary public or quasi-public use by condemnation; the owner must be fairly compensated. The right of the government to do this and the right of the private citizen to get paid is spelled out in the Fifth Amendment to the U.S. Constitution

Encroachment	Trespass: the building of a structure or construction of any improvements, partly or wholly on the property of another
Encumbrance	Anything that affects or limits the fee-simple title to property, such as mortgages, easements, or restrictions of any kind. Liens are special encumbrances that make the property security for the payment of a debt or obligation, such as mortgages and taxes.
Endorsement	The act of signing one's name on the back of a check or note, with or without further qualification
Equal Credit Opportunity Act	Federal law that prohibits lenders from discriminating when granting a loan based upon a borrower's sex, race, color, religion, age, marital status, handicap plus other items
Equity	The interest or value an owner has in real estate over and above the liens against it; branch of remedial justice by and through which relief is afforded to suitors in courts of equity
Equity of Redemption	The right to redeem property during the foreclosure period, such as a mortgagor's right to redeem
Equity Sharing	Where an owner-occupant and a nonowner investor pool their money to buy a home. A contract sets out the arrangements between the occupying owner and the nonoccupying investor.
Erosion	The wearing away of land by the action of water, wind, rain, or glacial ice
Escalation	The right reserved by the lender to increase the amount of the payments and/or interest upon the happening of a certain event
Escalator Clause	A clause in a contract providing for the upward or downward adjustment of certain items to cover specified contingencies
Escheat	The reverting of property to the state when heirs capable of inheriting are lacking
Escrow	The deposit of instruments and funds with instructions to a third neutral party to carry out the provisions of an agreement or contract; when everything is deposited to enable carrying out the instructions, it is called a complete or perfect escrow
Estate	As applied to the real estate practice, the term signifies the quantity of interest, share, right, equity, of which riches or fortune may consist, in real property. The degree, quantity, nature, and extent of interest that a person has in real property.
Estate of Inheritance	An estate that may descend to heirs. All freehold estates are estates of inheritance, except estates for life.
Estate for Life	A freehold estate, but not an estate of inheritance, but that is held by the life tenant for his or her own life or the life or lives of one or more other persons

Estate from Period to Period	An interest in land where there is no definite termination date but the rental period is fixed at a certain sum per week, month, or year. Also called a periodic tenancy.
Estate at Sufferance	An estate arising when the tenant wrongfully holds over after the expiration of his term. The landlord has the choice of evicting the tenant as a trespasser or accepting such tenant for a similar term and under the conditions of the tenant's previous holding. Also called a tenancy at sufferance.
Estate of Will	The occupation of lands and tenements by a tenant for an indefinite period, terminable by one or both parties without notice. Estates of Will are not recognized in California.
Estate for Years	An interest in lands by virtue of a contract for the possession of them for a definite and limited period of time. A lease may be said to be an estate for years.
Estimate	To form a preliminary opinion of value
Estimated Remaining Life	The period of time (years) it takes for the improvements to become valueless
Estoppel	A doctrine that bars one from asserting rights that are inconsistent with a previous position or representation
Ethics	That branch of moral science, idealism, justness, and fairness that treats of the duties which a member of a profession or craft owes to the public, to clients or patrons, and to other professional members. Various real estate trade associations have codes of ethics that govern their members.
Eviction	Dispossession by process of law. The act of depriving a person of the possession of lands, in pursuance of the judgment of a court.
Exchange	Officially called an Internal Revenue Code 1031 exchange that allows an owner to trade one property for another and to defer the income tax
Exclusive Agency Listing	A written instrument giving one agent the right to sell property for a specified time but reserving the right of the owner to sell the property without the payment of a commission
Exclusive Right-to-Sell Listing	A written agreement between owner and agent giving agent the right to collect a commission if the property is sold by anyone during the term of the agreement
Execute	To complete, to make, to perform, to do, to follow out; to execute a deed, to make a deed, including especially signing, sealing, and delivering; to execute a contract is to perform the contract, to follow out to the end, to complete
Executor/trix	A person named in a will to carry out its provisions as to the disposition of the estate of a person deceased

Expansible House	Home designed for further expansion and additions in the future
Expansion Joint	A bituminous fiber strip used to separate units of concrete to prevent cracking caused by expansion as a result of temperature changes
Expenses	Certain items that may appear on a closing statement in connection with a real estate sale
Facade	Front of a building
Fair Market Value	This is the amount of money that would be paid for a property offered on the open market for a reasonable period of time with both buyer and seller knowing all the uses to which the property could be put and with neither party being under pressure to buy or sell
Farmers Home Administration	An agency of the Department of Agriculture. Primary responsibility is to provide financial assistance for farmers and others living in rural areas where financing is not available on reasonable terms from private sources.
Federal Deposit Insurance Corporation (FDIC)	An agency of the federal government that insures deposits at commercial banks and savings banks
Federal Housing Administration (FHA)	An agency of the federal government that insures mortgage loans
Federal National Mortgage (FNMA) "Fanny Mae"	A private corporation whose primary function is to buy and sell existing mortgages in the secondary market
Fee	An estate of inheritance in real property
Fee Simple	In modern estates, the terms "fee" and "fee simple" are substantially synonymous. The term "fee" is of Old English derivation. "Fee-Simple Absolute" is an estate in real property, by which the owner has the greatest power over the title that it is possible to have, being an absolute estate. In modern use, it expressly establishes the title of real property in the owner, without limitation or end. The owner may dispose of it by sale, trade, or will.
Feudal Tenure	A real property ownership system where ownership rests with a sovereign who, in turn, may grant lesser interests in return for service or loyalty. In contrast to allodial tenure.
Feuds	Grants of land
Fidelity Bond	A security posted for the discharge of an obligation of personal services
Fiduciary	A person in a position of trust and confidence, as between principal and broker; broker as fiduciary owes certain loyalty that cannot be breached under the rules of agency
Filtering Down	The process of making housing available to successively lower income groups
Financial Intermediary	Financial institutions such as commercial banks, savings banks, mutual savings banks, and life insurance companies that receive relatively

small sums of money from the public and invest them in the form of large sums. A considerable portion of these funds are loaned on real estate.

Financing Statement   An instrument filed in order to give public notice of the security interest and thereby protect the interest of the secured parties in the collateral. (See Security Interest and Secured Party.)

Finish Floor   Finish floor strips are applied over wood joists, deadening felt and diagonal subflooring before finish floor is installed; finish floor is the final covering on the floor: wood, linoleum, cork, tile, or carpet

Fire Stop   A solid, tight closure of a concealed space, placed to prevent the spread of fire and smoke through such a space

First Mortgage   A legal document pledging collateral for a loan (see Mortgage) that has first priority over all other claims against the property except taxes and bonded indebtedness

First Trust Deed   A legal document pledging collateral for a loan (see Trust Deed) that has first priority over all other claims against the property except taxes and bonded indebtedness

Fiscal Controls   Federal tax revenue and expenditure policies used to control the level of economic activity

Fixity of Location   The physical characteristic of real estate that subjects it to the influence of its surroundings

Fixtures   Appurtenances attached to the land or improvements, which usually cannot be removed without agreement as they become real property—for example, plumbing fixtures or store fixtures built into the property

Flashing   Sheet metal or other material used to protect a building from seepage of water

Footing   The base or bottom of a foundation wall, pier, or column

Foreclosure   Procedure whereby property pledged as security for a debt is sold to pay the debt in event of default in payments or terms

Forfeiture   Loss of money or anything of value resulting from failure to perform

Foundation   The supporting portion of a structure below the first-floor construction or below grade, including the footings

Franchise   A specified privilege awarded by a government or business firm that awards an exclusive dealership

Fraud   The intentional and successful employment of any cunning, deception, collusion, or artifice, used to circumvent, cheat, or deceive another person, whereby that person acts upon it to the loss of his property and legal injury

Freehold	An estate of indeterminable duration, such as fee simple or life estate
Frontage	Land bordering a street
Front Foot	Property measurement for sale or valuation purposes; the property measures by the front foot on its street line each front foot extending the depth of the lot
Front Money	The minimum amount of money necessary to initiate a real estate venture
Frostline	The depth of frost penetration in the soil. Varies in different parts of the country. Footings should be placed below this depth to prevent movement.
Functional Obsolescence	A loss of value caused by adverse factors from within the structure that affect the utility of the structure
Furring	Strips of wood or metal applied to a wall or other surface to even it, to form an airspace, or to give the wall an appearance of greater thickness
Future Benefits	The anticipated benefits the present owner will receive from property in the future
Gable Roof	A pitched roof with sloping sides
Gambrel Roof	A curb roof, having a steep lower slope with a flatter upper slope above
General Lien	A lien on all the property of a debtor
Gift Deed	A deed for which the consideration is love and affection and where there is not material consideration
Girder	A large beam used to support beams, joists, and partitions
Grade	Ground level at the foundation
Graduated Lease	Lease that provides for a varying rental rate, often based upon future determination; sometimes rent is based upon result of periodical appraisals; used largely in long-term leases
Grant	A technical term used in deeds of conveyance of lands to signify an intent to transfer title
Grant Deed	A deed in which "grant" is used as the word of conveyance. The grantor impliedly warrants that he or she has not already conveyed to any other person, and that the estate conveyed is free from encumbrances done, made, or suffered by the grantor or any person claiming under him or her, including taxes, assessments, and other liens.
Grantee	The purchaser; a person to whom a grant is made
Grantor	Seller of property; one who signs a deed
GRI	Graduate, Realtors Institute

Grid	A chart used in rating the borrower risk, property, and the neighborhood
Gross Domestic Product (GDP)	The total value of all goods and services produced in an economy during a given period of time using resources located in the country
Gross Income	Total income from property before any expenses are deducted
Gross Rate	A method of collecting interest by adding total interest to the principal of the loan at the outset of the term
Gross Rent Multiplier	A figure that, times the gross income of a property, produces an estimate of value of the property
Ground Lease	An agreement for the use of the land only, sometimes secured by improvements placed on the land by the user
Ground Rent	Earnings of improved property credited to earnings of the ground itself, after allowance is made for earnings of improvements; often termed economic rent
Habendum Clause	The "to have and to hold" clause in a deed
Header	A beam placed perpendicular to joists and to which joists are nailed in framing for chimney, stairway, or other opening
Highest and Best Use	An appraisal phrase meaning that use which at the time of an appraisal is most likely to produce the greatest net return to the land and/or buildings over a given period of time; that use which will produce the greatest amount of amenities or profit. This is the starting point for appraisal.
Hip Roof	A pitched roof with sloping sides and ends
Holder in Due Course	One who has taken a note, check, or bill of exchange in due course: (1) before it was overdue, (2) in good faith and for value, (3) without knowledge that it has been previously dishonored without notice of any defect at the time it was negotiated to him or her
Holdover Tenant	Tenant who remains in possession of leased property after the expiration of the lease term
Homestead	A home upon which the owner or owners have recorded a Declaration of Homestead, as provided by statutes in some states; protects home against judgments up to specified amounts
Hundred Percent Location	A city retail business location that is considered the best available for attracting business
Hypothecate	To give a thing as security without the necessity of giving up possession of it
Impounds	A trust type of account established by lenders for the accumulation of funds to meet taxes, FHA mortgage insurance premiums, and/or future insurance policy premiums required to protect their security. Impounds are usually collected with the note payment.

Inclusionary Zoning	An ordinance that requires a builder of new housing to set aside a designated number of units for low- and moderate-income people
Income Approach	One of the three methods in the appraisal process; an analysis in which the estimated gross income from the subject residence is used as a basis for estimating value along with gross rent multipliers derived
Incompetent	One who is mentally incompetent, incapable; any person who, though not insane, is, by reason of old age, disease, weakness of mind, or any other cause, unable, unassisted, to properly manage and take care of him- or herself or property and by reason thereof would be likely to be deceived or imposed upon by artful or designing persons
Incorporeal Rights	Nonpossessory rights in real estate
Increment	An increase. Most frequently used to refer to the increase of value of land that accompanies population growth and increasing wealth in the community. The term unearned increment is used in this connection since values are supposed to have increased without effort on the part of the owner.
Indenture	A formal written instrument made between two or more persons in different interests
Indirect Lighting	The light is reflected from the ceiling or other object external to the fixture
Injunction	A writ or order issued under the seal of a court to restrain one or more parties to a suit or proceeding from doing an act that is deemed to be inequitable or unjust in regard to the rights of some other party or parties in the suit or proceeding
Input	Data, information, and so on, that is fed into a computer or other system
Installment Contract	Purchase of real estate wherein the purchase price is paid in installments over a long period of time; title is retained by seller, and upon default the payments are forfeited. Also known as a land contract.
Installment Note	A note that provides that payments of a certain sum or amount be paid on the dates specified in the instrument
Installment Reporting	A method of reporting capital gains by installments for successive tax years to minimize the impact of the totality of the capital gains tax in the year of the sale
Instrument	A written legal document created to effect the rights of the parties
Interest	The charge, in dollars, for the use of money for a period of time. In a sense, the "rent" paid for the use of money.
Interest Rate	The percentage of a sum of money charged for its use
Interim Loan	A short-term loan until long-term financing is available

Intestate	A person who dies having made no will, or one that is defective in form, in which case the estate descends to the heirs at law or next of kin
Involuntary Lien	A lien imposed against property without consent of an owner; for example, taxes, special assessments, federal income tax liens
Irrevocable	Incapable of being recalled or revoked; unchangeable
Irrigation Districts	Quasi-political districts created under special laws to provide for water services to property owners in the district; an operation governed to a great extent by law
Jalousie	A slatted blind or shutter, like a Venetian blind but used on the exterior to protect against rain as well as to control sunlight
Jamb	The side post or lining of a doorway, window or other opening
Joint	The space between the adjacent surfaces of two components joined and held together by nails, glue, cement, or mortar
Joint Note	A note signed by two or more persons who have equal liability for payment.
Joint Tenancy	Joint ownership by two or more persons with right of survivorship; all joint tenants own equal interest and have equal rights in the property
Joint Venture	Two or more individuals or firms joining together on a single project as partners
Joist	One of a series of parallel beams to which the boards of a floor and ceiling laths are nailed, and supported in turn by larger beams, girders, or bearing walls
Judgment	The final determination of a court of competent jurisdiction of a matter presented to it; money judgments provide for the payment of claims presented to the court or are awarded as damages
Judgment Lien	A legal claim on all the property of a judgment debtor that enables the judgment creditor to have the property sold for payment of the amount of the judgment
Junior Mortgage	A mortgage second in lien to a previous mortgage
Jurisdiction	The authority by which judicial officers take cognizance of and decide causes; the power to hear and determine a cause; the right and power a judicial officer has to enter upon the inquiry
Laches	Delay or negligence in asserting one's legal rights
Land Contract	A contract ordinarily used in connection with the sale of property in cases where the seller does not wish to convey title until all or a certain part of the purchase price is paid by the buyer; often used when property is sold on small down payment. (See Installment Contract and Installment Reporting.)

Land and Improvement Loan	A loan obtained by the builder-developer for the purchase of land and to cover expenses for subdividing
Landlord	One who rents property to another
Later Date Order	The commitment for an owner's title insurance policy issued by a title insurance company which covers the seller's title as of the date of the contract. When the sale closes, the purchaser orders the title company to record the deed to purchaser and bring down their examination to cover this later date so as to show purchaser as owner of the property.
Lateral Support	The support that the soil of an adjoining owner gives to a neighbor's land
Lath	A building material of wood, metal, gypsum, or insulating board fastened to the frame of a building to act as a plaster base
Lease	A contract between owner and tenant, setting forth conditions upon which tenant may occupy and use the property and the term of the occupancy
Leasehold Estate	A tenant's right to occupy real estate during the term of the lease. This is a personal property interest.
Legal Description	A description recognized by law; a description by which property can be definitely located by reference to government surveys or approved recorded maps. Examples: Lot, Block, and Tract; U.S. Government Survey; Metes and Bounds.
Lessee	One who contracts to rent property under a lease contract
Lessor	An owner who enters into a lease with a tenant
Level-Payment Mortgage	A loan on real estate that is paid off by making a series of equal (or nearly equal) regular payments. Part of the payment is usually interest on the loan and part of it reduces the amount of the unpaid balance of the loan. Also sometimes called an amortized mortgage.
Leverage	The use of borrowed funds to obtain an asset
Lien	A form of encumbrance that usually makes property security for the payment of a debt or discharge of an obligation. Examples: judgments, taxes, mortgages, deeds of trust, and so forth.
Life Estate	An estate or interest in real property that is held for the duration of the life of some certain person
Limited Partnership	A partnership composed of some partners whose contribution and liability are limited
Lintel	A horizontal board that supports the load over an opening such as a door or window
Liquidated Damages	A sum agreed upon by the parties to be full damages if a certain event occurs

Lis Pendens	Suit pending, usually recorded so as to give constructive notice of pending litigation
Listing	An employment contract between principal and agent authorizing the agent to perform services for the principal involving the latter's property; listing contracts are entered into for the purpose of securing persons to buy, lease, or rent property. Employment of an agent by a prospective purchaser or lessee to locate property for purchase or lease may be considered a listing.
Loan Administration	Mortgage bankers not only originate loans, but also "service" them from origination to maturity of the loan. Also called loan servicing.
Loan Application	The loan application is a source of information on which the lender decides whether to make the loan, defines the terms of the loan contract; gives the name of the borrower, place of employment, salary, bank accounts, and credit references; and, describes the real estate that is to be mortgaged. It also stipulates the amount of the loan being applied for and repayment terms.
Loan Closing	When all conditions have been met, the loan officer authorizes the recording of the trust deed or mortgage. The disbursal procedure of funds is similar to the closing of a real estate sales escrow. The borrower can expect to receive less than the amount of the loan, as title, recording, service, and other fees may be withheld, or he or she can expect to deposit the cost of these items into the loan escrow. This process is sometimes called funding the loan.
Loan Commitment	Lender's contractual commitment to a loan based on the appraisal and underwriting
Loan-Value Ratio	The percentage of a property's value that a lender can or may loan to a borrower. For example, if the ratio is 80%, this means that a lender may loan 80% of the property's appraised value to a borrower.
Louver	An opening with a series of horizontal slats set at an angle to permit ventilation without admitting rain or sunlight.
MAI	Member of the Appraisal Institute. Designates a person who is a member of the American Institute of Real Estate Appraisers.
Margin of Security	The difference between the amount of the mortgage loan(s) and the appraised value of the property
Marginal Land	Land that barely pays the cost of working or using
Market Data Approach	One of the three methods in the appraisal process. A means of comparing similar types of residential properties, which have recently sold, to the subject property.
Market Price	The price paid regardless of pressures, motives, or intelligence
Market Value	(1) The price at which a willing seller would sell and a willing buyer would buy, neither being under abnormal pressure; (2) as defined by the courts, is the highest price estimated in terms of money that a property will bring if exposed for sale in the open market allowing a reasonable

time to find a purchaser with knowledge of the property's use and capabilities for use

Marketable Title Merchantable title; title free and clear of objectionable liens or encumbrances

Material Fact A fact is material if it is one that the agent should realize would be likely to affect the judgment of the principal in giving consent to the agent to enter into the particular transaction on the specified terms

Mechanic's Lien A lien created by statute that exists against real property in favor of persons who have performed work or furnished materials for the improvement of the real estate

Meridians Imaginary north-south lines that intersect base lines to form a starting point for the measurement of land

Metes and Bounds A term used in describing the boundary lines of land, setting forth all the boundary lines together with their terminal points and angles

Minor Any person under 18 years of age

Misplaced Improvements Improvements on land that do not conform to the most profitable use of the site

Modular A building composed of modules constructed on an assembly line in a factory. Usually, the modules are self-contained.

Moldings Usually, patterned strips used to provide ornamental variation of outline or contour, such as cornices, bases, window and door jambs

Monetary Controls Federal Reserve tools for regulating the availability of money and credit to influence the level of economic activity

Monument A fixed object and point established by surveyors to establish land locations

Moratorium The temporary suspension, usually by statute, of the enforcement of liability for debt

Mortgage An instrument recognized by law by which property is hypothecated to secure the payment of a debt or obligation; the procedure for foreclosure in event of default is established by statute

Mortgage Contracts with Warrants Warrants make the mortgage more attractive to the lender by providing both the greater security that goes with a mortgage and a greater return through the right to buy either stock in the borrower's company or a portion of the income property itself

Mortgage Insurance Insurance against financial loss available to mortgage lenders to protect against loss resulting from default by borrowers

Mortgagee One to whom a mortgagor gives a mortgage to secure a loan or performance of an obligation; a lender. (See Secured Party.)

Mortgagor	One who gives a mortgage on his or her property to secure a loan or assure performance of an obligation; a borrower. (See Debtor.)
Multiple Listing	A listing, usually an exclusive right to sell, taken by a member of an organization composed of real estate brokers, with the provision that all members will have the opportunity to find an interested client; a cooperative listing
Mutual Water Company	A water company organized by or for water users in a given district with the object of securing an ample water supply at a reasonable rate; stock is issued to users
NAR	National Association of Realtors
NAREB	National Association of Real Estate Brokers
Narrative Appraisal	An extensive written report of all factual materials, techniques, and appraisal methods used by the appraiser to determine the value conclusion
Negotiable	Capable of being negotiated; assignable or transferable in the ordinary course of business
Net Listing	A listing that provides that the agent may retain as compensation for all sums received over and above a net price to the owner
Nominal Interest Rates	The percentage of interest stated in loan documents
Notary Public	An appointed officer with authority to take the acknowledgment of persons executing documents, to sign the certificate, and affix a seal
Note	A signed written instrument acknowledging a debt and promising payment
Notice	Actual knowledge acquired by being present at the occurrence
Notice of Nonresponsibility	A notice provided by law designed to relieve a property owner from responsibility for the cost of work done by a tenant on the property or materials furnished therefor; notice must be verified, recorded, and posted
Notice to Quit	A notice to a tenant to vacate rented property
Obsolescence	Loss in value resulting from reduced desirability and usefulness of a structure because its design and construction become obsolete; loss because of becoming old-fashioned and not in keeping with modern needs, with consequent loss in income
Offset Statement	Statement by owner of property or owner of lien against property, setting forth the present status of liens against said property
Open-End Mortgage	A mortgage containing a clause that permits the mortgagor to borrow additional money after the loan has been reduced, without rewriting the mortgage

Open Housing Law	Congress passed laws in 1968 and 1988 that prohibit discrimination in the sale of real estate because of race, color, religion, sex and handicap of buyers
Open Listing	An authorization given by a property owner to a real estate agent wherein said agent is given the nonexclusive right to secure a purchaser; open listings may be given to any number of agents without liability to compensate any except the one who first secures a buyer ready, willing, and able to meet the terms of the listing, or secures the acceptance by the seller of a satisfactory offer
Opinion of Title	An attorney's evaluation of the condition of the title to a parcel of land after examination of the abstract of title to the land
Option	A right given for a consideration to purchase or lease a property upon specified terms within a specified time
Oral Contract	A verbal agreement; one that is not reduced to writing
Orientation	Placing a house on its lot with regard to its exposure to the rays of the sun, prevailing winds, privacy from the street, and protection from outside noises
Overhang	The part of the roof extending beyond the walls, to shade buildings and to cover walks
Over Improvement	An improvement that is not the highest and best use for the site on which it is placed by reason of excess size or cost
Par Value	Market value, nominal value
Participation	In addition to base interest on mortgage loans on income properties, a small percentage of gross income is required, sometimes predicated on the fulfillment of certain conditions, such as minimum occupancy or a percentage of net income after expenses, debt service, and taxes
Partition Action	Court proceedings by which co-owners seek to sever their joint ownership
Partnership	A decision of the California Supreme Court has defined a partnership in the following terms: "A partnership as between partners themselves may be defined to be a contract of two or more persons to unite their property, labor or skill, or some of them, in prosecution of some joint or lawful business, and to share the profits in certain proportions"
Party Wall	A wall erected on the line between two adjoining properties, which are under different ownership, for the use of both properties
Patent	Conveyance of title to government land
Penalty	An extra payment or charge required of the borrower for deviating from the terms of the original loan agreement. Usually levied for being late in making regular payment or for paying off the loan before it is due.

Penny	The term, as applied to nails, serves as a measure of nail length and is abbreviated by the letter "d"
Percentage Lease	Lease on the property, the rental for which is determined by the amount of business done by the lessee; usually a percentage of gross receipts from the business with provision for a minimum rental
Perimeter Heating	Baseboard heating, or any system in which the heat registers are located along the outside walls of a room, especially under the windows
Personal Property	Any property that is not real property
Physical Deterioration	Impairment of condition. Loss in value brought about by wear and tear, disintegration, use, and actions of the elements.
Pier	A column of masonry, usually rectangular in horizontal cross section, used to support other structural members
Pitch	The incline or rise of a roof
Planned Unit Development (PUD)	A land-use design that provides intensive utilization of the land through a combination of private and common areas with prearranged sharing of responsibilities for the common areas
Plate	A horizontal board placed on a wall or supported on posts or studs to carry the trusses of a roof or rafters directly; a shoe, or base member as of a partition or other frame; a small flat board placed on or in a wall to support girders, rafters, and so on
Pledge	The depositing of personal property by a debtor with a creditor as security for a debt or engagement
Pledgee	One who is given a pledge or a security. (See Secured Party.)
Pledgor	One who offers a pledge or gives security. (See Debtor.)
Plottage Increment	The appreciation in unit value created by joining smaller ownerships into one large single ownership
Plywood	Laminated wood made up in panels; several thicknesses of wood glued together with grain at different angles for strength
Points	Under certain loans, discounts, or points, paid to lenders are, in effect, prepaid interest, and are used by lenders to adjust the effective interest rate so that it is equal to or nearly equal to the prevailing market rate (the rate charged on conventional loans)
Police Power	The right of the state to enact laws and enforce them for the order, safety, health, morals, and general welfare of the public
Power of Attorney	An instrument authorizing a person to act as the agent of the person granting it, and a general power authorizing the agent to act generally on behalf of the principal. A special power limits the agent to a particular or specific act as: a landowner may grant an agent special power of attorney to convey a single and specific parcel of property. Under the

provisions of a general power of attorney, the agent having the power may convey any or all property of the principal granting the general power of attorney.

Prefabricated House A house manufactured and sometimes partly assembled before delivery to the building site

Prepaid Items of Expense Prorations of prepaid items of expense that are credited to the seller in the closing statement

Prepayment Provision made for loan payments to be larger than those specified in the note

Prepayment Penalty Penalty for the payment of a mortgage or trust deed note before it actually becomes due if the note does not provide for prepayment

Prescription The securing of title to property by adverse possession; by occupying it for the period determined by law barring action for recovery

Present Value The lump-sum value today of an annuity. A $100 bill to be paid to someone in one year is worth less than if it were a $100 bill to be paid to someone today. This is because of several things, one of which is that the money has time value. How much the $100 bill to be paid in one year is worth today will depend on the interest rate that seems proper for the particular circumstances. For example, if 6% is the appropriate rate, the $100 to be paid one year from now would be worth $94.34 today.

Presumption A rule of law that courts and judges shall draw a particular inference from a particular fact, or from particular evidence, unless and until the truth of such inference is disproved

Prima Facie Presumptive on its face

Principal This term is used to mean either the employer of an agent or the amount of money borrowed or the amount of the loan

Principal Note The promissory note that is secured by the mortgage or trust deed

Privity Mutual relationship to the same rights of property; contractual relationship

Procuring Cause That cause originating from series of events that, without break in continuity, results in the prime object of an agent's employment producing a final buyer

Progression, Principle of The worth of a lesser-valued residence tends to be enhanced by association with many higher-valued residences in the same area

Promissory Note Following a loan commitment from the lender, the borrower signs a note, promising to repay the loan under stipulated terms. The promissory note establishes personal liability for its repayment.

Property The rights of ownership. The right to use, possess, enjoy, and dispose of a thing in every legal way and to exclude everyone else from interfering with these rights. Property is generally classified into two groups, personal property and real property.

Proration	Adjustments of interest, taxes, and insurance, on a pro rata basis as of the closing date. Fire insurance is normally paid for three years in advance. If a property is sold during this time, the seller wants a refund on that portion of the advance payment that has not been used at the time the title to the property is transferred. For example, if the property is sold two years later, the original buyer will want to receive one-third of the advance premium that was paid.
Proration of Taxes	To divide or prorate the taxes equally or proportionately to time of use
Proximate Cause	That cause of an event which, in a natural and continuous sequence unbroken by any new cause, produced that event, and without which the event would not have happened. Also, the procuring cause.
Public Trustee	The county public official whose office has been created by statute, to whom title to real property in certain states—such as Colorado—is conveyed by trust deed for the use and benefit of the beneficiary, who usually is the lender
Purchase and Installment Saleback	Involves purchase of the property upon completion of construction and immediate saleback on a long-term installment contract
Purchase of Land, Leaseback, and Leasehold Mortgages	An arrangement whereby land is purchased by the lender and leased back to the developer with a mortgage negotiated on the resulting leasehold of the income property constructed. The lender receives an annual ground rent, plus a percentage of income from the property.
Purchase and Leaseback	Involves the purchase of property subject to an existing mortgage and immediate leaseback
Purchase Money Mortgage or Trust Deed	A trust deed or mortgage given as part or all of the purchase consideration for property. In some states the purchase money mortgage or trust deed loan can be made by a seller who extends credit to the buyer of property or by a third-party lender (typically a financial institution) that makes a loan to the buyer of real property for a portion of the purchase price to be paid for the property. (In many states there are legal limitations upon mortgagees and trust deed beneficiaries collecting deficiency judgments against the purchase money borrower after the collateral hypothecated under such security instruments has been sold through the foreclosure process. Generally, no deficiency judgment is allowed if the collateral property under the mortgage or trust deed is residential property of four units or less with the debtor occupying the property as a place of residence.)
Quantity Survey	A highly technical process in arriving at cost estimate of new construction, and sometimes referred to in the building trade as the price take-off method. It involves a detailed estimate of the quantities of raw material (lumber, plaster, brick, cement) used, as well as the current price of the material and installation costs. These factors are all added together to arrive at the cost of a structure. It is usually used by contractors and experienced estimators.

Quarter Round	A molding that presents a profile of a quarter circle
Quiet Enjoyment	Right of an owner to the use of the property without interference of possession
Quiet Title	A court action brought to establish title; to remove a cloud on the title
Quitclaim Deed	A deed to relinquish any interest in property that the grantor may have
Radiant Heating	A method of heating, usually consisting of coils or pipes placed in the floor, wall, or ceiling
Rafter	One of a series of boards of a roof designed to support roof loads. The rafters of a flat roof are sometimes called roof joists
Range	A strip of land six miles wide determined by a government survey, running in a north to south direction
Ratification	The adoption or approval of an act performed on behalf of a person without previous authorization
Real Estate Association or Board	An organization whose members consist primarily of real estate brokers and salespersons
Real Estate Settlement Procedures Act	A federal disclosure law effective June 20, 1975, requiring new procedures and forms for settlements (closing costs) involving federally related loans
Real Estate Trust	A special arrangement under federal and state law whereby investors may pool funds for investments in real estate and mortgages and yet escape corporation taxes
Realtist	A real estate broker holding active membership in a real estate board affiliated with the National Association of Real Estate Brokers
Realtor	A real estate broker holding active membership in a real estate board affiliated with the National Association of Realtors
Recapture	The rate of interest necessary to provide for the return of an investment. Not to be confused with interest rate, which is a rate of interest on an investment.
Reconciliation	See Correlation
Reconveyance	The transfer of the title of land from one person to the immediate preceding owner. This particular instrument of transfer is commonly used when the performance or debt is satisfied under the terms of a deed of trust, when the trustee conveys the title that was being held on condition back to the owner.
Recording	The process of placing a document on file with a designated public official for everyone to see. This public official is usually a county officer known as the county recorder. The recorder designates the fact that a document has been given to him or her stamping it and indicating the

time of day and the date when it was officially placed on file. Documents filed with the recorder are considered to be placed on open notice to the general public of that county. Claims against property usually are given a priority on the basis of the time and the date they are recorded with the most preferred claim status going to the earliest one recorded and the next claim going to the next earliest one recorded, and so on. This type of notice is called constructive notice or legal notice.

Redemption Buying back one's property after a judicial sale

Refinancing The paying off of an existing obligation and assuming a new obligation in its place

Reformation An action to correct a mistake in a deed or other document

Rehabilitation The restoration of a property to satisfactory condition without drastically changing the plan, form, or style of architecture

Release Clause This is a stipulation that upon the payment of a specific sum of money to the holder of a trust deed or mortgage, the lien of the instrument as to a specific described lot or area shall be removed from the blanket lien on the whole area involved

Release Deed An instrument executed by the mortgagee or the trustee reconveying to the mortgagor the real estate that secured the mortgage loan after the debt has been paid in full. Upon recording, it cancels the mortgage lien created when the mortgage or trust deed was recorded.

Remainder An estate that takes effect after the termination of the prior estate, such as a life estate

Remainder Depreciation The possible loss in value of an improvement that will occur in the future

Replacement Cost The cost to replace the structure with one having utility equivalent to that being appraised, but constructed with modern materials and according to current standards, design, and layout

Reproduction Costs The cost of replacing the subject improvement with one that is the exact replica, having the same quality of workmanship, design, and layout

Rescission of Contract The abrogation or annulling of contract; the revocation or repealing of contract by mutual consent by parties to the contract, or for cause by either party to the contract

Reservation A right retained by a grantor in conveying property

RESPA Real Estate Settlement Procedures Act

Restriction As used relating to real property, this means that the owner of real property is restricted or prohibited from doing certain things relating to the property, or from using the property for certain purposes. Property restrictions fall into two general classifications—public and private. Zoning ordinances are examples of the former type. Restrictions may be created by private owners, typically by appropriate clauses in deeds, or in agreements, or in general plans of entire subdivisions. Usually they assume the form of a covenant or promise to do or not do a certain thing. They cover a multitude of matters, including use for residential or business purposes—for example, houses in tract must cost more than $100,000, and so on.

Retrospective Value The value of the property as of a previous date

Reversion The right to future possession or enjoyment by the person, or heirs, creating the preceding estate

Reversionary Interest The interest that a person has in lands or other property, upon the termination of the preceding estate

Ridge The horizontal line at the junction of the top edges of two sloping roof surfaces. The rafters at both slopes are nailed at the ridge.

Ridge Board The board placed on edge at the ridge of the roof to support the upper ends of the rafters; also called roof tree, ridge piece, ridge plate, or ridgepole

Right of Survivorship Right to acquire the interest of a deceased joint owner; distinguishing feature of a joint tenancy

Right of Way A privilege operating as an easement upon land, whereby the owner does by grant, or by agreement, give to another the right to pass over his land, to construct a roadway or use as a roadway; a specific part of his or her land; or the right to construct through and over the land telephone, telegraph, or electric power lines; or the right to place underground water mains, gas mains, or sewer mains

Riparian Rights The right of a landowner to the water on, under, or adjacent to his land

Riser The upright board at the back of each step of a stairway. In heating, a riser is a duct slanted upward to carry hot air from the furnace to the room above.

Risk Analysis A study made, usually by a lender, of the various factors that might affect the repayment of a loan

Risk Rating A process used by the lender to decide on the soundness of making a loan and to reduce all the various factors affecting the repayment of the loan to a qualified rating of some kind

Roman Brick Thin brick of slimmer proportions than standard building brick

Sale-Leaseback A situation where the owner of a piece of property wishes to sell the property and retain occupancy by leasing it from the buyer

Sales Contract A contract by which buyer and seller agree to terms of a sale

Sandwich Lease A leasehold interest that lies between the primary lease and the operating lease

Sash	Wood or metal frames containing one or more window panes
Satisfaction	Discharge of mortgage or trust deed lien from the records upon payment of the evidenced debt
Satisfaction Piece	An instrument for recording and acknowledging payment of an indebtedness secured by a mortgage
Scribing	Fitting woodwork to an irregular surface
Seal	An impression made to attest the execution of an instrument—for example, a notary public's seal
Secondary Financing	A loan secured by a second mortgage or trust deed on real property. These can be third, fourth, fifth, sixth—on and on, ad infinitum.
Section	Section of land is established by government survey and contains 640 acres
Secured Party	This is the party having the security interest. Thus the mortgagee, the conditional seller, the pledgee, and so on, are all now referred to as the secured party.
Security Agreement	An agreement between the secured party and the debtor which creates the security interest
Security Interest	A term designating the interest of the creditor in the property of the debtor in all types of credit transactions. It thus replaces such terms as the following: chattel mortgage, pledge, trust receipt, chattel trust, equipment trust, conditional sale, and inventory lien.
Seizin	Possession of real estate by one entitled thereto
Separate Property	Property owned by a husband or wife which is not community property; property acquired by either spouse prior to marriage or by gift or devise after marriage
Septic Tank	An underground tank in which sewage from the house is reduced to liquid by bacterial action and drained off
Servicing	Supervising and administering a loan after it has been made. This involves such things as collecting the payments, keeping accounting records, computing the interest and principal, foreclosure of defaulted loans, and so on.
Setback Ordinance	An ordinance prohibiting the erection of a building or structure between the curb and the setback line
Severalty Ownership	Owned by one person only; sole ownership
Shake	A hand-split shingle, usually edge-grained
Sheathing	Structural covering, usually boards, plywood, or wallboards, placed over exterior studding or rafters of a house

Sheriff's Deed	Deed given by court order in connection with sale of property to satisfy a judgment
Shopping Center, Regional	A large shopping center with 250,000 to 1,000,000 square feet of store area, serving 200,000 or more people
Sill	The lowest part of the frame of a house, resting on the foundation and supporting the uprights of the frame; the board or metal forming the lower side of an opening, as a door sill or windowsill
Single Agency	Where a broker represents only the buyer or the seller, not both, in a real estate transaction
Sinking Fund	Fund set aside from the income from property which, with accrued interest, will eventually pay for replacement of the improvements
SIR	Society of Industrial Realtors
Soil Pipe	Pipe carrying waste out from the house to the main sewer line
Sole or Sole Plate	A member, usually a 2-by-4, on which wall and partition studs rest
Span	The distance between structural supports such as walls, columns, piers, beams, girders, and trusses
Special Assessment	Legal charge against real estate by a public authority to pay cost of public improvements such as street lights, sidewalks, or street improvements
Special Warranty Deed	A deed in which the grantor warrants or guarantees the title only against defects arising during his or her ownership of the property and not against defects existing before the time of his or her ownership
Specific Liens	Liens that attach to only a certain specific parcel of land or piece of property
Specific Performance	An action to compel performance of an agreement—for example, sale of land
SRA	Designates a person who is a member of the Society of Real Estate Appraisers
SREA	Society of Real Estate Appraisers
Standard Depth	Generally the most typical lot depth in the neighborhood
Standby Commitment	The mortgage banker frequently protects a builder by a "standby" agreement, under which the banker agrees to make mortgage loans at an agreed price for many months in the future. The builder deposits a "standby fee" with the mortgage banker for this service. Frequently, the mortgage banker secures a "standby" from a long-term investor for the same period of time, paying a fee for this privilege.
Statute of Frauds	State law that provides that certain contracts must be in writing in order to be enforceable at law. Examples would be real property lease for more than one year or agent's authorization to sell real estate.

Statutory Warranty Deed	A short-form warranty deed that warrants by inference that the seller is the undisputed owner and has the right to convey the property and that the owner will defend the title if necessary. This type of deed protects the purchaser in that the conveyor covenants to defend all claims against the property. If the seller fails to do so, the new owner can defend said claims and sue the former owner.
Straight-Line Depreciation	Definite sum set aside annually from income to pay cost of replacing improvements, without reference to interest it earns
String, Stringer	A timber or other support for cross members. In stairs, the support on which the stair treads rest.
Studs or Studding	Vertical supporting timbers in the walls and partitions
Subject to Mortgage	When a grantee takes a title to real property subject to mortgage, he or she is not responsible to the holder of the promissory note for the payment of any portion of the amount due. The most that the grantee can lose in the event of a foreclosure is equity in the property. (See Assumption of Mortgage.) In neither case is the original maker of the note released from his or her responsibility.
Sublease	A lease given by a lessee
Subordinate	To make subject to or junior to
Subordination Clause	Clause in a junior or a second lien permitting retention of priority for prior liens. A subordination clause may also be used in a first deed of trust permitting it to be subordinated to subsequent liens as, for example, the liens of construction loans.
Subpoena	A process to cause a witness to appear and give testimony
Subrogation	The substitution of another person in place of the creditor, to whose rights the former succeeds in relation to the debt. The doctrine is used very often where one person agrees to stand surety for the performance of a contract by another person.
Substitution, Principle of	Affirms that the maximum value of a property tends to be set by the cost of acquiring an equally desirable and valuable substitute property, assuming no costly delay is encountered in making the substitution
Sum of the Years Digits	An accelerated depreciation method
Supply and Demand, Principle of	Affirms that price or value varies directly, but not necessarily proportionally with demand, and inversely, but not necessarily proportionally, with supply
Surety	One who guarantees the performance of another—a guarantor
Surplus Productivity, Principle of	Affirms the net income that remains after the proper costs of labor, organization, and capital have been paid, which surplus is imputable to the land and tends to fix the value thereof
Survey	The process by which a parcel of land is measured and its area is ascertained

Syndicate	A partnership organized for participation in a real estate venture. Partners may be limited or unlimited in their liability.
Take-Out Loan	The loan arranged by the owner or builder-developer for a buyer. The construction loan made for construction of the improvements is usually paid from the proceeds of this loan.
Tax-Free Exchange	Income property exchanged on an even basis for other income property that does not require a capital gain tax at the time
Tax Sale	Sale of property after a period of nonpayment of taxes
Tenancy in Common	Ownership by two or more persons who hold undivided interest, without right of survivorship; interests need not be equal
Tenants by the Entireties	Under certain state laws, ownership of property acquired by a husband and wife during marriage that is jointly owned. Upon death of one spouse, it becomes the property of the survivor.
Tentative Map	The Subdivision Map Act requires subdividers to submit initially a tentative map of their tract to the local planning commission for study. The approval or disapproval of the planning commission is noted on the map. Thereafter a final map of the tract embodying any changes requested by the planning commission is required to be filed with the planning commission.
Tenure in Land	The mode or manner by which an estate in lands is held
Termite Shield	A shield, usually of noncorrodible metal, placed on top of the foundation wall or around pipes to prevent passage of termites
Termites	Ant-like insects that feed on wood
Testator	One who leaves a will in force upon death
Threshold	A strip of wood or metal beveled on each edge and used above the finished floor under outside doors
Time Is the Essence	One of the essential requirements to the forming of a binding contract; contemplates a punctual performance
Title	Evidence that owner of land is in lawful possession thereof, an instrument evidencing such ownership
Title Insurance	Insurance written by a title company to protect property owner against loss if title is imperfect
Title Report	A report that discloses the condition of the title, made by a title company preliminary to issuance of title insurance
Title Theory	Mortgage arrangement whereby title to mortgaged real property vests in the lender
Topography	Nature of the surface of land; topography may be level, rolling, or mountainous

Torrens Title	System of title records provided by state law (no longer used in California)
Tort	A wrongful act; wrong, injury; violation of a legal right
Township	A territorial subdivision six miles long, six miles wide, and containing 36 sections, each one mile square
Trade Fixtures	Articles of personal property annexed to real property, but which are necessary to the carrying on of a trade and are removable by the owner
Trade-In	An increasingly popular method of guaranteeing an owner a minimum amount of cash upon sale of present property to permit the purchase of another. If the property is not sold within a specified time at the listed price, the broker agrees to arrange financing to purchase the property at an agreed-upon discount.
Treads	Horizontal boards of a stairway
Trim	The finish materials in a building, such as moldings, applied around openings (window trim, door trim) or at the floor and ceiling (baseboard, cornice, picture molding)
Trust Account	An account separate and apart and physically segregated from broker's own funds, in which a broker deposits funds collected for clients
Trust Deed	Just as with a mortgage, this is a legal document by which a borrower pledges certain real property or collateral as guarantee for the repayment of a loan. However, it differs from the mortgage in a number of important respects. For example, instead of there being two parties to the transaction, there are three. There is the borrower who gives the trust deed and who is called the trustor. There is the third, neutral party (just as there is with an escrow) who receives the trust deed and who is called the trustee. And, finally, there is the lender who is called the beneficiary because the lender benefits from the pledge arrangement in that in the event of a default the trustee can sell the property and transfer the money obtained at the sale to the lender as payment of the debt.
Trustee	One who holds property in trust for another to secure the performance of an obligation
Trustor	One who deeds property to a trustee to be held as security until the trustor has performed any obligations to a lender under terms of a deed of trust
Under Improvement	An improvement that, because of its deficiency in size or cost, is not the highest and best use of the site
Underwriting	The technical analysis by a lender to determine the borrower's ability to repay a contemplated loan
Undue Influence	Taking any fraudulent or unfair advantage of another's weakness of mind or distress or necessity

Unearned Increment	An increase in value of real estate resulting from no effort on the part of the owner; often caused by an increase in population
Uniform Commercial Code	Establishes a unified and comprehensive scheme for regulation of security transactions in personal property, superseding the existing statutes on chattel mortgages, conditional sales, trust receipts, assignment of accounts receivable, and others in this field
Unit-in-Place Method	The cost of erecting a building by estimating the cost of each component part, that is, foundations, floors, walls, windows, ceilings, roofs (including labor and overhead)
Urban Property	City property; closely settled property
Usury	On a loan, claiming a rate of interest greater than that permitted by law
Utilities	Refers to services rendered by public utility companies, such as water, gas, electricity, and telephone
Utility	The ability to give satisfaction and/or excite desire for possession
Valid	Having force, or binding force; legally sufficient and authorized by law
Valley	The internal angle formed by the junction of two sloping sides of a roof
Valuation	Estimated worth or price; estimation: the act of valuing by appraisal
Vendee	A purchaser; buyer
Vendor	A seller; one who disposes of a thing in consideration of money
Veneer	Thin sheets of wood
Vent	A pipe installed to provide a flow of air to or from a drainage system or to provide a circulation of air within such system to protect trap seals from siphonage and back pressure
Verification	Sworn statement before a duly qualified officer to correctness of contents of an instrument
Vested	Bestowed upon someone; secured by someone, such as a title to property
Void	To have no force or effect; that which is unenforceable
Voidable	That which is capable of being adjudged void, but is not void unless action is taken to make it so
Voluntary Lien	Any lien placed on property with consent of, or as a result of, the voluntary act of the owner
Wainscoting	Wood lining of an interior wall; lower section of a wall when finished differently from the upper part

Waive	To relinquish or abandon; to forego a right to enforce or require anything
Warranty Deed	A deed used to convey real property that contains warranties of title and quiet possession, and the grantor thus agrees to defend the premises against the lawful claims of third persons. It is commonly used in many states, but in others the grant deed has supplanted it because of the modern practice of securing title insurance policies that have reduced the importance of express and implied warranty in deeds.
Waste	The destruction of, or material alteration of, or injury to premises by a tenant for life or years
Water Table	Distance from surface of ground to a depth at which natural groundwater is found
Will	Instrument that leaves real estate of a decedent to an heir(s). Examples: witnessed will; holographic will; statutory will.
Wraparound Mortgage	Involves the borrower entering into a second mortgage. This arrangement represents the means by which the borrower can add to development without refinancing the first mortgage at substantially higher current rates.
Yield	The interest earned by an investor on his investment (or bank, on the money it has lent). Also called return.
Yield Rate	The yield expressed as a percentage of the total investment. Also called rate of return.
Zone	The area set off by the proper authorities for specific use, subject to certain restrictions or restraints
Zoning	Act of city or county authorities specifying type of use to which property may be put in specific areas

Index